The Law and Administration Relating to Protection of the Environment

D. ALASTAIR BIGHAM, M.A. (Oxon.)

of the Middle Temple, Barrister
Chartered Surveyor and
Chartered Land Agent
Fellow of the Institute of Arbitrators

London
Oyez Publishing

1973

©

OYEZ PUBLISHING LIMITED
OYEZ HOUSE, 237 LONG LANE
LONDON, SE1 4PU
1973

SBN 85120 1571

First published June, 1973

A/344.42

PRINTED IN GREAT BRITAIN BY
THE DEVONSHIRE PRESS LIMITED
TORQUAY

FOREWORD

CRITICAL awareness of the human environment is not a concern
peculiar to the present day. That we are so moved about the
condition and conservation of our surroundings is patent proof
of an earlier care, of a nurture by generations long past without
whose touch and husbandry we should have no environment worthy
of our desire. Ten years ago no one in Britain would have
understood the relevance of a Department of the Environment
as a major arm of the national Executive. When in the mid-
1960s the Natural Environment Research Council was no more
than an idea and a felt need, the word *environment* had for many
intimately concerned in the policy of the birth of the Council no
more than a topographical connotation. What is new today is an
awakening to realise that the environment we use and have
created has an anatomy of interdependent parts and functions.

Our fathers had worked in a sporadic manner, fashioning this
and fabricating that—the dimension of their consciousness, unlike
ours, did not reach to the totality, to the wholeness, of the human
environment. Nevertheless the heritage they left us, which is the
environment we now cherish and would improve, was itself the
artefact of guided law and rational policies. Those who would
comprehend the law as it stands today for the protection of the
environment will find an extensive web, ready woven, a gossamer
of statutory texts and case law stretching back into a past when in
the law of torts neighbour sought redress against neighbour for
nuisance of various kinds, when legislators focused their attention
on housing, on factory conditions and on the neglect of husbandry.
It was all environment. Much needs to be done in framing new
laws and policies to give expression to the implications of the present
awakening. But, be he politician, planner, legal practitioner or
surveyor, he who fails to know the law starts out on a false scent.
Besides which the law as it now stands is the sum and the substance
of the knowledge incumbent upon the present day practitioner to
profess.

That knowledge is here for the first time collated and analysed
by Mr. Alastair Bigham. A comprehensive practical treatise of
prime importance to the lawyer, the surveyor and the planner,

v

Mr. Bigham's work does not follow the orthodox pattern of the legal textbook and relate the law to the subject.   He relates the subject—protection of the environment—to the law.   He takes our hand and guides us: first to the administrative structure and the springs of policy-making; then to show how the environment is affected by industry and agriculture; thirdly, to man's activities manifest in transport, pollution and the built environment; and finally to problems of nature and her conquest by man.   Through it all runs the presentation of the law—factual, precise and readable.

I commend Mr. Bigham's book to the reader.

D. R. DENMAN
Professor of Land Economy

PEMBROKE COLLEGE,
CAMBRIDGE.

Lent Term 1973.

PREFACE

THE various means provided by the law for the protection or improvement of our environment are very considerable in their scope, although the sources relevant to a specific problem may, on occasion, be difficult to trace. Thus, it can be said that, with certain exceptions, most threats to our surroundings can be remedied with the aid of the law, *provided that* the correct administrative channels can be identified.

In the past few years much has been written about the practical problems relating to protection of the environment. These discussions have been of great interest, and the growth of constructive comment on the part of scientists is particularly to be welcomed. However, the views most usually expressed tend to be either of such a scientific nature, or to consist merely of generalised statements of moral or aesthetic values. These are, unfortunately, of limited assistance when one becomes practically involved in negotiation with administrative authorities, or in the conduct of a case on behalf of objectors at a public inquiry. The prime reason for this limitation is that it is a basic principle of the British systems of justice that "expert" views—whether of a technical or of an artistic nature—should be presented by the expert in person, so that he may then be open to further examination and cross-examination in order to test fully the value of his assertions. Thus, the expression of second-hand opinion, or of alleged fact without proof of validity, are afforded little weight.

My purpose, therefore, in writing this rather concentrated volume is twofold. First, I offer a consideration of the essentially practical difficulties which arise in seeking to protect or improve the human environment: these problems relate either to the actual process of persuasion of people (either individually, collectively, or in Ministerial form), or to the use of the law as it at present stands; and it is with this in mind that several of the chapters are divided into two parts—a preliminary discussion of theory and administration, and then a statement of the relevant legal provisions.

Secondly, I hope that this attempt to provide an overall view of the current situation may be of assistance in enabling the various sectors of the system of administration, and of the law relative to them, to be seen in context.   In the sometimes well-nigh impenetrable jungle of environmental administration this may serve to reduce the difficulty of " seeing the wood for the trees "—whereby painful collisions may, perhaps, be avoided.   In too many cases the public and the general professional practitioner are unaware of the rights which they, or the community as a legal entity, are entitled to enforce.

It is necessary to emphasise that the field of study encompassed by this book is not only large, and of somewhat uncertain periphery, it is also subject to rapid alteration as a result both of scientific and of Parliamentary activity.   So far as possible I have endeavoured to make recent amendments and additions, although a number of these have, of necessity, been incorporated as footnotes.   I trust that I may also be forgiven for remarking that many of the points of general principle which were originally drafted by me as long as two years ago have now been, quite separately, elucidated in recent reports by several Government Committees.   It is thus with mixed feelings of satisfaction and regret that such references have been included herein!

I should like to thank those who have given me help and encouragement in the preparation of this book, and in particular Professor D. R. Denman, Sir Desmond Heap, Mr. Harold Marnham, Q.C., Dr. Colin Kolbert, Mr. Francis Holland of the Country Landowners' Association, Mr. Leslie Ginsburg of the Civic Trust, and Mr. Christopher Parfitt and other members of the staff of the Polytechnic of Central London.   I am indebted to the Members, Secretaries and staff of a number of professional and other societies and institutions including notably the Royal Institution of Chartered Surveyors, the Royal Town Planning Institute, the Royal Institute of British Architects, the Nature Conservancy, and the National Trust for England and Wales.   I should also like to express my thanks to Mrs. Susanne Latourell for the extremely helpful and accurate way in which she typed the script.   But finally—and principally—I am grateful to my wife for her patience and encouragement.

2, *Harcourt Buildings,*
Temple, London.   ALASTAIR BIGHAM.

CONTENTS

ix

TABLE OF CASES

TABLE OF STATUTES

TABLE OF RULES AND ORDERS

[Entries are in chronological order]

CHAPTER 1

INTRODUCTION:
THE GENERAL CONTROL OF THE
ENVIRONMENT IN GREAT BRITAIN

THE purpose of this introductory chapter is to indicate the system of central and local government as it affects control of the environment; and to relate this to the application of the law and of matters of town and country planning theory and policy, so that the subsequent chapters in the book may be seen in context.

It must also be stressed (although mention of this has already been made in the Preface) that this work seeks to offer material which may be used as ammunition in any skirmish or major battle by those wishing to protect or improve the environment. The author has therefore avoided generalised quotations—since an expert witness, to be of real value, should usually be present at any hearing—and has arranged the majority of subsequent chapters in two parts. The first part of these chapters will consist of a commentary on matters of planning practice which may be used in material arguments. That is to say, matters which are purely comparative, and therefore questions of expert opinion, such as the relative rarity of a species of bird, are not included. The second part of each chapter is concerned with a selective statement of the law relating to each chapter subject.

Before proceeding further it is only fair to the reader to remark that the author has, regretfully, been unable to include variants of the law and administration which relate specifically to Scotland and Northern Ireland. The law as stated applies, in most cases, only to England and Wales, but in nearly every instance the substance (although not the source) will be the same in Scotland and Northern Ireland.

It is evident, since the greater part of any national system of law is concerned with the relationship between individuals, or between individuals and/or associations of individuals and the organs of government, that many aspects of both the common law and statutory law may influence the physical or mental position in

1

which a person may find himself.   For example, legislation relating to measures which may be taken against an individual who appears to be of unsound mind will clearly affect the living conditions of his immediate neighbours.   These extremities of the law must, however, be excluded, and the compass within which this book is written may be seen by reference to the index.

The author next wishes to stress that this particular chapter is designed with the layman, and to an extent the general practitioner, in mind; it is not intended for the expert, although it is hoped that various comments made may be of general interest.

The simplest approach to this discussion appears to be: (i) to outline the system, or systems, of national and local government in so far as they relate to protection of the environment; (ii) to refer briefly to the broad fields of environmental policy covered by the law; and then (iii) to indicate, in initial outline, the practical problems and strategy which may be involved in seeking either to prevent damage to the environment or to obtain a subsequent remedy.   These are, of course, more fully discussed in subsequent chapters.

Since the preparation of these pages, however, the Working Party appointed under the Chairmanship of the Countess of Dartmouth has completed its investigations into the human habitat in Britain, and has submitted a report to the Secretary of State for the Environment in which fifty-four formal Recommendations are made.   Clearly, recommendations of this nature, whether accepted in due course by the Secretary of State or no, are of at least important persuasive value in the furtherance of argument in any form of representation by members of the public and others.   The reader is therefore advised to consider carefully each of these short proposals, which are set out in Appendix B hereto.   However, it will be found to be of assistance firstly to read both the remainder of this chapter, and also to refer to the published version of the Working Party's Report [1] which sets out in simple language the principal physical (but not legal) problems currently affecting the environment in Britain.

---

[1] Report of the Working Party on the Human Habitat: Chairman, The Countess of Dartmouth; presented to the Secretary of State for the Environment in January 1972, and published by H.M.S.O. as " How Do You Want to Live? A Report on the Human Habitat."

1. The Systems of Government

(1) *The basic system, including the organisation of local government until 1st April, 1974*

It appears to be fashionable to lay the blame for damage to the environment at the door of a vague and uncertain body of persons known as " the planners "; yet relatively few people are able to identify them.   In fact there are broadly four types of system of administration involved.

Overall national government lies, of course, with the two Houses of Parliament, and it is said that, under our unwritten constitution, Parliament has unlimited authority.   Thus, the law may be altered even retroactively so that a crime committed some years earlier may cease to be a crime.   However, this power of the legislature becomes mingled with purely administrative functions in the persons of Ministers of the Crown.   Ministers may be empowered, under any given statute, to extend the force of legislation by making Ministerial Rules and Orders.   Yet they may also act administratively—and particularly so in the field of town and country planning —by taking " policy decisions," such as, for example, that a particular development within a Green Belt be approved in view of the overall national shortage of housing.

Town and country planning legislation[2] lays down that every Minister of the Crown has a positive duty to seek to protect the environment.   Thus, although the Secretary of State for the Environment, and the three other Ministers within his Department,[3] are primarily responsible for environmental matters, it is contrary to the express will of Parliament for any other Minister to fail to assess the significance of damage to the environment resulting from any administrative decision made by him.   In this sense, therefore, other Ministers such as those for Agriculture, Fisheries and Food, for Trade and Industry, or for Employment and Productivity, are also included amongst " the planners."   It will therefore also follow that it is within the function of the Secretary of State for the

---

[2] *Vide* effect of the Countryside Act, 1968, s. 37, together with Town and Country Planning Act, 1971, s. 48 (1) (*c*) (*d*) and (2), with Sched. 10 to the latter Act.

[3] Previously the separate Ministries of Housing and Local Government; Transport; and Public Buildings and Works.   The present three Ministers now acting under the general direction of the Secretary of State for the Environment are described as the Minister for Local Government and Development; Minister for Housing and Construction; and Minister for Transport Industries.

Environment to seek (or sometimes positively to require) the support of other Ministers in this respect.

The rearrangement of the governmental organisation which occurred in October, 1970, included, as already mentioned, the most valuable concept that the principal Ministries concerned with control of the environment be grouped together, now in the Department of the Environment, so that the functions co-ordinated therein include a general control of local government, and of housing, highways (including traffic) and town and country planning generally.   Public buildings and works are also within the Department.   However, consultative and administrative links must, of course, exist with other Departments and notably with those for agriculture, and trade and industry.

Below the level of government ministries it can broadly be said that three principal types of body having functions in relation to control of the environment now exist.   First, there are *advisory councils or committees*, consisting of members largely appointed by Ministers for the purpose of investigating local or national situations, and advising the relevant Minister.   These bodies have no legislative or administrative powers, although they may well exercise persuasion at other levels.   They include, for example, Regional Economic Planning Councils, which cover the whole of England, Scotland and Wales in ten regions, and report in confidence to the Secretary of State for the Environment.   Secondly, there are permanent *administrative and supervisory boards* which are appointed by various Ministers and are very largely autonomous— such as the Water Resources Board,[4] River Authorities, the National Coal Board, Electricity Boards, etc.   In addition there are other statutory undertakers, whose duty it is solely to provide services in a local area.   An example of a purely supervisory board, however, would be the permanent Inspectorate set up under the Factories Acts which has been responsible for the inspection of physical and working conditions in manufacturing industry for over a century. Thirdly, but equally as important as the first two in terms of status, there is the system of *local government*, consisting of councils of elected representatives, and staffed by employees of those councils.   However, it is essential to realise that the power of central government to direct [4a]

[4] Responsible for co-ordinating total national water availability.   But the Water Reorganisation Bill at present before Parliament (end-1972) proposes to alter the system of organisation of water authorities—see footnote 13a on p. 142.
[4a] e.g. by issue of circulars.

both the elected councils and also the local government employees is very considerable. The ultimate sanction lies in fiscal
measures since more than half the money spent by local authorities
comes from the national Exchequer and not out of local rates. This
control is exerted through the medium of (*a*) the annual audit, which
is carried out by a government auditor; or (*b*) the Chancellor of the
Exchequer's annual budget, which may reduce overall allocations
for specific local government purposes, or may re-allocate contributions as between particular (social) types of local authority.

Although, as has already been said, a great deal of law (both
statutory and otherwise) has an effect upon the environment, most
people tend to think only of the provisions made in Acts of Parliament, and by rules and orders made by Ministers under statutory
authority, these also tending to be described as " town and country
planning legislation." Except in the field of pollution, this is now
largely a correct assumption. The administration of systems of
town and country planning is now the responsibility of the Secretary
of State for the Environment, but with local planning authorities
and delegated authorities (i.e., until 1st April, 1974, county and
district authorities respectively), with very few exceptions, required
to make the initial decisions, subject to an overall power on the
part of the Secretary of State to overrule all such decisions. The
general responsibilities within the overall functions in local government of these authorities will now be considered preparatory to
outlining the administration of planning as part of these broader
duties.

At the time of writing, legislation is in progress for the purpose
of reorganising local government in order to adapt methods of
administration to modern sociological and economic needs. It is
also the hope and intention that such reorganisation will increase
the interest of the electorate in selecting and supporting their
candidates for local government office. For the period until 1st April,
1974, the present organisation will continue in being, and reference
will now be made to it—more especially because, from the standpoint of protection of the environment, it is a known rather than an
unknown quantity.

In simplest terms the United Kingdom is divided into counties,
which are the principal local authorities. Within each county
there are, at present, large numbers of districts; and below these,
as the smallest unit of population or area, there are administrative

parishes. The county councils are generally the prime authority for all local government functions save for two, namely, housing and rating.[5] These two important responsibilities lie with the district councils, together with a number of others which are theirs either in some instances by direct statutory authority, or, in others, by virtue of delegation agreements with the county council.

District and borough councils also have major responsibilities in terms of the Public Health Acts.

Administrative parishes have very minor local government functions which they exercise either through an elected parish council or, if no parish council exists, through a parish meeting. The parish will normally only be concerned with certain physical features within the parish, such as the provision of a village name sign, or the maintenance of a village playing field.

To the above short, and therefore not entirely accurate, description must be added three further points of classification. A county borough is a borough of sufficient size, which has been given the powers and duties of a county, and it will therefore carry out both the normal county council functions and will also act as rating authority and housing authority. Secondly, county districts (which, incidentally, never exist within county boroughs) are classified as urban districts and rural districts. Although some of the most ancient urban districts may once have been boroughs in their own right, and hold ancient charters, the principal point of distinction between an urban and a rural district is that, in certain circumstances, an urban district may be the highway authority for particular classes of roads. Thirdly, boroughs which are not county boroughs have powers and duties similar to those of urban districts—although the first citizen is described as a mayor rather than a council chairman.

The method of administration of town and country planning

This can be divided into two basic fields of activity, thus: (*a*) planning by means of restrictive controls as to new structures, or

---

[5] By way of explanation, it should be noted that a *rating authority* is an authority charged by statute with the duty of raising (i.e., obtaining payment of) the local general rate. This is a function of all district councils, and borough and county borough councils. The counties within which districts and boroughs lie have a statutory right to issue a precept to each district for a specified sum which with all other districts will collectively meet the county's estimated expenditure; but a county cannot levy a rate direct.

as to the alteration of structure or use of existing buildings or land; and (b) planning in positive form; that is, by creation of " development plans " for each distinct area of the country, whereby the future use (i.e., development or unchangeability) of every square metre may be charted or ascertained. These two separate mechanisms do, of necessity, impinge upon each other as follows:

To take (b), positive planning, first: it is provided (now in Part II of the Town and Country Planning Act, 1971) that " development plans " be prepared and drawn up.[5a]   It must, however, be noted here that, for a further short space of years, the precise form of development plans will vary from one part of the country to another. The reason for this is that, under the earlier Town and Country Planning Acts (1947 and 1962), development plans were required to consist of a written statement and a detailed scale plan (with larger scale inset plans, where necessary), and this type of development plan is still applicable (1972) to the greater part of Britain. It presents, however, a number of difficulties in that it is cumbersome to prepare and to revise; and, far more important, the precise designation of intended uses of the entire local planning authority area, which must be exactly delineated on the scale plan, produces great practical difficulty in terms of the effect upon property values. For example, the designation of a residential area, or of an area merely adjoining a residential area, for use for industry at some rather distant future date (say, twenty years) has a disastrous effect upon the saleability of existing dwellings.

Therefore, under the Town and Country Planning Act, 1968 (now Part II of the Town and Country Planning Act, 1971), it is provided that there be a gradual transition from the " old style " development plan to a " new style " development plan, such change to be carried out by each individual local planning authority at dates to be specified from time to time (and according to their local situation) by the Secretary of State for the Environment.

The new style development plans are to consist of two distinct phases—the *Structure Plan* and *Local Plans*. At the outset of preparation of the plan, however, a survey of the entire local planning authority area is to be carried out (1971 Act, s. 6). This survey is to include certain specific studies (s. 6 (3)), namely:

[5a] Administration is currently (1973) controlled by the Town and Country Planning (Structure and Local Plans) Regulations, 1972 (S.I. 1972 No. 1154).

(*a*) the principal physical and economic characteristics of the area, including present land use, and in relation to neighbouring planning authority areas;

(*b*) the size, composition and distribution of the population (whether resident or otherwise);

(*c*) the communications, transport system and traffic of the area (and in relation to neighbouring areas);

(*d*) " any considerations not mentioned in any of the preceding paragraphs which may be expected to affect any matters so mentioned ";

(*e*) " such other matters as may be prescribed or as the Secretary of State may in any particular case direct ";

(*f*) any changes already " projected " in any of the above.

The preparation of this survey is to be carried out in consultation with other authorities affected (s. 6 (4)), and fresh surveys may be required by the Secretary of State at any time (s. 6 (5)).

But the survey required by s. 6 does not form part of the text of the development plan, so that any reference to the survey made at any subsequent inquiry can only be either by way of interpretation in the absence of a clear meaning within the plan itself, or of merely persuasive effect.

Having prepared a full survey, the local planning authority must then proceed to the first phase of the development plan, that is completion of a *Structure Plan*. The Structure Plan is to be a written statement (s. 7) supported by explanatory diagrams—not scale plans—where necessary (s. 7 (3)). It will:

(*a*) formulate policy and general proposals in respect of the development and other use of land in that area (including measures for the improvement of the physical environment and the management of traffic);

(*b*) state the relationship of those proposals to general proposals for the development and other use of land in neighbouring areas which may be affected;

(*c*) deal with other matters as prescribed or directed by the Secretary of State.

The Structure Plan must also be made with reference to current economic planning policies for the region,[6] and to the local resources

---

[6] There are ten Economic Planning Regions in Britain.

likely to be available, together with other matters as may be directed (s. 7 (4) (*a*), (*b*), (*c*)).

Thus the Structure Plan will be seen to be a statement of policy rather than, as previously, a scale map of the area (supported by a written explanation) upon which the precise boundaries of land use were drawn. This avoids, therefore, such problems as the depression of land values ("planning blight") to a considerable extent, and also provides for far greater flexibility when periodic revisions of the plan become necessary. However, a special exception to this generalised approach is provided for (s. 7 (5)) although applicable only to localities where there is a special need for "comprehensive treatment" in the immediate future. These are to be provided for as "action areas" specified in the Structure Plan, and for which a *Local Plan* must be drawn up within a prescribed period.

The process of the initial survey and of preparation of the Structure Plan is to be carried out in close consultation with all local authorities concerned and also with the Department of the Environment. On completion of the Structure Plan by the local planning authority, it must be well publicised and all representations are to be considered by the county planning authority (s. 8 (1)). Copies of the plan must be made available for public inspection "not later than" the time of subsequent submission to the Secretary of State for approval (s. 8 (2)). The Secretary of State may refer the plan back to the local planning authority if he is dissatisfied (s. 8 (4), (5), (6), (7)), or he may (s. 9 (1)) either approve it, in whole or in part and with or without modifications, or reject it. As in most cases of submission for approval by the Secretary of State under town and country planning law, he is required (s. 9 (3)) to hear and consider any objections and may (in this case virtually certainly will) hold a local inquiry at which the local planning authority must be heard and at which other persons may be heard. (The reason for persons other than the local planning authority being afforded no absolute right to be heard lies merely in the practical difficulty that, if each individual in an area was able to insist upon making a statement, many inquiries could last for an utterly unreasonable length of time. However, the Department of the Environment Inspectors do not normally refuse individual requests.) It has also been indicated by the Secretary of State that, in future, local inquiries concerned with Structure (as opposed to Local)

Plans will be conducted in a more general and less, as it is put, " legalistic " manner. That is, expert witnesses will be permitted to speak on matters of general principle; they will be required to be less objective; and they will, presumably, be less exactly cross-examined. Whether or not such a change will produce satisfactory results remains to be seen. There is, at least, the danger that superficial theories will be more easily put forward by the more articulate planners and architects, and that these may be accepted but later found wanting.

(It must also be added that the following comment is included in the Dartmouth Working Party Report (Working Party Opinion, para. 2.39): " ' Strategic ' planning, as required by the 1968–69 Town and Country Planning Acts, has become an intellectual concept requiring its own special language. One result of this has tended to be that strategy is determined without public participation and then a presentation of the consequences, usually without alternatives, is made to local communities. Participation then becomes protest, with the usual pattern of embittered resistance, demonstrations, letters to newspapers, angry meetings, expensive delays and eventual revision of the plans.")

When the Structure Plan for a county is finally agreed by the Secretary of State (or in subsequent years—principally at five-yearly intervals—when revisions to Structure Plans take place) it is then necessary for the district authorities to prepare, in consultation with the county and the Secretary of State, their own Local Plans in accordance with the policy requirements of the Structure Plan (s. 11 (1), (2) and (9)). Local Plans will consist primarily of a map, which will be supported (as in the case of old style development plans) by written explanatory material. The principal map will be delineated on Ordnance Survey sheets, and may be supplemented by larger scale inset maps or diagrams (s. 11 (3), (5)). Separate Local Plans are permitted to be prepared for various different purposes for the same part of any area (s. 11 (4)). In the case of areas indicated as action areas in the Structure Plan, the local planning authority is to prepare suitable Local Plans (s. 11 (6)). Whereas at present both Structure and Local Plan functions are carried out by county and county borough authorities, as from 1st April, 1974, Structure Plans will be the responsibility of county planning authorities and, under this general aegis, Local Plans will be made by the new, enlarged, district planning authorities. The usual requirements as to consultation, publicity, opportunity for objections and representations, and approval or modification, etc., by the Secretary of State apply to the creation of Local Plans (ss. 12 to 14) as they do in the case of Structure Plans. It is also provided that local planning authorities " may at any time make proposals for the alteration, repeal or replacement of a local plan adopted by them, and may at any time, with the consent of the Secretary of State, make proposals for the alteration, repeal or replacement of a local plan approved by him " (s. 15 (1)). Thus it will be seen that in terms of protection of a local environment there may be two stages at which action can be taken in relation to the development plan: first, objections or representations (i.e., suggestions, etc.) may be made at the time of the development plan inquiry—both Structure Plan and Local Plan; and secondly, if the objections do not succeed, then a " political " type of campaign may be carried out in order to obtain a resolution of the local planning authority to alter, repeal or replace the plan or part of it. In addition, it should be borne in mind that, in all cases related to development plans, the Secretary of State has complete power (subject to consultation) to act on default of the local planning authority, or to take other initiatives. It should be added that the development of New Towns (which are created only following government decisions) is carried out under the New Towns Act, 1965. New Towns are, except as to the insertion into any existing development plan area of their total entity, beyond the provisions of general development plan legislation. That is to say, the local planning authority will not be at liberty to draw up a local plan to cover the proposed New Town. Development of such a town is the responsibility of its own Development Corporation, but on completion of the town this Development Corporation will be wound up and a traditional type of elected council will replace it.

It is now necessary to consider the other main function of town and country planning mentioned on pp. 6–7, that is (*a*) planning by means of restrictive controls. This presents an extremely large subject and only the salient features will be noted here. For a more comprehensive discussion the reader is referred to *An Outline of Planning Law* by Sir Desmond Heap, and to the text of the Town and Country Planning Act, 1971, Pts. III to V.

With the exception of certain types of construction (or engineering

operation) and changes of use, which are clearly defined,[7] all
" material [7a] development " requires express planning permission.
" Development " is defined at considerable length in s. 22 of the
1971 Act, which then goes on to specify, in s. 23, precisely in which
circumstances such development must have planning permission.
However, the fact that, by s. 23, the majority of actions within the
definition of " development " require permission does not prevent
the operation of the General Development Order or the Use
Classes Order (see footnote 7, *ante*) whereby the need for express
planning permission may be dispensed with in certain specific cases.
For convenience the full texts of ss. 22 and 23 of the 1971 Act are
set out in Appendix A, p. 320, *post*.

The form and content of applications for (express) planning permission is by s. 25 to " include such particulars, and be verified by
such evidence, as may be required by the regulations . . . (prescribed
under the Act) . . . or by directions given by the local planning
authority . . ." (under the Act).   In practice it is found that printed
forms are issued by the local planning authority for the area, and
that these may vary slightly in style, although not in content.   In
certain special areas as defined in the development plan, or where
the proposed development is not in accordance with the development plan, it is necessary to publicise a notice of the particular
application in the local press and by the posting of a copy of the
notice on the site (s. 26).   In other cases, however, it is not necessary
for the applicant (who need not be the owner or occupier of the
land) to publicise the fact of the application save that, in all cases
of proposed development, the owner (if the applicant is not the
owner) and any agricultural tenants of the land (s. 27) must be
informed in writing.   Thus it may happen that an adjoining
owner [8] may be entirely unaware of a proposed alteration to the
nature of adjoining land or use thereof until, permission having
been granted, the development is commenced.   However, he may
be fortunate enough to find that the local planning authority, as
part of the process of arriving at a decision, will seek his

---

[7] Under the Town and Country Planning General Development Order, 1973
(S.I. 1973 No. 31) and the Town and Country Planning (Use Classes) Order,
1972 (S.I. 1972 No. 1385).

[7a] Some development may not be deemed " material," and therefore may not
require planning permission.

[8] Except in Scotland

views.[9]   As will be seen in later chapters, certain special types of land or building, such as Conservation Areas, Green Belt land, Listed Buildings, Ancient Monuments, etc., are afforded various types of additional protection, including requirements as to publicising proposals.

Upon receipt of a planning application (which, in the case of building and engineering works, will need to be supported by a separate application for approval under Building Regulations so far as the proposed methods of construction are concerned), the local planning authority's planning department officers will examine the proposal including plans and elevations in the light of any particular qualities of the site and of the surrounding area. The officers will then report to their planning committee, making comments or recommendations as deemed to be desirable. The committee will consider the application and may either grant permission, refuse permission, or grant permission subject to specified conditions or limitations (the latter as to time). Most local planning authorities lay down certain basic " standard conditions " as to layout, design, private car parking, etc.

In the event of refusal, or of permission being granted only subject to conditions or limitations, it is open to the applicant to appeal to the Secretary of State for the Environment. Alternatively he may decide to put in a different proposal for development, or he may think it politic to delay matters for a certain period of time.

The process of appeal is as follows. Notice of appeal, under s. 36, is to be served upon the Secretary of State within such period as may have been specified under the development plan, but not being less than twenty-eight days (s. 36 (2)).[8a]   The rules of procedure are laid down in the Town and Country Planning (Inquiries Procedure) Rules, 1969 (S.I. 1969 No. 1092), and relate to both private hearings (if any) and to public inquiries in connection with planning applications, tree preservation orders, listed building consent, and consent under the Advertisement Regulations.

The Rules begin to function with the writing of a letter from the Secretary of State addressed to the local planning authority (r. 4). Upon receipt of this letter the local planning authority must at

[8a] Normally six months.
[9] See Appendix B, Recommendation 2.

once inform both the Secretary of State and the appellant (r. 4 (1)) of the names and addresses of any third parties who have made representations (by virtue of ss. 23, 26 and 27 of the 1971 Act), i.e., either as owners or agricultural tenants, or because of the proposed development being of " bad neighbour " type.[10]   If the Secretary of State decides to hold a public inquiry he must fix a date giving at least forty-two days' notice in writing to the appellant, the local planning authority and all such " Section 29 parties " (previously to the 1971 Act known as " Section 17 parties ") (r. 5 (1)).   However, shorter notice may be given if the appellant agrees in writing to accept it.

By r. 5 (2) the Secretary of State may (and generally will) require the local planning authority to publicise the holding of the inquiry and the appellant must also display on the site, for at least three weeks immediately prior to the inquiry, a notice stating that it is to take place.

Written statements of submissions must then be sent to the Secretary of State, the local planning authority's statement being known as a " rule 6 statement," a copy of which must be served on the appellant and all " Section 29 parties " at least twenty-eight days before the inquiry.   These parties, and any other interested person, are entitled to inspect and, where practicable, to take copies of the documents in the case (r. 6 (5)).   The " rule 6 statement " must also include a copy of any direction given by the Secretary of State as to restriction of traffic (r. 6 (3)).   Provision is made for the expression in writing of views held by any government department, such as, say, the Ministry of Agriculture, Fisheries and Food.   A copy of any written statement made by the local planning authority to the Secretary of State must be provided to the appellant, but statements by the appellant need only be communicated to the authority where the Secretary of State so directs.

Rule 8 provides for representation of the Department of the Environment itself, and r. 9 for any other government departments, at the public inquiry, if they so desire.

The only persons entitled as of right (r. 7 (1)) to appear at the inquiry are: the appellant; the local planning authority (but including an authority exercising delegated planning powers);

---

[10] Such as a proposal likely to produce unpleasant odours, etc.

" Section 29 parties "; a New Town corporation, where applicable; a joint planning board, where applicable (e.g., in the case of National Parks: see p. 293); and any person on whom, under r. 5 (2) (*b*), the Secretary of State has required notice of the appeal to be served.   Thus, in many cases, societies and associations concerned with protection of the environment (local or national) will have no positive right to be heard; but, in practice, Inspectors will tend to hear any person or body present at the hearing and expressing a desire to make a statement.   The making of a statement, however, will not normally be extended to include any actual right to examine or cross-examine witnesses.   However, where several persons have interests in common (say a society, or a residents' association, or group of inhabitants) it is normally arranged that they may be represented if they wish by counsel, solicitor, surveyor or any other person.

The actual procedure at the public inquiry is at the Inspector's discretion (r. 10 (1)) both as to persons to be heard—with the exception of those entitled as of right—and as to the order of proceedings.   He may also rule as to the late admission of documents and may adjourn the inquiry if he deems it desirable. Even where a person entitled to appear fails to do so, the Inspector may, at his discretion, proceed with the hearing (r. 10 (6)).

However, the proceedings must be in accordance with the " rules of natural justice " (that is, it must be a fair hearing for all those parties entitled to appear), and the order in which the parties are heard is likely to be: (1) the appellant, who will open his case and call witnesses; (2) the local planning authority, which opens, calls witnesses and makes a detailed closing address; (3) there interested persons, who state their cases, and (at the Inspector's discretion) call witnesses; (4) the appellant's detailed closing address.   It should be particularly noted that, at planning inquiries it is common practice for the initial statements of expert (or other) witnesses to be put in in writing but to be read by the witness himself.   This method is in contrast to the normal requirements of the rules of evidence in the courts, where witnesses may only refer to notes in order to refresh the memory.

After the inquiry the Inspector will, in most cases, prepare a report and recommendation for consideration by the Secretary of State for the Environment (i.e., of necessity, an official or committee acting on the Secretary of State's behalf). However, in certain smaller matters the Inspector may now, by virtue of powers afforded to the Secretary of State under s. 36 (8) of, and Sched. 9, para. 4, to, the Town and Country Planning Act, 1971, be appointed to determine the matter himself and without reference to the Secretary of State. In all other cases the Secretary of State must then arrive at a decision, and he is entitled to differ from his Inspector's recommendation. Thus he may grant or refuse permission, or grant permission subject to conditions or limitations, entirely as he deems fit. In a proportion of cases the decision of the Secretary of State may differ from his Inspector's recommendations for reasons of wider (say national) policy. But, where the Secretary of State proposes to come to a decision which differs from that of his Inspector, he must first inform the appellant, the local planning authority, and also any " Section 29 party " who in fact appeared at the inquiry; and must afford them an opportunity of making written representations (r. 12 (2)) within twenty-one days.

If, of course, the Secretary of State receives any fresh evidence, then any of the above three categories of party may, as of right and within twenty-one days, call for the inquiry to be reopened (r. 12 (3)).

Finally, the Secretary of State will give a decision in writing, copies of which document must be sent to the appellant, the local planning authority, " Section 29 parties," and to any other person who has actually appeared at the inquiry and has asked to be notified (r. 13 (1)). The written decision is normally in letter form addressed to the appellant, and must be accompanied either by a copy of the Inspector's report or by a summary of the Inspector's conclusions and recommendations.

General comment as to planning control

At present [10a] all local planning authorities are either county or county borough councils. Any planning powers exercised by district or borough councils [11] are so exercised solely by virtue of periodic agreements between the district or borough and the county council whereby these powers are delegated. The precise

[10a] Until April, 1974.
[11] But not county borough councils.

system of delegation has varied considerably from county to county and, in some, overmuch responsibility has been retained by the county council and county planning committee; whereas in other counties an additional, intermediate, stage of delegation has been developed consisting of area planning committees which are made up of agreed proportions of county council and district council elected members. Area planning committees generally deal with proposals for most estate developments and matters such as Green Belt sites, whereas district planning committees recommend to their district councils decisions as to, say, single house developments, and the addition of private domestic garages, etc. However, the largest or most obviously controversial planning proposals, together with proposals for development plans, are dealt with by recommendations in the report of the county planning committee to the county council. In theory, in almost every case, it is the relevant *council*— county or district, etc.—which makes each planning decision and does so by voting for the adoption of the report of their planning committee. Matters which are not accepted are referred back to the committee. In special circumstances, however (as in the case of extreme urgency), the chairman of the council, or more frequently the chairman of the planning committee, may be given power to act *ad hoc* in relation to a specific anticipated situation. In the case of both area and county planning committee deliberations, recommendations—which are persuasive only—are normally received from the district council in whose area the land is situated.

At the top of the planning tree there is, however, the Secretary of State for the Environment, who may direct or advise any local planning authority, and who may alter any decision upon grounds of policy—save where he would thereby be *ultra vires* his powers under any statute. However, in so acting, the Secretary of State (or, for that matter, any Minister) must ensure that the case has been considered in accordance with the rules of natural justice. For example, an Inspector appointed to hear a planning appeal must hear fully the appellant, " Section 29 parties," and the local planning authority. He may, at his discretion, hear objectors and other interested parties. If the Inspector fails to hear the parties legally entitled to be heard, any decision eventually made by the Secretary of State without further hearing will be null and void, and the matter will have to be heard again from the outset.

In terms of protection of the environment, it is also important to realise that a given factual situation may well offend several statutes simultaneously. The most obvious examples arise in circumstances related either directly or indirectly to housing, where the given facts may be breaches under the Housing Acts (the principal Act being the Housing Act, 1957), the Public Health Acts (the principal Act being the Public Health Act, 1936), the Highways Acts (the principal Act being the Highways Act, 1959), and under town and country planning legislation (principally the Town and Country Planning Act, 1971, but extending to several others of different forms of title). By way of fictitious example, this situation could arise where, say, the owner (or occupier) of a Listed Building constructed a small extension to it without obtaining approval either for planning purposes or under the Building Regulations, and did so in such a way as to create and occupy a basement flat in which ventilation and drainage, etc., were substandard, the extension incidentally also extending onto land which although not part of a metalled road was, in fact, a grass verge and part of a public highway.[11a]

Various statutes, not strictly designed for town and country planning purposes, may thus be used to achieve an aim in protecting local amenities.

A further example may assist. A dwelling house can be extended by way of " permitted development "[12]—that is, providing the extension lies " within the curtilage "[13] of the dwelling house it may be constructed without express planning permission to a size of not exceeding 50 cubic metres (1,750 cu. ft.), or one-tenth of the existing volume of the house, whichever is the greater,[14] but

---

[11a] At least six separate breaches of statutory provisions thereby arise.

[12] " Permitted development " is provided for under the Town and Country Planning General Development Order, 1973 (S.I. 1973 No. 31) which stipulates twenty-three classes of permitted development.

[13] " Curtilage " is defined by the Court of Session in a Scottish case, *Sinclair Lockhart's Trustees* v. *Central Land Board* (1950), 1 P. & C.R. 195; affirmed (1951), 1 P. & C.R. 320, thus, " The ground which is used for the comfortable enjoyment of a house or other building may be regarded in law as being within the curtilage of that house or building, and thereby as an integral part of the same although it has not been marked off or enclosed in any way. It is enough that it serves the purpose of the house or building in some necessary or reasonably useful way." Also see *Stephens* v. *Cuckfield R.D.C.* [1960] 2 Q.B. 373 (C.A.).

[14] Development within the curtilage of a dwelling house is permitted under Class I of the General Development Order; see footnote 12.

subject to a maximum of 115 cubic metres (4,000 cu. ft.) and with certain limitations as to height.   Assume, therefore, that such action were taken in our fictitious case, and that the extension entirely destroyed the only acceptable view of an ancient church door.   If it could be established that the form of construction of the extension contravened the Public Health or Highways Acts,[15] then an order could be obtained for its removal.

It is not possible to pursue detailed explanations of the inter-related effects of these various types of legislation, but one further factor in this context must be borne in mind.   As a result of the history—some of which is ancient—of the development of local services, the functions of local authorities are divided in various ways which may not be immediately evident to the layman.   By the seventeenth and eighteenth centuries various localities had quite separate local boards fulfilling their own distinct functions.   Thus, the Poor Law was administered by the parochial overseers of the poor, the setting up of turnpike roads by turnpike trustees, the provision and maintenance of local drainage systems by yet another body, and so on.   These various functions were gathered together by Acts of Parliament during the nineteenth century and the majority allocated to newly-formed " local authorities " although, where in a given locality the need for a specific service was seen to lie beyond the limited boundaries of local authorities, statutory undertakers—such as water boards[16]—were separately set up. Towards the end of the last century greater co-ordination between elected local authorities was deemed to be necessary, and Parliament therefore created administrative counties,[17] which were given supervisory powers in various, but by no means all, of the local government functions, together with other more direct powers—as exemplified in recent years by town and country planning legislation.

It will assist a broad understanding of the system of local govern-ment, and thereby of some of the forces influencing the environment, if approximate lists giving the most usual committees of county and district, or borough, councils (pre-1974) are set out as below:

[15] If, say, the natural daylight to the extension were inadequate, or that it stood upon a public footpath which was classified as a " highway."
[16] i.e. for the collection, purification and supply of domestic water.
[17] Local Government Act, 1888.

County Council Committees	*District (or Borough) Council Committees*
Finance	Finance and General Purposes
General Purposes [18]	—
(Policy) [19]	(Policy) [19]
Education [20]	Education [20]
Highways [21]	Highways/Works [21]
—	Housing [22]
Estates [23]	—
Lands [24]	Parks
Planning [25]	Planning [25]
Special Development [26]	—
Health [27]	Health [27]
Police	—
Fire Brigade	—
Welfare Services [28]	Welfare and Children's [28,29]
Children's [29]	—
Libraries and Museums [30]	Museums, Concert Halls etc. [30]
	(possibly)
Small Holdings [31]	—

[18] Includes consideration of Parliamentary matters, such as Private Bills, on behalf of the county.

[19] These may be formally constituted or merely informal.

[20] Powers of decision lie solely with the county education authority, although boroughs may be invited to act in certain capacities, and school boards, appointed by the county, generally select and appoint staff.

[21] As already mentioned, highways may be Ministry, county or district (borough) roads.

[22] The largest function of a district or borough, to build and manage housing for rent (sale may also be permitted under current legislation).

[23] Management of county-owned property, such as the county council offices, police stations, local libraries, etc.

[24] Land owned by the county, which will include parks, other than district parks or National Parks.

[25] At present the district (or borough) planning committees have only powers delegated from the county. After 1st April, 1974, both county and district planning committees will exist in their own right (see p. 22).

[26] Where these committees exist their aim is to co-ordinate the wishes of the individual committees involved (e.g., planning, highways, education, police, etc.) in the formation of a plan for improvement or development of a large or difficult area; such as to re-habilitate a small town centre, or to site a community centre with medical and social service units, etc.

[27] Counties and districts (or boroughs) appoint Medical Officers for Health.

[28] Including the management of old people's homes, etc.

[29] Including the taking into care of children during temporary or permanent inability of the parents adequately to provide a home; and the management of children's homes.

[30] Counties provide libraries and museums, but some boroughs may own and manage their own local museums, concert halls, etc.

[31] Small holdings are agricultural lettings ranging between as little as a fraction of an acre to, say, 150 acres in size. They were set up by statute after the 1914–18 war in order to provide a "farming ladder" up which tenants might, possibly, progress.

County Council Committees	District (or Borough) Council Committees
Diseases of Animals [32]	—
National Park [33]	—
Local Taxation [34]	—
Staff [35]	—
Selection [36]	—
(Civil Protection) [37]	—
Other and *ad hoc*	Other and *ad hoc*

(2) *Reorganisation of local government in* 1974

Finally, in relation to the organisation of local government, there remains to be noted the proposed alterations to be applied as from 1st April, 1974. This is contemplated in the Local Government Act, 1972.[38]

Very briefly, the main structure will be as follows. The one-tier units (that is, the present county boroughs) will cease to exist. These authorities having been removed there will be two levels of operational local authorities, described as *counties* and *districts*, throughout England and Wales. A number of the existing counties will be reduced in size [39] and/or boundaries adjusted, and a total of 39 English, 8 Welsh, and 6 Metropolitan (excluding Greater London) counties will then exist. As stated, six of these will be described as " Metropolitan Counties " and will contain " Metropolitan Districts "—Greater London being excluded from the reorganisation. In metropolitan counties and metropolitan districts

[32] Diseases of animals are those upon which there is a statutory duty to report, and in relation to which regular checks must be carried out.

[33] National Parks may be managed, by statutory right, by an independent national park committee, but in many instances this committee is content to operate as a committee or a sub-committee to the planning committee of the county council.

[34] Local taxation is *not* rating, since this is a function only of district councils: it is concerned largely, at present, with motor tax.

[35] The staff committee selects and appoints council staff, other than principal officers such as the clerk, treasurer, county medical officer, chief planning officer, etc.

[36] The selection committee recommends the allocations of elected council members to appropriate committees.

[37] Civil protection committees existed by statute in all counties until disbanded by the last Labour Government. A number of counties have felt that a skeleton organisation should be maintained, and financed out of very limited allocations in the annual budget out of which the rate precept is fixed.

[38] As foreshadowed in the White Paper, " Local Government in England," Cmnd. 4584; and the Consultative Document, " The Reform of Local Government in England and Wales," published in February, 1971.

[39] An average size, with the exception of Metropolitan counties, will be about 300,000 people.

the functions of each will be very slightly different from those of ordinary counties and districts. The proposed metropolitan counties will be: Greater Manchester; Merseyside; Tyne and Wear; South Yorkshire; West Yorkshire; and West Midlands (including Coventry).

The preparation of *Local Plans* and the application of planning controls—that is, the power to grant or refuse planning permission or to take enforcement action against unauthorised development (including use) of land or buildings—will become the function primarily of the new district councils; although certain powers of approval or refusal may be reserved to the county authority in special cases or in special areas, where these are deemed necessary to ensure the fulfilment of the general strategy for the county, and are approved as such by the Secretary of State for the Environment.

Thus the new enlarged district councils will have a much increased function. It is to be hoped that this will be carried out with the same degree of impartiality and suppression of commercial self-interest as has commonly been the case amongst county planning authorities until now. One of the advantages (although there are also other disadvantages) in the fact that members of county councils are at present drawn from widely-dispersed electoral areas is that the opportunity for the establishment of self-interested groups (whether for private or public purposes) is minimal.[40]

As to other rearrangements of functions under the new organisation,[40a] *housing* (that is, responsibility for reduction of the local housing waiting list, and for the construction and management of council-owned dwellings) will continue to lie with districts; although the counties will have certain reserve powers. *Education, libraries,* and *personal social services* will continue to be controlled at county level, except in the metropolitan counties (other than Greater London), where they will be the responsibility of the metropolitan districts. *Highways*—which are at present divided as between (*a*) motorways, special roads and most trunk roads, for which the Secretary of State for the Environment (previously the Minister of Transport) is the " highway authority "; and (*b*) county roads; and (*c*) district and borough roads—will continue upon the present basis, save that

[40] Unlike the arrangement in the United States of America.
[40a] As to these allocations, see Pt. IX of the Local Government Act, 1972.

district councils may be empowered to maintain " urban " roads.[41]
These " urban " roads are defined as roads which are subject to a
speed limit of not exceeding 40 m.p.h. or are otherwise streets in
an urban area, but which are not trunk or classified roads. In
addition, the powers of maintenance of footpaths and bridleways
will be transferred from the county to the district councils, subject
to a reserve power as to overall county networks.

So far as environmental *health* functions are concerned, district
councils will continue to be concerned with food safety, hygiene,
clean air, nuisances, enforcement of the Offices, Shops and Railway
Premises Act, 1963, port health, slaughterhouses, and some other
related matters. They will be responsible for the collection of
refuse, but refuse disposal will be a function of county authorities:
this is an efficient division of responsibility due to the increasing
difficulty in finding sites for tips. Although, at the present time,
the administration of domestic water supply, sewerage and sewage
disposal is provisionally left with districts, these are related to a
national problem of water organisation (the purpose of the Water
Resources Board), and alterations may be anticipated in due time.
Lastly, so far as district authority functions are concerned, they will
continue as *rating authorities*, and as responsible authorities in the
application of *building regulations*.[42] *Police forces*, *traffic control*, and
fire services will be county responsibilities.

2. The Broad Fields of Environmental Policy covered by the Law

Although a few very early statutes [43] were created either to protect
natural resources, or to prevent various unpleasant activities (such
as disposal of domestic sewage into certain specific city streets), the
real concept of the need for the community as a whole to improve
or protect the environment has arisen only since about 1800. It
became evident that these measures were essential during the

---

[41] Until April, 1974, many such districts or boroughs may only appoint a highways
engineer individually approved by the county authority.
[42] The National Building Regulations, 1972, made by virtue of ss. 4 and 6 of the
Public Health Act, 1961, ss. 53, 61 and 62 of the Public Health Act, 1936, and
s. 24 of the Clean Air Act, 1956. They replace previous local authority byelaws throughout the country (save for Greater London) and impose a minimum
standard of building construction, including matters of height of rooms, size of
windows, sanitation, constructional measures for fire prevention, etc.
[43] As early as the fourteenth century.

Industrial Revolution, as a result of the physically dangerous and harmful effects of many manufacturing processes, together with the rapid increase in population.[44]   Until the development of manufacturing industry, by far the greater part of the population had lived and worked in the countryside—where the bounty of nature served to heal and prevent many physical evils, and where the danger of infection was less acute, due to the scattered population.

However, the new industrialists created both factories and hastily-constructed towns in which to house their workers. Many of these dwellings were of such poor layout and design that they became slums almost at once. By 1848 the Public Health Act imposed certain duties in relation to sewers, drains, etc.; and by 1851 the Labouring Classes Lodging Houses Act attempted to improve conditions in lodging houses. Measures were taken to prevent the escape of poisonous substances from factories by the Alkali, etc., Act, 1863, which enabled the Minister of Works to create an Alkali Inspectorate (which still continues in being).[44a] Local authorities were empowered to create local building byelaws under the Public Health Act, 1875, and removal of unhealthy groups of buildings became possible under the Housing of the Working Classes Act, 1890.

The present broad policies relating to control of the environment by application of legal powers and sanctions can only be sketched in outline here, but it is hoped that the following few pages may assist an understanding of subsequent chapters.

The purpose in planning the use of urban and rural areas throughout Britain is, ideally, to achieve the maximum possible standard of environment, as required by the inhabitants of these islands at any given time. This means that, in order to protect or to improve some areas of the land mass and inland and coastal waters, other areas must be increasingly used for less pleasant purposes. The Department of the Environment will presumably therefore aim so to co-ordinate the planning decisions of local planning authorities that (bearing also in mind the democratic process of election of local councils) the best possible overall national environment can be achieved. Thus, some areas which are already firmly committed to industrial use, and which have a satisfactory

[44] Population of the United Kingdom in 1800 was only about 10½ million, compared with about 56 million today.
[44a] Now styled the Alkali and Clean Air Inspectorate.

modern infrastructure [45] to support it, will probably be required to continue as industrial areas. At the other extreme, areas of open country which are in satisfactory—that is, reasonably productive—use for agriculture should, so far as possible, remain so used in order to meet (at least in part) national food requirements.

Thus, in order to attempt to achieve an ideal balance of land use, many interlocking factors have to be taken into account. These factors are investigated in county planning authority surveys carried out prior to making any development plan, and they are also investigated by the regional economic planning councils and boards who advise the Secretary of State for the Environment, as already mentioned. It may still not be entirely inappropriate to say that, in the geographical sense, one man's meat may be another man's poison; and the eventual proposals emerging from the deliberations of a local planning authority will, to a correct and democratic extent, represent the desires of the majority of the electorate of that council. (Nevertheless, the usual duty to act according to conscience and, at the same time, to apply knowledge and experience in the making of a decision will be exercised by members of the council.) Even then, however, a development plan as proposed by a local planning authority is subject to amendment by the Secretary of State for the Environment, who will, in turn, apply such measures of knowledge, experience and overall national interest as he believes to be appropriate. Although at present " old style " development plans, made under the Town and Country Planning Act, 1962, Part II,[46] still cover a large part of England and Wales, all future development plans will be in the " new style " introduced by the Town and Country Planning Act, 1968.[46] In the " new style " system (as already indicated at p. 22, *ante*), districts will be permitted to make their own local development plans.

In considering the achievement of a suitable balance one must bear in mind the weight of existing needs. An area of heavy industry will tend to create a rather larger area of land which is

---

[45] " Infrastructure " is an expression used by town and country planners to refer to the basic services and physical requirements needed to support any development (or existing use) of land. Thus, the most obvious items of infrastructure for, say, a housing area would be roads, drainage, lighting (including adequate power for street lighting), sufficient school places for the children of the housing area, social services generally, shopping facilities, public transport, and even recreational and sporting facilities; together with many other items.

[46] Now consolidated in Part II of the 1971 Act.

not really suitable for housing purposes; yet, as a corollary, it can be said that areas of industry and housing must exist within a reasonable distance of each other in order to meet labour requirements. Where the industry can be classified as " light industry " (that is, broadly speaking, of a type which will not unduly disturb a residential area in terms of noise, smoke, fumes, etc.), then the planning ideal can be achieved, namely of a ready source of employment close at hand, wherein also some of the problems of personal transportation are reduced. (Further reference to pollution is made below.)

In order to consider problems relating to the environment, and to attach the relevant legal remedies and sanctions to these problems, a series of more distinct viewpoints will be adopted in later chapters. Since the productive activities of mankind, such as the growing of food, the manufacture of goods for sale, and the extraction of minerals from the earth, are the prime influences upon our environment, these will be considered in the next three chapters of this work (namely, Chapter 2—Industry, including Service Industries; Chapter 3—The Countryside—I: Agriculture and Forestry; and Chapter 4—Extractive Industries).

These will be followed by a consideration of the means of transporting people, raw materials and finished products (Chapter 5—Transport—a necessary link), and by four chapters on the pollution caused by waste products and noise.

Having considered the basic essentials related to food and the means of industrial production, the matter next discussed is that of the planning and control of the places in which we elect—or may be forced of necessity—to live and work (Chapter 10—Residential and Shopping Areas; and Chapter 11—Offices).

Finally, in the rest of the book, the major specialised aspects of protection of particular environmental assets are considered—that is, those largely visual or historical attributes which are of value to mankind for aesthetic, sociological and psychological reasons, such as a beautiful landscape, pleasingly designed buildings and places which are a reminder of Britain's long history. These final four chapters range between control of the design of new buildings to the means of protection of ancient buildings, and the means of protection of the countryside. Protection of wild life is to be found in Chapter 15.

So far as existing planning needs are concerned, the population of Great Britain continues to rise and this, together with the increasing international commercial competition—which results from the new industries being created in the developing countries, and from immensely competitive Japanese efficiency and prices—renders it ever more essential to improve upon and expand British industrial production. Thus, the demand for housing and for industrial development represents an always rising target. At the same time, the situation is complicated, first, by an intense reluctance on the part of the average factory worker to move his home to another part of the country, even in the face of widespread unemployment; and secondly by the large areas of obsolete, or obsolescent, industry which are relics of this country's early lead in the world industrial revolution.[47] In this sense it can be claimed that the traditional industrial areas in Germany have, in the long run, benefited by their virtual obliteration during war-time bombing.

Partly, indeed largely, as a result of lack of employment in the Northern parts of England, and in Scotland, there has been a very considerable migration of people to the London area and home counties, and this in itself has accentuated housing and industrial problems. These problems will be further aggravated within the next few decades by the certain effects of entry into the European Economic Community, which will include a considerable increase in cross-Channel traffic in both goods and persons, and will result in a desire further to industrialise Kent, Surrey, Sussex and Hampshire. The ungainly size of London and its suburbs and other dormitory areas has presented increasing problems in terms of commuter and commercial traffic, as will be seen in Chapter 5.

It has, however, been the policy of recent governments to attempt to stem the tide of migration from the North, and particularly from the North East. Various government departments have been moved from London to those areas of England, both as part of a general scheme for decentralisation, and also as a token gesture. The creation of four of the five new metropolitan counties may well accelerate prospects of a revival of trade through the North Eastern ports direct to North West Europe.

The question of selection of the correct channels for the export of finished goods and for the import of raw materials is exceedingly complex, and much delay in decision has been experienced in

[47] See Appendix B, Recommendations 34, 37, and 38.

recent years, as governments have alternated in colour and have, until recently, avoided decisions as to the siting of " containerised " ports.[48]   The basic need is to site ports having deep water berths and specially designed wharves in such a way as to reduce inland traffic demand, and it may be that, in certain parts of Great Britain, it is preferable to ignore the present ports and industrial areas, and to stress the development of Maritime Industrial Development Areas (" MIDAS ").[49]   However, these decisions—as in the case of virtually all planning decisions on the siting of industry and general commerce—are inevitably related to the development of national and local road networks, and the revival of other forms of transport.

The question of housing is also of major importance.   As already stated, dwellings must be positioned for reasonable accessibility to centres of employment, yet the centres of many (if not most) of our towns and cities have long since ceased to provide adequately for this need.   In smaller towns, dwellings have tended to be converted to, or replaced by, shops and offices; and in large cities a great many residential areas have either declined to below the average modern requirement, or have deteriorated into slums declared as such by their housing authority.   In many ways, this complete deterioration can be more easily remedied.   As will be seen in Chapter 10, such areas may either be declared clearance areas,[50] or may be compulsorily acquired by the housing authority.   This then enables the area to be demolished and cleared, ready for redevelopment. In such cases, and also in the development of virgin land as, say, New Towns,[51] the planner and architect may have, so to speak, a clear canvas.   In recent years a fairly wide range of patterns have been applied to such canvases; not always with success.

To endeavour to summarise the points of discussion mentioned in this section of this chapter, it may be said that the law and the system of administration seek first to protect the individual and the community from harmful acts (or omissions) in terms of pollution, nuisance and the generally unneighbourly use of land; and secondly they seek either to improve physical conditions, or to prevent deterioration of physical conditions, by means of town and

[48] Containerised goods traffic is discussed in Chapter 5; see p. 89.
[49] See Chapter 5, Transport.
[50] See p. 206 for definition.
[51] Created under the New Towns Act, 1965.

country planning controls.   However, since solution of these problems is frequently a matter of reaching the best possible form of compromise—that is, between desires as to amenity on the one hand and commercial and material necessity on the other, the law is heavily influenced by matters of policy.   Thus, whereas it can be said that the carrying out of a building operation will (with certain exceptions)[52] require planning permission and that enforcement action can be taken to ensure demolition in the absence of such planning permission, yet the question of whether or not permission *ought to be granted* is seldom defined by the law, and will almost invariably be decided as a matter of desirable policy in the national (or sometimes local) interest.

Such decisions as to policy are made in the light of certain basic needs.   These are: the improvement of the national or regional economy; the distribution of population and employment; the tendency of towns to sprawl ever outwards; the need for urban renewal and reconstruction; the dispersal of population and industry (in relation to pollution and services); the protection and further development of agriculture; the need to exploit mineral deposits; the need to maintain and improve the flow and access of various types of traffic; and the need to preserve and improve amenities generally.

3. Practical and Strategic Problems

The purpose of this section is to set out, in the simplest possible terms, the practical problems in dealing with (*a*) the prevention or removal of a situation (including pollution), structure or other thing which is damaging to the environment; or (*b*) the securing of protection of a positive asset which is enhancing the environment; or (*c*) seeking to improve a local environment through the medium of a development plan, or by similar measures.

It will be evident from a study of the earlier parts of this chapter that, in terms of strategy, the battle for protection of any local amenity should, where possible, first be joined at the development plan inquiry stage.   If the development plan incorporates the protection of a given situation or asset, then the burden of proving a case for change on the part of, say, a developer is very much increased.   (As to this, Recommendations 1 to 5 in Appendix B

[52] See p. 12, and footnotes 7 and 7a thereon.

are particularly relevant, but Recommendation 4 will present practical difficulties.)

It may also be appropriate to say that it is generally advisable to avoid the placing of any public servant in a position in which he must commit himself in absolute terms, and particularly so if in writing. Such a commitment will immediately tie his hands and (unless he has exceeded his powers or is wrong as to his understanding of the law or the facts) will render a change of decision virtually impossible without subsequent reference to the committee or council to which he is responsible. (The same may apply at Parliamentary level.) Such a committee will incline towards supporting their staff, in the absence of any clear reason why they should not do so. It is, therefore, often of great advantage to muster as much support as possible—both in the form of reasoned and material argument, and in the form of public opinion—before a firm official line is adopted, in the hope that the officer concerned may thereby be encouraged to find means of justifying a recommendation which supports the particular cause.

However, once an inflexible position has been adopted by the authority concerned (be it a local planning authority, a Minister, a statutory undertaker or some other administrative board) the following factors will apply.

First, the fullest possible information should be obtained: this is an essential of any form of warfare or contest. The information must be accurate, and therefore initial data should be checked both as to sources and in relation to any conflicting facts or opinions. It is, for example, unlikely to be sufficient for one local inhabitant alone to hazard the view that a certain factual situation existed twenty years ago, or that, in his view, a particular building is an example of the best architecture of its period. Whereas *strength* of local opinion is, as will be seen later, of great value, expert opinion can normally only carry weight when put forward by an acknowledged expert.

After some thought, the author takes the view that it would be unwise to attempt to list, in a book of this general nature, those items of information usually required for use in planning inquiries, or for other purposes, such as pollution control. The reason for this decision is that, even in the case of the simplest planning appeal —say a single dwelling on a single site—a very great deal of information may, in given circumstances, be required, and these requirements can only be gauged from experience. For example, drainage of the site may or may not be relevant, dependent upon either the possibility of a gravity flow, or the availability, at economic cost to the local rate fund, of a pumping system.

The physical and aesthetic or historical features of the site and/or structure itself must first be considered. The needs of the immediate area must then be assessed; and subsequently (in certain cases) the overall needs of the region generally must be borne in mind. This latter area of information will certainly only be obtained by reference to official publications or statutes (such as, for example, " The Strategic Plan for the South East "[53] in the case of sites in London and the South East of England), together with evidence obtainable from witnesses who are expert in the functions of town and country planning, or of transport, or of pollution control, etc. It may be relatively easy to produce sufficient evidence of mere strength of local opinion as to the effects of development upon the immediate vicinity; but consideration of, say, housing needs in London and the South East relative to the Metropolitan Green Belt will necessitate an accurate discussion of statistics relating to the population and population changes, communications, industrial and commercial needs, agricultural production where applicable, and many other factors.

It may be of some assistance to mention a few of the more common planning factors which may assist an Inspector conducting a planning appeal inquiry in arriving at his conclusions.

The local development plan should be examined to verify the purpose for which the site has been zoned, and also the various purposes intended for adjoining and other sites in the locality. The presence of any special restrictions or policies, such as conservation areas, listed buildings, Green Belt land, tree preservation orders, areas of outstanding natural beauty, National Park land, etc. (all as discussed in later chapters) should be carefully noted. Any latent or patent physical defects in the site should be assessed and recorded. In constructional terms any local tendency towards soil subsidence, flooding or poor drainage facilities generally may or may not have been taken in issue under the building regulations application, and should not be ignored in the planning argument. The question of vehicular access—volume of passing traffic, gradient,

[53] Published H.M.S.O., 1970.

traffic site lines, nearness to hazards such as sharp bends—will also be very relevant, although this will generally have been considered by the highways surveyor for the local planning authority. Danger to old people, children and animals should be noted.

What is described as the " infrastructure " of the area is also of importance. This includes a great many items of public and private services which are normally required in connection with the particular type of development. Thus, domestic housing areas require supplies of water, electricity and, possibly, gas, together with some hygienic system of foul drainage. They also require public transport to run within a reasonable distance (e.g., houses for people less likely to have private cars should be on or near bus routes; commuters need train services, etc.). Shops having, in total, a fairly wide range of wares must be reasonably accessible, together with various static services such as hospitals, schools, post offices, libraries, welfare clinics, etc. In addition, other types of mobile service are essential, including district nurses, social services, police, fire, and ambulances. All these services, both static and mobile, are ultimately related to the adequacy of the local road system, as well as to the existence of public transport.

So far as the design and appearance of a new, or altered, structure is concerned, it must be borne in mind in terms of strategy that a developer may decide to strengthen his case by offering to modify elevations, or size or layout, and by proffering tree screens and various forms of camouflage. Equally, a conditional approval may be granted, subject to the developer's acceptance of such variations. These possibilities should always be anticipated and assessed.

Considerably more could obviously be said, but it is hoped that the various lines of thought so far indicated will assist in encouraging a flexible and thorough consideration of environmental problems. It therefore only remains to refer to one important item of strategy, the use of public opinion.

Unlike matters of law heard in the courts, the element of administrative (i.e., governmental) policy is always relevant in planning and environmental matters. Even in pollution control it may be deemed economically advisable to permit a certain excess of contamination in the interests of industry as a source of national income. In planning cases the balance may often be swung by sheer weight and sincerity of local, or national, public opinion. The permanent loss of an amenity may be considered to be unjustified even in the light of a considerable short-term advantage. However, it is important to realise that evidence of local opinion must be convincing in character. Thus, an eccentric zealot may, upon giving evidence, actually weaken a case—more especially if the impression is given that only local eccentrics take the particular view, and that the ordinary person is unconcerned. Again, if objectors wish to record their views in writing for submission to the local planning authority or to the Secretary of State, it is infinitely more impressive if a few hundred personally written letters can be achieved, than where a few hundred signatures are appended to a mass petition. Protection societies serve a most useful purpose by their sheer existence, since they are able to mobilise support at shorter notice, and are also generally in a position diplomatically to select the most appropriate witnesses for any given purpose.

CHAPTER 2

INDUSTRY
(INCLUDING SERVICE INDUSTRIES)

1. General

The siting (or re-siting) of industry, and the administrative
mechanisms employed for accomplishing this purpose, are of
critical importance in Britain, due to two factors of about equal
significance. First, the need to earn foreign currency by manufacture of goods for export is now fundamental to our economy:
without a considerable and expanding flow of exports it would not
even be possible to feed[1] the present population. Secondly, the
small land area comprised in the British Isles renders it essential
that industrial sites be most carefully selected, not only from the
standpoint of protection of the environment, but also in order to
avoid the incidental waste of land capable of use either for
agricultural production or for dwellings.

In order to keep pace with foreign industrial competition (which
exists both in the form of sales competition in new markets as they
open up in developing countries, and also in terms of economy in
methods of manufacture which can result in competitive price-
cuts) it is evident that new industry must be sited with a view to the
availability of economic and efficient transport systems for both
incoming raw materials and motive fuel, and for outgoing finished
goods. In addition there must be ready availability of suitable
labour; and the more sophisticated the techniques to be employed,
the higher the quality of work-force required.

To this must also be added the special needs of certain types of
manufacture, such as the use of soft or hard water or the necessity
for relatively clean air.

And lastly, in this initial outline, one must note the additional
difficulty, more acute in Britain than in almost any other country,
which results from our early leadership in the world industrial
revolution, namely, the existence of many areas of entirely outdated,

---

[1] At present almost half of the food consumed in Britain has to be imported.

34

and even partially abandoned, industrial conurbations.[2] Further, these areas of obsolete or obsolescent industry were originally served by a transport system based upon railway and waterway services, which have been permitted over many decades to become increasingly inefficient and uneconomic due, in part, to failure to invest in order to meet modern requirements and techniques.[3]

Within the framework of the geographical problems referred to above, the following factors will require to be considered by the local planning authorities and by the Department of the Environment in arriving at a national strategy for the location of industry and at individual Structure Plans for the area of each local planning, i.e., county level, authority—that is to say, under the " new style " development plans introduced by the 1968 Town and Country Planning Act and re-enacted by way of consolidation in the Town and Country Planning Act, 1971.

(*Note*: In considering the following matters, however, the reader should also refer to the Recommendations, numbers 30, 31, 34, and 36 to 38, put forward by the Dartmouth Committee, for the text of which see Appendix B, p. 325; but, in so doing, it may be found preferable to read initially the remainder of this chapter.)

Clearly, it is necessary to trace all existing factories in the planning area, and to evaluate their present output and future requirements. Provision will generally have to be made (according to the evidence available) (i) for anticipated expansion of each industrial plant; *or* (ii) for reduction in size in the light of any falling demand for products; *or* (iii) merely for modernisation of buildings and/or equipment in order to reduce production costs and overheads or to avoid pollution of the environment. The existing pattern of industry in any given area will also influence the form of any new types of manufacture in terms of the availability of suitable employees. Thus, a firm contemplating a heavy industrial plant may find the labour market more readily tapped in an area in which

---

[2] See Appendix B, Recommendations 34, 37 and 38.

[3] It is, for example, surprising that commercial interests have failed, until recently, to realise that the carriage by canal of bulk cargoes of many types can be achieved with maximum economy, due to reduction of labour (i.e., one bargeman piloting a long barge, or string of barges, in place of a large number of lorry drivers transporting the same total bulk of cargo). Providing the element of labour cost does not become excessive the speed of travel is in many ways irrelevant once a regular and frequent flow of cargo is achieved at the point of destination. See also Appendix B, Recommendation 36.

heavy industry already exists. And, upon the same line of argument, a town in which a particular craft or technological skill has
a tradition will be better equipped to accommodate new factories
of a similar, or related, type.

However, the local planning authority will, in general, tend to
have only a persuasive function in encouraging development of
new factories, since the ultimate initiative will come from the
investors in private or public companies. The attitude adopted
by the local planning authority as to the suitability of zoning, or
individual siting, of various types of industry (ranging from heavy
to light industry and from, say, oil ports and refineries to service
industries such as computer centres), will, however, serve either to
encourage or discourage investment in a given locality.   This aspect
of local planning authority policy is, of course, most significant in
relation to protection of a particular local environment, whether
from the standpoint of pollution or of scenic and other aesthetic factors.

Again, the local planning authority, in conjunction with the
various highway authorities and the Department of the Environment, may adopt a policy for a local transport system (including
roads, railways, canals and air traffic) which tends either to encourage or to discourage expansion of industry in that locality.   In
fact, circumstances may exist in which the *avoidance* of certain routes
for trunk and local roads will act as a more effective deterrent to
industrial development than will constant refusal of speculative
planning applications.

Persuasive influences upon the zoning of industry

In addition to the factors already considered the following
matters should be borne in mind.

(a) Financial incentives

Regional, or more local, development of industry may be deliberately influenced by financial incentives provided by the national
government, and this is principally related to local employment
needs.   These needs are indicated in considerable detail by monthly
returns supplied to the Department of Employment and Productivity
from every local Employment Exchange Area, wherein are stated
the numbers of unemployed persons and also estimated numbers of
employed persons.   These are further sub-divided into types of
employment.   For the purposes of development plan surveys these
statistics are used by comparison with wider regional, and also

national, figures. They are also used in studies of comparable monthly and yearly trends, and are further divided as between male and female employees.

The normal categories of industry used for these purposes are as follows:

(i) *Extractive Industry:*
 1. Agriculture, forestry and fishing
 2. Mining and quarrying

(ii) *Manufacturing Industry:*
 3. Food, drink and tobacco
 4. Chemicals
 5. Metal manufacture
 6. Engineering and electrical goods
 7. Shipbuilding and marine engineering
 8. Vehicles
 9. Metal goods not elsewhere specified
10. Textiles
11. Leather, leather goods and fur
12. Clothing and footwear
13. Bricks, pottery, glass, cement, etc.
14. Timber, furniture, etc.
15. Paper, printing and publishing
16. Other manufacturing industries

(iii) *Service Industry:*
17. Construction
18. Gas, electricity and water
19. Transport and communications
20. Distributive trades
21. Insurance, banking and finance
22. Professional and scientific services
23. Miscellaneous services
24. Public administration and defence

It would not be appropriate to seek to discuss these categories in detail in a work primarily related to environmental matters, but the following comments may be relevant. In general it would appear that the categories are selected essentially from the standpoint of types of employee. For example, members of a branch office of an insurance company may not be familiar with banking procedures, but will be people tending to have the same characteristics in terms of interest and mathematical ability as bank employees. Further, there may, in a given area, be a close relationship between the activities of various separate categories, such as between category No. 1, forestry, and No. 14, timber, furniture, etc.; or again, between No. 1, agriculture, and No. 3, food, etc. (in terms of cheese or butter making); or between categories Nos. 5–9 inclusive.

It should also be remarked, in regard to town and country planning, that in some areas the extent of activity in category No. 2, mining and quarrying, may tend to decrease as natural resources are worked out: but, equally, that other mineral resources may be increasingly, or newly, tapped as transport facilities improve, or as a relatively rare mineral (such as copper) becomes more expensive on the world market.

As to category No. 17, the construction industry, this activity is inseparably linked with the rate of rise in prosperity, general productivity, and population of the area. Thus, for example, whereas the rate of construction may be increased by industrial stimulation in an area declared to be a " development area," [4] the rate of construction in many other areas which tended to be principally concerned with the service industries has tended to decrease in direct relation to the decline in such service industries which has been deliberately induced by the imposition of Selective Employment Tax. However, by virtue of s. 122 of the Finance Act, 1972, Selective Employment Tax will be abolished with effect from 1st April, 1973.

It must, however, be emphasised that the statistics referred to in the employment classifications are interpreted by the Department of Employment and Productivity by careful reference to other (annual) returns which are completed by local factories. These returns are designed to provide information in confidence to the Department. Accordingly, the completed forms are coded for identification and used in their coded state in order to obscure the name of the individual factory. Thus, the information provided about the size of installations, number of employees and rate of productivity is concealed from any potential competitors.

On a similar principle, local planning authorities generally make it a matter of policy not to provide over-specific information to inquirers who intend to consider investment and development in

[4] See p. 39, *post.*

the local planning authority area, and in particular to avoid the provision of the names and addresses of existing factories in that area. Nevertheless, one of the functions of a county planning officer's department is to offer general advice to those potential developers who request it and to indicate whether or not a particular enterprise would, in their view, be, in the long run, of value to the locality.

Reference has already been made to development areas. These are areas declared by order of the Secretary of State for Employment and Productivity, by virtue of s. 1 of the Local Employment Act, 1972, to be areas in which the extent and type of unemployment is deemed to warrant a special encouragement of growth of manufacturing industry, and, therefore, in which the Exchequer will make special grants and loans available to concerns seeking either to set up entirely new industry (including moving to the area from other parts of Britain), or to construct considerable extensions to plant and machinery, thereby increasing the labour force required. So far as the United Kingdom is concerned, the declared *development areas* consist of the whole of Scotland; almost the whole of Wales (i.e., excluding small areas in Flint and Denbigh and in the Cardiff and Monmouth areas); the entire Northern Economic Region,[5] with a small exception near the city of York; about half the county of Cornwall (i.e., the entire area of the county west of Plymouth, but extending eastwards along the north coastal belt); certain western areas of Devon; the Merseyside area of Lancashire; two further areas in the northern parts of the Yorkshire and Humberside Region. In some cases, as in the Plymouth development area, it is the Government's intention that the expansion of manufacturing industry within the development area itself will also provide employment for the population inhabiting the surrounding largely agricultural sub-regions.[6]

It is relevant to interject here that, in some cases, the declaration of a development area is an acceptance in principle that the industrial worker may be most reluctant to leave his home town or locality, even for the prospect of extremely profitable employment in another part of the country.

In addition, other areas may be designated intermediate

---

[5] Northumberland, Durham, Cumberland, and the Northern parts of Yorkshire and Westmorland.
[6] As to Regional Economic Planning Councils and sub-regions see p. 42.

areas (also by s. 1 of the above Act) and receive modified assistance. [6a]

Nevertheless, there is a strong element in Government policy which, where possible, leans towards the encouragement of new industry at the most suitable centres from the standpoint of transport services, and notably as to export facilities.   There has also, in recent years, been consideration given to the development of Maritime Industrial Development Areas (" MIDAS "—perhaps a sinister pseudonym).   These are intended to be industrial complexes designed round major existing or future seaports, in order to provide a saving in transport costs (both in terms of cost per mile and also in terms of highway and railway capital investment cost) in relation particularly to those types of manufacture which are principally concerned with large-scale export and/or the use of imported raw materials.   The areas which have, at various stages, been favoured for the possible development of " MIDAS " have included the Humber, Cardiff and Newport, the Clyde, and the Lower Medway.   By way of example, the scale of development mooted for, say, the Medway would cover 8,000 acres, with a possible need for new homes to be specially constructed in the region of about 70,000 dwellings.[7]   However, no doubt firmer policies may develop during the next decade as the more precise commercial requirements resulting from membership of the European Economic Community become known.

The orientation of Government policy is also assisted by information, advice, and diplomatic activity originating from *Regional Economic Planning Councils* which exist for each of the ten Economic Planning Regions into which Great Britain [8] is now divided, separate provision having been made for Northern Ireland.   The relevance of the functions of Economic Planning Councils to industry in the particular context of the environment will now be briefly discnssed, but reference should also be made to Chapter 1 as to economic planning in relation to town and country planning generally.

(*b*) *Regional Economic Planning Councils*

The constitution of the Regional Economic Planning Councils

[6a] Intermediate Areas and Derelict Land Clearance Areas Order, 1972 (S.I. 1972 No. 421), as amended by S.I. 1972 No. 585.

[7] But see Appendix B, Recommendations 30 and 31.

[8] i.e., England, Scotland and Wales.

may well be altered as part of the process of modernisation of the present structure of local government; but at present the Economic Planning Councils consist of members entirely appointed by the Secretary of State for the Environment; that is, they are individually selected and none sit as delegates (*per se*) from local authorities. Selection is intended to be based upon the member's knowledge and experience and . . . "They are drawn from both sides of industry and from the local authorities, and also include individuals expert in various fields " [9] (the latter including academic and professional experts).

The Economic Planning Councils have 25 to 30 members and they are also assisted by Planning Boards which are made up of "representatives in each region of the principal departments concerned with regional planning. The Boards work under the chairmanship of the senior representative of the Department of the Environment in the region." [9] However, it must also be noted that the Department of the Environment has recently developed a more localised system whereby there is a senior *town and country planning* administrator (a permanent civil servant) having an office situated actually within each region.

In view of the earlier discussion of the functions of Regional Economic Planning Councils,[10] it will suffice to say here that they are concerned with both the urban and the rural economy within the region; and that they are charged with recommending (but not implementing) the broad policies for economic planning for that region. So far as possible the Economic Planning Councils are to have two-way discussions with industrial interests and others, and to publish reports of their researches and policies. However, it must also be emphasised that all members of Economic Planning Councils and (virtually) all experts (such as county planning officers, county surveyors, chairmen of local chambers of trade, etc.) who are consulted are first required to sign declarations under the Official Secrets Act, 1911, and subsequent Orders thereunder. There is thus strict control over public discussion and speculation in relation to problems under consideration at any given time. Bearing in mind that about a third (if not more) of the total membership of such a council may tend to be drawn by appointment from the members or officials of local authorities, difficulties must

[9] Circular of Department of Economic Affairs, June 1968.
[10] Chapter 1.

arise in the minds of such members when current problems happen to become the subject of debate by their local authority council. However, the need for strictly confidential investigation and discussion by Economic Planning Councils may well arise from time to time, and economic speculation or unnecessary public alarm should be avoided by these means.

The formal link between the Economic Planning Council in any region and other statutory authorities may be provided for by means of Standing Conferences, consisting of appropriate area associations, or directly with single local authorities where necessary.

In any event, it is open to local planning authorities to arrange to form Joint Advisory Committees, consisting of delegates from adjoining counties and county boroughs; these delegates being taken partly from elected councillors or aldermen and partly from officers of each authority.[11]   In addition, it is common practice for Economic Regions to be divided into permanent sub-regions which are delineated on the ground upon a basis of having distinct sub-regional problems.

The basic information obtained by the permanent staff of each Regional Economic Planning Council is largely of the same type as the statistical data amassed by local planning authorities, but the former will have additional value in that it may be combined and collated so as to provide overall studies of areas, sub-regions, and of the region as a whole, thereby making comparisons beyond the confines of county boundaries.

In addition to an analysis of the structure and output of manufacturing industries within the region, the Economic Planning Council will also be concerned with a study of localised dependence upon the various types of manufacture, and in forecasting change and development under a given range of circumstances.   This will also be related to studies of the regional extractive industries, i.e., mining and quarrying, agriculture, forestry and fisheries; and of energy supplies; ports and communications generally; and office activities. Each of these will also be related to the present and potential capacity of the construction industries in the region.   In addition it will be necessary to consider the need to develop the tourist trade (both for national use, and as a source of foreign currency); to protect special amenities (such as National Parks, Nature Reserves,

[11] Such Joint Advisory Committees have no power to legislate, but members report back to their own local authorities.

etc.); and to extend facilities for education and vocational training, for medical and hospital services, and for local recreation (the arts, sport and general entertainment).

It will be seen, therefore, that the recommendations of a Regional Economic Planning Council should be based upon a " global " view of the region, and that some declared policies as to environmental matters may be based upon studies and information which may not be immediately evident (or even available) to the protectionist in the immediate vicinity of an affected area.

To summarise the objectives of an analysis, for both economic planning and town and country planning purposes, it may be said that the principal aims should be: to conserve any valuable resources which may be adversely threatened by development; to develop useful resources and to encourage such development; to remove undesirable things or to reverse undesirable trends (either as a matter of urgency, or as the opportunity arises at a later date, dependent upon the degree of such undesirability); to reserve land for anticipated needs, whether for future public or private use, and in order to ensure suitable location; and generally to seek to plan well in advance in order to minimise future problems.

(c) Local authorities and industrial estates

It should be mentioned that upon a very much smaller scale than the matters discussed hitherto in this chapter it is not uncommon for local authorities, at county district or county borough level, to encourage the development or the re-location of industry in a locality by arranging for the development of industrial (or " trading ") estates. Many of these estates are relatively small in overall size and are laid out and constructed either with the aid of funds raised by the local authority or, more frequently, by the employment of private developers who are required to submit a scheme as to layout, design and rental terms to the local authority. In general, estates of these types contain buildings designed for flexibility in use by light industry, together with supporting storage and office facilities. The buildings therefore tend to be laid out to a standard size, within a systematic road layout, and to be let to industrial tenants, each for a fixed term.

2. Legal Controls

There are now two parallel, but distinct, systems of control over proposed industrial development. In addition to the usual planning controls (which require the applicant to submit either initially an outline, or in any event a detailed planning application),[12] it was found necessary to impose an extra means of supervision upon the growth of manufacturing industry directly through central government.

The system was introduced by the Town and Country Planning Act, 1962 (ss. 38, 39 and 40), and was elaborated by the Control of Office and Industrial Development Act, 1965 (ss. 19 to 22) and the Industrial Development Act, 1966 (ss. 22 to 27). However, these provisions have now been consolidated and are to be found in Part IV of the Town and Country Planning Act, 1971, ss. 66 to 72, together with the provisions as to enforcement of planning control now re-enacted in Part V of the same Act.

The practical effect of this legislation was originally that, throughout England and Wales, and (by the Local Employment Act, 1960) Scotland, whenever development was proposed consisting either of the erection of an " industrial building " of one of the " prescribed classes," [13] or of a change of use whereby premises not being an industrial building of one of the prescribed classes should become such an industrial building (s. 67 (1) of the 1971 Act), in either case in excess of a specified area of " industrial floor space," [14] then an Industrial Development Certificate had to be obtained from the Department of Trade and Industry prior to making the normal type of planning application.

However, the position has been modified by the Town and Country Planning (Industrial Development Certificates) Regulations, 1972 (S.I. 1972 No. 904) and 1973 (S.I. 1973 No. 149), whereby Industrial Development Certificates are no longer required in a considerable number of employment exchange areas. These areas constitute parts of the Northern, the Merseyside, the Welsh and the South Western Development Areas, together with the Scottish Development Area excepting Edinburgh, Leith and Portobello, and also Skelmersdale New Town. With regard to the

---

[12] Save where development is of a type authorised by the Town and Country Planning General Development Order, 1973 (S.I. 1973 No. 31) or is carried out under the Town and Country Planning (Use Classes) Order, 1972 (S.I. 1972 No. 1385). As to the meaning of " development " see Chapter 1, at p. 12, and Appendix A, at p. 320.

[13] See p. 46.

[14] See pp. 45–47, and notably p. 47.

remainder of Great Britain, Industrial Development Certificates (I.D.C.s) are required whenever the exemption limit of industrial floor space is to be exceeded. Again, however, the exemption limit figure to be applied depends upon the part of the country in which the proposed development is to be situated, since *two* limits now exist by virtue of the Town and Country Planning (Industrial Development Certificates: Exemption) (No. 2) Order, 1972 (S.I. 1972 No. 996). Thus, an exemption limit of 15,000 square feet [15] is applied throughout the country *with the exception of*: (*a*) those areas already referred to as entirely exempt; and (*b*) those areas specified in the Schedule to the last-mentioned Order, in which case the exemption limit is now 10,000 square feet. The areas given in this Schedule are: Greater London; the administrative counties of Bedford, Berkshire, Buckingham, Essex, Hampshire, Hertfordshire, Kent, Oxford, Surrey, East Sussex and West Sussex; the municipal borough of Poole (Dorset); and the county boroughs of Bournemouth, Brighton, Canterbury, Eastbourne, Hastings, Luton, Oxford, Portsmouth, Reading, Southampton and Southend-on-Sea.

It is of interest that many areas which had a previous exemption limit (under the superseded Order, S.I. 1970 No. 1849) of only 5,000 square feet, have now a very considerably increased exemption limit of 15,000 square feet. These areas include: the administrative counties of Cambridgeshire and the Isle of Ely, Herefordshire, Huntingdon and Peterborough, Leicestershire, Lincoln, Norfolk, Northamptonshire, Rutland, Salop, Staffordshire, East Suffolk, West Suffolk, Warwickshire, and Worcestershire. They also include the county boroughs of Birmingham, Burton-on-Trent, Coventry, Derby, Dudley, Great Yarmouth, Ipswich, Leicester, Lincoln, Northampton, Norwich, Solihull, Stoke-on-Trent, Walsall, West Bromwich, Wolverhampton, and Worcester (as originally listed in the Schedule to the Order of 1970).

The provisions as to the application of an exemption limit according to the amount of industrial floor space to be developed require further explanation, and can be briefly set out as follows:

(i) No formal step may be taken in a planning application until an I.D.C. is obtained, since it is provided that a copy of the certificate must accompany such an application and, in the absence of this document, the local planning authority is not permitted to

---

[15] Metric measurements are not used in the Order.

entertain the application.   However, initial informal discussions
may take place with the officers of the local planning authority and,
in any event, the application for an I.D.C., although addressed to
the Secretary of State for Trade and Industry, is generally transmitted via the local planning authority.

(ii) The expression "prescribed classes" means such types of
manufacturing industry as the Secretary of State for Trade and
Industry may by order prescribe.   To date the "prescribed classes"
include all types of manufacturing industry.

(iii) The meaning of "industrial building" is given in s. 66 of
the 1971 Act.   It is "a building used or designed for use:—

(*a*)   for the carrying on of any process for or incidental to any of
the following purposes, that is to say—

(i)   the making of any article or of part of any article; or

(ii)   the altering, repairing, ornamenting, finishing, cleaning, washing, freezing, packing or canning, or adapting for sale, or breaking up or demolition, of any
article; or

(iii) without prejudice to the preceding sub-paragraphs,
the getting, dressing or preparation for sale of minerals
or the extraction or preparation for sale of oil or
brine;

(*b*)   for the carrying on of scientific research,

being a process or research carried on *in the course of a trade or business*."

It is also provided (s. 66 (2)) that any premises which, within
the context of s. 66 (1), are designed as ancillary to the above uses
of other premises or are comprised in the same building or the same
curtilage, are to be treated as similarly used.

Thus "industrial building" for the purposes of control under
Part IV of the 1971 Act is defined by the use to which it is intended
to be put, and the purpose of such use must be in connection with a
"trade or business."   However, it must be noted that "trade or
business" does not mean simply for commercial purposes, so that
a charitable workshop, even running at an overall loss, will be
subject to industrial development control unless none of the products
are for ultimate sale.   In order to complete the definition, s. 66 (3)
then defines an "article" as "an article of any description,
including a ship or vessel"; a "building" includes part of a building; and "scientific research" "means any activity in the field of
natural or applied science for the extension of knowledge."

(iv) The reference to "industrial floor space" is interpreted (s. 68 (3)) as follows: "the floor space comprised in an industrial building or industrial buildings of the prescribed classes." The floor space area in fact referred to is to be measured externally, that is, so as to include exterior or party walls.[15a] The stipulation that all such proposed industrial floor space in excess of 15,000 and 10,000[16] square feet shall require an I.D.C. is given in s. 68 (1) of the 1971 Act, as amended, and provision is also made, by s. 69 (1), whereby the Secretary of State may, by order, from time to time, direct that s. 68 (1) be amended as to the area of floor space down to a minimum figure of 1,000 square feet.

(v) It must finally be remarked, as part of this explanation of the general statement on p. 44 *et seq.*, that special provision is made to prevent the evasion of control by piecemeal development. Any industrial development which is proposed either within an intended planning application, or which is related to a site on which earlier planning approvals have been granted on or after 1st April, 1960, is to be subject to an Industrial Development Certificate whenever the total industrial floor space, i.e., proposed and "related development" together, will exceed a total of 15,000 square feet (or 10,000 square feet if applicable). The precise definition of "related development" is set out in s. 68 (4) and, broadly, includes other buildings within the same scheme or project, whether due to be developed simultaneously or not.

No appeal lies from a refusal by the Secretary of State[17] to grant an Industrial Development Certificate, save in the comparatively rare case of an appeal on a point of law only to the High Court.

In considering whether or not to grant an I.D.C., the Secretary of State[17] is to base his decision upon whether the development proposed "can be carried out consistently with the proper distribution of industry . . ." and ". . . shall have particular regard to the need for providing adequate employment in development areas" (development areas are as specified in s. 15 of the Industrial Development Act, 1966; that is, areas in which the encouragement of local employment and industrial development is of particular importance, and which are accordingly specified as such by the Department of Trade and Industry). In this connection the exemption from

---

[15a] Presumably to the mid-point of a party wall, if in dual ownership.
[16] *Ante*, p. 45.
[17] Secretary of State for Trade and Industry.

I.D.C. requirements of the development areas specified in the Schedule to S.I. 1972 No. 904 and S.I. 1973 No. 149 (see p. 44, *ante*) will be in mind.

In deciding upon whether or not to issue an I.D.C., the Secretary of State for Trade and Industry will not be directly concerned with town and country planning questions, but rather with matters of national employment and with national (or regional) industrial output.   It accordingly follows that, in theory at least, the existence of an I.D.C. has no direct effect as to policy considerations upon the exercise of a purely town and country planning decision to be arrived at solely by the local planning authority.   However, two important factors must be noted.   First, provision is made for the attachment of restrictions or conditions to an I.D.C. at the discretion of the Secretary of State.[17]   If these are attached they must subsequently be included in any subsequent terms imposed upon the planning permission if granted by the local planning authority: if the planning permission is inconsistent with the terms of the I.D.C., the I.D.C. is to prevail (s. 71 of the 1971 Act).   But secondly, there is no requirement that following the issue of an I.D.C., planning permission be granted.   It is entirely open to the local planning authority to refuse permission of any sort.   However, the existence of an I.D.C. will tend to encourage the applicant to appeal to the Secretary of State[18] upon purely *planning* grounds; and, invariably, the fact that an I.D.C. has been granted will be used as a point of argument at the subsequent planning inquiry.   In a sense this facility represents a weakness in the system, since the I.D.C. may have been granted without consideration of local amenity factors.   However, it may be possible to reach a compromise on a given site whereby the local need for manufacturing industry can be met but subject to strict conditions as to, for example, user and screening of the proposed factory.

[18] Secretary of State for the Environment.

CHAPTER 3

THE COUNTRYSIDE — I:
AGRICULTURE AND FORESTRY

1. General

The progressive loss of rural environment is, clearly affected by those general factors already discussed in the first chapter of this book, including the demands of and control of development in various ways as discussed individually in other chapters.[1] Further, the particular question of legal control of the balance between the requirements of rural conservation and of the national need for recreation in the countryside is considered in detail in Chapter 15, The Countryside—II: Conservation and Recreation. However, it may be appropriate here to indicate very briefly the influences exerted upon our open country.

The rural environment is primarily influenced by the demands made upon it, and these demands may be listed as follows:

(A) The needs of agriculture in the widest sense, that is including traditional farming,[2] horticulture, intensive food production (such as broiler chicken rearing, mushroom growing and intensive veal calf rearing), and also forestry. These factors will be considered in the present chapter, with the exception of pollution by agricultural waste products (Chapters 7 and 8).

(B) The demands, in an intensively industrialised country such as Britain, for industrial and commercial development as an essential requirement of national economic survival (as to which see Chapters 1, 2 and 4).

(C) The demands, particularly resulting from (B), for an improved and intensified transport system (as to which see Chapter 5).

(D) The demands, also resulting from (B), for domestic housing, and medical and social service buildings (as to which see Chapter 10).

(E) The demands of the non-agricultural population made upon the countryside in terms of a variety of recreational activities, that

---

[1] For example, Industry, Chapter 2; Housing, Chapter 10.
[2] For example, dairy, mixed, hill farming, etc.

is, both for physical and for mental recreation, as stated above (as to which see Chapter 15).

In the national sense, it is clearly necessary to strike an accurate balance between the need to maintain economic growth and commercial prosperity, and the equally important requirement in a relatively small island that open land be retained, so far as possible, both for food production and also to offer a degree of peace of mind to the individual together with space for physical recreation.

At present the striking of such a balance is not very finely controlled, due to the fact that there is no overall assessment of the comparative values of areas of rural land as such. In other words, although certain well-known areas have been classified as Green Belts or as National Parks, and other rather lesser-known smaller areas are defined as Areas of Outstanding Natural Beauty, or Nature Reserves, etc., by far the greater part of the countryside is classified as merely " white land." That is, land which has been deliberately excluded from commitment as to policy by the local planning authority when drawing up the development plan (and, in the case of an approved plan, has been similarly treated by the Secretary of State for the Environment). Thus, most agricultural land is afforded no special protection in development plans and is open to applications for development. It follows that any assessment, even when made by the Department's planning Inspector at a local planning appeal, tends, of necessity, to be based upon a very localised inspection of the appeal site and the more immediate vicinity.

The threat offered to the countryside under the present classification may be illustrated by considering the use, or lack of use, of the protection which can be given by local planning authorities by means of the creation of Conservation Areas under the Civic Amenities Act, 1967. Although many local planning authorities have, much to their credit, created scores of Conservation Areas within their counties, others have created hardly more than can be counted on the fingers of one hand; and these latter have not in every case the excuse that there is little to conserve in their part of the country. It must further be noted that, although the classification " Conservation Area " is provided under the Civic Amenities Act, it is clearly stated in that Act that such an area is not intended to be solely urban or to be restricted merely to places of architectural or historic interest but, in fact, that the Act will apply to other areas having a "special character." Thus, a Conservation Area may cover an open space, such as a village green, or a mill leat, or an ancient battlefield. It is possible that in such areas actual buildings may be non-existent, or insignificant.

Bearing in mind the general lack of any overall presumption, in planning terms, that agricultural land should be afforded any pre-classified special protection, it is necessary now to consider in more detail the present limited extent of (and the machinery for) the restriction of non-agricultural development proposed to be carried out upon agricultural and other rural land. (But this discussion will exclude comment about the general national mechanism used for planning the siting of industry so as to meet national industrial needs, which has already been considered in Chapter 2: Industry.)

As explained later in the present chapter there are, in fact, certain defined areas in the British countryside over which various special guardian angels watch. The *areas of outstanding natural beauty* and the conditions applicable to their agricultural development are set out on pp. 63 to 65. See also Chapter 15: The Countryside—II, p. 308.

Conservation Areas are relatively small, isolated areas designated by the local planning authority under s. 1 of the Civic Amenities Act, 1967. They are created on the initiative of the local planning authority with formal notice to the Secretary of State. Where the authority fail to act, the Secretary of State may direct them so to do. The precise conditions as to any planning permission granted within these areas are considered in Chapter 13: Conservation Areas and Buildings of Architectural and Historic Interest.

National Parks were created by the National Parks and Access to the Countryside Act, 1949, and these will be considered in greater detail, in conjunction with both conservation of various types and recreation, in Chapter 15: The Countryside—II: Conservation and Recreation. Therefore, suffice it to say here that there are now ten National Parks (for list of which see p. 292) which together total in area about 5,258 square miles and thus amount to about one-tenth of the area of England and Wales. They are, however, situated largely in the most remote parts of the country. In terms of the demands upon the countryside made by industry and urban-based development generally, however, no specific additional powers of restriction are given either to the local planning authority or to the Secretary of State, although it is to be their policy (as required by the Act) to be more stringent in granting planning approval and to limit the expansion of villages in the National Parks to very moderate further growth. It is also expected that new buildings should be of traditional designs and in traditional materials except where the cost would be unduly high. However, despite this general statement of principle given in the Act, there still exists a considerable danger within National Parks in the case of " permitted development " under the General Development Order, 1973. But with the exception of loopholes applicable to permitted development, it can generally be said that about one-tenth of the total countryside is fairly strongly protected against industrial and urban development.

Green Belt Areas will be considered in detail in Chapter 14 but the comment should be made here that the total of all such areas amounts to about 5,735 square miles in England (not Wales), and thus constitutes about 10 per cent. of the total countryside. However, these areas (particularly in the London Green Belt) cannot always be said to be genuinely rural in character. Certainly, from the standpoint of the agriculturalist, they do not always present the ideal environment for farming, due to the incursions of urban population, for whose benefit the Green Belt exists. Further, by their nature, Green Belts may tend to alter in order to permit gradual expansion of the urban core. They are also frequently subject to the most intense pressures, at one extreme in terms of demand for high-quality housing and, at the other (as they become less " green " in character), in terms of the siting of light industry.

There remain, within our chequered countryside, certain other special types of area in which industrial and urban-based development would not be welcome. These are as follows: *Nature Reserves* created under Pt. III of the National Parks and Access to the Countryside Act, 1949, and controlled by the Natural Environmental Research Council. These reserves may also be created by local planning authorities in consultation with the said Council; and they may be compulsorily purchased by the Council (further consideration of their use is given elsewhere: see index). *Areas of Special Scientific Interest* in England, Wales and Scotland may be made the subject of voluntarily negotiated agreements between the Natural Environmental Research Council and owners, lessees or occupiers of land, by virtue of s. 15 of the Countryside Act, 1968. Consultation in this regard is to take place between the said Council and the local planning authority before such agreements are concluded. The agreement may provide for the carrying out of work in the interests of science upon the land and for the restriction of the activities of the owner, tenant or occupier. Areas in the vicinity of Royal Palaces and Royal Parks also require special consultation with the Secretary of State.

The last category of land having a special characteristic of ability to resist, to a limited extent, industrial and urban-based intrusion is that owned by the *National Trust* for England and Wales, as also the National Trust for Scotland. The purpose of the Trust is, of course, to preserve but also to offer the fruits of such preservation to interested members of the public, and the matter is further considered in Chapter 15: The Countryside—II: Conservation and Recreation, although some purely urban properties are owned by the Trust. The total area in England and Wales in the ownership of the National Trust is about 570 square miles.

The following approximate and generalised statement as to open country within the United Kingdom may be of assistance. It is, however, emphasised that, so far as the author is aware, an accurate statistical analysis cannot be made due to certain overlapping of the various classifications of protected land.

It was estimated in 1964 that the total area of what might broadly be described as " agricultural " or " open " land (which was made up of arable land, pasture, rough grazing and common land) in the United Kingdom amounted to about 48,614,000 acres (say 75,178 square miles) of which 29,234,000 acres (say 45,678 square miles) were in England and Wales. In the case of England and Wales— the total land area of which is 58,340 square miles—it will be seen that a balance of 12,662 square miles is, broadly speaking, " non-agricultural." But, out of this, a further approximately 7,000 square miles is now used for forestry, leaving a final remainder of about 5,660 square miles (almost one-tenth of the total surface) devoted to urban and industrial land, roads, airports, reservoirs and a multitude of other uses.

Out of the 52,678 square miles of agricultural-type land (i.e., including 7,000 square miles of forestry) however, fairly substantial areas are now protected in various ways and to greater or lesser degrees. These areas cannot be shown as a percentage of the whole, since they tend to overlap. Thus, a National Park may include a large area of afforestation; or a country park may include an area of outstanding natural beauty, etc.

Referring, therefore, to total areas within each statutory category for purposes of protection, the following list [3] may be stated (in relation to England and Wales alone).

(1) *Areas in which statutory powers of protection are very considerable:*

(i) The ten National Parks total about 5,258 square miles.

(ii) Areas of Outstanding Natural Beauty total about 4,464 square miles.

(iii) National Trust-owned property amounts to about 570 square miles, with a further thirty-three square miles of which the Trust has tenancies.

(iv) Country Parks [4] in total amount to about thirty-two square miles.

(v) National Nature Reserves amount to about 425 square miles.

(vi) Land held by Naturalists' Trusts consists of a further approximately eighteen square miles.

(vii) A large number of Private Nature Reserves, which are officially recognised by the Countryside Commission, also exist, but a record of their total area does not seem to be readily available.

(viii) Many hundreds of Conservation Areas, as designated by local planning authorities, exist, but vary very greatly in size, although the largest will seldom exceed say ten acres. (The total area is not known.)

(2) *Areas in which there is a presumption against development but over which no statutory restrictions apply:*

(i) Green Belt Areas [5] exist round a large number of major cities and larger towns. The Metropolitan [6] Green Belt amounts to 850 square miles and this is to be extended by fifteen per cent to about 980 square miles. [6a] However, although the presumption against development (and particularly against industrial or commercial development) in a Green Belt Area may be validly given as a reason for refusing planning permission, or for refusing to grant permission on appeal, there is no actual restriction imposed upon the granting

---

[3] See index as to further discussion of each type of area.

[4] i.e., broadly speaking relatively small areas designated by local planning authorities but treated rather similarly to National Parks, save that specific means of extra protection against development do not apply.

[5] See Chapter 14.

[6] London.

[6a] The counties adjoining Greater London had, in their development plans, proposed a total of a further approximately 400 square miles of land, which would have given 1,200 square miles in all.

of permission if the local planning authority or Secretary of State for the Environment so pleases.

(ii) " White land " is generally land lying outside urban or village areas, and on which it is assumed that the current user will continue. In other words, if the land is at present used for agriculture it is presumed that such use will continue but, again, there is no requirement that planning permission should not be granted, in fact, for any purpose which may be the subject of an application. But see p. 334.

(iii) Crown and Duchy lands are subject to special provisions and are, virtually, beyond the control of local planning authorities. Thus, although it will generally be assumed that agricultural use will continue in rural areas, the Crown Commissioners or Duchy Stewards are at liberty to implement other forms of use.

(iv) Government Departments' lands equally lie beyond the strict control of local planning authorities and in certain areas, such as tracts of land used for training or operational purposes by the Ministry of Defence, development may take place which is not consistent with continuation of virgin land or agriculture. However, local planning authorities are now at least notified of any proposed development, in accordance with the provisions of Circular No. 80/71, Development by Government Departments, and they may lodge an objection within two months which could (or may not) result in a public inquiry. These provisions, whilst deemed to be an improvement upon those in the former Circular 100, are commented upon rather adversely by the Dartmouth Committee (Section 4 of their Report, at para. 4.58).

Influences of industrialisation.—The general picture, and future pattern, of use of the British land mass must also be viewed in the context of the present rate of re-development of industrial and other urban areas. This aspect is further emphasised by the comments in the Dartmouth Committee Report, notably in Section 6, Industry and Commerce, at paras. 6.41 and 6.42, which read as follows:

" The quality of the environment is an important factor in the industrial attraction of an area, and is certainly taken into account by any industrialist when considering the establishment of a new plant. There is an obvious link between a poor environment, economic depression, unemployment, and outward migration. National policies which offer inducements to industrialists to locate new factories in such areas could be justified on social grounds alone.

However, there is a complementary need for positive environmental improvement.   Only when these twin objectives, social and
environmental, find a place in our policies, will they be truly
effective in creating economic prosperity in what are usually classified as depressed areas.   The benefits of efficiency are undeniable,
and the potential of technological power is enormous.   But as
economic productivity increases, so will the exploitation of resources,
and the physical disruption of the environment.   This could result
in a great concentration of urban conurbations and the massive
erosion of the countryside."

These comments by the committee should be read in the light of
their Recommendations 30 to 38 (see Appendix B); reference may
also be usefully made to paras. 6.30, 6.31 and 6.38 of the Report.

The present tendency to develop industry in the South of England,
and notably in the locality of Southampton and the Severn valley
(Bristol and northwards), is stimulated by the anticipated construction of major, containerised ports; that is, ports with berths designed
to take ships of greater draught and length, having also facilities
for handling large cargo containers which are designed to be packed
at the factory of origin, shipped, unloaded, transferred to heavy road
vehicles for delivery to places of destination, and finally unpacked.
For a further discussion of the general problem of the location of
industry and of transport services, reference should be made to
Chapters 2: Industry, and 5: Transport.

It will be seen, therefore, that the maintenance and protection
of the countryside is a problem to be met in the national context
and is directly related to national economic and industrial planning.
Much of the information used in such planning is provided by
Regional Economic Planning Councils (see Chapter 1), yet it is
submitted that these councils are seldom, if ever, concerned with the
balance to be struck between the ceaseless demand for new industrial and commercial sites and the maintenance of the countryside,
which is said to be basically the concern of local planning authorities
and the Secretary of State for the Environment.

With the extensive abandonment of the very considerable networks created largely in the nineteenth century for the transportation of goods by both rail and canal, the economy of Britain is
increasingly reliant upon development of a system of fast motorways
and other major roads.   The worldwide tendency towards the
oversea shipment of containerised cargo further restricts the ability

of British Railways to handle such large consignments on the rolling stock and rail gauges available, so that the presence of immense, articulated cargo container lorries upon the roads is rapidly increasing. Suggestions have been made from time to time in recent years that abandoned railway tracks should be converted to roadways for the exclusive use of lorries, but (possibly for reasons of commercial competition) such lines have been gradually sold off to adjoining owners. The value of such routes for cargo carried by road might, in some parts of the country, have been extremely high if one bears in mind the fact that many railway lines were constructed at vast expense in terms of taking the best and shortest routes available, and in the formation of gradients. In Cornwall, for example, most communication was by sea until the development of the railway, due to the herringbone structure of the peninsula, which rendered, and still renders, road communication difficult and sometimes hazardous.

2. The Needs of Agriculture

The current technical and economic needs of the agricultural industry are considered at some length in the following pages, principally because the author takes the view that, since eighty per cent. of the population of Great Britain consists now of urban dwellers—and possesses a predominance of voting power—it is of great importance that there should be a broader understanding of rural problems. This need for understanding arises not only in relation to matters of protection of our environment, but also because the national economy relies to a very considerable extent upon the production of food for home consumption. About half of Britain's food supply is at present imported and this proportion may tend to increase relative to the rise in total population.

The war of 1939 to 1945 made it essential that, during those years, the maximum possible production of home-grown foodstuffs be developed, and this acted as the initial spur to widespread mechanisation. In the past three decades there has been, therefore, a general change from the literal use of " horse " power (combined with steam power for threshing and a few other machines) to the use of the internal combustion engine in tractors, combine harvesters, forage harvesters, etc.

The old traditional appearance of a countryside and of farm buildings, shaped over the centuries by the needs of a relatively

large and inexpensive labour force, has been inevitably altered by
the demands of modern machinery and by the increasing scarcity
and relative cost of skilled agricultural workers.   Thus, for example,
the cut and laid hedge has become more expensive and more
difficult to achieve; and the thatched roof is an increasingly rare
and expensive scenic luxury.   In addition, the use of large machines,
such as combine harvesters, six-furrow multiple ploughs, and wide
corn drills, has made it necessary, in all arable areas in which the
contours of the land do not hinder their use, to increase the size of
fields from, say, ten acres to forty acres or more.

Equally, the increased productivity of mixtures of specially bred
grass strains has produced a pattern of work and field layout in
most grass-growing areas based upon the sowing of three-year,
two-year and even one-year grass leys.   That is, a suitable mixture
of grass strains is designed and sown with the object of obtaining
maximum production during a three-year, two-year or single
season period.   Such leys can be " undersown " to a corn crop:
that is, the grain and grass seeds are sown at the same time, the
corn rises above the grass and is harvested, leaving the grass ley to
continue and develop for cutting or grazing the following (say)
spring.

Thus, the need for the previously general use of permanent
pasture has become very much reduced (if not altogether abandoned) on most farms, other than those generally described as
" hill farms."   The economic need to cultivate those grass fields
which may have been permanently under grass for centuries or
decades has, in itself, caused an increase in field size.   In most
areas strip grazing by means of a movable electric fence has been
used for the past twenty years and, more recently, " paddock
grazing " has been introduced.   In both cases (and particularly in
the latter), a very large field may be cultivated and seeded to a three-
year ley, and temporary fences then set up to confine the grazing
stock as required.   This enables the grass to be grazed intensively
and in rotation over each section of the field, thereby reducing
waste by treading in or fouling.   Intensive grazing and periodic
fertilising also encourage more rapid re-growth and greater total
production.

Again, a large area of grass can be used, if the farm is suitably
equipped with buildings, for " zero-grazing."   In this case the stock
are seldom put out to pasture even in summer, but are housed in yards

throughout the year, the grass being cut and carried to the yard. This method reduces wastage, enables the grass to be heavily and more frequently fertilised, and avoids the loss of production which would otherwise result from stock such as a milking herd having to walk from field to milking parlour. (Whether or not the consequent lack of fresh air and exercise may weaken future generations of cattle is beyond the scope of this book.) The advantages of zero-grazing are, of course, also to be weighed against the additional costs in terms of labour and transport.

However, the most obvious change in feeding technique is the virtually universal adoption of the use of silage as a winter bulk feed. This method involves the cutting of young grass in the spring and summer, by means of a forage harvester which chops it into short lengths and loads the crop (by blowing) into a high-sided trailer. The grass is then carted to a clamp, generally adjoining the yard to be used for wintering stock, where the silage is made by stacking and compacting into a solid mass, the operation being carried out under carefully controlled conditions as to temperature and acidity. A further improvement in the maintenance of quality of the silage consists in the sealing of the clamp with polythene sheeting. The stock then generally feed direct from the face of the clamp during the following winter, thus avoiding the need to cut and carry bulk fodder. The use of this system has eliminated the pre-war method of providing bulk feed in the form of root crops (turnips, swedes, etc.), which had to be chopped and fed in mangers, and has thus eliminated a heavy labour requirement. In addition, a good grass ley may yield not only up to three or more cuts for silage, but will also provide useful grazing, or a cut of hay, later in the year.

Intensified methods also apply to grain crops. Whereas a traditional " rotation " of crops required that only a proportion of the farm be under corn at any one time (the remaining parts being used for stock and other crops of a type which rejuvenated the soil ready for corn in later years), many areas of England have grown grain crops year after year for the past twenty-five years.[7] This has been made possible by the heavy use of artificial fertilisers. As a result the total grain crop per holding may now have increased by as much as twelvefold over pre-war figures.

[7] As to the pollution aspect, see Chapter 8, at p. 166 *et seq.*

It will be obvious from the above very brief discussion of cropping methods that not only have field sizes been required to be vastly increased, but also that the types of farm buildings now required are radically different from those previously considered for centuries to be acceptable. The traditional patterns of farming provided for the storage of grain in sacks in barns, the housing of wintering cattle in stalls, and of pigs in small sties; storage of cattle fodder root crops was largely in clamps in the open, and the storage of hay and straw was in stacks protected from the weather by thatch.

In contrast, the modern method of grain storage is principally in very large (say thirty-ton) metal bins after mechanical drying to avoid mould or spontaneous combustion which would otherwise develop during the storage period. Handling of grain is now in bulk from the combine harvester, thence to a trailer, thence (by means of mechanical augers, blowers and chutes) to the grain dryer, and thence to the grain storage bin. Alternatively, grain may now be stored moist in a sealed tower silo if the purpose is to feed the grain to stock rather than to sell-on.

Even the storage of potatoes has now followed the earlier methods used for apples and other fruit, whereby specially designed temperature-controlled and fumigated storage buildings are employed.

Thus, the traditional agricultural buildings, so much an accepted part of the British rural scene, have, in many cases, tended to fall into disrepair; and have been replaced by new, bulky, and sometimes unsightly structures. In this respect it may be reasonable to comment that even the highly mechanised requirements of modern dry grain bulk storage can, with reasonable care, be achieved (often without additional cost) by the erection of bins and equipment within traditional barns and other outbuildings. In such cases the life of the metal structures may even be extended by protection from the weather, and the cost of demolition for site preparation saved.

The use of stock housing for dairy herds and beef cattle tends to be greater in parts of Scotland and the North of England where the normal grazing season is shortened by snow and inclement weather. In certain grassland areas it is economic to house stock on slatted floors so as to avoid the need for straw as litter. But even in milder climates it has become the general custom to house dairy herds in covered yards for four or five months of the winter, where the herd can be " self-fed " from a silage clamp, and can be machine-milked in a dairy under the same roof. By these means the labour demand is vastly reduced and the milk yield increased.

The general principle that the yield can be proportionately greater relative to fodder consumption (i.e., the " conversion ratio " is said to be higher) where the animals are housed so as to prevent excessive loss of body heat, combined with reduction in exercise, has now been generally adopted in what is called intensive stock housing, the stock being kept in specially designed or modified buildings in which, as a result of insulation and thermostatically controlled air conditioning, the temperature and humidity can be regulated. This method of housing is commonly employed for pig rearing and fattening, veal calf rearing, broiler chicken rearing, and intensive egg production, but it also extends to the rearing of other types of stock in varying degrees according to local climatic conditions. In Scotland and the North of England even sheep have been housed in slatted-floored buildings during winter months. The rate of growth, and also the proportion of young stock successfully reared from birth, is certainly much increased by these methods and, particularly in the case of broiler chickens and egg layers, this is further extended by the breeding of special strains designed to give maximum growth or production under such intensive conditions.

It should, nevertheless, be realised that disease resistance can be increased in young stock by rearing out of doors and at higher altitudes; and also, of course, that productivity (notably in milk production) is most strongly influenced by hereditary factors.

To conclude this short discussion, it should be appreciated by those concerned with the planning and protection of the rural environment that the following factors must now inevitably influence the method of operation of the average farm:

(i) The world food shortage [7a] is an inducement to all countries to seek full and intensive agricultural production, so far as is compatible with the maintenance of reasonable quality of the end products and therefore with the careful continuation of suitable hereditary factors, whether in animal or vegetable.

(ii) The low return upon capital invested in British agriculture

[7a] But the significance of the " Green Revolution " which commenced in about 1967 should be noted. The introduction of improved plant strains, notably of rice, and the continuing improvements in irrigation, have already begun to ease the situation: see " Only One Earth ", by Barbara Wood and René Dubos— an official United Nations Report, published by Penguin Books, 1972—notably Chapter 11 (i) thereof.

today renders it financially impossible for many farmers and horticulturalists to revert to traditional (and perhaps more nutritious)
methods of production, such as hand hoeing to avoid the use of weed
killers, and the extensive use of well-rotted farmyard manure.   The
high cost of agricultural land, which has been produced by investors
wishing to hedge against inflation, also leads to maximum use of the
total area available, and results in tree-felling and the removal of
hedgerows, duck ponds and other rural features.

(iii) The high cost of labour (although low in comparison with
the engineering industry) and of the maintenance and fuelling of
farm machinery has led to intensive time and motion study, and
this has resulted, on efficient farms, in the reduction in double-
handling of crops and fodder and in transportation.   This change
requires that most farm buildings be very carefully sited in relation
to the layout and use of the holding, roadways, available drainage,
water supply, etc.   Thus, for example, an ancient, but isolated,
barn may become in practical terms of little use to the
farmer.

Lest it be thought that the author believes that agriculture in
Britain should be governed solely by commercial principles which
will override the needs of mankind as to the rural environment, it
must be stressed that, although the agriculturalist must work on a
proper economic basis, it is still the separate duty of any government
to protect those features in the countryside which are of benefit, but
which offer no economic return.   It is therefore necessary that
Parliament, the Secretary of State and local planning authorities
together continue to assess the value of rural features in terms of
aesthetic, historic and psychological importance.   Thus, whilst no
one has as yet proposed that all village greens be put under the
plough, or be converted to concrete car parks, it is certainly
necessary that a decision be made as to whether or not the
removal of ancient (even, in some cases, literally pre-historic)
hedgerows be allowed to continue at the rate of 5,000 miles per
annum.

In terms of development related to agriculture itself, where the
building is to be upon agricultural land and comprised in an
agricultural unit, and is also to be of a type likely to be undertaken
on a normal farm, then planning permission is not required except
where the structure exceeds certain dimensions.   This general
right of the farmer to build or carry out engineering operations for

the benefit of his farming enterprise is afforded under Class VI of the Town and Country Planning General Development Order, 1973 (S.I. 1973 No. 31).   Subject to certain reservations as to areas of outstanding natural beauty, the only restrictions which will require that planning permission be obtained for agricultural buildings are where the proposed structure exceeds 465 square metres in area, *or* is within 25 metres of the metalled portion of a trunk or classified road, *or* exceeds 12 metres in height.   However, the Dartmouth Committee recommends (see Appendix B hereto, Recommendation 35) " The National Farmers Union and the Department of the Environment should co-operate to draw up a form of planning control for farm buildings."

The extent of the latitude at present permitted in relation to construction for agricultural purposes is further illustrated by reference to the statutory conditions governing agricultural tenancies, whereby a tenant, if refused permission by his landlord to erect a new agricultural building, may insist upon the matter being referred to the Agricultural Land Tribunal, and the Tribunal may order that the tenant be permitted to construct it, although, of course, at his own expense.

It is also worthy of note that, in an attempt to reduce the capital cost of modern farming, it has become fairly common in some areas to use relatively temporary timber buildings or semi-portable structures, such as " cow-kennels," which were first developed on the Duchy of Cornwall Estate.   These obviate the need for the large and expensive roof of a covered yard and may well, by strategic siting, be so employed as to avoid the necessity to obtain planning permission which would have been required for a single building of sufficient size to house the same number of cattle.

In addition, however, where the agricultural development proposed is within an area of outstanding natural beauty as specified in the Town and Country Planning (Landscape Areas Special Development) Order, 1950 (S.I. 1950 No. 729), the development must not be carried out without fourteen days' prior notification to the local planning authority which may, within that period, require an application to be made.

The areas of natural beauty so far specified are:

In Caernarvonshire: Urban District of Betws-y-Coed, and Rural
    Districts of Gwrfai, and of Naut Conway.
In Cheshire: Rural District of Tintwistle.

In Cumberland: Urban District of Keswick, and Rural Districts of
Cockermouth, of Ennerdale, of Millom, and of Penrith.
In Derbyshire: Urban District of Bakewell, and Rural Districts of
Bakewell, and of Chapel-en-le-Frith.
In Lancashire: Rural District of Ulverston.
In Merioneth: Urban District of Dolgelly, and Rural Districts of
Dolgelly, of Deundraeth, and of Penllyn.
In Westmorland: Urban District of Lakes and of Windermere, and
Rural Districts of North Westmorland, and of South West-
morland.

Having indicated the limited extent to which planning controls
and the more positive aspects of town and country planning apply
to agriculture, it is also necessary to mention that a number of
other factors which are within the control of either central or
local government have a bearing upon the operation and economy
of an agricultural holding. At the present time the Minister of
Agriculture, Fisheries and Food is empowered to make grants for the
improvement of a holding and these are of particular significance
in connection with buildings and equipment. If a grant is required,
application must be made, and written approval received, before
any building or engineering operations are commenced. Where
restrictions upon discharge of effluent and drainage may apply, the
approval of the relevant River Authority must be obtained before
the Ministry can in turn approve the scheme for grant purposes.
It is the duty of the Minister's officers to ensure that the grant of
public money is justified in terms of the economic viability of the
project, including sound systems of construction (also using durable
materials) and of subsequent operation. The majority of such
projects which are dependent partly upon a grant are discussed in
the very early stages between the agricultural occupier (owner and/
or tenant) and the Ministry's advisory officers, who are, of course, in
a position to draw upon local and national experience and information. In approving a grant, however, the Ministry of Agriculture,
Fisheries and Food is not officially concerned with the purely town
and country planning aspects of the case, although the officers
dealing with it are permitted to increase the grant total to allow
for any reasonable additional cost of, say, cladding materials of a
colour or texture more suited to the site. However, it is not, for
example, the concern of the Ministry, in approving, say, an intensive
veal calf building, to consider whether the structure would be

acceptable in an area of outstanding natural beauty, or whether the probable increase in traffic serving the site would be advisable in local circumstances.

The matter of intensive housing of stock is, however, influenced indirectly by local and national government in terms of liability for rating. The possibility (or probability) of rating all agricultural buildings is now under discussion but, at the present time, those buildings which are used " solely " in connection with agricultural operations (as defined in the Rating and Valuation (Apportionment) Act, 1928, s. 2) are exempt from rating, whereas those used for " factory farming " are rateable.[8]

3. Forestry and Tree Preservation

(1) *General considerations*

It may not be fully appreciated by the layman that commercial forestry, and amenity tree planting, are highly technical fields of work—a fully qualified forester will have taken seven years from the date of commencing to study for a degree until completion of training—so that the character of a given landscape, or the character of a smaller area created by the planting of specimen trees, will be influenced by many factors which are not directly related to the ultimate appearance, or amenity, of the locality. In other words, the hands of the forester may be tied by forces unseen by the preservationist. These forces will now be very briefly discussed.

In Britain, man has been engaged in clearing forest for purposes of farming, and for defence, for at least a thousand years. In the natural state, these islands (in total absence of the needs of man) would be largely covered by deciduous forest and areas of scrub and thicket. Probably the only large tracts of open land would be on some of the high hills and mountains, and possibly on the areas of early settlement, which were selected by man because of their open space—and thus greater safety—such as Salisbury Plain. Nevertheless, it must be remarked that recent experience has shown that on the Sussex Downs a large farm could in the course of fifty years revert from arable land to " impenetrable blackthorn and brambles." [9] The existence of traditional farmland thus depends

---

[8] *W.& J. B. Eastwood, Ltd.* v. *Herrod (Valuation Officer)* [1968] 2 Q.B. 923.
[9] *Agriculture*, vol. 43, No. 6, September, 1956, at p. 258, by G. D. Nightingale. Also substantiated by more recent, and controlled, experiments by the Ministry of Agriculture, Fisheries and Food.

upon constant and continuous cultivation, including the maintenance, where applicable, of perennial grasses stimulated by grazing
and the cutting of hay and silage, etc.

However, the days when natural forests could be relied upon to
produce a satisfactory timber supply are long past.   The Industrial
Revolution has changed the face of British forestry in three main
respects.   First, the maintenance of enormous Royal Forests,
initially preserved for hunting (both for sport and for food), was
continued for several centuries longer than might have been the
case, due to the need for suitably-shaped and selected oak branches
for the construction of ships' frames, when the " wooden wall " of
the Navy was essential for defence, and wooden ships the means of
world trade.   Secondly, the Industrial Revolution inspired vast
undertakings in civil engineering, such as the construction of canal
and railway networks; and these and industry itself consumed vast
quantities of timber for props and other more permanent uses.
Thirdly, the Industrial Revolution, and the parallel essential of
improved health and sanitary services, have permitted a tenfold
increase in the population of these islands, thereby causing a proportionate rise in the numbers of dwelling houses—in most of which
timber is essential for roof and floor construction, and general
joinery.

These forces had induced, during the nineteenth century, a need
to produce timber as a methodically planted and cultivated crop—
although in many areas the cultivation of beech and oak can best be
carried out by natural or semi-natural regeneration under mature
trees.

However, the indigenous trees of Britain, being almost entirely
of deciduous species, tend to be slower-growing than coniferous
softwoods.   Conifer crops may, in some cases, begin to produce a
worth-while initial source of income from the age of twenty years
onwards, whereas a planted crop of oak may take 120 years or more
to reach a stage for economic sale, principally on maturity.

The two world wars during the present century served to re-
emphasise the need to produce large volumes of cheap, homegrown
softwoods (i.e., conifers), and the face of Britain has accordingly
changed vastly in the past hundred years.   This change has been
further accelerated by the importation of foreign hardwoods and
softwoods, which have rendered relatively unimportant the local
growth and supply of certain types of hedgerow tree.   Thus, elms

were once essential for local use for durable purposes (such as farm troughs and mangers), and were widely used—although often vulnerable to woodworm—for floor boards. Beech, however, has such excellent qualities for turning and for furniture construction that it continues to be grown in small, continuous woods to supply local furniture-making trades. Equally, other indigenous timber, such as ash, willow and poplar, has specialised uses.

However, so far as the environment is concerned, the type of local woodland is very much controlled by local growing conditions of soil and climate. In other words, certain species will not prosper on acid soils, whereas others will fail to produce an economic yield on strongly alkaline soils. Equally, some species will grow more rapidly and to a greater mature size in a moist climate, whereas others may be more susceptible than usual to disease under such conditions. In general, a weakly-growing tree will be more readily damaged by bacteria, fungus and insect pests.

It can therefore be argued that, if it is intended to depart from the natural, native afforestation of any area—for example oak or beech, etc.—by the planting of conifers, it is essential that the correct species for local conditions be selected.

It is appropriate to mention at this point the special values that individual trees or groups of trees may have in deliberately enhancing or preserving local amenity. Thus, a suitably sited tree or group of trees may add an essential visual balance to a building or complex of buildings, or may soften the impact of an elevation in a given setting. This function is now the active concern of modern landscape architects. It is of interest that it is now possible to transplant,[10] without undue expense, semi-mature trees of, say, 30 feet in height.

Considerable research has also been carried out as to means of improving the appearance of unsightly industrial wastelands and—of even greater practical importance—stabilising potentially dangerous features, such as slag heaps. As mentioned elsewhere in this book, various forms of vegetation may be used to bind and to clothe the surface of heaps of industrial waste. So far as trees are concerned, the local climate will influence choice of species (i.e., moist, dry, air polluted, etc.), but in general it has been found that Corsican

---

[10] Subject to pruning and preparation of the root system for about twelve months in advance.

pine and Scots pine, or birch, or elder, will grow if planted on disused colliery spoil heaps. In the case of those areas of reinstated open-cast mining which may be found to be unsuitable for agriculture, Corsican pine and larch have produced satisfactory yields. These latter two species are also more suitable than others in most areas of industrial air pollution. It is also well known that plane trees flourished in central London even before clean air zones were declared. However, the effects of air pollution vary with both source and local climate, and reference should be made to various specialised reports.[11]

More detailed reference is made elsewhere to the agricultural values of hedgerows and to the shelter-belts on farms, but it should be noted here that, although large hedgerow trees will generally tend to reduce the yield of arable or grass crops beneath their branches, well-selected and carefully cultivated individual specimens can, on occasion, produce a greater margin of profit in the long term than average farm crops on an equivalent small area. This, however, will depend upon the species and quality of the tree and, to some extent, upon accessibility to a local timber merchant. In any event, the loss of hedgerow trees will radically alter the scenic character and wildlife of a rural area.

For these various reasons related to local conditions, combined with the urgent need to encourage an increase in overall production, the Forestry Commission was set up by the Forestry Act, 1919. This and later Acts were largely repealed and replaced by the Forestry Act, 1967, which, together with ss. 23 and 24 of the Countryside Act, 1968,[12] now constitutes almost the entire statutory source of law in relation to forestry. However, as will be seen later, the 1967 Act has been modified in regard to tree preservation orders by the Trees Act, 1970.

During the 1914–18 War about 450,000 acres of woodland were felled. In 1925, the Forestry Commission actively took over about 120,000 acres. By 1948, following the Second World War, it was found that, out of a total of nearly 3·5 million acres of woodland in the United Kingdom, 1,300,000 acres had become either scrub,

---

[11] " Atmospheric pollution and its influence on British Forests " by R. Lines, *Y Coedwigwr*—the magazine of the University College of North Wales, 3 (3), 1958–59.

[12] But s. 23 is excluded in regard to the New Forest, Hampshire, by the New Forest Act, 1970, s. 1 (2).

devastated or felled, and that 60 per cent. of our total hardwood had been cut. The post-war policy was therefore to increase the total woodland acreage to 5 million, of which 3 million would require to be planted on bare ground previously not used for timber production. By 1956 almost a million acres had been planted by the Forestry Commission, and the total now under direct Forestry Commission-controlled State ownership is about 3 million acres. Of this about 1,797,000 acres are planted, 312,000 acres are awaiting planting, and 886,000 acres represent necessary supporting land which is largely used for agriculture (including upland grazing) or is unplantable, and a small proportion represents forest nurseries.

In addition to State Forests, there is something in excess of 2,687,000 acres of privately owned woodland, giving a total woodland area in Great Britain of about 4,484,000 acres, or 7·6 per cent. of the land surface.

By s. 1 (2) of the Forestry Act, 1967, the duty of the Commissioners is to promote the interests of forestry, the development of afforestation, and the production and supply of timber and other forest products in Great Britain; and, by s. 1 (3), " The Commissioners' general duty includes that of promoting the establishment and maintenance in Great Britain of *adequate reserves* of growing trees."

The prevalence of coniferous plantings has, not unnaturally, induced public criticism as a result of the dramatic changes in the appearance of landscape which almost invariably result from the felling of deciduous woodland and replanting with conifers. However, the Commission has, in recent years, agreed to increase the proportion of deciduous plantings, and that care should be taken in arranging blocks of newly planted coniferous woodland so that they take into account, and do not conflict visually with, the contours and other natural features of the area. (It should be noted, however, that, for purposes of cultivation, felling and extraction, trees are generally planted in lines, and that straight lines dividing woodlands into blocks are necessary not only for access, but also as a fire precaution.) In addition to the shape and style of planting, variety can, where soil and climatic conditions permit, be introduced by mixed planting, either in a pattern of rows, or in groups: this mixture of species will, however, increase the difficulty and cost of felling and extraction in most cases, because one species will generally reach maturity before the other. However, in principle, the extremely dark foliage of Corsican pine can be relieved by the paler foliage of, say, Lawson's cypress, or larch (the latter being deciduous). Dangers of " wind-blow " must also be considered: in other words, certain species will be more deeply rooted, particularly under various specific soil conditions, and may be used to protect those of less secure habit. In addition, the choice of mixture of species may be influenced by the precise timber requirements of a local market.

It is, unfortunately, not possible in a book of this nature to discuss the basic economic and physical requirements of forestry to an extent sufficient for practical use in a public inquiry, but reference may be made to a number of reliable and very readable textbooks, as indicated in the footnote.[13]

An important factor to be appreciated, however, is that the margin of profit (if any) to be obtained from forestry even on a large commercial basis is so small and so speculative that there is an essential need for " economy of scale." Further, that care must be exercised in producing what is called a forest programme, whereby the costs of cultivation are well spread from year to year, and whereby also there should result a continuous and even flow of mature produce commencing many decades in the future. This requires a forecast of demand for a particular type of timber, this demand being in part related to any more localised manufacturing market. In addition, matters of estate duty relief upon standing timber may arise, and influence the times of planting and felling, but these technicalities cannot be discussed here.

With these basic problems of economics in mind, it has been government policy, since the inception of the Forestry Commission, that both technical advice and the various alternative forms of advice and management by the Commission and related forestry grants should be available to private landowners. Thus, woodlands may be " dedicated " (now under s. 5 of the 1967 Act); or, alternatively, made subject to an Approved Woodlands Scheme (s. 4); or they may benefit from a Small Woods Planting Grant (s. 4).

The *Dedication Scheme* (s. 5) affords the most comprehensive assistance, but requires the owner to enter into a covenant or agreement to the effect that the Commission will undertake to

---

[13] Say, the various works of N. D. G. James, M.C., M.A., F.R.I.C.S.; or " Practical Forestry for the Agent and Surveyor " by Cyril E. Hart, M.A., F.R.I.C.S. (1962, *Estates Gazette*).

manage his woodlands for the main purpose of timber production in accordance with an agreed plan of operations, which will be carried out under the control of the landowner's own skilled staff. The owner binds himself and his successors for a long period of years, and will thus cease to have sole discretion as to the types of tree to be planted. It is accepted, however, that questions of sport and amenity must not be totally overridden by the Forestry Commission. Dedication permits the Commission to provide financial aid in the form of Planting Grants [14] and of annual Management Grants.[15] Dedication also exempts the particular woodland from the need to obtain Felling Licences (*post*) and prevents the application of Tree Preservation Orders (*post*). Further, it excludes compulsory acquisition of the land if this acquisition is solely for forestry purposes.

An *Approved Woodlands Scheme* (s. 4) is applicable to owners who do not wish to part with their rights of management for a long period under a Dedication Scheme, but are prepared to manage their woodlands in accordance with a plan approved by the Forestry Commission. Approved Woodlands Schemes also enable Planting Grants to be available on the same scale as for a Dedication Scheme, but these are payable as to three-quarters in the year of planting, and one-quarter five years later. No Management Grant is available.

Small Woods Planting Grants (s. 4) are designed to cover small woods, or other small areas of land deemed to be suitable for tree-planting, subject to various different limitations as to the size and type of area to be planted and the size and type of woodland owned. The scale and basis of grant is as for an Approved Woodlands Scheme; and, as in that case, no Management Grant will be payable.

It is also of significance in agricultural areas that grants may be obtained from the Ministry of Agriculture, Fisheries and Food (or the Department of Agriculture and Fisheries in Scotland) under s. 34 of the Agriculture Act, 1970, for up to fifty per cent. of the approved cost of establishing " shelter-belts " on upland stock-rearing farms. Also, on other farms, up to one-third of the cost of establishing shelter-belts is available under s. 32 of the Agriculture

[14] £23·175 per acre successfully planted, replanted or restocked, etc.
[15] £1·0625 per acre for first 100 acres; £0·7125 per acre for the next 100 acres, and £0·4375 per acre thereafter.

Act, 1957.   However, these grants cannot duplicate other grants under the Small Woods Scheme—although a higher rate may be obtained in relation to agriculture, if this is selected in preference to an agricultural grant.

In addition, the Forestry Commission can offer technical advice through their regional Conservators of Forests.

Reference has already been made to *Felling Licences* and *Tree Preservation Orders*.   These systems of control function separately, but are each of importance in terms of protection of the environment.

In the environmental sense, the felling of trees, or the felling and replanting with other species, can affect local physical conditions in addition to local visual amenity.   For example, extensive conifer planting on the West Coast of Scotland has completed a progressive change from a form of croft farming which was common until the depredations of sheep grazing enforced by (largely absentee) land-owners, to an afforested area now functioning as a source of cheap timber; but more important, as a catchment area for water for hydro-electric schemes.   In other words, trees have been used to bring down air-borne water in areas where it may be conveniently collected for the generation of electric power.   Equally, dramatic climatic changes have been induced in, for example, Norfolk, Suffolk, and Essex by, on the one hand, the planting, and on the other the extensive felling, of trees; the effects of which have been related to the strong winds and dust erosion which may follow the excessive drying-out of soil.

(2) *Legal controls for the preservation of trees and woodlands*

The control of felling and replanting of trees rests partly with the Forestry Commission and partly with the local planning authority, either or both of which bodies may prevent felling or may require an undertaking as to replanting.   The systems operate independently, but are inter-related, as follows:

Felling Licences are issued by the Forestry Commission and, under s. 9 (1) of Pt. II of the Forestry Act, 1967, it is an offence to fell any growing (i.e., not dead) tree without a licence, subject to certain important exceptions: a licence will not be required where the felling is by the occupier of the land on which the trees are, or by the land-lord of the occupier, provided either that the trees (any number) have a diameter of not exceeding 4 inches [16] and the felling is carried

---

[16] Measured 5 feet above ground.

out in order to improve the growth of other trees (s. 9 (3) (*a*)), or alternatively, the aggregate cubic content of the trees which are felled (by the occupier or his landlord) does not exceed 825 cubic feet (Hopus) in any quarter of a calendar year and the aggregate so felled which is also sold does not exceed 150 cubic feet in any quarter (or such larger quantity as the Commissioners may in a particular case allow) (s. 9 (3) (*b*) (i), (ii)).

Further, regardless of whether the " person felling " is the occupier or his landlord or not, a licence will not be needed for the felling of trees not exceeding 3 inches in diameter; or, in the case of coppice [17] or underwood, 6 inches in diameter (s. 9 (2) (*a*)). Also (s. 9 (2) (*b*)) the felling of fruit trees, or trees standing on land comprised in an orchard, garden, churchyard or public open space, or (s. 9 (2) (*c*)) the topping or lopping of trees or the trimming or laying of hedges, may be done without a licence. It should, perhaps, be noted that, as a result, trees in public parks may be vulnerable; and that trees in, say, streets may be lopped excessively (and even fatally) with impunity.

In addition to the above exemptions from licensing, felling may be carried out to prevent danger or to abate a nuisance (s. 9 (4) (*a*)); or to comply with a statutory obligation (s. 9 (4) (*b*)); or when required by an Electricity Board in relation to a main transmission line (s. 9 (4) (*c*)). It is also important to note that trees may be felled in relation to *development authorised by planning permission* under the Town and Country Planning Act, 1971 (s. 9 (4) (*d*) of the 1967 Act). Further, the Commissioners are empowered to make Regulations providing for additional exceptions (s. 9 (5)) from the need to obtain a felling licence.

Application for a felling licence is made to the Commissioners (represented by the local Conservator of Forests) in writing and in prescribed form (s. 10). The Commissioners may then grant a licence subject to conditions as to felling and/or replanting (s. 10 (5)). The licence will continue in force for such period as specified therein, but for not less than one year from the date on which

---

[17] Large areas of coppiced woodland still exist in localities where these were once essential to provide hazel and ash rods for the making of hurdles for sheep pens. Such pens were used for grazing sheep upon root crops, but this method of sheep farming has been virtually abandoned due to the high labour cost. Nevertheless removal of coppiced woodland may radically affect visual amenity, until replanting has taken effect.

it is granted (s. 10 (3)).   If a licence is refused, the Commissioners
may at any subsequent time alter their decision (s. 10 (5)).   Refusal
must be notified in writing and the grounds for the decision included
(s. 10 (6)).   In such cases the applicant will have a right both
to appeal to the Minister of Agriculture, Fisheries and Food (or the
Department of Agriculture in Scotland) (s. 16) or, alternatively, he
may claim compensation from the Forestry Commission (s. 11).
Where the applicant appeals to the Minister, the Minister will
appoint an independent committee to hear the case and to report
thereon.   The Minister will then arrive at a decision either to
grant or to refuse the licence, or to grant it subject to conditions.
Again, compensation may be claimed.

The Commissioners also have powers to direct that felling be
carried out where they deem this necessary to prevent deterioration
of timber, or to improve the growth of other trees (s. 18).

If a tree is felled without licence the person who fells it is liable
to a penalty upon summary conviction of not exceeding £10 or
twice the sum which appears to the local magistrates' court to be
the value of the tree, whichever is the higher (s. 17 (1)).   Proceedings must, however, be instituted within six months of the " first
discovery of the offence by the person taking the proceedings,
provided that no proceedings shall be instituted more than two
years after the date of the offence " (s. 17 (2)).

In the case of trees which are subject to Tree Preservation Orders
(*post*), the Commissioners must, on receipt of an application for a
licence, give notice in writing to the local planning authority; and
this is to apply even where the intention is to refuse a felling licence
(s. 15 (1)).   If, however, a licence is granted it will constitute
valid authority to override a Tree Preservation Order (s. 15
(6)).

Tree Preservation Orders are now made under ss. 59 to 62, 102,
103, 174 and 175 of the Town and Country Planning Act, 1971,
and they may be designed either to prevent felling of a tree or group
of trees or area of woodland; or to ensure that, if felling is permitted,
suitable re-planting will be carried out.

By s. 59 it is " the duty of the local planning authority," in
granting planning permission for any development, to ensure that
adequate provision is made, by means of conditions, for the preservation or planting of trees.   Thus " if it appears to a local planning
authority that it is expedient in the interests of amenity to make

provision for the preservation of trees or woodlands in their area " they " may "[18] make a Tree Preservation Order (s. 60 (1)). These conditions may relate not only to felling, but also to topping, lopping or wilful destruction of trees; and they may also require the re-planting, in prescribed manner, of a woodland area felled in the course of forestry operations. However, as already mentioned, the Forestry Commissioners have power to issue a felling licence, or to require the carrying out of felling as part of a *plan of operations previously approved* by the Commission and currently in force (s. 60 (7), (8)).

There are, however, two types of Tree Preservation Order in terms of immediacy of effect. The normal method of creation of an Order involves fairly considerable delay, and a more rapid procedure may be employed in the case of urgency—as where a potential developer has already begun to fell an area of woodland which will result in loss of local amenity.

The procedure for the making of a normal Tree Preservation Order is laid down in part in subss. (4) and (5) of s. 60, and in the Town and Country Planning (Tree Preservation Order) Regulations, 1969. It is important to note that if, in the process, any objection to the Order is received and not withdrawn, then the Order will " fail to have effect " until it is confirmed by the Secretary of State for the Environment. The tree or trees for which protection is sought are therefore in a vulnerable position[19] for a considerable period. Under the Regulations the local planning authority must first make the Order and deposit a certified copy, together with supporting maps or plans, the form of these documents being specified in reg. 5 (*a*). Copies must also be sent to the Conservator of Forests, and to the District Valuer, together with a list of persons affected (reg. 5 (*b*)). In addition, copies must be served upon the owners and occupiers of the land affected by the Order and on any other person known to the authority as being entitled to work by surface working any minerals on the land, or entitled to fell any trees or woodlands thereon. Further, a notice stating the grounds for making the Order, the place at which it is available for public inspection and the right of objection within

[18] It is, apparently, not mandatory that they do so.
[19] Subject, of course, to the need to obtain a felling licence, if applicable. Note that a tree of visual or historic significance may be of under 825 cubic feet in volume.

twenty-eight days must be served with each copy of the Order.   If
any objection is lodged, the Order will only take effect if confirmed
by the Secretary of State for the Environment and notified to the
owners and occupiers.   Appeal on a point of law lies to the High
Court.   If no objection is lodged, the Order may be confirmed by
the local planning authority itself after a period of not less than
forty-two days (s. 60 (5) (*c*) of the 1971 Act; reg. 6 (1)).   Once
effective, an Order prohibits the felling, topping, lopping and wilful
destruction of the trees, except with the consent (which may be
conditional) of the local planning authority.   In areas where
forestry (cropping) operations are necessary, the Order may permit
this, and allow for replanting.   Where this is not practicable, the
owner may, in certain cases, serve a purchase notice under s. 18 of
the Town and Country Planning Act, 1971.   This situation is also
aided by ss. 174 and 175 of the 1971 Act, whereby the Secretary of
State may provide compensation to an owner required to replant in
the interests of amenity; compensation being payable by the
Exchequer, following application through the local planning
authority.

The above commentary is clearly not comprehensive, but it will
be evident that, the machinery for making an Order being rather
cumbersome, planning authorities may tend to refrain from embarking upon it in marginal cases, particularly where they have in mind
that, as with all crops, trees should be felled at maturity, rather than
after onset of decay.   However, the principal problems arise where
trees may be indiscriminately felled to clear building sites and, for-
tunately, such cases of urgency are now provided for by *provisional
Tree Preservation Orders*, made by virtue of s. 61 of the 1971 Act,
whereby a local authority may cause an Order to operate forthwith
and for a period of six months, or until the Secretary of State
confirms, or refuses to confirm, such Order.   In such cases an
Order can be made before a survey of the woodland is carried
out.

Finally, if a tree which is subject to a Tree Preservation Order
(other than where a tree to which the Order applies is part of a
woodland) is " removed or destroyed," or is so removed or destroyed
due to dangerous decay, etc., " it shall be the duty of the owner of
the land, unless . . . the local planning authority dispense with this
requirement, to plant a tree of an appropriate size and species at the
same place as soon as he reasonably can " (s. 62 (1)).   Subsequently,

the Tree Preservation Order will continue in respect of the replacement tree. It is presumed that the provisions of s. 62 will apply to clumps of trees which were originally planted in the process of " landscape gardening," since these are not " part of a woodland."

CHAPTER 4

EXTRACTIVE INDUSTRIES

1. General Considerations

It is not within the province of this book to discuss the economic value to Britain of the extractive industries as seen in the context of international trade and the balance of payments. Yet it should be remarked that this country is now feeling the adverse effects of a combination of our early leadership in the Industrial Revolution two centuries ago, and the relatively small size of the land mass comprising these islands and supporting a large population. The following general comments may be of assistance in placing later discussion of the law in a practical context.

As the import prices of raw materials rise and the population expands, so also increases the need to exploit such native sources of materials as remain to us; but against this must be set the further need (which is in some respects indirectly economic as well as purely aesthetic) to protect the environment.

At the most elementary level, the image in the public mind surrounding the extractive industries generally is of areas of the country in which heaps of spoil and slag dominate the scenery, and in which towns and villages, many of which were constructed in the last century, are depressing in design and atmosphere. In addition various forms of mineral extraction (such as open-cast coal mining) have removed large areas of the agriculturally productive surface in certain localities.

In more modern terms, however, the position may be stated thus. It is the policy of the present and recent governments that the reclamation of derelict land is to receive support and financial aid from the Exchequer, so far as this can be afforded. However, the question of cost to the nation is not merely a matter of expenditure on improvement of living and working conditions, since it is well established that the population, and particularly the younger sector of the population, tends to migrate from a derelict area, thereby (a) reducing the potential for the industrial rehabilitation of that area; and (b) increasing the demand in other parts of the country for development of industry and housing upon productive agricultural land.[1]

Valuable work has been carried out in the development of techniques either for the levelling of spoil heaps where possible, or for the covering of such heaps with vegetation, to be followed eventually by tree planting.[2]

In addition, and probably as a result of public awareness of environmental problems, representatives of the major extractive industries have tended to accept that the mineral extractor has a duty (in the national sense) to reinstate or back fill old workings so that the area concerned will have a use either for agriculture or for some other purpose, whether this be recreational (such as a golf course or park), or as a site suitable for industrial development, housing or other purposes. It will be appreciated that both agricultural land and building land thus created have a calculable commercial value and that, particularly in some of the more industrially active areas, the selling price of sites for factory construction is extremely high. In addition, the provision of new areas for recreation is of value in terms of the facilities necessary for a modern community. Certain types of recreational land (such as golf courses) are also capable of providing substantial income.

Against this must be set a full realisation of the extent of the problem, as clearly set forth at a recent conference held by the Civic Trust at Stoke-on-Trent in April, 1970.[3] Government statistics, as at the end of 1968, show that in Britain as a whole there were about 128,000 acres of derelict land (England 93,930 acres; Wales 19,041 acres; Scotland 15,000 acres); and further, that the extent of dereliction produced in the period 1964 to 1968 had actually *exceeded* the amount of reclamation by about 5,000 acres. However, it must be noted that the figures stated do not relate solely to the extractive industries but include areas of land abandoned by outdated manufacturing industries or by disused railway lines and the like. Nevertheless, it has been stressed that these government statistics are based upon an extremely restrictive definition of dereliction, and that a far larger area is, in fact, seriously spoiled and

---

[1] See Appendix B, Recommendations 34, 37 and 38.

[2] Such cultivation requires the initial development of humus (a " top soil ") upon a largely barren or inert surface. This can now be achieved by the use of chemicals, imported earthworms, and the planting of special grasses, etc.

[3] " Reclamation of Derelict Land, Report of Civic Trust Conference," April, 1970. Published by the Civic Trust.

degraded by industry.   In the West Riding of Yorkshire, to give a
rather more extreme example, the official area of derelict land in
1966 was 3,428 acres; yet the local planning authority's survey of
the problem had revealed, for that year, a total of about 24,083
acres of spoiled and degraded and derelict land.

About 6,000 acres of land, mainly agricultural in use, are taken
annually for the extraction of minerals other than coal.   The area
taken annually for the dumping of colliery waste amounts to about
500 acres, but the statutory requirements governing the National
Coal Board and the iron ore industry have ensured that, in theory
at least, open-cast mining of these two types is carried out only with
continuous back filling as the work progresses.[4]   In short, the combined effect of extraction, dumping and of other dereliction merely
resulting from disuse is that the total annual increase in the area
of derelict land in Britain is now (1971) about 3,000 acres.[5]

Considerable effort to restore land has been made by various
sectors of the extractive industries and by certain local authorities,
and these are referred to in the Civic Trust's Report of the Conference,[6] but it is emphasised that long-term development planning
will be required in order to achieve a more substantial effect.

The extent of the increase in national requirements from the
major extractive industries may be seen in the following Table:

UNITED KINGDOM MINERAL EXTRACTION
(Thousand Tons)

(A) *Increases:*	1950	1968
Sand and Gravel	39,302	106,027
Limestone	24,964	75,383
Ironstone	12,271	12,610
Clay, Shale	23,585	34,782
China Clay	735	2,621 [7]

---

[4] Between 1960 and 1970 the National Coal Board restored 50,000 acres at an
average cost of £200 per acre; between 1951 and 1970 the ironstone industry
restored a similar acreage.

[5] The estimated cost, if an attempt were made to remove, and also continuously
to reinstate, all derelict land in Britain by 1980 would amount to about £15 million per annum.   The national expenditure from public, as distinct from commercial, sources at the present time (i.e., Exchequer and local authorities
combined) is only about £6 million.

[6] See footnote 3, p. 79.

[7] Extraction of china clay requires the washing of the mined material so as to
leave eight tons of waste (to be surface tipped) for every ton of usable clay
dispatched from the quarry site.

(B) *Decreases:*	*1950*	*1968*
Coal: Deep mined	204,140	165,000
Open cast	12,190	7,100

The considerable increase in extraction of sand and gravel (and of other building materials) reflects the rapid acceleration in what now tends to be called the " built environment," which already represents ten per cent. of our land area.

In addition there are many other useful and valuable substances to be obtained from the British land mass and, clearly, in cases of extreme rarity and industrial value, a very localised disturbance of the environment may be more readily justified in the national interest. It is not appropriate to attempt to give an extensive list of such mineral substances, but certain factors should be borne in mind. Metallic ores are generally of particular value and may often warrant the cost (in the widest sense of the word) of mining. By way of example, commercial quantities have been found and mined in Cornwall of the following metalliferous ores: tin, copper, tungsten, arsenic, zinc, lead, silver, iron, uranium, etc. In other areas sand and gravel, stone (including special and rather rare types suitable for non-skid road-surfacing, known as " road metal ") and other construction materials may be of great national importance. In addition there are rarer minerals which have particular chemical or physical properties which are essential for use in certain industrial processes, and for which substitutes have not yet been developed: examples include fuller's earth. Salt and brine are also extracted from inland and coastal sources.

Lastly, in this short practical discussion of the problems of extractive industries in relation to dereliction, the general question of the *transportation of materials* is of extreme significance. First, the siting of extractive industry is clearly influenced by the comparative valuation of cost of production, and cost of carriage of the minerals from source to market, or to local factory. Secondly, the practicability of reinstatement of excavated areas is related (*a*) to the proportionate volume of the top soil or other excavated strata available for back filling as extraction proceeds; and (*b*) to the availability of some suitable type of waste material for tipping into the void. Thus, national and regional studies of the location of waste materials and of costed transport facilities are necessary. In recent years some waste tips which had previously been considered as environmental liabilities, such as the fly ash from power stations, have become saleable assets for road and other construction. More recently this has been extended to colliery waste in suitable locations, which may now be used as a fill for motorway embankments. It is also increasingly appreciated that disposal of domestic or factory waste generally may often be more advantageously done by use as filling material than by expensive incineration.

Thus it is necessary to plan for waste material disposal on a regional and national basis, and this aspect will, no doubt, be increasingly considered in relation to the transportation system in general, more particularly in view of the impetus given to collaboration between local planning authorities under Pts. I and II of the Town and Country Planning Act, 1971 (see below).

Direct financial aid for " areas of derelict land " may also be made available under the Local Employment Act, 1972, ss. 8 (6) and 14 (1). [7a]

2. Legal Controls

In theory at least, the extraction of minerals has been largely controlled since 1948 by virtue of the Town and Country Planning Act, 1947, as continued by provisions in the Town and Country Planning Act, 1962. It is now also subject to rather different provisions under the Town and Country Planning Act, 1971.

Under the two earlier of these Acts it was required that every local planning authority carry out a survey or surveys of their area and draw up a development plan in which the locations of existing and proposed mineral workings could be defined. Further, the provisions relating to planning control ensured that planning consent must be obtained in relation to any digging or reinstatement operations. However, it was not a positive requirement that the local planning authority collect and collate all possible facts about mineral workings in their survey, although they were asked in particular to deal with information under thirteen headings, including " minerals." Although the Minister could amend a development plan proposal, he had no firm assurance that a full investigation as to mineral extraction had been made.

Under the " new style " development plans now gradually being introduced area by area (1973) by successive regulations under the

[7a] See Intermediate Areas and Derelict Land Clearance Areas Order, 1972 (S.I. 1972 No. 421), as amended by S.I. 1972 No. 585.

Town and Country Planning Act, 1971, what may, at first sight, appear to present a more peripheral approach to the information to be provided in the (development plan) survey by the local planning authority does, in fact, impose a stricter requirement.   The 1971 Act, by s. 6 (1), states that the local planning authority must institute a survey of their area " examining the matters which may be expected to affect the development of that area or the planning of its development . . . and to keep all such matters under review." These matters are to include (s. 6 (3)) the principal physical and economic characteristics of the authority's area, including the principal purposes for which land is used, and their effect upon neighbouring areas.[8]

Thus, the local planning authority, in conducting the required statutory survey preparatory to the drawing up of a development plan (i.e., both " structure " and " local " plans under the 1971 Act), must ensure that information is obtained about significant mining and quarrying within the local planning authority area. They must then include in their proposed plan suitable provisions to cover future extractive operations.   These provisions must, under both old and new style development plans, be made available for comment by county district councils (where these apply); and, if under the new style requirements, they must be made available for comment by persons or groups which are likely to want to make representations, thus following the recommendations of the Skeffington Committee on Public Participation in Planning (1969).

It is also significant that, where a development plan provides that land is to be used for the winning and working of minerals, " *compulsory working rights* " may be obtained by application to the High Court, under s. 265 of the 1971 Act read in conjunction with the Mines (Working Facilities and Support) Act, 1966 (which latter repealed and replaced earlier legislation on the subject).   Under these Acts, the applicant wishing to work mineral rights, or to obtain ancillary rights so as to render this possible, such as the right to let down the surface or to obtain a water supply, must first obtain

---

[8] For a concise description of the functioning of the old and new style development plans see *Planning Law and Procedure* by A. E. Telling, at pp. 47 to 70.   The provisions of the new style development plans are to be applied under the Town and Country Planning Act, 1971, Pt. I, and the Town and Country Planning (Structure and Local Plans) Regulations, 1972 (S.I. 1972 No. 1154); and these Regulations are well explained in the Department of the Environment Circular No. 44/71.

the approval of the Secretary of State for Trade and Industry and the Secretary of State for the Environment, who may then refer the case to the High Court if they so agree.   However, the order can, in general, only be made where the court is satisfied that the applicant has an interest in the minerals (see below); and that, in the absence of an order, some parcels may probably be left permanently unworked; and that the necessary rights cannot be obtained by negotiation between the parties; and, finally, that the right to extract the said minerals should be granted in the national interest.   (In the case of coal and certain other minerals, however, it is not necessary to establish either the lack of ability to negotiate an agreement or that there may be a permanent residue left unworked in the absence of an order.)

As to the question of the applicant's interest in the minerals, it should be noted that, where a development plan specifically allocates land for mineral working, any person may apply for the right to work it (that is, he need not previously have a financial interest in the said minerals) providing that the High Court deems that such extraction would be in the national interest.   Nevertheless even where such an application is supported by a court order, the usual right of the local planning authority, jointly with the Secretary of State for the Environment, to attach specific conditions to a planning permission will still exist.

In terms of the application of the detailed provisions of the Town and Country Planning Acts, the Town and Country Planning General Development Order, 1973 (S.I. 1973 No. 31),[8a] and the Town and Country Planning (Use Classes) Order, 1972 (S.I. 1972 No. 1385), mining and quarrying are deliberately put into a peculiarly ambivalent position by virtue of reg. 3 of the Town and Country Planning (Minerals) Regulations, 1971 (S.I. 1971 No. 756). (*Note*: These Regulations do not however apply to the mining operations of the National Coal Board.)   Regulation 3 specifies that mining and quarrying shall be treated (with exceptions discussed below) as a development operation rather than as a " use " of the land, and thus it places such operations on a similar footing to engineering or building construction projects.   However, for practical reasons, reg. 4 (*b*) also recites that mineral development

[8a] Replacing the similarly-named Order of 1963 (S.I. 1963 No. 709), as amended.

shall be treated as a " use " in respect of the ability to impose conditions as to the *length of time* for which the operations may be carried on (s. 30 (1) (*b*) of the 1971 Act). The regulation also provides that planning permission may be granted to enable a mining use already instituted to be continued.

Thus, the local planning authority may limit the time-span allowed for any given mining or quarrying, and they may require the carrying out of works on such land if these appear to be relevant to the " proposed development " (s. 30 (1) (*a*) of the 1971 Act)— such as the progressive back filling of excavation at a specified rate throughout the operation or that the site be screened by trees; or that special access routes for lorry or railway traffic be constructed and/or used. In addition they may also require that on completion of the period of time granted as part of limited planning permission any buildings or works erected under that permission be then removed or altered.

In short a local planning authority may grant planning permission subject to such conditions as they think fit (s. 24 (2) (*b*) of the 1971 Act), provided the conditions are valid conditions in the planning context as distinct from some other context. If the local planning authority or the Minister mistake or misuse their powers however *bona fide*, the courts can interfere by declaration or injunction (*Pyx Granite Co., Ltd.* v. *Ministry of Housing and Local Government* [1958] 1 Q.B. 554 (C.A.), reversed upon other grounds [1960] A.C. 260 (H.L.)). By the Town and Country Planning General Development Order, 1973, art. 7 (4) (*a*) (i), the reasons for imposing any conditions must be stated, but the courts cannot disturb a policy decision providing the correct factors had been taken into account (*Fawcett Properties, Ltd.* v. *Buckingham County Council* [1959] Ch. 543 (C.A.); affirmed [1961] A.C. 636 (H.L.)). To give a separate example, it would clearly be invalid for a local planning authority to attach as a condition of a planning permission a requirement that the land excavated be made available for acquisition by the local authority at a purely nominal price, the financial factor not being a valid planning provision. [9]

Once the period of limited planning permission has expired, *enforcement notices* may be issued by the local planning authority requiring demolition or alteration of any buildings or works, or the

[9] For a concise further discussion of the general principle see *An Outline of Planning Law* by Sir Desmond Heap, 5th ed., at pp. 114 to 120.

discontinuance of operations (s. 87 of the 1971 Act); and, subject to a right of appeal to the Secretary of State (under s. 88), any person who subsequently uses, or permits the use of, land in contravention of the notice is guilty of an offence (under s. 89 (5) of the 1971 Act) for which the maximum penalties are: upon summary conviction £400 and £50 a day thereafter, and upon indictment no limit.   It is further provided (by reg. 5 of the Minerals Regulations) that such enforcement notice can be served in respect of non-compliance with a condition at any time within four years after the non-compliance has become known to the local planning authority.

A factor operating in the mineral extractor's favour is, however, provided by reg. 6, which states that s. 118 (1) of the 1962 Act (now s. 164 (1) of the 1971 Act) shall apply to mineral workings: thus, where permission to develop is subsequently revoked or modified, compensation becomes payable by the local planning authority. But the regulation also provides a modification that a claim for expenditure or loss shall not be entertained under the said subsection in respect of buildings, plant or machinery unless the claimant can prove that he is unable to use such buildings, plant or machinery, or to use them except at the loss claimed.   Provision is then made that, for this purpose, the Lands Tribunal may give directions that such claim be severed from the remainder of the claim and be dealt with at a later date.   Further, by reg. 8, provision is made for apportionment of values for compensation purposes between that part of the land comprised of " minerals " and the remainder in cases where the mineral rights have been sold off separately.[10]

Thus, it will be observed that most of the inadequacies[11] in legal control of the extractive industries result not from insufficiency in the statutory provisions, but from the physical and technical changes which occur over the years and which thus render the conditions attached to any given planning permission in some way inappropriate.   For example, conditions imposed twenty years ago often did not take into account the vast increase in size and capacity of excavating machinery, together with the resultant capacity to back fill progressively.   It has therefore been suggested that a system

[10] The remainder of the Minerals Regulations is concerned with the method of assessment of compensation for loss of development value.

[11] It must, however, be noted that in the case of mining operations carried out *by the National Coal Board*, tipping of colliery waste cannot be restricted since special provisions apply Class XX, para. (iii), of the General Development Order specifically to this activity.

should be developed, and generally agreed, whereby conditional planning permissions can be varied periodically in relation to the improvement in techniques of mining and other factors: the problem here, however, is to ensure that the economic assessment (both as to capital investment and as to running costs and income) of the applicant can be sufficiently protected against future modifications in the planning permission.

CHAPTER 5

TRANSPORT

Those factual and legal problems which relate to pollution caused by the various forms of modern transport are discussed in Chapters 8 and 9.[1] The purpose of this present chapter is rather to consider those factors which tend to influence the location of transportation systems—that is, the positioning of routes and networks and the positioning of points of generation of internal traffic, such as principally seaports and airports. It must, however, be emphasised that, in this respect, this chapter is intended merely to be a " plain man's guide " to the more common problems and theories involved: that is, it does not purport to discuss, beyond a mere mention, considerations of statistical analysis of traffic flow, or the degree of possibility (in terms of cost) of the introduction of more modern forms of locomotion, such as moving belt pedestrian walkways, or electronically controlled (regulated) road vehicles.

For convenience, transportation services may be divided into passenger transport and freight transport; but, in addition and in parallel, they may also be divided into (1) incoming and outgoing oversea surface transport; (2) incoming and outgoing oversea air-borne transport; (3) long- and medium-distance transport within Great Britain; (4) short-distance transport for commuter passengers (notably in the London and other major conurbation areas) or local delivery services for goods.

Each of these divisions will now be considered, firstly in relation to town and country planning administration and principles (headed " General "); and secondly as to legal control.

1. General

(1) Oversea surface transport

The present means[2] of carriage oversea of passengers and freight may be either by ship or by aircraft, or (more recently) by a combination of these, namely hovercraft.

---

[1] Pp. 158, 177.
[2] But a channel tunnel, or bridge, is visualised.

It should be interjected at this stage—although it is not directly in connection with the town and country planning aspect of protection of the environment—that the methods of operation (such as stowage of cargo and pilotage, etc.) of each of the above-named types of transport (i.e., of individual ships, aircraft or hovercraft) is governed by separate and distinct codes of conduct and law. In other words, the legal liabilities in relation to (a) the conduct of ships' masters or captains of aircraft, etc., together with (b) the contractual conditions and tortious acts in relation to carriage of passengers, and (c) the contractual conditions and tortious acts in relation to cargo, are subject to separate and distinct codes of law according to the type of " craft " involved. In the case of hovercraft, however, there is a peculiar amalgam of legal codes, whereby maritime law applies to cargo, whereas the Civil Aviation Acts apply to passengers.

The method of operation of merchant shipping has changed radically during the past twenty years. The rapid increase in freight handling and ships' operational costs resulting from rising labour charges have necessitated radical alterations, wherein cargo increasingly tends to be " containerised." That is, goods are crated in large containers at the factory of origin, and remain so crated until arrival at their ultimate (probably inland) destination. Such containers are generally of sufficient size to be carried as a single unit forming the entire load of a large, articulated lorry or trailer; or, alternatively, of a rather similar size suitable for carriage on a railway flat truck. The principal effects of this method are that the total number of units of cargo to be handled is reduced, and that this handling is now largely by mechanical means. Thus, modern ships tend to be either bulk carriers for such cargoes as oil, grain, or metallic ores, or to be of what is called " containerised " design, to permit easy lowering into stowage position with minimum need to manhandle or stow by hand. (There is, however, one arresting factor in these developments, namely, the existence of countries throughout the world in which labour is still extremely cheap, and where mechanical handling would be not only unjustified economically, but would be inadvisable in political terms.)

In conjunction with the modern design of docks arise two factors which are of basic significance in terms of town and country planning, namely (a) the need to construct (or create by alteration) deep water channels and berths sufficient to take the new deep-draught bulk carrier or containerised ships[3]; and (*b*) the need to handle the increasing volume of total cargo at ports by means of pipelines, augers, cranes and other mechanical (as distinct from manual) methods. It will thus be appreciated that many of the traditional dock areas, as in London, Liverpool, Bristol and elsewhere are, of necessity, outdated due to inability physically to increase the depth of navigational channels and of berths. Added to this there arises the problem of reduction in labour force requirements, which necessitates partly schemes for retraining locally for other occupations, and partly the migration of dockworkers to the new containerised ports.

This need has also resulted in the concept of the development of Maritime Industrial Development Areas (" MIDAS ") in suitable parts of the country. A " MIDA " would consist of a very large dock complex developed in conjunction with an immediately adjoining industrial area. The types of manufacture initially to be encouraged in (or allocated to) such an area would be mainly those concerned with large-scale export and/or with the use of large quantities of imported raw materials, but the growth of subsidiary industry would also be anticipated. Additionally, the presence of oil-receiving depots and refineries, or of other sources of industrial fuel supply, such as natural gas or (to a lessening extent) coal, would reduce the incidental costs of powering factories. It will thus be seen that the development of MIDAS would assist the national environmental situation by reducing problems of transporting raw materials, products and fuel over road, rail, canal or pipeline networks. Further, the development of an airport for cargo aircraft within such a complex would tend to reduce the rate of increase of overland flights, which, at present, tend to be generated by mixed freight and passenger airports.

The modern methods of ship and cargo handling render it possible to offer a much quicker turn-round of each vessel, and thus to reduce the total number of berths required. It must also be remarked that, as a result of the immense growth in size and the related problems which arise in terms of navigation (not least the distance required in which to stop a tanker or to alter course in an emergency), discharging and loading of bulk oil is now carried out by pipeline at the seaward end of very long jetties, and not within the confines of a conventional port.

In relation to cross-channel traffic to the Continent special

[3] See Appendix B, Recommendations 31 and 32.

considerations apply. The most significant change during the period from 1955 has been the growth, at a rate of over 13 per cent. per year, in the carriage by sea of cars—crossing primarily for tourism, but also for business purposes. Clearly this volume will further increase now that Britain has entered the European Economic Union. The ports in Britain concerned with this traffic are of small to medium size, and are of the traditional type. In addition to conventional shipping, hovercraft are now extensively used for this purpose. However, the extent of surface travel over the channel will be greatly reduced with the advent of a channel tunnel or bridge. If a tunnel is constructed the type of transport used will, for the foreseeable future, be in railway form, so as to avoid many of the problems of ventilation of fuel waste gases. Such a tunnel or bridge would, obviously, have a very basic influence upon the road and rail networks of both Britain and Continental Europe.

To summarise the position from the standpoint of the environment, it should therefore be borne in mind that, if it is desired to prevent a seaport development on the grounds that it will spoil or endanger local amenity, it will be necessary to establish that the national need for bulk carrier or containerised berths can be met in other areas where environmental damage will be less significant. In the case of smaller vessels, however (such as those acting as channel car ferries), the practical range of choice for harbour expansion may be far greater.

The operation of seaborne passenger services (as distinct from car ferrying) has traditionally been through Southampton and, to a lesser extent (and on the Atlantic routes), from the Mersey and the Clyde. However, the total volume has greatly decreased as a result of the improvements in air travel. In town and country planning terms, therefore, the problems of increase in road and rail traffic related to oversea passenger services have tended to develop in connection with: (a) cross-channel car ferries; (b) transport to major airports; and to be potentially concerned with the possibility of a channel tunnel or bridge.

(2) Oversea airborne transport

The increase in total air traffic has been extremely rapid in recent years and it was calculated that even in the period 1956 to 1966 there had been an annual rate of increase of aircraft movements from the four major British airports (Heathrow, Gatwick, Stansted and Prestwick) of 7·6 per cent.   It was also forecast that there would be acceleration in the rate of growth in passenger travel, and more particularly in non-scheduled tourist services; in cargo services; and in air taxi services.   However, it is believed that the bulk of medium distance air freight will continue to be carried in mixed passenger-cargo aircraft.   But it must be borne in mind that successful development of designs for VTOL[4] and STOL[5] aircraft and modern airships[6] might radically alter the requirements—in particular in relation to the environment—as to future airports.

At the present time a very high proportion of Britain's inter-national air traffic uses airports in the South East of England, due to the amount of traffic actually originating in the Metropolitan region; that is, in terms of (*a*) passengers, and (*b*) freight which tends to be the products of light industry (as opposed to the heavy industry products of, say, the industrial Midlands).

It is not the intention of the author to enter upon an exhaustive discussion of the merits and demerits of the various sites proposed for a third London airport—or even to discuss whether or not such a third airport will be necessary in the light of possible VTOL and STOL developments—but brief reference will be made to the prac-tical needs to be met in the siting of any new airport in any part of Great Britain.

The selection of an airport site should involve the striking of a fair balance between (*a*) the amenity needs of any local (or more general) population,[6a] and (*b*) the reasonably accurately estimated compara-tive costing of a range of possible sites.   The methods of airport costing have become extremely sophisticated, and involve a cost-benefit analysis.   That is, briefly, a balanced comparative assess-ment of the capital cost of the airport and of transport systems (roads; railways, whether conventional or monorail; taxi aircraft, etc.) required to both serve and to service it; together with the running costs of such services; and together with a factor represent-ing the value of the time per journey for each air passenger.   It may be said, in non-technical language, that these factors are now customarily reduced to formulae whereby the relative values may

---

[4] Vertical take off and landing.

[5] Short take off and landing.

[6] Gas-filled airships have great weight-carrying capacity.

[6a] Also, as to air pollution, see Chapter 8, at p. 165, and as to noise, see Chapter 9, at p. 184; and as to adverse " physical factors " generally, see pp. 117 to 118 (The Land Compensation Bill).

be assessed. To this calculation is added a further formula which is said to represent the values of amenity existing in the locality of any proposed airport, together with an estimate of the extent to which this may be affected by both aircraft and ground traffic generated by an airport. In this latter respect, however, it must be evident that such a rule of thumb estimate must be purely objective in nature; that is, it cannot allow for the susceptibility—or sensitivity —of the particular local population which is under consideration. By way of fictional example, it is possible that the inhabitants of a New Town, if recently moved from London, may find themselves oblivious to additional aircraft noise, whereas people who have lived the whole of their lives in an atmosphere of rural quiet may find themselves unable to sleep or to concentrate. It is therefore of the greatest importance that members of a local population who feel strongly opposed to any probable effects of aircraft noise should ensure that evidence of the strength of local opinion is adequately demonstrated at any local consultation or inquiry.

In view of the complexity (or sophistication?) of the modern means of cost-benefit analysis of potential airport sites, and in view of the volume and variety of evidence recently received in relation to the future third London airport, the author does not propose to attempt to pursue this discussion in technical terms: rather to say that unless extremely strong and extensive public opinion can be aroused (and strength of local public opinion is a valid ground for decision in a town and country planning matter), evidence of such opinion must always be related to a cost-benefit analysis and objectors should seek expert professional advice at an early stage. Where, however, this strength of opinion is eventually deemed (by the Cabinet) to be sufficient, the normal, relatively short-term, basis of cost-benefit analysis will be set aside. In other words (at the time of writing at least), the choice of the Foulness site for the third London airport has become related not to immediate costs and immediate benefit, but to the probable long-term cost-amenity benefits to London and the South East of England generally.[7]

[7] The Roskill Commission which was appointed in 1969 to investigate sites and to recommend to the Government a site for the third London airport, spent two years in surveying and evaluating 78 sites, which ranged from Hullavington (near Bristol) in the West to Woodbridge (near Ipswich) in the East, and from Newark (near Grantham) in the North to the Isle of Wight in the South. The short-listed sites were Cublington, Thurleigh, Nuthampstead and Foulness, the last-named now having been selected by the Government.

The legal controls applicable to the siting of runways and the allocation of flight paths (i.e., direction and altitude) are considered in part 2 of this chapter, *post*, and pollution by aircraft noise in Chapter 9 at p. 184.

(3) *Long- and medium-distance transport within Great Britain*

The principal forms of transport used for long- and medium-distance travel are: road, rail, air, and waterborne (the latter including both coastal shipping and inland waterway carriage).

The author has regretfully decided that he should not discuss all of these alternatives in detail, but that space should be allocated principally to a careful analysis of the system of road transport. As regards the use of the national railway system, it may suffice to say that, as a result of a policy adopted by several successive Governments in recent years, the previous, extremely comprehensive Victorian network (perhaps the most comprehensive in Europe), has been to a very considerable extent dismantled. No doubt this was considered desirable in economic terms—in view, principally, of the high and ever increasing cost of railway personnel—but there is now a firm opinion emerging that even a very substantial subsidy from the Exchequer would be justified in terms of improvement of the environment, and of personal safety, in relation to the mounting volume of road traffic. However, the purpose of this book is not to crusade in worthy causes so much as to provide material for legal argument; and it is felt that to embark upon an involved statistical discussion in favour of a re-expansion of the railway network would not be of sufficient value in relation to the space available, since the present clear and uncompromising Government policy can only be altered by Parliamentary action.

The inland waterways are in a slightly better position than the railways because, in this case, there is no policy of deliberate contraction, but rather one of rehabilitation of canals and docks in so far as this can be justified in terms of an increased volume of local user. But there does not appear to be any stated intention to re-activate long-distance routes, such as, for example, from Bristol to London. Routes of this type would, however, be of value in taking bulk loads off the road network; and, if a reliable flow of deliveries at points of destination were achieved, then the actual speed of travel would, in the case of the majority of bulk cargoes, be material only if the cost of barge crews became too high relative to the value of goods carried.

The internal air services available in the British Isles are, of course, very much limited by capital cost and availability of suitable airport sites. It is submitted that the air services between London and the major industrial and commercial centres are at present sufficient to meet average demand—although this demand may itself be influenced by availability. The South West of England would certainly benefit from an extended service, and indeed this would probably assist in the growth of industry within development areas in that part of the country. The environmental considerations affecting the siting and use of airports are discussed in an earlier section of this chapter; and also, as to pollution, including noise, in Chapters 8 and 9.

The present national policy for transport stems from a White Paper on Transport Policy (Cmnd. 3057) published in July, 1966, which was followed by a series of more specialised White Papers published during 1967, on " Railway Policy " (Cmnd. 3439), on " Transport of Freight " (Cmnd. 3470), and on " Waterways " (Cmnd. 3401). The policies put forward in these White Papers were subsequently embodied in the Transport Act, 1968. A further White Paper on " The Reorganisation of the Ports " (Cmnd. 3903) was presented to Parliament in January, 1969. In addition to the White Papers, a statement of policy was issued jointly by British Railways and the Minister of Transport in March, 1967.

Road transport and the road network.—It is now an accepted principle of road network design that, for long- and medium-distance travel, the provision of fast motorways between major centres of industry and population is not, in itself, enough, since a higher proportion of time is statistically found to be wasted by traffic passing through towns rather than on the stretches of road between them. Thus, the provision of ring roads (once called bypasses) has become an essential factor in road network design. Further reference will be made to ring roads under part (4) in discussing short-distance and commuter transport, but it may be remarked here that, in the case of larger cities, there may well be (in existence or intended) three concentric ring roads, the outer ring being designed to carry traffic which wishes entirely to skirt (or bypass) the conurbation, the inner routes being designed to take medium-distance traffic having business within the conurbation itself.

It must be said that one of the principal advantages to be gained by the formation, in October, 1970, of the Department of the Environment—which thus brought the functions of the Ministries of Housing and Local Government, Transport, and Public Building and Works under the overall supervision of the Secretary of State for the Environment—is that a far more effective liaison between those responsible for town and country planning and for highways, railways and other forms of transport can be obtained.   It should be noted that the Ministers responsible for the functions of the former Ministries of Housing and Local Government, Transport, and Public Building and Works were given fresh titles and functions in October, 1970, namely: Minister of Local Government and Development; Minister of Housing and Construction; and Minister for Transport Industries.   The matter of improved liaison was, and is, of considerable importance, since the tendency until 1970 had been for local highway authorities (counties, boroughs [7a] and districts) to be concerned primarily with matters of cost of construction, repair and maintenance of highways, and with road safety, rather than to take the needs of town and country planning as an essential starting point for highway design and adaptation.   This deficiency tended, on occasion, also to relate to more major highway construction, such as the pre-planning of motorways, which were the responsibility of the Ministry of Transport, and as a result, several of our major motorway routes consist now inadequately of only two-lane dual carriageway, whereas other sections of motorway are tending to be used to a lesser extent than had been anticipated.   However, in several counties, additional county council committees (called, for example, a " Special Development Committee ") have existed for a number of years, the purpose of which has been to encourage effective liaison between those committees and their chairmen which are primarily concerned with the planning of a local environment.   Such a committee will probably consist of the chairmen and vice-chairmen of the county council and of the planning, highways and finance committees, together with some other members and, from time to time, some further chairmen of committees co-opted for the purposes of a particular project only.

In considering the effects of long- and medium-distance roads (which for this purpose will be taken to be non-urban roads) upon

[7a] Until April, 1974.

the environment, the principal factors to be taken into account are first the speed, flow and destination of the traffic carried upon them; and secondly the resultant effects in terms of pollution (including noise, vibration, vehicle headlamps and exhaust fumes), together with the build-up of traffic in inhabited areas, including village high streets.

In further considering the problems of a national road network in relation to the general strategy for transport as set out in all the above policy documents, the Minister of Transport prepared, in 1969, a Green Paper, " Roads of the Future: A New Inter-Urban Plan," in which the salient features were discussed, and a proposed strategy put forward, upon which the general public (including interested organisations) were specifically invited to comment. The Green Paper was supported by a series of maps showing the route strategy proposals for England as a whole, together with four separate but integrated maps indicating regional strategy proposals for each of the eight Economic Planning Regions[8] in England (but not Wales or Scotland).

Following receipt of public comment, a further White Paper, " Roads for the Future; the New Inter-Urban Plan for England " (Cmnd. 4369), was published in May, 1970. (Similar proposals were also published for Scotland and for Wales in the White Papers, " Scottish Roads in the 1970s " (Cmnd. 3953), published in March, 1969; and, earlier, " Wales: The Way Ahead " (Cmnd. 3334), published in July, 1967.)

The essence of the inter-urban road plan can be stated briefly as follows. A comprehensive national system of trunk roads is to be provided (completed) upon which commercial traffic and private cars will be able to move freely, and on which delay and congestion (it is perhaps optimistically said) will have been " virtually eliminated." This relief is, of course, directly connected with the present " associated economic loss."

In the decade 1960 to 1970, the volume of traffic using inter-urban trunk roads had more than doubled, to about 21,000 million vehicle miles,[9] and the prospect of a continuing rise in the ownership of

---

[8] The Regions are: South Eastern; South Western; East Anglia; East Midlands; West Midlands; Yorks and Humberside; North West and Northern.

[9] " Vehicle miles " is a measure of traffic volume representing the average mileage travelled by one vehicle in one year multiplied by the number of vehicles registered in the country.

private cars (quite apart from rising industrial and commercial needs) must be anticipated. In 1970 there were about 11 million private cars, [9a] and it is estimated that there may well be as many as 20 million by 1985. Since 1964 the annual rate of expenditure on road construction has exceeded £360 million, with the result that the approximate total mileage of motorways in England and Wales by the end of 1972 is 1,000 miles, [10] together with an equivalent length of other dual-carriageway trunk roads.

The design of the national network has been revised following comments on the Green Paper, and is now set out in Maps " A " and " B " annexed to the White Paper. Map " A " gives a " Route Strategy Network for England " and relates this to existing major urban areas together with areas shown as designated or proposed for new or expanded towns, such as the Central Lancashire New Town, Corby New Town, Bracknell New Town, and Harlow New Town —a total of 24 urban areas in all. However, it has been emphasised that the network as shown on Map " A " is, in fact, not the entire requirement for the strategy, since the complete concept also encompasses a very considerable scheme for improvement of many other existing roads to dual carriageway standard; also the provision of new and improved links to the primary network from centres of population and industry; and also measures to relieve or improve certain parts of the earlier constructed motorway network (e.g., M1 and M4) where the capacity is inadequate.

Map " B " emphasises, within the general strategy, the existing and proposed motorways and trunk roads, and relates these to large areas of the country in which *feasibility studies* of certain routes are in progress. These feasibility studies are shown as being carried out in the following areas: north of Leeds; between Doncaster and Grimsby; between Preston and Burnley; east of Blackpool; between Manchester and Sheffield; north west of Derby; between Coventry and Leicester; in a large area stretching from Worcester and Gloucester in the west, to Birmingham in the north, to Oxford in the south and to Luton in the east; north east of Bristol; in the entire area within an approximate radius of twenty-five miles from central London, but also stretching in a corridor as far as Luton; between Barnstaple and Taunton; north of Winchester; south west of Basingstoke; and, finally, east of Southampton.

[9a] Private cars only: not all vehicles.
[10] The total of 1,000 miles for England, Wales *and Scotland* was achieved in 1971.

However, as comprehensive regional strategies become further developed (i.e., following the advices of the Regional Economic Planning Councils) certain relatively minor amendments to the national network may become necessary. In addition, the siting of the third London airport at Foulness will affect the rate of future development in the areas east of London.

In terms of any measures which may be contemplated for protection of a local environment, it must also be noted that the routes as depicted in Map " A " of the White Paper are entirely diagrammatic, and that precise lines will not be known until declared by the Secretary of State for the Environment or until compulsory purchase orders are made and, subject to the usual public local inquiry procedure, approved. It is, however, specifically stated in the White Paper (Cmnd. 4369), at para. 22, that:

" In selecting routes for new and improved roads full account will be taken of environmental and amenity questions including the conservation of historic areas. New roads do improve the total environment although, inevitably, amenity is reduced in some areas and for some people. The aim will be to safeguard and, indeed, to enhance both amenity and environment to the maximum possible extent. Road plans will be most carefully co-ordinated with local authorities' development plans, use will be made whenever possible of derelict land, whenever it proves practicable and economic, suitable material from unsightly waste tips will be utilised in the actual construction of roads." [10a]

The relative priorities of various parts of the total network may vary from time to time, and the stated policy as to this is that sufficient flexibility of choice on the priority of individual routes shall be reserved to the Secretary of State. The White Paper, in para. 25, states:

" The intention is to retain sufficient flexibility of choice on the priority of individual routes and schemes to enable full account to be taken of future development in national, regional and local planning. The primary consideration will continue

[10a] But there has recently been considerable complaint about the method employed in terms of the right of public objection in connection with the Oxford to Warwick section of proposed motorway, the line of which has been taken in extremely short lengths, thereby rendering an *overall* objection to the total route nugatory, and enabling the Department of the Environment to oppose any deviation in the light of resultant increase in cost.

to be the economic benefits to be derived from reduction of congestion and accidents but due weight will be given, in determining priorities, to the need to support economic development in all regions."

It is also recognised that a higher proportion of expenditure on roads will have to be allocated to those within urban areas (see Part (4) of this chapter, p. 105, *post*).

A more recent statement of the Government's intention was, however, made by the Secretary of State for the Environment in a Written Answer in the House of Commons on 23rd June, 1971. This did not negate any part of the above-mentioned policy as to the national road network, but enlarged upon it and made certain emphases. Briefly, the Answer included a statement that the Government intended to extend motorway construction in order to ensure that the national network shall include a total mileage of motorways of 2,000 by the early 1980s. Within this general proposal it was emphasised that the purpose is to "achieve environmental improvements by diverting long-distance traffic, and particularly heavy goods vehicles, from a large number of towns and villages, so as to relieve them of the noise, dirt and danger which they suffer at present." Secondly, the comprehensive network to be obtained by the early 1980s will be based upon " strategic routes to promote economic growth." Thirdly, it is the intention to link the more remote and less prosperous regions with this national network; and, fourthly, it is intended to ensure that every major city and town with a population exceeding 250,000 will be directly connected with the strategic network, together with provision that all towns with a population of over 80,000 will lie within 10 miles of the network. Fifthly, the strategic network will serve all major ports and airports, including the future third London airport at Foulness. Sixthly, it is specifically stated as policy that " as many historic towns as possible " will be relieved of through traffic. The Secretary of State enlarged upon this latter point as follows:

" The Government have given especially sympathetic consideration to the traffic relief of historic towns. The network of strategic routes and the individual improvements planned will benefit almost all the historic towns listed by the Council for British Archaeology and which are on trunk roads. The C.B.A. list includes 105 historic towns which are on trunk roads. Of these, 84 will have been relieved of through traffic by the early 1980s, either by the planned network or by individual schemes already announced. Many other historic towns, although not on the trunk road network, will nevertheless benefit from the diversions of traffic on to the main strategic routes. Through traffic is, of course, only one cause of urban congestion and due weight will also be given to the needs of historic areas when considering future principal road schemes which local authorities may propose."

The plans, as at the date of the Written Answer, envisaged an increase in the total number of vehicles (of all types) on the roads in England and Wales from 15 million to about 22 million by 1980, and are designed to meet this situation.

It was also emphasised that the road network

" will be continuous and, subject only to the decisions we have still to take about the trunk road network in the vicinity of a very few towns where special studies are in hand, it will be possible to drive direct from one point on the network to any other entirely on high-standard trunk roads."

In addition, reference was made to the fact that the choice of schemes had been taken in the light of the views of the National Ports Council, to the effect that adequate access to the major docks be provided well within the time-span of the present plans (i.e., early 1980s), and " in most cases by the mid-1970s."

Appended to the Written Answer was a list of some fifty-three new major road improvement schemes together with four feasibility studies; and also four illustrative, but diagrammatic, maps showing: the Primary Trunk Road network by the early 1980s; Trunk Road Network and Individual Improvements by the early 1980s; Trunk Road Network Historic Towns relieved; and Major Ports Served by the Network (these latter being: Tyneside, Teesside, Hull, Immingham, Preston, Liverpool, Manchester (ship canal), Ipswich, Felixstowe, Harwich, Tilbury, Bristol, London, Dover and Southampton).

It should also be mentioned that the planning of the national road network has been based upon the now highly technical method of appraisal known as cost/benefit analysis, in which the present and estimated future figures as to traffic needs, accidents, overloading of routes and economic loss upon every section of trunk road are taken into account, and these are related, within the analysis, to any planned changes in the pattern of industry or of population. The technique is essentially linked to the direct economic benefit to be derived from any part of the total network, or proposed network. The probable traffic flows upon any hypothetical part of a road network are now, as stated in the Appendix to the Green Paper,

"... based upon calculations of the traffic on every section of the trunk road or principal road system and of the changes in traffic flow which would take place if parts of that system were improved or replaced by new roads. To calculate the traffic the Department relies upon relationships between factors which generate traffic—population, vehicle ownership, distance between centres of population—and the actual traffic which occurs in practice. The estimates obtained in this way form a representation (or model) of the vehicle flows on the roads.

For the purposes of the model the information which is used includes details of about 1,400 zones of population; all links in the network of trunk and principal roads (generally each link represents the road between two junctions on the trunk or principal road system); and the characteristics of each link—width, number of side roads, average travelling speed. The traffic which would be generated from each population zone to every other is calculated and assigned to routes. The result is a calculation of the traffic on every part of the *existing* road system. This representation of the traffic can be checked against known traffic flows and the model adjusted to closely match reality.

When the model gives a satisfactory representation of the traffic flows on the *existing* network it can be used to project *future* traffic flows, taking into account changes in the road pattern and expected increases in population and numbers of vehicles. For the purposes of the present" [Green Paper, 1969] "study the projection can be made to the early 1970s (to cover those roads which are firmly in the existing programme and are not at issue in the network under consideration). A further projection can then be made to the 1980s assuming the completion of a new network in the intervening period. The redistribution of the traffic and the resulting direct economic benefits can then be assessed and set against the capital cost to yield the *cost/benefit return* resulting from the investment. Different networks can be dealt with in this way and the results compared. The effect can also be calculated for individual proposals of sufficient size—a reasonably long route or a particular regional network—to assess the relative worth of a particular part of the network or the interdependence of the effects of several improvements on one another."

The process is said by the Department to be more complex than as outlined above, and it is stated that further details of the method will be published in due course.

Within these calculations, the actual cost of construction of the road itself is more significant than it may appear to the layman. For example, selection of one route may involve a considerable amount of levelling-up to ensure traffic safety and drainage. In some areas it may be economic to obtain and move soil for embankment construction, in others such construction would only be possible if materials were carried a very great distance. Again, in some areas the removal of soil to create cuttings may provide a local, and thus economic, means of obtaining material for local embankments. In addition, the provision of vehicles, machinery and construction materials along the proposed line of a motorway may only be practicable if a large number of rural lanes are widened and " improved " to permit access by this type of traffic. It follows, therefore, that (apart from questions of traffic generation from centres of population, etc.) it may be necessary to strike a balance between the shortest possible length horizontally measured (i.e., a straight line) and deviation from this as a result of earth-moving problems.

The cost of motorway or new three lane dual carriageway construction is now, in general, so high (average of £954,000 per mile)[11] that it may be found that a perfectly sound case upon amenity or preservationist (e.g., archaeological) grounds will eventually be discounted in favour of a very large saving in cost to the national Exchequer. It is therefore important to realise that the protectionist should seek, at a relatively early stage, the professional advice of a highway engineer specialising in this particular type of problem, since the ultimate argument at a public inquiry is most likely to turn upon a detailed discussion as to methods of

[11] At March, 1972.

construction and the related cost. The Ministry will invariably design the route on a basis of the regulations governing gradients, camber, and suitable radii for bends to take traffic at specific speeds; but it is not unknown for an appellant, when convincingly advised by an expert, to obtain an alteration of the proposed route even where the alternative may be admittedly of a very slightly lower standard. In other words, the Secretary of State for the Environment may exercise a certain limited amount of discretion in balancing physical design requirements with environmental needs.

It may also be appropriate at this stage to mention that there is an increasing awareness of the value of archaeological excavation, particularly now that radio-chemical analysis can be used to place a scientifically accurate date upon objects, and thus upon ancient human settlements, found. The Department of the Environment is therefore encouraging the provision of grants for the rapid excavation of sites lying in the path of a new road, and it is presumed that the co-operation of the construction contractors may be expected within reasonable limits.

Finally in relation to the road system outside urban areas, it must be remarked that about one-fifth of the population of England lives in villages, or the countryside generally. In fact, since 1951 over a million people have moved from urban into rural areas. The problems caused by the increase in traffic and the " improvement " of roads in and near villages have been stressed by the Council for the Protection of Rural England in a recent booklet, *The Future of the Village*. In extreme cases trunk roads pass through the village centre; in others the village is bypassed by a motorway or major dual carriageway route at so short a distance that local amenity is still affected; and in others the small commercial life of the village (based, for example, upon a village shop, inn, and small garage and petrol station) may decline as a result of a fast bypass. In the latter instance, a catchment area for shoppers and other customers may be simply cut off by a trunk route, which either renders physical access impracticable or dissuades drivers who would have to cross it. In some cases, however (e.g., Honiton) the village or small town has, generally at its own request, been signposted on the bypass route or motorway as a " service area," providing as indicated, say, petrol, meals and hotel accommodation.

One of the remedies against overmuch through, or tourist,

traffic recommended by the Council for the Protection of Rural England is the erection of toll or other gates on roads leading to villages. However, in such cases it would be essential first to attempt to estimate the sources of village income from trade, and the probable effect upon it.

(4) *Short-distance transport for commuter passengers and for the local distribution of goods*

The commercial life of the larger cities in Great Britain, and more especially of London, is now, and will remain, dependent upon a daily influx of office, shop, and (to a lesser extent) industrial workers. It is well known that the square mile of the City of London proper—which is one of the major financial centres of the world—is virtually devoid of a resident population, and is occupied outside office hours by a very small number of people, many of whom are caretakers for office and warehouse buildings, although a number of modern blocks of flats have been built during the past decade. Thus, it is an inescapable problem that efficient and (in terms of the total national wage bill) reasonably economic forms of " commuter " transport be provided. This daily movement of the population from the suburban and countryside areas surrounding major cities relies upon an inter-related combination of public transport services and the private motor car. The public services consist of overground and underground railways, and buses (including on the River Thames a small number of water buses). In view of the brevity of this book, it is not proposed to discuss in any detail the planning of the future of the conventional and underground railway systems. In the former case the national network has, as is all too well known, drastically contracted in recent decades, although not in relation to the areas in which daily commuters normally live. At the same time, matters of public and private nuisance have tended to decrease as a result of the replacement of coal-burning engines by diesel locomotives, and the great reduction in shunting yards. In the case of the underground system, existing and new lines (such as the Victoria Line in London) have relatively little effect upon the conditions of living of persons other than passengers, save that certain dwellings and other buildings in the immediate vicinity of high-level underground lines may be affected by vibration.

It must, however, be remarked that the method of use of the

railways is now affected by two more modern problems: the probable need to park a private car at the home station, and the probable need, due to lack of space, for passengers to spend part, or the whole, of a relatively longer journey standing than hitherto. It is therefore submitted that commuter travel will benefit from either (*a*) increased speed (as by, say, the use of monorail trains); or alternatively (*b*) particular consideration being given to the longer-distance commuter passenger who may wish, and indeed need, to work whilst on the train.

So far as the underground train networks are concerned, it is essential to avoid the over-saturation of existing stations caused by development of too great a density of offices (in terms of office floor space and thus personnel), as discussed in Chapter 11—Offices.

The remainder of the subject of short-distance commuter transport and of the local distribution of goods is related to problems of road traffic. It is evident, particularly in the light of experience in the United States, and of similar symptoms which are rapidly developing in this country, that the increase in the number of vehicles per unit of area of carriageway can eventually be such that the flow of traffic virtually ceases. This has two effects. First, the time spent in travel becomes totally uneconomic. And secondly, the commercial value of an urban centre becomes so debased (due to traffic strangulation causing business customers to go elsewhere) that the heart of a town is, in effect, rendered a desert, containing the lowest possible standard of housing and little else.

The use of the motor vehicle in urban areas is, increasingly, restricted by inefficient traffic circulations, and these inefficient circulations in themselves progressively degrade human life within the area. It is evident that the traditional arrangements of streets (and particularly the " high street ") between blocks of buildings is now outdated. Therefore the major flows of traffic must be canalised into specifically designed circulatory systems, in connection with which will be developed systems for the parking of vehicles, and for the transportation of people; such as, for example, overhead walkways with moving escalators. Having designed such circulatory systems, it will be necessary to limit the future access of road vehicles, but to equate both the circulatory system and the number or volume of vehicles to the requirements of the particular town. That is, to assess the needs according to an analysis of local trade, industry, commerce, and the pattern of domestic housing. The commercial (and thus, the related domestic) requirements of a town may increase, or decrease, in the future. Where an increase can be confidently predicted, it becomes possible to allow for a far more imaginative treatment of vehicular traffic in laying out future areas, and thereby in possibly reducing the pressures upon existing localities. In any event, it is evident that the planned change in use of certain areas within an existing town—such as warehouse areas becoming office areas—may reduce the pressure of traffic, or at least the number of heavy vehicles. Positive recommendations are given in Appendix B, Recommendations 22 to 29. The " loop " system whereby through traffic is excluded from a city centre is of particular significance, and is referred to in footnote No. 1 to that Appendix.

Development plans for large urban areas should be supplemented by " transportation plans," and thereby ensure that traffic circulation becomes integrated in all considerations of town planning. Within such a transportation plan there are four possible means of control of traffic: either (*a*) by the exclusion from defined zones of all vehicles which have not been licensed to enter them; or (*b*) by charging (by means of electronically operated meters) for the use of a road; or (*c*) by subsidising public transport to the extent that it acts as a financial inducement to avoid the use of cars; or (*d*) as at present, the use of parking restrictions, or the provision of car parks in the most appropriate places within the area. Thus, it may often be inadvisable to incorporate car parks in new office buildings, since this will encourage the use of private cars. New buildings should be considered from the standpoint of the minimum essential traffic to be generated by them, but provision should be made for the off-street parking of essential delivery vehicles.

Clearly, priority must be given to the creation of improved systems of public transport, which should be both convenient to the individual, and relatively cheap. The system should be designed to deal principally with movement of the population at peak periods; as also should restrictions upon non-essential road traffic.[12]

The problem of road traffic in towns is not merely one of inconvenience to individual drivers of vehicles or (equally) to pedestrians, since part of the solution must lie in a very great increase in the number and size of primary distributor roads passing through urban areas where this cannot be avoided. Inevitably the provision, or

[12] See Appendix B, Recommendations 26, 27 and 28.

improvement, of such roads must often injure or destroy existing local amenities. It is not, however, always appreciated that the creation of a primary route may also destroy a clearly defined local urban community—that is, a community centred round such traditional points as public houses, churches, shops, or even types of housing area, such as a group of Georgian streets or squares. The destruction may result either from an actual physical division into two sectors; or from a perhaps psychological division created by a flyover road which does not actually stop-up existing streets. This problem relates also to " environmental management," which is discussed in the Report of the Steering Group and Working Group appointed by the then Minister of Transport, which was published as long ago as 1963, and entitled " Traffic in Towns." The matter is considered in paras. 467 to 469. It is suggested that, if a given local environment can be improved by management—that is, by the removal of extraneous traffic from such specific areas—and by re-organisation of the system of internal movements of traffic and pedestrians (e.g., by overhead pedestrian ways, etc.), then the flow of traffic will also be improved, since more road space will be available to it.

Whereas positive development (with certain exceptions) requires the active consideration of the local planning authority and the granting of permission, there is at present no adequate means whereby the owner or occupier of property affected by a sudden increase of traffic permanently diverted along his street or road can obtain a public inquiry. Thus, he is in a position to object to, say, a new petrol filling station or to most other new buildings (whether connected with traffic generation or no), yet he can do no more than lobby his local elected representative if a traffic circulatory system is proposed or altered (see paras. 470 and 471 in " Traffic in Towns "). However, provision has been made by regulation whereby highway authorities proposing to alter the *direction* of flow of traffic, or to close public streets to vehicular traffic, must advertise the fact and post notices in the thoroughfares affected. If objections follow, a public inquiry will normally be held.

In addition, in semi-urban and rural areas, the local population may object to extensive development of a site, yet on appeal permission may be granted by the Secretary of State, whereby a very marked increase occurs in the volume of traffic on roads in the locality. Thus, the local ratepayer may find that not only is his environment altered (most frequently in order to meet the national housing shortage), but that he will also be required to pay, at some future date, an increase in contribution to the district or county rates for the cost of widening and improvement (including, perhaps, lighting) of these roads. However, at least in such cases an opportunity is afforded for the hearing of local objectors at the planning appeal inquiry.

In order to provide for the effective planning, or redevelopment, of the urban environment it is, therefore, essential that full use be made, by the Department of the Environment, of the new machinery whereby the planning of transportation systems, and the zoning and design of the various types of buildings, can be seen as one entity. The future need for multi-level design of vehicular traffic and pedestrian traffic systems clearly requires a far greater degree of integration of buildings (as, for example, in the Barbican complex in the City of London), and this in turn requires greater co-operation between private developers. It also necessitates, in " twilight areas," intervention by local authorities in order to provide a sufficient degree of finance and co-ordination, since individual owners may be entirely unable to arrange an economic basis either for re-development or for the prevention of yet further traffic deterioration.

To put the problem in the simplest (or perhaps in over-simple) terms, it may be said: (*a*) that traffic should be both able and required to bypass all towns at which it has no need to call; (*b*) that, within towns, a " cell " pattern should be developed, whereby traffic can flow unimpeded round the periphery of each " cell," in a one-way system (i.e., " no right turns "); (*c*) within each " cell " there should be afforded the maximum possible amenity (e.g., pedestrian precincts with separate access for private cars or commercial vehicle deliveries); and (*d*) that separate provision should be made for the movement of pedestrians at levels above or below the road traffic routes, and giving direct pedestrian access to (or through) buildings.

At the same time, however, it is evident that where the existing forms of architecture and amenity are worthy of protection, then they must be retained wherever possible. Mankind owes a greater debt to his past—and to the feeling of stability and security which this affords—than appears to be recognised by many developers, and not a few town planners and architects. The rate of crime and broken marriages in many New Towns should be evidence enough of this instinctive need.   And to this basic requirement should be added the more sophisticated argument that care should be taken to avoid, where possible, the virtual destruction of the aesthetic character, importance and balance of existing (often ancient) buildings, by re-development upon adjoining sites of new buildings of excessive height.

Further, in towns, or urban areas, of historic interest it is necessary (if the value of the town is to justify protection) that the numbers, weight and speeds of vehicles be kept to a minimum practicable level, and that through traffic be prevented.   In addition, streets and areas which are already used predominantly by pedestrians should be converted to pedestrian use only.   For a further discussion of preservation of the amenity of an historic town the reader is referred to *Traffic in Towns*, Pt. 3 (pp. 112–123).

2. Legal Aspects

Considerable latitude is allowed in terms of development of those transport undertakings in general which are the responsibility of statutory undertakers.   This power to develop land without (broadly speaking) the need to obtain planning permission from the local planning authority is provided by the Town and Country Planning General Development Order, 1973 (S.I. 1973 No. 31). By Class XVIII of the 1973 Order it is permitted under Art. 3 (but subject to conditions [13]) to develop:

A. As part of *railway and light railway undertakings* if required for the movement of traffic by rail and carried out by the undertakers on the operational land of the undertaking [14] *except* the construction of railways, or the construction or alteration so as materially to affect the design of any (*a*) station or bridge, (*b*) hotel, (*c*) residential

---

[13] Art. 3 (3): " The permission granted by this article and Schedule 1 to this Order shall not, except in relation to development permitted by Classes IX, XII or XIV in the said Schedule [notably repairs to unadopted streets and development by local highway authorities], authorise any development which requires or involves the formation, laying out or material widening of a means of access to an existing highway which is a trunk or classified road, or creates an obstruction to the view of persons using any highway used by vehicular traffic at or near any bend, corner, junction or intersection so as to be likely to cause danger to such persons."

[14] *East Barnet U.D.C.* v. *British Transport Commission* [1962] 2 W.L.R. 134; 12 P. & C.R. 127.

or educational building, or building to be used for manufacturing or repairing work unless situated wholly within the interior of a railway station, (d) car park, shop, restaurant, garage, petrol filling station or other building provided in pursuance of . . . [certain powers under the Transport Acts, 1962 and 1968], which is not situate wholly within the interior of a railway station. Thus, certain works can have the effect of facilitating the return to use of a disused railway line.

B. As part of a *dock, pier, harbour, water transport, canal or inland navigation undertaking*, if required for the purposes of shipping, including embarking, disembarking, loading, discharging or transport of passengers, livestock or goods, where the work is carried out by the statutory undertakers, or by their lessees, in, on, over or under the operational land of the undertaking, *except* the construction, etc., or alteration so as materially to affect the design or external appearance of structures as described in (a) to (c) of A above.

Provision is also made to permit the spreading of dredgings.

F.[15] As part of *tramway or road transport undertakings*, if required in relation to any of the following: overhead wires, etc., in relation to "public vehicles"; tramway tracks, drains and pipes in relation to tramways; telephone apparatus, huts, stop signs required in relation to " public vehicles "; provision of passenger shelters, etc.; any other development carried out on operational land of the undertaking unless (a) materially affecting the external appearance, etc. (as before), or (b) involving erection of a structure exceeding 15 metres (50ft.) in height or exceeding an earlier structure replaced thereby, or (c) certain other development in connection with omnibus or tramway stations under the Transport Acts, 1962 and 1968.

G. As part of *lighthouse undertakings*.

And notably:

H. As part of undertakings of the *British Airports Authority*. (*Note*: The operational land of this Authority is at present limited to the airports at London (Heathrow), Gatwick, and Stansted, and does not extend to other airports in Great Britain.) Development, by the Authority, of operational land of the undertaking, being development which is required in connection with provision by the

---

[15] Paragraphs C to E inclusive refer to water, gas and electricity undertakings, in that order.

Authority of services " necessary or desirable " for the operation
of an aerodrome, *other than:*

    (i)   the construction or erection, or the reconstruction or altera-
tion so as materially to affect the design or external appearance of (*a*) any hotel, or (*b*) any buildings (not being
buildings required in connection with the movement or maintenance of aircraft or with the embarking, disembarking,
loading, discharge or transport of passengers, livestock or
goods at an aerodrome); and

    (ii) the construction or extension of runways.

Thus, in relation to heading H., it will be seen that, with the
exception of the construction or extension of runways (which
requires planning permission), the British Airports Authority has,
under the General Development Order, 1973, very considerable
powers of development without the need to apply to the local
planning authority for planning permission in cases where the
proposed development relates to the purposes *shown in parenthesis*
in sub-para. (i) above, i.e., broadly where related to the movement
of aircraft and passengers. However, the former Ministry of
Housing and Local Government and the Welsh Office have given
an important assurance in relation to the environment, in Circular
No. 55/68 (dated 31st October, 1968), thus:

" 3. The Ministers and the British Airports Authority recognise that development at an airport may well have a marked
effect on other planning proposals for the area, and that
whenever possible there should be prior consultations between
the Authority and the local planning authority. The Authority
has therefore given the following written undertaking to the
Ministers:

' The British Airports Authority recognise that development
at an airport can have a marked effect on the amenity of
adjoining land, and on other planning proposals for the area.
It therefore gives this undertaking that, notwithstanding the
permission granted by the amending order, it will consult with
the local planning authority before carrying out any development for which permission is given by that order, save in the
case of minor works urgently needed to enable the airport to
function efficiently.'

4. The Ministers are confident that this arrangement will
provide local planning authorities with an opportunity to

comment on development proposed by the Authority no less effectively than was the case when the airports were vested in the Ministry of Aviation."

To the above assurances should be added the commentary which relates to pollution by noise and the need to consult with representatives of the local community, as to which see Chapter 9.

It will be appreciated that there exists a great deal of law governing the creation, discontinuation, diversion, repair and methods of use of highways, all of which will directly or indirectly have a bearing upon the amenities of a local community, or of the country as a whole. However, in view of the general nature of this book it is proposed only to refer here to those aspects of the law which are most likely to exert a strong influence upon physical changes in the environment. For more detailed discussions the reader is referred to the sources given in the footnote below.[16] It may also be of assistance first to mention the general framework of the law relating to highways.

The common law deals extensively with highways, and many rights and duties thereunder are of ancient origin. Although certain aspects of the common law are still significant, for most practical purposes there has been a great deal of statutory codification, and this has been largely consolidated in the Highways Act, 1959 (which also, rather surreptitiously, introduced several alterations in earlier statutory law), but is now extended by the Highways Act, 1971 (July), and the Town and Country Planning Act, 1971 (October), Pt. X (which latter also amends ss. 50, 77 and 78 (2) of and Sched. 7 to the Highways Act, 1971).

The 1959 Act contains the following: Part I broadly defines " highway authorities," [17] together with their functions; Part II

---

[16] *The Encyclopedia of Highway Law and Practice* (Sweet & Maxwell) and, as to road traffic, *The Encyclopedia of Road Traffic* (Sweet & Maxwell); also *Law of Highways* by Pratt and MacKenzie, 21st ed., 1967.

[17] By the Local Government Act, 1972, ss. 186–188, the highway authorities after April, 1974, will consist only of: the Secretary of State for the Environment; counties (rural and metropolitan); and districts—the latter only as to " urban roads," footpaths and bridleways. At present the division is broadly as follows:

(1) The Minister of Transport (now Secretary of State for the Environment), for trunk roads; or for any other if so provided by statute; or for a road constructed by the Minister (unless otherwise provided);

(2) A county borough council, for all highways within their borough, except those for which the Minister is highway authority;

relates to trunk roads, special roads,[18] county roads and county
bridges, and particularly to the wide powers given to the
Secretary of State for the Environment, previously Minister of
Transport; Part III deals with the creation of highways[19] (including
public rights of way); Part IV deals with the maintenance of highways, and relates to financial powers in connection with repair;
Part V is concerned with improvement (widening, provision of
roundabouts, etc.) as distinct from repair, and also the introduction
of safety provisions, lighting, etc.; Part VI states the powers in
relation to the stopping-up or diversion of highways (but note that
these are amended and extended by the Town and Country
Planning Act, 1971, and the Highways Act, 1971); Part VII is
concerned with lawful and unlawful interference with highways,
that is, with powers to carry out repair works upon adjoining land,
to excavate for repair of services (gas, water, electricity, drainage,
etc.), and to proceed against persons obstructing or damaging the
highway; Part VIII relates to the creation of new streets, and to
creation of any necessary byelaws governing their use; Part IX
governs the making up and repair of private streets, and for their
widening, etc.; Part X provides extensive powers (subject to the
certified approval of the Secretary of State) for the compulsory or
negotiated acquisition of land for purposes of highway construction
or improvement, and for the transfer or extinguishment of private
rights and duties over such land; Part XI makes financial provisions
for contributions by the various (levels of) highway authorities and
by the Exchequer, according to the type of road [20] and the purpose

(3) A non-county borough or an urban district, for all highways within their
borough or district, except roads where the Minister or the county are highway
authorities;

(4) A county council, for all highways situate within all rural districts in the
county and for county bridges, but not for highways for which the Minister is
authority; the county is also authority for " county roads," i.e., those roads
which although lying within non-county boroughs, boroughs, or urban districts
are " classified roads " or similar (see s. 21 of the Act for the circumstances
in which highways are designated " county roads "). But, in boroughs
or urban districts exceeding 20,000 population, the local council may, subject
to certain requirements, claim the right to maintain a county road;

(5) Parish and rural district councils are not highway authorities, but have
certain rights and duties (s. 116 (3)).

[18] A " special road " means a highway provided in pursuance of a scheme under
s. 11 of the Act, that is, roads reserved for particular classes of traffic.

[19] But s. 50 in Pt. III is amended by the Town and Country Planning Act, 1971

[20] e.g., trunk and special roads, county roads, and district roads, etc.

of the expenditure [21]; and, finally, Part XII contains miscellaneous and supplementary provisions including, for example, powers to require gas or water pipes to be moved, power of the Secretary of State to conduct experiments, provisions for (public and other) inquiries, for the service of notices and for the imposition of penalties following convictions under the Act. There are also 26 Schedules [22] to the Act, dealing principally with the form of various orders made under the Act and the form of particulars of information when required.

It will, however, be appreciated that the 1959 Act was designed to consolidate a total of fifty-four earlier statutes dating from as early as A.D. 1530.

Reference has already been briefly made to the Town and Country Planning Act, 1971, and the Highways Act, 1971, and these two enactments are of particular significance in a study of the environment, since they are concerned with the creation and design of new, or improved, highways, the impact of which upon local amenities may be very considerable.

To take first the Highways Act, 1971, the purpose of this legislation is to enable the Secretary of State for the Environment and the highway authorities to expedite the construction and improvement of trunk roads and motorways by use of a simplified and more rapid procedure. (It should be noted that the length of periods in which objections must be lodged has been shortened (ss. 14 to 16).)[23]

The powers of local highway authorities are increased in terms of construction and improvement of highways in relation to:

side roads which cross or join classified roads (s. 1), which may be stopped-up or diverted;

stopping-up of private access if causing danger to traffic (ss. 2 to 9);

the diversion of navigable and non-navigable watercourses and the construction of bridges over and tunnels under such watercourses (ss. 10 to 13);

the securing and delineation of a " centre line " [23a] for new highways (s. 17) (which must be notified by the Secretary of State

---

[21] e.g., construction, improvement, maintenance, drainage, etc.

[22] Of which Sched. 7 (as to " blight ") is amended by the Town and Country Planning Act, 1971.

[23] Broadly, a reduction from 3 months to 6 weeks.

[23a] i.e., the centre line of the intended route for a new road.

to the relevant highway authority in writing and by indica-
tion on a map before compulsory acquisition can be commenced but may deviate from the line by not exceeding
55 yards on either side, as may be specified in the scheme or
order);

the provision of walkways (e.g., ways over or ways under highways, or over or through buildings (s. 18));

the provision of barriers (s. 19) and footbridges (ss. 20 and 21);

the drainage of existing highways (s. 22) (by means of, say,
soakaways on adjoining land) and the provision of means of
protection against the " hazards of nature " (such as snow)
(s. 23);

the provision of picnic sites and public conveniences for users of
trunk roads (s. 26) (*Note*: this may now be carried out by
the Secretary of State, and subsequently managed by a local
authority; this power compulsorily to acquire sites and to
finance loans for such projects out of Exchequer funds is of
great value since, previously, county and other local authorities were not financially in a position to find sufficient funds
for such purposes. The cost of piping water to, and main-
taining, an isolated public convenience is, however, extremely
high, and local ratepayers quite naturally show reluctance
to increase local rates for the accommodation of holiday-
makers who may, in certain areas, offer no source of income
to the locality);

and

the provision of areas for parking heavy goods vehicles may now
be carried out by highway authorities (s. 30).

Part II of the Highways Act, 1971 (ss. 31 to 43), is concerned
principally with the increase in the control by a highway authority
over the method of operation of building contractors upon sites
adjoining highways.

By Pt. III (ss. 47 to 56) of the same Act the powers are increased
for the acquisition of land, or of rights over land not actually
acquired but in fact used in connection with a highway. By s. 49,
however, if the extent of the rights acquired can be held to justify it,
the land-owner can compel acquisition by the highway authority of
the land itself.

Further, s. 50 amended the law in relation to " planning blight "
where this arose from the acquisition of land, or of adjoining or

adjacent land, for highway purposes. This section is now re-enacted in ss. 192 and 194 of the Town and Country Planning Act, 1971, under which Act the provisions as to planning blight are given in ss. 193 to 207 inclusive. In so far as blight caused by acquisition for highway purposes (i.e., for construction, alteration or improvement of highways) is concerned, a person who claims that he has an interest in the land, but is unable to sell such interest " except at a price substantially lower than that for which it might reasonably have been expected to sell " (s. 193 (1)), may serve upon the highway authority a notice (in prescribed form) requiring that authority to purchase his interest. It is appropriate to mention at this point that, although as the law stands (December, 1972) there are rather severe limitations upon the rights of owners of land to require purchase by the authority, the Land Compensation Bill at present before Parliament provides for considerable extension of the right to claim compensation, and this is intended to be made retroactive to 17th October, 1972. The Bill provides for the extension of the right to compensation to cases where the mere *use* of highways, aerodromes, and other public works produces " adverse physical factors," such as noise, vibration or fumes; and these rights arise regardless of whether or not any part of the claimant's property (whether he be owner or occupier) has actually been acquired as part of the public works. In the case of highways, the date upon which such a claim can be lawfully established will be the date on which the relevant section of road is first used by public traffic. (It should incidentally be noted that any " physical factors " caused by road traffic collisions, etc., are specifically excluded!) The calculation of compensation is to be based upon the reduction in value of the affected property, and the matter, as in other cases of compensation resulting from public works, may be referred to the Lands Tribunal.

Part II of the Bill provides for the mitigation of the injurious effects of public works—whether highways, airports or other types—by means of the making of grants for sound insulation and other purposes by the relevant authority: previously, such payments had been the concern of the Secretary of State for the Environment direct. In addition, such public works authorities are empowered to acquire land in excess of their basic requirement, where the extra land is to be used specifically to mitigate the physical effects of the works, such as by the construction of sound baffles, tree planting, or alteration of the type of private user in the immediate vicinity.

Certain special problems arise in connection with the severance of farms and other agricultural holdings by new motorways and trunk roads, and these give rise to particular considerations in terms of valuation for purposes of compensation.   The majority of the factors to be mentioned below also apply in terms of compensation arising out of acquisition or severance of land (including urban sites) generally, but are more significant in practical terms when related to rural and agricultural land, and thus to protection of amenity.   Clearly, if a farm is severed by a major road, the movement of stock and machinery may be rendered impossible unless an underpass or suitable bridge can be provided.   Further, if the fields severed from the main holding are insufficient in area and/or agricultural capacity, it may be deemed uneconomic to provide such an underpass or bridge.   The problem may be particularly acute where the farm steading (i.e., house and farm buildings) virtually alone is cut off from the bulk of the farm.   Such a circumstance will greatly increase problems of movement of stock, fodder, crops, fertiliser and machinery, and may also have incidental effects during the construction of the highway (such as the pollution of milk in the dairy).   It will therefore be seen that, in certain cases, a radical alteration of the shape and size of holdings may ensue, either necessitating the rearrangement of tenanted farms on an estate, or the sale or purchase of parts of owner-occupied farms.

The methods of calculation of compensation are based upon rules clearly laid down previously in the Lands Clauses Acts and now in Part I of the Compulsory Purchase Act, 1965.   Broadly, compensation will include the value of the land (or interest in land) purchased for highway purposes, together with any damage suffered by severance; an allowance for the increased cost of operating the farm as a result of the severance; damage suffered by loss of privacy, noise, and injurious affection [24] caused by the execution of authorised works.   The latter will also apply to adjoining or adjacent owners from whom no land has actually been acquired.

In addition to the existing provisions under the 1965 Act, however, the new Land Compensation Bill (*ante*) makes certain very considerable concessions to agricultural owners and/or tenants. When an agricultural holding is severed by a road in such a way as seriously to affect the holding's physical and economic operation, the

---

[24] As to " injurious affection," and the counterpart " betterment," see *Compulsory Purchase and Compensation* by D. M. Lawrance and Victor Moore (Estates Gazette)

Bill provides that the highway authority may now be required to purchase the entire holding.   In other situations, " blight " notices may become applicable to agricultural land, whereas this has not been possible hitherto.   Thus, where the value of the land is depressed, or private sale at a fair price rendered impossible, as a result of zoning in a development plan or the fixing of a centre line for a future road, then the owner of a farm, or other type of agricultural unit, will be in a position to require the entire unit to be purchased by the responsible authority.   The Bill further assists agricultural occupiers (tenants or owners) who move away as a result of any of the above mentioned circumstances, by providing for " farm loss payments," which are designed to aid the farmer in setting up in a new holding.

Where the agricultural occupier remains on a holding which is adversely affected in the various ways already referred to, the negotiations in connection with compensation will include consideration of a variety of accommodation works, such as underpasses, bridges, fences, gates, cattle grids, lay-bys, hedges, tree screens, special means of access generally, additional surface water drainage, etc., and it must be borne in mind that if the claimant is eventually put in a better position than he was in regard to any specific items, these items will constitute " betterment," and be set off against the total compensation he would otherwise be due to receive.   Nevertheless, it is preferable that the majority of these accommodation works be carried out by the highway authority contractor, since it will then be the authority's responsibility to rectify any defect. This may be of particular importance in relation to drainage, since motorways and large trunk roads will collect immense volumes of surface water, and difficulties have from time to time arisen where the soakaway systems for such roads have entirely disrupted the drainage from stock housing, yards, and the farm-house.   In order to solve such problems, early liaison at the preconstruction stage between the highway authority, the land owner and the local river authority may be essential.

The initial negotiations as to the amount of compensation to be payable are conducted between the claimant (owner, tenant, etc.) and the district valuer, the district valuer being assisted by estimates and recommendations in most cases provided by the county surveyor.   In the absence of eventual agreement the claimant is entitled to apply for the case to be heard by the Lands

Tribunal.[25]   (A general discussion in relation to the above may be found in *Modern Methods of Valuation of Land, Houses and Buildings* by Lawrance, Rees and Britton, 5th ed., 1964, at pp. 384 to 389.)

The owner of a holding affected by a motorway or trunk road should employ a qualified and experienced valuer to act on his behalf, and should also request that he negotiate for the maximum possible in ancillary works.   Thus, fences should be of best quality (i.e., sawn heart of oak posts, not concrete, and with timber rails rather than wire susceptible to eventual corrosion); quickset hedges will supplement fences and last a century or more if cut or cut and laid; and tree screens may be of great value in reducing both the glare of headlamps and, to an extent, noise of traffic.[26]

---

[25] *Not* the Agricultural Land Tribunal!

[26] Problems arise in foxhunting country, where normal wire mesh fences will be surmounted by hounds, and the cost of higher fences may be uneconomic.

CHAPTER 6

POLLUTION OF THE ENVIRONMENT — GENERAL

Nuisance; Negligence; Rule in Rylands v. Fletcher

(NOTE: This general chapter should be read in conjunction with each of the subsequent three chapters on pollution)

In February, 1970, a Royal Commission on Environmental Pollution was set up, under the chairmanship of Sir Eric Ashby. The Commission is authorised upon a continuing basis to inquire into any matters which they may think of value in this field, or which are referred to them by any of Her Majesty's Secretaries of State or Ministers.

The Commission's first White Paper, which was presented to Parliament in May, 1970, was entitled " The Protection of the Environment: The Fight Against Pollution " (Cmnd. 4373). It considered the practical and scientific problems arising out of the most common types of pollution. The Government's priorities in terms of action to be taken were stated in the White Paper as follows: " First, to take such action as will maintain and improve the health of the public where this is demonstrably affected; secondly, to safeguard the health of the public where it may or may not be affected (because there are many fields where certainty in this question is not possible) and thirdly, to act where pollution affects the ordinary pleasure and contentment of people in the quality of their life."

The second major step in recent Government action to combat pollution (as well as to co-ordinate and improve the positive planning of the environment) has been the setting-up of the Department of the Environment as in overall control of the (now renamed) three Ministries of Local Government and Development, Housing and Construction, and Transport Industries.

At present the law relating to the various forms of pollution is complicated and confused. The remedies available vary and overlap between those offered by the courts at common law and in equity and those offered (frequently concurrently) by statute or by Ministerial Rule and Order, or even by Ministerial " advisory " circulars.   It is, therefore, not practicable to attempt an analysis of the subject of pollution under " sources of law "; nor even by type of origin of each form of pollution.   Accordingly the broad topic will be discussed under the following general headings:

A.—(The present Chapter): *General.*   In brief outline (and with the exception of the law relating to pollution of water) the general Common Law, Equitable and Public Health legislative remedies.

B.—(Chapter 7): *Water.*   Pollution of fresh water, including water for domestic supply; and pollution of the sea and beaches.

C.—(Chapter 8): *Air*; and *Land.*   Special statutory provisions relating to pollution of (1) the air; and (2) land.

D.—(Chapter 9): *Noise*; and *Nuclear Pollution.*   Special statutory provisions relating to pollution by (1) noise; and (2) nuclear contamination.

The non-statutory remedies against (potentially) all types of pollution are founded principally upon actions in tort[1] for nuisance, both public and private; but the facts of any given case may indicate that it would be preferable to sue, solely or additionally, in negligence; or under the rule in *Rylands* v. *Fletcher*; or even under the special principles governing, for example, liability for animals.

Each of these aspects of the law takes up many pages in general reference books on the law of torts, and it would be inappropriate to attempt a full discussion here.   It is proposed, therefore, to indicate briefly the lines of action which *may* be available, but with the strong reservation that no step should be taken without a full discussion of the facts of the particular case so as to enable accurate professional advice to be given.

Where actions will lie in tort, they may have an advantage over statutory remedies,[2] in that the courts may, in most cases, either award damages (which can be substantial) or they make a discretionary order requiring the defendant to refrain from his activities, or requiring him to carry out some positive action.[3]

---

[1] A civil wrong, exclusive of contract.

[2] Which are usually initially orders to the offender on pain of a fine, but may, in some cases, include compensation to persons suffering damage.

[3] Such remedies are awarded at the discretion of the court, i.e., may be withheld.

The availability of damages or an injunction varies according to the type of tort, and a brief outline is given below which must, due to brevity, be not entirely accurate.

1. Nuisance: Public and Private

Pollution may, amongst other things, constitute either a *public nuisance* or a *private nuisance*. A public nuisance is a crime, but it is also a tort for which an individual may in the right circumstances be able to recover damages, or obtain an injunction. A public nuisance can be defined as " an act or omission which materially affects the reasonable comfort and convenience of life of a class of Her Majesty's subjects." [4] The layman should note that the court will need to interpret this definition in the light of the facts of the particular case. Thus " reasonable comfort and convenience " will not necessarily be interpreted as the plaintiff may wish; and a " class " is a matter of fact, meaning, in non-legal terms, a definable section of the public in the area affected. Public and private nuisances are dissimilar in many ways, and some distinctions can be seen as follows:

(1) *Public nuisance*

If a case is to be established as a public nuisance, a number of people in the given area must be seen to be affected and each and every one of them must be so affected. But the pollution must not be too widespread, since it is necessary to prove that the class of Her Majesty's subjects (say the population of a village) is living in less than usual comfort or convenience compared to the public in larger areas of Britain generally. If this can be established, then criminal proceedings may be brought by way of indictment against the offender; and proceedings are, in fact, generally brought by the Attorney-General acting " in the public interest." Concurrently the Attorney-General may, by an action in the civil division of the High Court, obtain an injunction against the offender whereby he is ordered to refrain, or to act, as necessary. Failure to comply is then subject to imprisonment for contempt of court. In the case of criminal proceedings against a corporate body (such as a company or local authority) a fine is generally imposed; but, in some instances, individual officers, such as a company secretary or managing director, may be subject to imprisonment.

[4] *A.-G.* v. *P.Y.A. Quarries, Ltd.* [1957] 2 Q.B. 169, 184.

As to damage or inconvenience suffered by an *individual* as a result of a public nuisance, a civil action in tort can be brought, but only when the plaintiff is able to prove that he has suffered particular damage over and above that caused to the public at large.[5] Clearly, instances of public nuisance are experienced by a section of the public whilst they are upon what may be called " public land," such as a highway, or in relation to the water in a navigable river. Equally, however, the persons affected may be upon private land at the time in the sense that it may be appropriate for the Attorney-General to commence an action, or criminal proceedings, on their behalf on the basis that they are all affected as inhabitants of an affected area.   Nowadays this action is rather less frequently taken by the Attorney-General since, in many instances, the local, or other, authority may have adequate statutory powers to deal with the situation.[6]

It is important to note, however, that proceedings in relation to public nuisance essentially require a class of persons to be affected.   Therefore, in many cases, an individual sufferer can only rely upon an action for private nuisance, and this type of remedy is hedged around with certain well-established rules of law, which will be discussed below.

(2) *Private nuisance*

This can, in legal terms, be of two kinds.   Either (a) a wrongful disturbance of an easement or other servitude connected with land [7]; or (b) an " act of wrongfully causing or allowing the escape of deleterious things into (onto) another's land, as, for example, the escape of water, smoke, smell, fumes, gas, noise, heat, vibrations, electricity, disease germs, animals and vegetation." [8]

Broadly, it can be said that these escapes must cause damage either (a) to the land (or to things thereon) or (b) to the occupier of the land.   Also that the escape (not the damage) must, in most cases, have occurred over a substantial length of time.   A single escape causing even substantial and permanent damage will only

---

[5] *Halsey* v. *Esso Petroleum Co., Ltd.* [1961] 2 All E.R. 145.

[6] See p. 133 *et seq.*

[7] Which will seldom relate to actions arising out of pollution and will not be discussed in this work.

[8] *Salmond on Torts*, 15th ed., at p. 65.   Also escape from land occupied by the defendant may not always be necessary, as where the private nuisance is caused in a navigable river or harbour—*Southport Corporation* v. *Esso Petroleum Co., Ltd.* [1954] 2 Q.B. 182.

be actionable as nuisance (as the law now stands) in cases where the nuisance caused could be " reasonably foreseen." [9]   However, single escapes, if of " things likely to do damage if they escape " and which have been brought onto the land (occupied by the defendant) his servants or agents, will present a good cause of action, not in nuisance in the general sense, but under the rule in *Rylands* v. *Fletcher* (see below).

At the present time an action in private nuisance can only be brought successfully by either (*a*) the occupier of land (usually the owner-occupier, or lawful tenant, and not a person merely present as a licensee [10]); or (*b*), in the case of permanent damage to the property, by the owner who is not in occupation (i.e., a landlord, etc.) where the damage is reflected in the ultimate value of the property to him (i.e., the reversionary value [11]).

The reference above to the " occupier " is, thus, significant. The wife of an occupier has been held unable to recover damages for personal injury where a cistern fell upon her as a result of vibrations caused by an engine operating on the defendant's adjoining premises.[12]   Yet a holidaymaker who has taken even a one-week tenancy of premises could, as lawful occupier, recover in nuisance.[13]

Again, if the source of the nuisance happens to be upon the land occupied by the plaintiff (due to no fault of his) he is unable to recover in nuisance, although he may have a cause of action against the wrongdoer for, say, trespass.

The general maxim applicable to nuisance is that a man must not make such use of his property as " unreasonably and unnecessarily " to cause inconvenience to his neighbour [14] (the assessment of the words quoted will be a matter for the court to decide in any given case).   And the court will need to consider both the type of harm and the gravity of harm caused by the escape, together with the frequency of escape, in order to assess whether the facts constitute an actionable nuisance.

Thus, questions of evidence are of great importance, and the

---

[9] *The Wagon Mound (No.* 2) [1967] A.C. 617.

[10] Licensee: e.g., a visitor or tradesman.

[11] *Shelfer* v. *City of London Electric Lighting Co.* [1895] 1 Ch. 287, 318.

[12] *Malone* v. *Laskey* [1907] 2 K.B. 141.   But see also *Cunard* v. *Antifyre, Ltd.* [1933] 1 K.B. 551.

[13] It is probable that possession without title would be adequate as in the case of a squatter.

[14] *Sic utere tuo ut alienum non laedas.*

courts tend to be more ready to provide a remedy where the nuisance causes physical damage to property, in contrast to personal inconvenience, discomfort and suffering.[15]   This takes into account the realistic factor that a person cannot expect an unsalubrious area to be made more pleasant simply because he chooses to live there and to bring an action.   Nevertheless, if the area is not unsalubrious (for the plaintiff's purposes) with the exception of the nuisance complained of, the plaintiff may succeed even against a defendant who has been happily using adjacent premises for years without causing offence to others.[16]   However, " What would be a nuisance in Belgrave Square would not necessarily be so in Bermondsey." And, again, an exceptionally sensitive plaintiff, even where the sensitivity has a good commercial or technical basis, cannot expect a remedy for a nuisance which would not affect others less sensitive.[17]

If one looks at the common-law remedies for nuisance as applicable to cases of environmental pollution, there are clearly certain gaps in the protection afforded to individuals and to the public, but these have been, to a great extent, filled by legislative (principally statutory) remedies provided progressively over the past hundred years.   By and large the withholding of remedy under the law of nuisance has valid legal principles.   In other cases, where remedy is in fact afforded, certain defences are denied to the defendant which would otherwise weaken a plaintiff's case.   Thus it is no defence to plead that the plaintiff agreed to, or came to, the nuisance[18]; nor that some act (even of a third party) had precipitated the nuisance, unless this could not have been foreseen by a " reasonable man "[19]; nor that the defendant's actions were for the public benefit[20]; nor that the locality was suitable for the defendant's activities[21]; nor that others were doing the same so as to aggravate

---

[15] *St. Helens Smelting Co.* v. *Tipping* (1865), 11 H.L.C. 642, 650.

[16] *Sturges* v. *Bridgeman* (1879), 11 Ch.D. at p. 865; accepted by the Court of Appeal in *Polsue & Alfieri, Ltd.* v. *Rushmer* [1907] A.C. 121.

[17] *Robinson* v. *Kilvert* (1889), 41 Ch.D. 88.   Storage of brown paper susceptible to heat, but plaintiff could not recover.

[18] i.e., *volenti non fit injuria* not applicable to this defence.   *Sturges* v. *Bridgeman* (1879), 11 Ch.D., at p. 865, etc.

[19] i.e., *novus actus interveniens* not applicable to this defence.

[20] *Shelfer* v. *City of London Electric Lighting Co.* [1895] 1 Ch. 287, 316.

[21] *St. Helens Smelting Co.* v. *Tipping* (1865), 11 H.L.C. 642; but, as already said, subject to the fact that a nuisance causing only personal discomfort, as distinct from damage to property, is tested by the actual local standard of comfort.

the nuisance (e.g., pollution by a group of factories [22]); nor that the defendant, his employees or agents (including, say, building contractors) had exercised care and skill.[23] Nevertheless the courts will require reasonable " give and take " between the parties,[24] in the absence of " malice." [25]

Certain special rules apply which arise out of the terms of occupation of property, in some cases relating to the plaintiff, and in others to the defendant, and these matters may well affect the existence or absence of a valid case. Thus, as already stated, qualified legal advice should always be sought at the outset when an action in nuisance is contemplated. For example, the defendant may have a prescriptive right, i.e., by twenty years' user, to create a private (but not a public) nuisance. Again, the occupier may have quite innocently taken on liability (jointly with the original perpetrator) for a nuisance on acquiring property.[26] Or again, liability for a sudden and single event causing a nuisance may be avoided if caused by a latent (but not a patent) defect.[27]

Turning from the common-law action for nuisance, two further solutions may apply. First, there is a general right to take steps personally to discontinue (abate) a nuisance, but this must be carefully exercised in case a counter-action for trespass arises. Secondly, the discretionary remedies for nuisance, already mentioned, of injunction and mandatory injunction are applied by the courts according to different rules and principles from the common-law remedies discussed above. The court may consider that a particular nuisance, although perhaps meriting the award of damages, is yet of too slight a nature to warrant an injunction. An injunction will only be granted if the injury is of so material a nature that either (*a*) it cannot be adequately compensated for by damages, or (*b*) continuance of the nuisance is of a permanently, or increasingly, mischievous character so that it constitutes a constant, or constantly

---

22 *Lambton* v. *Mellish* [1894] 3 Ch. 163. Each is separately liable.

23 *Salmond on Torts*, 15th ed., at p. 79; and *B.C. Pea Growers* v. *City of Portage La Prairie* (1964), 49 D.L.R. (2d) 91, 94.

24 *Bamford* v. *Turnley* (1862), 3 B. & S. 62, at pp. 83–84; approved *Trevett* v. *Lee* [1955] 1 W.L.R. 113, 122.

25 In the tortious sense of intent or of degree of negligence: compare *Christie* v. *Davey* [1893] 1 Ch. 316 and *Hollywood Silver Fox Farm, Ltd.* v. *Emmett* [1936] 1 All E.R. 825.

26 *Wilkins* v. *Leighton* [1932] 2 Ch. 106.

27 *Noble* v. *Harrison* [1926] 2 K.B. 332.

recurring, grievance.[28] Slight decrease in the value of property will not furnish grounds for an injunction [29]; and an injunction will not be granted to restrain the " ordinary and reasonable use " of premises for purposes not in themselves noxious, even though some annoyance is, and will be, caused [30]; unless this annoyance is sufficient to amount to an actionable nuisance (as defined earlier in this chapter).[31] But, in the case of, for example, noxious and offensive fumes which do substantial damage to property (as by destroying trees) an injunction may be granted, even if there is no dwelling or place of employment in the affected area.[32]

However, a distinction must be drawn in the case of the rights of riparian owners (i.e., owners of the land adjoining and including part of a stream or river), who are entitled at common law to receive their water in its " natural state," i.e., uncontaminated by, for example, factory waste. These riparian owners can obtain an injunction against the polluter [33]—providing, of course, that they are able to prove the real source of the pollution; and this may present difficult problems of evidence. If the source can be proved in relation to a sufficient degree of pollution to constitute an actionable nuisance, then the fact that others are also offending will be no defence.[34]

A prescriptive right to pollute a stream can be obtained at common law; but a prescriptive right to contravene a statute cannot be acquired.[35]

The above principles as to streams and rivers also apply to the pollution of underground water.[36]

(3) *The Rule in Rylands* v. *Fletcher* [37]

The rule in *Rylands* v. *Fletcher* imposes absolute or strict liability

---

[28] *A.-G.* v. *Sheffield Gas Consumers' Co.* (1853), 3 De G.M. & G. 304.

[29] *A.-G.* v. *Nichol* (1809), 16 Ves. 338, at p. 342.

[30] *Ball* v. *Ray* (1873), 8 Ch.App. 467; *Christie* v. *Davey* [1893] 1 Ch. 316; cf. *Hollywood Silver Fox Farm, Ltd.* v. *Emmett* [1936] 2 K.B. 468.

[31] *Sturges* v. *Bridgeman* (1879), 11 Ch.D. 692, at p. 701, etc.

[32] *Wood* v. *Conway Corporation* [1914] 2 Ch. 47; *St. Helens Smelting Co.* v. *Tipping* (1865), 11 H.L.C. 642.

[33] *A.-G.* v. *Birmingham* (1858), 4 K. & J. 528; *Crossley* v. *Lightowler* (1867), 2 Ch.App. 479.

[34] *Crossley* v. *Lightowler* (1867), 2 Ch.App. 479.

[35] *Hulley* v. *Silversprings Bleaching and Dyeing Co., Ltd.* [1922] 2 Ch. 268; *Green* v. *Matthews & Co.* (1930), 46 T.L.R. 206.

[36] *Ballard* v. *Tomlinson* (1885), 29 Ch.D. 115.

[37] *Rylands* v. *Fletcher* (1866), L.R. 3 H.L. 330.

upon the occupier of land who brings and keeps upon it anything likely to do damage if it escapes.   Such an occupier is bound at his peril to prevent its escape, and is liable for all the direct consequences of its escape, even if he has been guilty of no negligence.

Clearly, this rule is not intended as a substitute for the general principle of the law of nuisance.   In some respects it offers a wider remedy than nuisance, since the latter must be to some extent continuous, or at least present a threat of continuity.   The *Rylands* v. *Fletcher* case was based upon the sudden (and entirely unforeseen) escape of the bulk of water stored in a newly-constructed reservoir, which penetrated old and disused mineshafts and thus flooded other mineworkings owned by the plaintiff.   There had been no negligent act or omission for which the defendant could be held responsible, and he was unaware of the existence of the disused shafts.   The essential elements are, however: (i) the defendant is occupier of land; (ii) the " thing " which escaped must be deemed (by the court) to be such as is " likely to do damage if it escapes."   This latter factor is, to an extent, a matter of opinion and it is here that the court can apply flexibility to the otherwise strict rule.   An examination of those cases in which the rule has been applied is no guide to probabilities on the facts of any future case, since the " things likely to do damage " have variously included: water, trees, chimney stacks, motor-cars, fire, electricity and chemicals; and it may equally be said that, on the facts of many occasions of escape, these could not be things likely to do damage.   Again, this factor of likelihood has been (in some ways rather surprisingly) extended to escaping vibrations[38]; and to escaping caravan dwellers (whose caravans were upon a site owned by the defendant).[39]

Further variability from the strict rule was introduced by the principle that " natural " uses of land should not be subject to liability (in the absence of negligence).   Thus, certain things may be upon land and escape without incurring liability under *Rylands* v. *Fletcher*, such as vermin, poisonous weeds, and water[39a]— although in specific instances there may be either a statutory remedy or liability in nuisance.   Nevertheless, liability under the rule will

---

[38] *Hoare & Co.* v. *McAlpine* [1923] 1 Ch. 167.   But not followed in *Barette* v. *Franki Compressed Pile Co.* [1955] 2 D.L.R. 665; and contrast *Malone* v. *Laskey* [1907] 2 K.B. 141, where plaintiff was not occupier.

[39] *A.-G.* v. *Corke* [1933] Ch. 89, where an injunction was granted to restrain an owner from licensing such dwellings on his site.

[39a] e.g., water which has *not* been deliberately accumulated.

arise where such natural but dangerous things are artificially and deliberately accumulated, such as collection of rainwater in a reservoir.[40] Where such accumulation is caused by artificial but unintentional means the law is uncertain and this together with the rather complicated rights exercisable by the occupier of land intended purely to protect his own property will not be discussed further here.[41]

A brief comparison of the law of nuisance with the rule in *Rylands* v. *Fletcher* can be made as follows:

(i) In nuisance the plaintiff must be the occupier (or, exceptionally, the owner) of land: under *Rylands* v. *Fletcher*, he need have no connection whatsoever with the occupation of land, he may be a passer-by.

(ii) A private nuisance can be legalised by twenty years' prescription: under *Rylands* v. *Fletcher* there is no precedent as to this.

(iii) Inevitable accident (i.e., " not avoidable by any such precautions as a reasonable man, doing such an act then and there, could be expected to take ") can be a defence so as to establish " reasonable user " in nuisance: under *Rylands* v. *Fletcher* the stricter principle of Act of God (those occurrences which man has no power to foresee or prevent) applies.[42]

(iv) The perpetrator of a nuisance need not actually be occupier of the premises (e.g., he may be a building contractor on the site): under *Rylands* v. *Fletcher* all cases so far decided have been against occupiers only.

(v) In certain cases of nuisance, liability will only arise where there is also negligence: under *Rylands* v. *Fletcher* the element of negligence is irrelevant to liability.

(vi) Certain factors are essential to proof of liability under the rule in *Rylands* v. *Fletcher* which are not essential to the tort of nuisance. These are: (*a*) there must be an accumulation and an escape; (*b*) the user of the land must be

---

[40] *Rickards* v. *Lothian* [1913] A.C. 263; and *Crown Diamond Paint Co., Ltd.* v. *Acadia, Ltd.* [1952] 2 D.L.R. 541—the bringing upon land of industrial water (i.e., under pressure) is not a " natural user."

[41] Note, however, that the occupier of land is liable for the act of another if he " adopts " a nuisance even by failing to take action to abate it—*Sedleigh-Denfield* v. *O'Callaghan* [1940] A.C. 880.

[42] *Nichols* v. *Marsland* (1876), L.R.Ex. 265, 280.

" non-natural " (in the legal sense); and (c) the escaping object must be " potentially dangerous."

2. Negligence

To conclude this brief discussion of the common-law remedies for pollution, a short reference should be made to the tort of negligence. (Despite the increasing development of " safari parks " and other similar institutions, the special branch of the law relating to liability for animals will not be discussed within the limited scope of this book.)[43]

Negligence can exist either (a) as a tort in itself, or (b) as a factor in the commission of other torts, such as nuisance or trespass. It can, in both instances, be defined as: the breach of a legal duty of care owed by one person to another, as a result of which injury is caused to the other. As a tort in itself, it can, in the context of pollution, be best illustrated by a fictitious example, as where the plaintiff's neighbour, in process of spraying a bed of weeds adjacent to his boundary, either intentionally or wantonly also sprays the plants upon the plaintiff's land. Clearly, providing there is direct evidence of the defendant's actions, it will be possible to sue in negligence; equally under the rule in *Rylands* v. *Fletcher*; and, subject to the limitations as to period of escape and forseeability, in nuisance.

In negligence the plaintiff must show that the defendant was under a legal duty to take care; whereas in nuisance the defendant will be liable whether or not he was under such a duty, and the decision of such a case will be based upon whether or not the defendant has been reasonable in his use under all the circumstances. But it is essential to realise that, in negligence, lack of foreseeability may be a defence, whereas this is generally not so in nuisance.[44]

3. Public Health Legislation

The scope of public health legislation is immense, and only a brief reference may be made to it in a work of this nature. It is suggested (at least to the layman) that where it appears from the following pages that public health powers may relate to a given

---

[43] Reference should be made to " *Salmond* " or *Winfield on Torts* or, for a more detailed discussion, to *Clerk and Lindsell on Torts*, etc.

[44] *The Wagon Mound* (*No. 2*) [1967] 1 A.C. 617.

problem under consideration, reference should be made to a legal adviser, and to *Halsbury's Laws of England*, or *Lumley on Public Health*. The basic concept behind common-law nuisance was that there should be a remedy available to the public or to the individual for general inconvenience caused by the defendant. The law was not primarily concerned with those types of nuisance which represented pollution (as we now know it) or which constituted a danger to human health.

Separate legislation therefore developed (even as early as 1388) the purpose of which was generally (*a*) to reduce the risk of serious epidemics (such as cholera), and (*b*) to reduce the drain upon the Poor Law resources of local communities which tended to result from illness. The need for such measures increased in direct relation to the size and density of urban communities in which, in addition, the proportion of persons able to afford to protect themselves by means of an action at common law was extremely small. Therefore, following a report by the Poor Law Commissioners in 1838, a special Royal Commission was set up and (in 1845) it was recommended that local authorities be formed for the purpose of controlling and developing water supplies and drainage schemes, and for the cleansing and repairing of streets. It followed that the first Public Health authorities were created, and these were local responsibilities but under central government supervision. Such Public Health authorities were gradually incorporated within the general functions of local government and, in 1936, the Public Health Act consolidated and amended a mass of public health legislation. The purpose of this Act was stated by the Parliamentary Committee responsible for it as covering:

" the provisions of a strictly public health character relating to the prevention and treatment of disease, that is, as regards environment, such matters as drains and sewers, buildings, water supply and the abatement of nuisances, and as regards personal hygiene to such matters as the provision of hospitals, maternity centres, etc."

Certain public health matters, such as those concerned with streets, were not included, but many were subsequently dealt with in various later statutes, such as the Highways Act, 1959, and the Public Health Act, 1961. In addition, the creation of the National Health Service by the National Health Service Act, 1946, removed many of the functions relating to personal health and hygiene from the field of local government. It should further be noted that a separate Public Health (London) Act, 1936, applies to London.

It will be seen from this short history that many special duties and powers of the local authority, such as the duty to cleanse streets or to provide public lavatories, may have a bearing upon pollution and the environment generally; but many others are irrelevant to this book, such as matters relating to food and drugs, or to weights and measures.

With some exceptions, public health administration is the function mainly of either county boroughs or, elsewhere, county districts; but in terms of overall responsibility county councils are directly concerned. These latter have, for example, a statutory duty to appoint a county medical officer of health, who must make an annual report to the council on the sanitary circumstances, sanitary administration, and vital statistics of the county, and must supply a copy thereof to the Minister of Health.

The functions of a borough or district council, under the Public Health Act, 1936, include the use of valuable powers to require disclosure of full information as to the ownership and occupation of any premises; and they may also authorise a council officer to enter any premises at all reasonable hours in order to ascertain whether there is, or has been, on or in connection with the premises, a contravention of the provisions of the Act, or of any byelaws made by the local authority thereunder.

Offences under the Public Health Act, 1936, may be prosecuted, under the Magistrates' Courts Act, 1952, before a magistrates' court, which court may impose a fine, and also fix a daily penalty where the offence continues. (The provisions for such prosecutions are slightly different in London from the remainder of England and Wales.)

The more precise application of the Public Health Act, 1936, to given forms of pollution will be considered in the ensuing three chapters, but it should be noted that most subsequent legislation defines any breach of statutory requirements in terms of an offence under the 1936 Act. Thus, such offences are described as " statutory nuisances," and the power (and duty) to abate them is conferred upon the local authority where (and only where) speedy action appears to be necessary in order to protect the health of the community. Such a " statutory nuisance " need not necessarily interfere with personal comfort; but it can only arise from a private source: that is, it cannot (by definition) arise from public works, such as sewers or sewage works constructed by the local authority. Whether or not a statutory nuisance exists is a question of fact for the magistrates, and in this respect duration of the nuisance may be a relevant consideration. Nevertheless, the matters declared (by s. 92 of the 1936 Act) to be capable of constituting a statutory nuisance are clearly defined. The footnote as to " nuisance " below must be emphasised in this connection, but the following are statutory nuisances.

1. Any premises in such a state as to be prejudicial to health or a nuisance.[45]

2. Any animal kept in such a place or manner as to be prejudicial to health or a nuisance.[45]

3. Any accumulation or deposit which is prejudicial to health or a nuisance.[45]   Certain statutory defences apply here.

4. Any dust or effluvia caused by any trade, business, manufacture or process and being prejudicial to the health of, or a nuisance to,[45] the inhabitants of the neighbourhood.   Here it is a defence that the best practicable means have been employed for prevention.

5. Any workplace which is not provided with a sufficient means of ventilation (or in which this is not maintained), or which is not kept clean, or which is overcrowded so as to be prejudicial to those employed therein.

6. Any pond, pool, ditch, gutter or watercourse which is so foul or in such a state as to be prejudicial to health or a nuisance.[45]

7. Any part of a watercourse, not being a part ordinarily navigated by vessels employed in the carriage of goods by water, which is so choked or silted up as to obstruct or impede the proper flow of water and thereby to cause a nuisance [45] or give rise to conditions prejudicial to health.   (But note that a landowner is not, either at law or by statute, responsible for the natural silting up of a natural watercourse.)

8. Any well, tank, cistern or water-butt used for the supply of water for domestic purposes which is so placed, constructed or kept as to render the water therein liable to contamination prejudicial to health.

[45] In this, statutory, context " a nuisance " must affect the public health; a matter which merely interferes with personal comfort cannot, even if found to be a nuisance in the common-law sense, constitute a statutory nuisance.

9. A tent, van, shed or similar structure used for human habitation which is in such a state or so overcrowded as to be prejudicial to the health of the inmates; or the use of which gives rise to a nuisance [46] or to conditions prejudicial to health.

10. Any " smoke nuisance " if it is a nuisance [46] to the inhabitants of the neighbourhood; but save as to special provisions discussed in Chapter 8 (Pollution of the Air).

11. A shaft or outlet of an abandoned mine, or a quarry, where these constitute a danger to the public by reason of their accessibility from a highway or place of public resort.

In respect of all the above statutory nuisances, certain relief is given in favour of heavy industries, such as iron and steel, coal, etc.

It will be appreciated that, in addition to the restrictive powers relating to statutory nuisances, local authorities are charged, by the 1936 Act, with a range of positive functions in the services provided for the community, and that the Act requires that these facilities must be so provided to certain defined, or definable, standards. In addition to the prevention and control of disease, the services in relation to hygiene and sanitation include: the provision of baths and washhouses; scavenging; provision and cleansing of public conveniences; atmospheric cleanliness [47]; destruction of pests; the provision of public sewers and sewerage installations, and provision of drains. [48] In respect of sewers and sewerage systems outside London, powers are provided for the compulsory acquisition of land to be used for such purposes; and for the adoption of private sewers. The statute also covers the protection of such installations, both against the discharge of deleterious matter (or also surface water) into them; and against physical damage whether by construction of buildings over them, by excessively heavy vehicles, by malicious damage, or by negligent acts generally. Within Greater London, however, even more detailed statutory control is imposed, and reference as to this should be made to Part II of the Public Health (London) Act, 1936.

It is appropriate also to comment at this juncture that (outside Greater London) a local authority may deal with any offensive ditch or pond if likely to be prejudicial to health, by draining, cleansing or covering it, or by other means of prevention, provided that they do

[46] See footnote 45, p. 134.
[47] See Chapter 8, Section 1, Pollution of the Air.
[48] See Chapter 7, Pollution of Water.

not interfere with any private right or with public drainage, sewerage or sewage disposal works (s. 343 of the Public Health Act, 1936). Within Greater London the position is governed by the Public Health (London) Act, 1936, s. 83 (1) (*a*), and is rather similar, save that a private person, whether owner or occupier, may be required to construct a proper drain to relieve the situation, or execute other works within a time-limit specified in the relevant statutory notice.

Also within the field of public health provision is made for the control of *offensive trades* (again, with separate legislation for Greater London) which require the consent of the local authority. Within a borough or urban district such permission is required to carry on the trade or business of: a blood-boiler, blood-drier, bone-boiler, fat extractor, fat-melter, fellmonger, glue-maker, gut-scraper, rag and bone dealer, size-maker, soap-boiler, tallow-melter, tripe-boiler or any other trade, business or manufacture which has been declared to be an offensive trade (i.e., declared by the local authority to be so and confirmed by the Secretary of State for the Environment). A penalty for breach of not exceeding £50 may be imposed upon summary conviction (s. 107 (1)). In addition to offensive trades, special provisions are applied to the use and storage of inflammable substances and to rag flock and other filling materials.

In conclusion, this general discussion of public health legislation must include reference to the control of building construction. Until 1966 local authorities (i.e., borough and district councils) in England and Wales, save for London, each made their own building byelaws, by virtue of s. 61 of the Public Health Act, 1936. By virtue of ss. 4 to 11 of the Public Health Act, 1961, these were replaced throughout the country (save for the Inner London Boroughs, to which the London Building Acts and byelaws still apply) by the Building Regulations, 1965, now 1972 (S.I. 1972 No. 317), made by the Secretary of State for the Environment. The purpose of these regulations, put very broadly, is to ensure that any new, or altered, structures are of stable, sound and generally suitable construction and materials; that the space surrounding buildings, lighting, ventilation and dimensions of rooms are of a prescribed minimum standard; and that private sewers and drains related to them, sanitary appliances, refuse disposal systems, and water supplies shall also be to specified standards. In addition, the construction and materials employed must meet certain criteria in relation to fire hazards, including the retarding of any escape of fire into other property.

4. Compensation for Adverse Effects of Public Works

Where public works, such as for example new roads, or new or extended airports, create what are described as adverse " physical factors "—such as noise, vibration, fumes, traffic headlamp glare, etc.—compensation is to become payable by the relevant public works authority.   This is the intention of the new Land Compensation Bill at present before Parliament (February, 1973), which provides for compensation based upon the reduction in value of premises, whether to an owner or to an occupier, where these adjoin, or are adjacent to, the public works.   Since these situations arise principally in relation to matters of transport, the Bill is more fully described in Chapter 5, Transport, at pp. 117–119.   However, it must be stressed here that the adverse " physical factors " envisaged by the pending legislation may equally be related to other types of public works, such as, say, sewage plants or power stations.

CHAPTER 7

POLLUTION OF FRESH WATER; POLLUTION OF THE SEA AND BEACHES

1. Pollution of Fresh Water, including Water for Domestic Use

It is preferable to discuss the question of water pollution under a composite heading to include both common law and statutory law, since these are in this instance closely interwoven. In addition, the legal position in any given case is especially influenced by the physical location of the polluted water.

Thus liability for pollution of water varies according as it may be (1) in a " natural " watercourse (i.e., a stream, river, or natural lake fed by them; or tidal waters[1]); or in a defined or definable underground watercourse (see p. 140); or (2) percolating through underground strata but in no definable channel (see p. 146); or (3) in artificial watercourses or artificial lakes (see p. 147); or (4) water intended for domestic use—that is, in a waterworks or local (water) authority water main (see p. 148).

(1) *Water in natural watercourses*

The common-law and discretionary remedies against pollution of streams and rivers[2] have ancient origins, since these watercourses have long met several basic needs of man, in terms not only of water supply, but also (until comparatively recently) of both food and transport. Special rights have been, and still are, vested in the riparian owners (i.e., owners of the river banks and bed and tenants holding under them: generally the ownership extends to the mid-line of the stream, save where the landowner has both banks). Riparian owners thus have both special rights and special duties as between each other.[2a] However, it must be noted that persons other than riparian owners can, in more limited circumstances, have a right of

---

[1] " Tidal waters " are those river waters which are subject to the regular ebb and flow of the ordinary highest tides; but where " fresh water prevails " in the admixture, the river is said to be non-tidal.

[2] Including lakes fed by them.

[2a] These rights may now be at risk under the proposed terms of the Water Reorganisation Bill, 1973.

action at common law, as for example: for the disturbance of the enjoyment of a fishery, including oyster beds; or where a person is entitled to receive a supply of underground percolating water which becomes contaminated. Again, a person or persons other than a riparian owner, such as an angling association, may acquire a right to receive uncontaminated water.

A riparian owner may be restrained by injunction from altering the " natural quality " of the water in the stream either by pollution,[3] or by merely raising its temperature,[4] or by changing it from soft to hard water.[5] In cases of this type it is unnecessary for a lower (i.e., down-stream) riparian owner to prove that he has suffered actual damage in order to succeed in an action; and it is also no defence to prove that others have contributed to the pollution. Further, although it is possible to acquire a prescriptive common-law right to pollute a stream, this is nowadays seldom of value as a defence because it has also been held that the prescriptive right does not justify contravention of the Rivers (Prevention of Pollution) Acts, 1951, 1960 and 1961,[6] which are very broad in their compass and, amongst other things, make it an offence to discharge sewage effluent into a stream so as to interfere with the flow thereof or to pollute its waters. (For further detail see *post*, p. 144.) Such a contravention of these Acts is a statutory nuisance and may be restrained by injunction.

Again, even where a common-law prescriptive right to pollute can be established without being subject to the Rivers (Prevention of Pollution) Acts, this will not permit of any increase in the volume of pollution.

With regard to one specialised aspect of river pollution, it is an offence, under the Salmon and Freshwater Fisheries Act, 1923, s. 8 (1) (together with the Rivers (Prevention of Pollution) Acts, 1951 and 1960), for any person to put into waters containing fish, or into any tributaries thereof, any liquid or solid matter to such an extent as to cause the waters to be poisonous or injurious to fish, unless either he does so in exercise of a legally authorised right, or he has been so doing in continuation of the method of use of

---

[3] *Pride of Derby and Derbyshire Angling Association* v. *British Celanese, Ltd.* [1952] 2 All E.R. 1326.

[4] *Tipping* v. *Eckersley* (1855), 2 K. & J. 264; and *Pride of Derby, etc., supra.*

[5] *Young* v. *Bankier Distillery* [1893] A.C. 691.

[6] *Hulley* v. *Silversprings Bleaching Co.* [1922] 2 Ch. 268, 282; *Green* v. *Matthews* (1930), 46 T.L.R. 206.

particular premises prior to 18th July, 1926 (in which case, however, he must also take practical steps, if at reasonable cost, to minimise injury to fish).

Underground water flowing in defined channels is subject to the law as stated above for surface streams,[7] but water which is percolating underground in no defined stream is subject to rather different rules, both as to pollution and abstraction.[8]   It should also be noted that ditches (i.e., channels dug for the purpose of draining land) are not generally " watercourses "; but the legal interpretation will be based upon the degree of drainage in the sense of volume, or flow, of water.[9]   Thus, for example, a winterbourne [10] should be classified as a watercourse and not a ditch, and is so defined by s. 11 (1) of the Rivers (Prevention of Pollution) Act, 1951. The significance of classification as a " ditch " lies in (*a*) that the common-law rights and liabilities of riparian owners do not apply to a ditch; and (*b*) that considerably greater latitude as to the discharge of effluent, etc., is permitted under several statutory provisions.

Turning from the more general common-law and equitable situation in relation to natural watercourses, it must be noted that further complications (and perhaps confusion) arise as a result of a variety of statutes.   The paragraphs discussing these alternatives will be distinguished as below, for ease of choice of remedy:

Alternative (*i*)

By s. 3 (2) (as amended) of the Alkali, etc., Works Regulation Act, 1906, it is an offence punishable by a fine of £100 [11] upon summary conviction and by further fines of £20 per day during which the offence continues (or per day upon resumption thereof within a period of three months following the first conviction) to release chemical waste from a " scheduled industry " (i.e., scheduled under this Act), whether into water or otherwise " so as to cause nuisance."   Curiously, action under this Act must be taken in the county court, and not before the magistrates (s. 17).   The person

---

[7] *Chasemore* v. *Richards* (1859), 7 H.L.C. 349.

[8] See p. 146, below.

[9] *Phillimore* v. *Watford Rural Council* [1913] 2 Ch. 435.

[10] A winterbourne carries a very considerable volume and flow of water in winter, but may be completely dry in summer.

[11] It may be preferable to take action under the Rivers (Prevention of Pollution) Act, 1961, where maximum penalties are heavier.   See *post*, p. 144.

aggrieved should set this in motion by lodging a complaint with the local sanitary authority, who should then pursue the matter by informing the Secretary of State for Health and Social Security (under whom the Alkali Inspectorate functions). It should be noted that the owner's liability under the Act is not absolute, in the sense that it may be discharged upon conviction of his servant or agent, provided that the owner can establish that he personally has exercised " due diligence " to comply with the Act. Nevertheless, the owner of such a scheduled works may require the local authority to provide (but at the owner's expense), and to maintain, a suitable drain or channel discharging into the sea or a river, in order to avoid or reduce such pollution (s. 3 (3)); this discharge must not, however, be contrary to the Rivers (Prevention of Pollution) Acts, 1951 and 1961.[12] In the event of the local authority agreeing to undertake such works as above, they will have such powers as apply to the providing and laying of public sewers (s. 3 (3)), although subject to the payment of compensation by them " to any person for any damage sustained by him by reason of the exercise of . . . [such] . . . powers; and such compensation shall be deemed part of the expenses to be paid by the owner making the request . . ." (s. 3 (4)).

Alternative (ii)

The Public Health Act, 1936, s. 259 (1), enacted that a statutory nuisance shall exist (*a*) where a pond, ditch, gutter or watercourse is so foul as to prejudice health or constitute a nuisance; or (*b*) where a watercourse is choked or silted up so as to obstruct or impede the flow in such a way as to be either a nuisance or to give rise to conditions prejudicial to health. And the effect of the above subsection is further supported by s. 259 (2), which provides that any person who " throws or deposits any cinders, ashes, bricks, stone, rubbish, dust, filth or other matter likely to cause annoyance into or in any river, stream or watercourse, or who suffers any such act to be done," [13] shall be liable, upon summary conviction, to a penalty of not exceeding £2 (s. 296) and a daily penalty may also be fixed by the court where the offence continues (s. 297). However,

---

[12] i.e., no discharge without consent of the River Authority, even in the case of discharges in existence prior to inception of the 1951 Act.

[13] But mere failure by a landowner to keep a natural stream flowing through his land free from obstruction by natural causes is not an " act or default "—*Neath R.D.C.* v. *Williams* [1951] 1 K.B. 115; [1950] 2 All E.R. 625.

the proceedings may only be commenced by either the " party aggrieved " or the council or byelaw authority for the district, except where the written consent of the Attorney-General is obtained by some other person (s. 298). The provisions of s. 259 are also extended to canals (" waterways ") by the British Waterways Act, 1965, s. 14.

In addition, the local authority (and also the parish council) may " take steps to deal with " any pond, pool, ditch, gutter or place containing, or used for the collection of, any drainage, filth, stagnant water, or matter likely to be prejudicial to health, by draining, cleansing or covering it, or by other means: and, in so doing, they will not prejudice their right to take any subsequent legal action (s. 260). In the case of an offending adjoining local authority the aggrieved authority may obtain an order from a court of summary jurisdiction requiring matters to be rectified (s. 261). There are also special provisions in regard to ditches and culverts in built-up or urban areas (ss. 262–264).

Alternative (iii)

On the face of it, it might be considered that Alternatives (i) and (ii) already offer an adequate range of powers and remedies, but it became obvious in the course of the inquiries of the Proudman Committee, supported by surveys as early as 1958, that a proper national control of water and drainage had become essential in order to remedy existent and future water shortages. The Committee's report (1962) resulted in an extension of the Water Act of 1945 by the Water Resources Act, 1963. Under this latter Act the then Minister of Housing and Local Government was required to set up a Water Resources Board to manage the resources of England and Wales, and to establish " River Authorities " to deal in fact no longer with individual rivers (as had the discontinued River Boards), but with groups of river basins.[13a] The Minister is also required to formulate national policy with regard to the augmenting and redistribution of water resources in England and Wales. The term " water resources " is defined by s. 2 of the Act. In relation to any

[13a] But the Water Reorganisation Bill at present before Parliament (1973) provides for the replacement of the Water Resources Board by a National Water Council, and for setting up nine Regional Water Authorities and a Welsh National Water Development Authority, to replace the existing River Authorities. See also Department of Environment Consultative Paper "The Amenity Use of Water Space and the Reorganisation of the British Waterways Board."

area it means " water for the time being contained in any source of supply in that area." " Source of supply " means any inland water (i.e., not the sea) and any underground strata, including strata into which a well or borehole has been sunk. However, by s. 2 (3), isolated lakes, ponds or reservoirs (or groups of the same), which do not discharge into any further inland waters, are not subject to the Act. Thus, a municipal reservoir filled, say, from a single spring, and from which water was only drawn off by piped main supply, etc., would not be subject to control under the Act, save for a possible limitation if, in this example, the source were from underground strata which could be tapped elsewhere. (For further reference to the rights conferred under this Act to impound water, see p. 151, footnote 38.)

The significance of the above explanation in relation to water pollution may be seen upon consideration of Pt. VII (ss. 72–82) of the Act. By s. 72, it is unlawful to discharge into underground strata by means of a well, borehole or pipe[14] any " trade effluent or sewage effluent " [15] or any " poisonous, noxious or polluting matter," except with the consent of the River Authority. Such consent shall not, however, be unreasonably withheld; but may be given subject to conditions as set out in s. 72 (2). There is a right of appeal to the Minister (s. 72 (6)), who may either decide the matter himself or may, by order, set up a tribunal (s. 116). To date, no such order has been made. The Minister's decision shall be final.[16]

Consents given by the River Authorities may allow for transition to eventual cessation (s. 73), or they may be revoked or varied (s. 74); and a register of consents must be kept by every River Authority (s. 75), thereby enabling any unauthorised pollution to be readily identified.

The same River Authorities now control aboveground waters as a result of having taken over (by s. 5) (*a*) the functions of the old river boards which had earlier been exercised by virtue of s. 4 of the River Boards Act, 1948 (and which provided for the transfer to the boards of functions relating to land drainage, fisheries, river pollution

[14] Thus, not natural seepage from a normal water pond.
[15] As defined in the Rivers (Prevention of Pollution) Act, 1951.
[16] Section 117 provides that the decision " shall not be questioned in any legal proceedings whatsoever," but it is well established that an application for a prerogative order of prohibition, certiorari or mandamus may always be made to the High Court where the Minister's decision may be contrary to the rules of natural justice, etc.

and other matters); and (*b*) the functions of the old river boards exercised under s. 8 of the 1948 Act of navigation authorities, conservancy authorities and harbour authorities; and (*c*) functions under the Rivers (Prevention of Pollution) Acts, 1951 and 1961, together with various other statutory provisions.

By s. 2 (1) of the Rivers (Prevention of Pollution) Act, 1951, it is an offence:

(*a*) to cause or knowingly to permit any poisonous, noxious or polluting matter to enter a " stream ";

[" Stream " includes any river, stream, watercourse or inland water (whether natural or artificial), except that it does not include a lake or pond which does not discharge into a stream, or a sewer vested in a local authority, or (in general) into tidal waters (which include an enclosed dock which adjoins tidal waters).]

(*b*) to cause or knowingly to permit[17] to enter a stream any matter so as to tend either directly or in combination with other similar acts (whether his own or another's) to impede the flow . . . in a manner liable to lead to a substantial aggravation of pollution due to other causes . . . ;

(*c*) where conditions have been imposed as to a discharge into a stream, any breach of such stated conditions shall also be an offence.[18]

Further, the liability of local authorities is increased above those of other persons in this respect, in that wherever there is a discharge of the types described into a " stream " (as defined) from any public sewer or sewage disposal works, the local authority is to be deemed either to cause or knowingly to permit it.   Proceedings under this and related statutes may only be instituted by either the appropriate River Authority, or the Director of Public Prosecutions.

The maximum penalties for offences under this Act (s. 2 (7), as amended by the Rivers (Prevention of Pollution) Act, 1961, ss. 8 (3), 15 (4) and Sched. 2) are:

(*a*) for a single offence upon conviction upon indictment, a fine not exceeding £200;

(*b*) for a single offence upon summary conviction, a fine not exceeding £100 [19];

---

[17] *Allen* v. *Whitehead* [1930] 1 K.B. 211.
[18] Added by the Rivers (Prevention of Pollution) Act, 1961, s. 1 (8).
[19] As amended by the 1961 Act, s. 8 (1).

(c)   upon repetition of an offence following an earlier conviction upon indictment, either up to six months' imprisonment,

or a fine not exceeding £50 per day of the repetition or continuation,

or a fine in total not exceeding £500 (whichever fine is the greater),

or both fine and imprisonment, as above;

(d)   upon repetition of an offence following an earlier summary conviction, either up to three months' imprisonment,

or a fine not exceeding £10 per day of the repetition or continuation,

or a fine in total not exceeding £100 (whichever fine is the greater),

or both fine and imprisonment.

A further means of protection of an individual stream or any part of a stream is provided by s. 119 of and Sched. 12 to the Water Resources Act, 1963.   Under this section (which replaces earlier enactments) the River Authority is empowered to make byelaws. The penalties prescribed by the Act (s. 79 (8)) are:

(a)   for a single offence upon summary conviction, a fine not exceeding £20;

(b)   for a continuing or repeated offence after such a conviction, upon summary conviction, a fine not exceeding £5 for each day on which it is so continued.

The procedure for bringing such a byelaw into effect is somewhat exacting.   The River Authority must obtain confirmation of the byelaw by the Minister (Secretary of State for the Environment) or appropriate Ministers (Secretary of State for the Environment and the Minister of Agriculture, Fisheries and Food) and, at least one month prior to application for such confirmation, the River Authority must publish notice of their intention in the *London Gazette* and in one or more local newspapers; and must also send a copy of the byelaw to every local authority whose area is in, or partly within, the River Authority area.   In addition, for the same period, a copy must be made available for public inspection at all reasonable hours; and a printed copy be supplied free of charge to any person "appearing to be interested."

If the Minister or Ministers receive any written objection, then a byelaw (made under this section) cannot be confirmed without a local inquiry.

It should also be noted that where an offence under the Water Resources Acts, 1963 and 1971 (which also extend beyond pollution to matters of unlawful abstraction of water), is proved to have been committed by a corporate body " with the consent or connivance of, or to be attributable to any neglect on the part of, any director, manager, secretary or other similar officer . . . etc." he, as well as the body corporate, shall be guilty of the offence and shall be liable to be proceeded against and punished accordingly (1963 Act, s. 118 (3), (4)).

(2) *Water percolating through underground strata but in no definable channel*

At common law no action will lie for the abstraction or diversion of underground water which merely percolates through the soil but does not run in a definable channel.[20]   Nevertheless the owner (and presumably also a tenant) of land has a right of action if such water is polluted, as in *Ballard* v. *Tomlinson*,[21] where the plaintiff's well became polluted by sewage which had contaminated the percolating water.

But the lack of remedy at common law is now partly counteracted by ss. 23 to 25 of the Water Resources Act, 1963, which make it an offence (subject to certain special exceptions) to abstract water from underground strata without the licence in writing of the appropriate River Authority.   In this respect, however, no statutory right to bring a civil action is conferred upon a person suffering damage.

Discouragement of pollution of percolating water is, however, extended by the creation of an offence under s. 72 of the Water Resources Acts, 1963 and 1971, whereby it is unlawful to discharge any trade or sewage effluent, or any poisonous, noxious or polluting matter, into underground strata if without the consent of the relevant River Authority for the area; or, equally, to so discharge in a manner contrary to any conditions imposed in such a consent.   The offence is punishable either upon indictment or upon summary conviction by a fine of £100 (s. 72 (8)).   Certain provisions are made in the Act for a time-limit upon the granting or refusal of consent (s. 72 (1)); and for appeals to the Secretary of State for the Environment (s. 72 (3)).   Provision is also made for the revocation or variation of an existing consent.   Thus, by s. 74 (1), an application may be made by any person to the River Authority for such revocation or variation; or the River Authority may itself take the initiative.   In the former

[20] *Dickinson* v. *Grand Junction Canal Co.* (1852), 7 Ex. 282.
[21] (1885), 29 Ch.D. 115, C.A.

case, the River Authority is to reach a decision within three months
or, failing this, the authority is to be deemed to have refused to make
the variation (s. 74 (3)).   Once a decision is made (or deemed to be
made) by the River Authority time runs as to the right of appeal to
the Secretary of State and this period is to be provided for by
regulation, which at present permits the minimum period prescribed
by the Act, namely 28 days.[22]

(3) *Water in artificial watercourses or lakes*

For the sake of clarity, it should be emphasised at the outset that
the statutory controls already referred to in relation to natural
watercourses [23] apply equally to artificial watercourses.[24]

As to the common-law position, in general the owners of the banks
of an artificial watercourse or lake cannot acquire riparian rights
over the stream, and they will therefore not be able to claim the
normal riparian right to receive water " in its natural state."   Thus,
they will only be able to sue those other owners who pollute the
watercourse to such an extent as to cause a public nuisance, and
this may be difficult to establish: no right will exist to sue merely for
pollution.[25]   Further, an easement can be created either by agreement or prescription to discharge polluting matter into an artificial
stream (but not into a natural watercourse, *ante*), although it has
been held that this must not " considerably " enlarge the pollution
thereof.[26]   But the validity of the latter limitation may be ques-
tionable.

There is, however, an important factor to be borne in mind in the
case of those watercourses which may have their origins in a natural
stream which has become enclosed by artificial banks or by roofing
over; or, indeed, where the watercourse is known to have been
created artificially but with the intention, as proven by subsequent
user, that the owners of the banks shall have riparian rights.[27]   In

---

[22] Water Resources (Miscellaneous Provisions) Regulations, 1965 (S.I. 1965 No.
1092), reg. 4.

[23] Page 139 *et seq.*

[24] But, in some cases, excluding local authority sewers.

[25] *Whaley* v. *Laing* (1857), 2 H. & N. 476; *Paine & Co., Ltd.* v. *St. Neots Gas and Coke
Co.* [1939] 3 All E.R. 81.   Note also that a non-riparian owner taking water
from a natural stream by means of conduits has no natural rights to sue riparian
owners who pollute the natural stream and, thus, the conduit water—*Ormerod*
v. *Todmorden Mill Co.* (1883), 11 Q.B.D. 155.

[26] *McIntyre Bros.* v. *McGavin* [1893] A.C. 268.

[27] Except where the artificial watercourse was intended only to be of a temporary
nature—*Burrows* v. *Lang* [1901] 2 Ch. 503; *Greatrex* v. *Hayward* (1853), 8 Ex. 291.

these instances it is well established that riparian rights will exist, so that the same remedies against pollution will exist as in the case of a natural stream.[28]

(4) *Water intended for domestic use*

A factual comment should be made at the outset, namely that, at the present time, the extent of pollution of rivers is such (despite the marked improvement in many cases, and notably in the River Thames) that water undertakers are forced to incur the expense of construction of reservoirs in upland areas which might otherwise be avoided.[29]   It is, however, encouraging that it is now technically possible to monitor river pollution by the installation of computer-operated meters at strategic intervals in the stream.   These are fully automated to take regular (say half-hourly) samples of water which are tested and, if below a given degree of pollution, discharged. When and if a sufficiently polluted sample is found, the machine will retain it and will then automatically connect an alarm system to the River Authority office.   Thus it will be possible to investigate pollution without delay and also to establish the stretch of river between meters in which the source of pollution must lie.

As already stated, liability for pollution of water which is intended for domestic use (in that it is in course of treatment in a waterworks or has been supplied to a public water main for domestic purposes) is a matter principally of public health law.   The subject will, therefore, be considered only in outline in this book, and the reader should refer to more specialised sources where necessary: some of these are noted below.[30]

The general responsibilities of the local water authority are governed by the Public Health Act, 1936.   This requires that the water in any waterworks (i.e., following treatment) which is intended for domestic use shall be " wholesome."   The expression means, virtually, suitable for human consumption, and is the only practicable requirement, since, in the scientific sense, " pure " water can only be obtained by distillation into sterilised containers.   The judicial interpretation of the description " wholesome " in this context is

[28] *Sutcliffe* v. *Booth* (1863), 32 L.J.Q.B. 136; *Baily & Co.* v. *Clark, Son and Morland* [1902] 1 Ch. 689.

[29] As to the acquisition of valleys for reservoirs, a more equitable future distribution may result from legislation proposed under the Water Reorganisation Bill.

[30] *The Public Health Encyclopaedia* (Sweet & Maxwell); *Coulson & Forbes, Law Relating to Waters*; *Lumley's Public Health*; and more shortly, *The Law on the Pollution of Waters*, by A. S. Wisdom.

to be given " a fair, large and liberal construction," and can thus extend to include water to which a small proportion of fluoride has been added.[31]

The term of art " pure water " is, however, employed by statute in relation to water in a public water main, in the requirement that the water shall be " pure " at the point of connection with a private supply. This is an absolute statutory duty under the Water Act, 1945, s. 28. It follows that the question of the exercise or not of " due care " is irrelevant to the requirements of the Act (although the rule in *Donoghue* v. *Stevenson* does apply[32]), since the existence of a statutory duty does not extinguish the common-law duty unless there is an express provision or necessary implication to that effect.[33] In the event of a statutory breach in this regard it has been held that only the ratepayer (or tenant as occupier if he does not pay the rates) can recover.[33] Where, however, the impurity of the domestic water supply results from the *negligence* of the water undertakers they will be liable in damages not only to the ratepayer but also to others affected on the ratepayer's premises.[34]

As to *private sources of water supply* where the water is, or is likely to be, used for domestic purposes, the local authority is empowered,

---

[31] *A.-G. of New Zealand* v. *Lower Hutt Corpn.* [1964] A.C. 1469 (P.C.). In this case the local water was deficient in fluoride, in that the proportion of this element present was well below the " world average," so that the water was deemed, by the Privy Council, to remain " wholesome " even after addition of fluoride.

[32] The rule in *Donoghue* v. *Stevenson* [1932] A.C. 562: the plaintiff became ill as a result of having drunk ginger beer (from an opaque bottle) in which she subsequently found the decomposed remains of a snail. The drink had been purchased by a third party, so that contractual liability did not then apply. In finding in favour of the plaintiff, the House of Lords stated a rule, thus: " A manufacturer of products, which he sells in such a form as to show that he intends them to reach the ultimate consumer in the form in which they left him with no reasonable possibility of intermediate examination, and with the knowledge that the absence of reasonable care in the preparation and putting up of the products will result in injury to the consumer's life or property, owes a duty to the consumer to take reasonable care."

[33] *Read* v. *Croydon Corporation* [1938] 4 All E.R. 631. The ratepayer's infant daughter contracted typhoid. The infant daughter claimed damages in respect of pain and suffering, and the ratepayer claimed in respect of special damages incurred as a result of his daughter's illness. *Held* (*inter alios*) that there was no contractual duty to supply the water to the infant daughter; and that the breach of statutory duty conferred a right of action upon the ratepayer only.

[34] *Barnes* v. *Irwell Valley Water Board* [1939] 1 K.B. 21, where the water supplied in the water board's main was " pure " but was plumbosolvent and, as a result of passing through the lead pipes in the plaintiff's own house, produced lead poisoning in the ratepayer and his wife, both of whom recovered damages.

by s. 140 of the Public Health Act, 1936, in cases where the water is, or is likely to become, so polluted as to be " prejudicial to health," to apply to a court of summary jurisdiction for a summons; the court may then direct that the supply be permanently or temporarily closed (s. 140 (2)).   If the person against whom the order is made fails to comply the court may then authorise the local authority to rectify the fault and to charge the cost to the person in default (s. 140 (3)).   Further, by the Water Act, 1945, s. 21, where a person is guilty of any act or neglect whereby a spring, well, borehole or adit, the water from which is used or likely to be used for human consumption or domestic purposes, or for manufacturing food or drink for human consumption, is polluted or likely to be polluted, such person may, upon summary conviction, be subject to a fine not exceeding £5 per day for continuation after conviction; or, upon conviction on indictment, a fine not exceeding £200, and in continuing offences, as above, a further £20 per day after conviction. There is, however, a specific provision that no restriction shall be placed upon the cultivation of land in accordance with the principles of good husbandry; and that the reasonable use of oil or tar upon a highway shall not constitute an act leading to an offence provided that the highway authority has taken reasonable steps to prevent pollution of water from such causes.

The general scope of responsibility of statutory water undertakers[35] is set down in the Water Acts, 1945 and 1948.   These Acts enable the undertakers to pass local byelaws and to apply Model Byelaws[36] to protect against the pollution of any water, whether surface or underground, and to compel the owner or occupier of any premises in their area to carry out repairs so as to prevent pollution of their water.[37]   If the owner or occupier fails to comply, the statutory water undertakers may (subject to a right of appeal to the Secretary of State for the Environment) carry out such works and recover the cost from the owner or occupier as a civil debt.   In addition, the byelaws may provide for a fine upon summary conviction of not exceeding £20 and a further fine of not exceeding £5 per day for a continuing offence after conviction.   And, lastly, statutory water undertakers have power either to acquire land or to enter into

---

[35] i.e., supplying water by virtue of the Public Health Act, 1936, as amended; and the Water Act, 1948.

[36] Series XXI has been published.

[37] Water Act, 1945, s. 18.

agreements with owners and occupiers of land in order to prevent the pollution of water supplies.[38]

2. Pollution of the Sea and Beaches

(1) *General comment*

At a recent international conference in London[39] it was emphasised by the Secretary of State for the Environment that by far the main world source of pollution of the sea is from rivers carrying industrial and other effluent, and sewage. Thus, although the occasional (but not infrequent) discharge of oil from tankers or other vessels whilst at sea receives at present the greatest publicity, and in particular when holiday beaches are contaminated, it should be our first priority to reduce the ever-rising flow of pollution from rivers. This urgency is directly related to the need to solve the world food problem, since it is increasingly clear that the seas must be farmed. Although the areas of most rapid fish growth tend to be in those parts of the world where there is an up-current from the extremely deep oceanic water, local fisheries in shallow seas are also of increasing importance. The real significance of the need to control sea pollution may be illustrated. In terms of protein production, it is estimated that it takes 100 tons of small fish to develop 10 tons of edible (i.e., nettable) fish, and that 10 tons of fish meal from such netted fish would only produce 1 ton of, say, chicken meat. Again, certain types of sea life actively concentrate toxic substances, and notably metals such as mercury which is found increasingly in fish.

(2) *Discharge from estuaries*

The purpose of this subsection is to indicate any special aspects of the law which relate to pollution emanating from estuaries (i.e., originating in inland waters but affecting the sea), and further discussion of off-shore and deep sea pollution will be found in subsection (3).

The responsibility for control of estuarial pollution is, in a sense, divided. It is the duty of the District Sea Fishery Committees for England and Wales,[40] of which there are eleven, to exercise vigilance

---

[38] Water Act, 1945, s. 22.

[39] United Nations Delegates Conference, London, July, 1971.

[40] For constitution of such committees under the Sea Fisheries Regulation Act, 1966, see *post*, p. 154.

and control over sea fisheries in national and territorial waters.   The definition of territorial waters is accepted as waters extending three nautical miles from the coast, but it is possible that "national waters" for the purposes of sea fishing extend at least to the exclusive fishery limits laid down in the Fishery Limits Act, 1964, s. 1, namely six miles, and may even extend to the "outer belt" (again, s. 1) of twelve miles from the coastline.   (The Scottish coastal waters have no such committees and control is only achieved by extension of the powers of River Authorities over estuaries and certain limited coastal waters.)   Thus, in the case of England and Wales, effective control over estuaries and the waters in the vicinity of estuaries depends essentially upon effective co-operation between the relevant District Sea Fishery Committee and the relevant River Authority or Authorities.   Whilst byelaws may be made by the Committee (*post*, p. 154), real control of estuarial pollution lies with the River Authority.   Provision for this is made in the Rivers (Prevention of Pollution) Acts, 1951 and 1961.   By the latter Act, the Secretary of State may now extend the effect of ss. 2 to 6[41] of the earlier Act to any "tidal waters," including enclosed docks or parts of the sea as may be specified by him in the order.   Such orders set out with precision, and by reference to Ordnance Survey charts, the limits of the specified areas: they do not have a blanket coverage of the entire coastline.   Further, it should be noted that such orders can only be made upon the application of either the River Authority or of "some other person appearing to the Minister to be interested."[42]

The procedure for obtaining such an order is: that the application must set out the proposed order in draft form (which may then be modified by the Minister); that notice of intention to make the application must first be given in the *London Gazette* at least one month before it is actually made; and that a copy of the application must be kept at the offices of the River Authority where public inspection (free of charge) is to be possible "at all reasonable hours."   Further, where the applicant is not the River Authority, he must supply copies to the River Authority free of charge.

The estuaries and coastal waters falling under the control of River Authorities as a result of the above orders—namely "controlled

---

[41] *Ante*, p. 139.
[42] An uncertain description!

waters " [43]—can be supervised by the said authorities not only in relation to the flow from the river itself, but also as to any outlets for sewage or industrial waste which run, or are intended in the future to run, into the tidal estuary or into controlled waters on the sea coast. In such cases any proposals to alter existing outlets, or to bring into use new outlets, must be approved by the River Authority. Such approval cannot be unreasonably withheld, but may be granted subject to conditions. These conditions must be recorded in a register kept by the authority and this is to be open for inspection by " any person appearing [to the authority] to be interested in the outlet." The statutory provisions as stated above are derived from three sources. [44]

(3) *Discharge of sewage or other noxious or polluting matter into the sea from land-based installations, etc.*

In considering the sea in general (together with tidal estuaries) in terms of the law, a clear distinction must be drawn between (*a*) estuaries and " controlled waters " [45] and (*b*) the remainder of the sea, that is including both coastal waters and deep sea or oceanic waters.

At common law there is no right to discharge sewage into the sea where such discharge causes a nuisance to another, [46] and such an activity cannot be rendered lawful by prescription. But, where no nuisance can be proved, a common-law right to discharge into the sea will exist.

The occupiers (or licensees) of oyster beds have successfully maintained actions for trespass and nuisance where the discharge of sewage by a local authority has been in the vicinity of the beds and has thus rendered them unfit for use. [47] Again, an injunction will lie against the pollution of oyster beds. [48]

---

[43] These comprise most of the tidal estuaries of England and Wales and are listed in the Schedule to the Clean Rivers (Estuaries and Tidal Waters) Act, 1960.

[44] Section 7 of the Rivers (Prevention of Pollution) Act, 1951; together with the Rivers (Prevention of Pollution) Act, 1961, other than ss. 1 to 3; and together with the Clean Rivers (Estuaries and Tidal Waters) Act, 1960.

[45] " Controlled waters " are artificially designated and may include open sea: see subs. (2) of this part of this chapter.

[46] *Hobart* v. *Southend-on-Sea Corporation* (1906), 75 L.J.K.B. 305. But nevertheless a grant of such a right may, in given circumstances, be presumed—*Somerset Drainage Commissioners* v. *Bridgewater Corporation* (1899), 81 L.T. 729, at p. 730.

[47] *Owen* v. *Faversham Corporation* (1908), 73 J.P. 33.

[48] *Foster* v. *Warblington U.D.C.* [1906] 1 K.B. 648.

It will be seen, therefore, that those local authorities who still discharge sewage into the sea do so in reliance upon the fact (*a*) that an actionable nuisance cannot be proved; and (*b*) that no statutory provision or order is, at present, being transgressed; or, occasionally (*c*) that there exists a local or special Act of Parliament, Royal Charter, letters patent, prescription [48a] or immemorial usage.

In general, therefore, control of land-based discharges along those parts of our coasts which are away from estuaries and controlled waters will only arise where an initiative is taken either in bringing an action for nuisance (which may be difficult to establish in terms of evidence, frequency and extent, etc.); or by the Minister making an order in relation to the particular coastal area.   Thus, the public using beaches contaminated as a result of piped discharge of sewage into the sea will sometimes be unable to prevent or alter this until a clear case of infection and serious illness is established.   This situation continues, no doubt, as a result of the sometimes extreme financial problems which would arise should small seaside towns or villages attempt to undertake the installation of sewage disposal plants, but it should be noted that grants or loans may be made by the Exchequer for this purpose.

Where, however, the pollution can be proved to be affecting any recognisable sea fishery (which may, again, be difficult to establish in practice), the relevant District Sea Fishery Committee for the area [49] is empowered under the Sea Fisheries Regulation Act, 1966, to make, subject to the approval of the Minister,[50] a suitable byelaw. This power applies to any " solid or liquid substances " (s. 2), but contravention of such a byelaw can only be subject to a maximum fine upon summary conviction of £50 or, in the case of a second or subsequent conviction, of not exceeding £100.

The District Sea Fisheries Committees consist (by s. 2 of the 1966 Act) of county and/or borough council members, at least one member of the River Authority, and of representatives of " fishing interests," including owners of fisheries, fishing-boat owners, fishermen and fish merchants, etc.   The proportions of these members are as directed by the Minister of Agriculture, Fisheries and Food.

The most significant forms of coastal pollution in terms of annual volume at the present time are domestic sewage, industrial

[48a] But not a prescriptive right to cause a *nuisance.*
[49] Eleven areas for the coastal waters of England and Wales.
[50] Minister of Agriculture, Fisheries and Food.

waste and cooling water (i.e., heated) discharged from power stations.

(4) *Discharge from vessels at sea*

In practice the discharge of polluting matter from vessels at sea can be divided into: discharge by accident (notably of oil tanker cargoes or their tank washings, and of fuel oil from oil-fired ships in general); discharge by intent (notably of tank washings); and the deliberate dumping of industrial waste (including radioactive materials, chemicals and other solid scrap).[51]

It will be evident that any discharge or dumping which is carried out in the open sea beyond any territorial waters can only be controlled by international agreement. The major maritime countries therefore subscribe to the Inter-Governmental Maritime Consultative Organisation (IMCO), which has agreed to certain conventions in order to control the operation of tankers and other ships at sea. By the International Convention for the Prevention of Pollution of the Sea by Oil, it is agreed that the owners of tankers and other ships at sea will pay compensation for damage caused by oil spills, and special consideration is given to such discharges in the North Sea and English Channel, together with much of the North Atlantic, since these areas have great concentration of shipping. So far as British jurisdiction is concerned, the Oil in Navigable Waters Acts, 1955 and 1963, as amended by the Oil in Navigable Waters Act, 1971, prohibit the discharge of oil, or mixtures containing oil, into prohibited sea areas, or into United Kingdom territorial waters (i.e., the three-mile limit) or inland waters navigable by seagoing vessels. The 1971 Act has two main purposes. It amends the earlier Acts so as to enable the United Kingdom to give effect to changes agreed internationally in the International Convention for the Prevention of Pollution of the Sea by Oil, 1954 (Cmnd. 4347: May 1970), and it also enables the British government to take action in the case of oil pollution casualties against any ship in territorial or internal waters and against any United Kingdom ship elsewhere. As to foreign ships on the high seas, it applies within certain limits permitted by the Order in Council. This latter provision follows

---

[51] Certain vessels are chartered for the specific purpose of dumping sewage sludge and industrial waste in the open sea beyond territorial waters, and it is recognised by the Department of the Environment that much of this material is highly toxic.

the agreement between coastal sovereign states by the International Convention relating to Intervention on the High Seas in Cases of Oil Pollution, Accidents and Collisions. This was signed at Brussels in November, 1969, together with the International Convention on Civil Liability for Oil Pollution Damage. The latter Convention is put into effect by the Merchant Shipping (Oil Pollution) Act, 1971, which imposes strict liability upon a shipowner for oil pollution damage in the United Kingdom (including Northern Ireland and the Channel Islands), subject to certain exceptions, such as an act of a third party (s. 2), and to a limit as to liability which is related to the ship's tonnage (s. 4). Also, ships carrying a bulk cargo of oil are compelled to insure against liability (s. 10) and to obtain a certificate to this effect from the Secretary of State for Trade and Industry (s. 11).

The sanctions applicable to these offences operate both against the ship's master and against the shipowners, and these have been increased by the Oil in Navigable Waters Act, 1971, and the Prevention of Oil Pollution Act, 1971, whereby a shipowner and/or ship's master may be liable upon summary conviction to pay a fine of not exceeding £50,000, or upon conviction on indictment to an unlimited fine.

To reinforce these, it is also provided that ships must report any discharge of oil into the waters of a harbour (Oil in Navigable Waters Act, 1971, s. 1) and oil records must be kept by the ship's master and be subject to regulations to be made by the Department of Trade and Industry (s. 7). The records concern the loading, discharge and other operations relating to oil. The purpose is to ensure that any accidental or intentional discharge into the sea or other waters can be traced, and failure to keep such records is subject to a fine not exceeding £500 on summary conviction; and, where false records are kept, to a similar fine or imprisonment for up to six months, or both. Where conviction is upon indictment, imprisonment may be for up to two years.

It is also provided elsewhere that the Exchequer will bear 50 per cent. of the cost of clearing oil-contaminated beaches, this to be carried out by local authorities. The responsibility for the tracking and dispersal of oil slicks at sea lies, however, with the Department of Trade and Industry.

A further distinct statutory control is provided by the Sea Fisheries (Shellfish) Act, 1967. By this, the Minister of Agriculture,

Fisheries and Food may make an order for the establishment of oyster and mussel fisheries on the sea bed or in estuarial or tidal waters, whereby grantees are specified to operate them. Once such beds are established it becomes an offence under s. 7 of the Act to deposit ballast, rubbish or any other substance upon them, and such an offence is punishable by fines of £2, £5 and £10 for first, second and third and subsequent offences respectively. The same section also provides that an offender " shall be liable to make full compensation."

As stated in relation to land-based discharges, the powers of District Sea Fisheries Committees are governed by the Sea Fisheries Regulation Act, 1966, and these committees may make byelaws[52] for prohibiting or regulating the deposit or discharge of any solid or liquid substance detrimental to sea fish[53] or to sea fishing.[54] Contravention is subject to a fine on summary conviction (as already mentioned in relation to discharges or dumping from land) of £50 or, in the case of second and subsequent conviction, not exceeding £100.

[52] Sea Fisheries (Byelaws) Regulations, 1938 (S.R. & O. 1938 No. 1182).
[53] Includes sea fish (but not salmon or migratory trout) and lobsters, crabs, shrimps, prawns, oysters, mussels, cockles and other kinds of crustaceans and shell fish.
[54] See also Radioactive Substances Act, 1960, s. 9 (1), (2) and Sched. 1, Pt. I.

CHAPTER 8

POLLUTION OF THE AIR; POLLUTION OF LAND

1. Pollution of the Air

The first of the series of Acts of Parliament leading up to the modern statutory law governing air pollution was the Alkali Act, 1863. This Act created a national Alkali Inspectorate, which has remained charged with the inspection of all " works " (factories) concerned in the production of substances the manufacture of which may involve the release of " noxious fumes and smoke." In addition, the Act and its successors imposed restrictions upon the escape of these substances not only from the factory building and site, but also from the production lines themselves, thereby protecting employees in such works.

The principal Act at present in force is the Alkali, etc., Works Regulation Act, 1906,[1] the more precise application of which is by virtue of ss. 2, 7 and 8 and Sched. 1, as amended by the Clean Air Act, 1956, s. 17 (4) and Sched. 2. The Schedule to the 1906 Act provides a list of " noxious and offensive gases " (ranging from, for example, muriatic acid to volatile organic sulphur compounds), together with a list of " scheduled processes " which the Act requires to be controlled. These two lists have since been extended by a number of Ministerial orders made by virtue of s. 4 (1) of the Public Health (Smoke Abatement) Act, 1926; and certain obsolete processes have been removed by orders made under the Clean Air Act, 1956, s. 17 (3). In fact, the principal current list of gases and of " works " is now to be found in the Alkali, etc., Works Order, 1966 (S.I. 1966 No. 1143),[1a] which represents the fruits of the deliberations of the Alkali Inspectorate (now the Alkali and Clean Air Inspectorate) at their centenary conference.

The penalties applicable to contravention and enforcement of the conditions required by the 1906 Act are fines of £100 upon summary conviction; and a further £20 per day for a continuing emission or

---

[1] As to water pollution under this Act, see Chapter 7.
[1a] Extended by S.I. 1971 No. 960, of the same title.

for emission which has continued since an earlier conviction. The present penalties are by virtue of s. 16A of the 1906 Act (i.e., as amended by the Clean Air Act, 1956, s. 17 (*a*) and Sched. 2). In this instance, the action, although criminal in nature, has (peculiarly) to be brought in the county court.

Probably the prime importance of the 1906 Act now lies in the need for the highly technical and specialised knowledge which has been developed, and made available by the Alkali and Clean Air Inspectorate.[2] This Inspectorate was originally under the control of the Local Government Board and subsequently the Minister of Health, but since 1951 it has reported to the Minister of Housing and Local Government and, thus, since 1970, to the Secretary of State for the Environment.

The more general function of protection against air pollution in the wider sense—that is, due to combustion of heating fuels—has been introduced by the Clean Air Acts, 1956 and 1968. These two Acts impose controls upon the " emission of dark smoke," whether by industry or by domestic fuel consumers. The Acts are to be read together and their combined effect is as follows. Emission of " dark smoke " (that is, smoke as dark as, or darker than, Shade 2 on the Ringelmann Chart, in accordance with the 1956 Act, s. 34 (2)) from a chimney of any building is an offence. But, by the 1968 Act, s. 1, this is extended to any emission (whether from a chimney or not) from industrial or trade premises. However, there are certain exemptions from both these provisions. By the Dark Smoke (Permitted Periods) Regulations, 1958 (S.I. 1958 No. 498) the emission of dark smoke from chimneys is permitted for limited times during any given eight-hour period, and this can be shown in tabular form:

| | *Permitted Period of Dark Smoke: in eight-hour period* | |
No. of Furnaces Served by one Chimney	*Normally*	*If Soot-Blowing*
1 furnace only	10 minutes	14 minutes
2 furnaces	18 minutes	25 minutes
3 furnaces	24 minutes	34 minutes
4 furnaces	29 minutes	41 minutes

[2] *The Times*, in an editorial of 4th June, 1971, called for a reduction of secrecy as between the Inspectorate and the general public to enable any relaxation which results in a higher degree of pollution in a given locality to be publicised.

Further, by the Clean Air (Emission of Dark Smoke) (Exemption) Regulations, 1969, the production of dark smoke is permitted under certain restricted circumstances, providing that this is done strictly in accordance with conditions of burning as defined in the Regulations.

The circumstances to which this permission under the Regulations applies are:

(i)   Building site clearance (but in no event to include the burning of rubber, flock or feathers).

(ii) Burning of containers of toxic substances.

(iii) Burning of waste explosives or of animal or poultry carcasses where these have been slaughtered in order to combat a disease epidemic.

(iv) Burning of tar, pitch, etc., in the course of surfacing or re-surfacing (e.g., roads, flat roofs, etc.); and research into the causes of and control of fires; and fire fighting training.

The conditions (which will be defined below) under which each of the above is permitted fall into three categories, A, B and C, all, or some, of which apply to each circumstance, thus:

Circumstance (i)—Conditions A, B and C.

Circumstance (ii)—Conditions A, B and C.

Circumstance (iii)—Conditions A and C.

Circumstance (iv)—Condition C only.

These conditions are specified as follows:

Condition A: That there is no other reasonably safe and practicable method of burning.

Condition B: That burning is carried out so as to minimise smoke.

Condition C: That burning is under direct and continuous supervision of the occupier of the premises, or of a person authorised by him.

In addition to these controls as to user, there are a number of restrictions imposed upon the design of both industrial/commercial furnaces and chimneys, and of domestic hearths, boilers and chimneys. The installation of any furnace (other than domestic furnaces of less than 55,000 Btu/hr) is prohibited unless the design is such as to provide smoke-free combustion (1956 Act, s. 3). Further, the height of chimneys is to be subject to the specific approval of local authorities, bearing in mind the purpose of the chimney, the position and type of any neighbouring buildings, and the levels and conformation of the surrounding land (1956 Act, s. 10, and Ministry of

Housing and Local Government Circular No. 64/56). This applies nationally, with the exception of Greater London, where the matter is controlled under the London Building (Amendment) Act, 1935. In addition, s. 6 of the 1956 Act (as amended by ss. 3 and 6 of the 1968 Act, and the Clean Air (Measurement of Grit and Dust from Furnaces) Regulations, 1971 (S.I. 1971 No. 161), and Clean Air (Emission of Grit and Dust from Furnaces) Regulations (S.I. 1971 No. 162)), requires that a grit arresting plant, of a pattern approved by the local authority, must be fitted where the burning of solid fuel or pulverised waste is to exceed 100 lb. per hour. As an additional precaution, the height of industrial chimneys serving any furnace exceeding $1\frac{1}{4}$ million Btu/hr can be controlled under s. 6 of the 1968 Act. Any chimneys of lesser capacity fall under the (National) Building Regulations, 1972. A subsequent circular (Clean Air: Tall Buildings and Industrial Emissions, No. 69/65) stresses that local planning authorities should pay particular attention to the siting of any new tall buildings near existing chimneys, where these chimneys aggregate a continuous rating of 450,000 lb. steam per hour or over, as in the case of a small power station, upwards. In these instances the advice of the Chief Alkali Inspector is to be sought.

Having laid down the requirements as to design and permitted types of combustion a final precaution is added by Parliament in the form of s. 7 of the 1956 Act read with s. 5 of the 1968 Act, which requires that the owner of a furnace, upon receipt of a notice in writing from the local authority, shall, within six weeks, measure the dust, grit and fumes emitted. The method for so doing is set out in the Clean Air (Measurement of Grit and Dust) Regulations, 1968 (S.I. 1968 No. 431), and fully explained by reference to British Standard 3405 of 1961 together with the publication (H.M.S.O. 1961) *Measurement of Solids in Flue Gases*.[3] If the local authority itself wishes to carry out such measurements it must give forty-eight hours' notice to the chimney owner.

The provisions of the Clean Air Acts are more widely known in so far as they relate to the creation of *smoke control areas*. These may be declared by a local authority by virtue of s. 11 of the 1956 Act; or, if the local authority fails to act, the Secretary of State may by s. 8 of the 1968 Act, require them, after due consultation, so to do. The process for creation of smoke control areas is, very briefly, as follows:

[3] The British Coal Utilisation Research Association. Authors: P. G. W. Hawksley, S. Badzioch and J. K. Blackett.

The local authority must first discuss the local fuel supply position with the relevant sources of supply (National Coal Board, Gas Boards,[4] Electricity Boards, fuel distributors).   The authority must then obtain a broad assessment of the likely need for structural alterations to furnaces, hearths and flues and submit a report as to the above to the Secretary of State.   This report is to include a map defining the proposed area, and is to indicate the numbers and types of building (i.e., domestic, commercial, industrial and other, together with a list of Government buildings affected).   An estimate of the probable cost of grant aid (*post*) is to be given, and the date from which the proposed order is intended to apply.   If the Secretary of State agrees in principle, he will then require a detailed survey to be carried out by the local authority, and it is suggested by the Secretary of State that this should always begin with a public relations operation, involving discussions with local voluntary bodies (such as the Townswomen's Guilds, W.R.V.S., etc.), and that exhibitions be organised.   The local authority's resolution making a Section 11 order is subject to approval and confirmation by the Secretary of State (1968 Act, s. 10 (4)), as explained below. The local authority's resolution to make such an order must be advertised in the local press and in the *London Gazette*, and copies must be posted conspicuously in the area affected for at least six weeks prior to the Secretary of State's confirmation.[5]   During this time objections may be lodged with the local authority and, if not withdrawn, these will be considered by the Secretary of State, who may either order a public inquiry or provide " other means of hearing objections."

After six weeks the order is to be submitted to the Secretary of State for approval, together with any outstanding objections, and supported by rather more detailed information, including a further map, lists (by type) of buildings and of Government Department buildings affected, and a schedule of the grants payable in each individual case.   But, by Circular 77/65, " Smoke Control Areas: Estimates and Final Costs," the local authority need no longer specify the details of appliances necessary for each building.   The

4 The White Paper, Cmnd. 4375, states that a number of otherwise obsolescent gas works are being continued in operation so as to provide coke, etc.

5 There is no prescribed form for a Smoke Control Order, but a model is given in App. I to the Minister's Memorandum: " Clean Air Act, 1956—Memorandum on Smoke Control Areas " (1956, reprinted 1961).   The order must specify date of commencement and list the buildings affected.

Secretary of State will then either confirm, modify or refuse the order.

The grants (referred to earlier) in aid of structural adaptations or for the provision of new appliances for use in dwelling-houses are set out in Annexe E (Conditions of Grant) to Circular No. 3 of 1962, " Smoke Control Areas." These are available partly from the local authority and partly from the Exchequer. Where any adaptation to a dwelling-house or to its fireplaces is necessary so as to meet the order, the local authority must pay 7/10ths of the expenditure and may pay the cost in full. The Exchequer (following specific approval by the Secretary of State under the 1956 Act, ss. 22 to 31) will then reimburse the local authority as to 4/10ths. Thus, if the dwelling-house is privately owned, the occupier or owner will be required to find only 3/10ths of the cost; and, if owned by the local authority, the authority will find 6/10ths (the Exchequer the balance). However, if there is need for an appliance, which is " fixed yet readily removable," then, although the grant will be paid in the proportions as above, only half (i.e., 7/20ths) will be paid initially to the owner or occupier, the balance (i.e., 7/20ths) being payable two years after the order. In such event, the second instalment is payable to the then current occupier. If the appliance is bought on hire-purchase, the grant will not extend to cover payment of interest or other charges.

If the non-occupying owner of a dwelling-house refuses to agree to the adaptations, the tenant can apply to the county court for a court order regardless of any terms in his tenancy agreement. He may also recover part of the cost from the lessor. Where, however, the property is rent-controlled, the lessor may then increase the rent by eight per cent. of the expenditure reasonably incurred (after deduction of grant).

Failure voluntarily to carry out works of adaptation is met by a notice duly served under s. 12 (2) of the 1956 Act, and if this is not complied with, the local authority may do the work and recover 3/10ths of the cost; but this recovery of the cost may be waived, by virtue of the Act, if the local authority so resolves. The liability to pay if required to do so by the local authority rests upon either the occupier or owner according to the terms of the tenancy, and the matter, in case of conflict, may be referred by the local authority to the magistrates' court by virtue of the Public Health Act, 1936, s. 290 (or under a corresponding provision in Greater London).

Alternatively, however, the county court may again become involved in order to authorise the local authority to carry out the works regardless of the terms of the tenancy.

The other practical effects of an order by the Minister upon a Smoke Control Area are as follows: (i) it becomes an offence to sell solid fuel of other than " authorised fuel " type for use in such an area (1956 Act, s. 34 (1)).   The vendor must, however, be proved to have known that the purchaser so intended (1956 Act, s. 27). (ii) The occupier of premises becomes liable if he produces black smoke regardless of whether or not he is aware of the type of smoke, but he may validly argue that he had no knowledge of the existence of the order, since he had received no oral or written warning from the local authority (1956 Act, s. 30).   This is a curious reversal of the principle that ignorance of the law is normally no valid excuse, whereas ignorance of fact may be so.   However, the purpose of the Act in this instance appears to be to ensure that the local authority informs all inhabitants, at the outset, of a smoke control order.

The penalties imposed as to dark smoke from chimneys (1956 Act, s. 27) are: (i) in the case of a private dwelling, £20 (or £100 if " more than one " chimney smoking); (ii) in the case of trade or commercial properties, £100 and/or up to three months' imprisonment.   These penalties are to be imposed by the county court, which may, at the same time, order remedial works to be carried out.

Where the dark smoke arises from bonfires a less severe penalty is imposed (1956 Act, s. 16) of a maximum fine of £10 plus £5 for each day the offence is continued.

The effect of the Clean Air Acts is further extended by the Clean Air (Emission of Grit and Dust from Furnaces) Regulations, 1971 (S.I. 1971 No. 162) which, for the first time (by reg. 4 and Sched. 1) specify the maximum permitted quantities of grit and dust which may be emitted by an industrial furnace in terms of pounds weight per hour.   The highest rate listed, 250 lb. per hour, applies to a furnace (burning solid matter) of 475,000 lb. steam/hr.

A draft order has been published, and a public inquiry held, to add five noxious processes which produce poisonous fumes to those required to be registered under the Alkali Act, 1906, as amended, notably a number of plastic and mineral processes; and also in relation to the discharge and storage of oil and the primary melting of aluminium.

The remaining sources of air pollution are from the combustion of *fuel used in propulsion of land vehicles and aircraft,* and from dust. The latter will be discussed in the second part of this chapter—The Pollution of Land.

In effect the principal source of pollution from exhaust gases is from motor vehicles, but it is particularly significant that there appears to be no statutory remedy against the emission of " dark smoke " from aircraft, although the larger type of " non-jumbo " jet aeroplane (e.g., Boeing 707) is said to emit, on take-off, as much as the exhausts of 1,000 cars for the equivalent period of time.   This is clearly a matter of public concern.   For the sake of completeness, it should be remarked that there appears also to be no restriction upon emission of smoke and fumes from railway engines (diesel or steam) or from ships' funnels; but the pollution caused is so proportionately slight that legislation would hardly be justified.

Control of motor vehicles as to exhaust gases lies entirely with the Department of the Environment by various rules and orders made under s. 40 of the Road Traffic Act, 1972 (previously under s. 64 of the Road Traffic Act, 1960), namely, the Motor Vehicles (Construction and Use) Regulations, 1973 (S.I. 1973 No. 24).[6]   These require that " compression ignition engines " be constructed so as " to prevent any avoidable emission of smoke or vapour " (regs. 31 to 34).   In the case of solid fuel motor vehicles (e.g., steamrollers), there must be an appliance to trap sparks and grit, and also a means of prevention of the deposit of ashes and cinders upon the road (reg. 35).

The method of checking the rate of emission of exhaust fumes is, at present, purely visual, but instruments are being developed for use in the annual motor vehicle road test.   As to diesel engines specifically, the Minister has agreed on a British Standard (BS/AU 141) of manufacture, and this will, in due course, be enforced by regulation.   As yet there is no legislation to control emissions from the gas combustion vehicles which may be expected to become generally used on the roads in the next decade.[7]

The penalty for contravention of regs. 31 to 35 is imposed under

---

[6] Replacing the similarly named Regulations of 1969 (S.I. 1969 No. 321) as amended.

[7] The increase in use of electrically driven, battery supplied vehicles especially in towns is also to be anticipated, and will have the immense advantage of almost total avoidance of air pollution and of noise.

s. 41 of the Road Traffic Act, 1972, and consists of a fine of £50 upon summary conviction.

A continuous study of air pollution from all sources was initiated by Circular No. 12/61 which invited local authorities to participate by either taking measurements themselves under the said scheme; or contributing towards the cost of the services provided (in taking comparative measurements) by the Department of Scientific and Industrial Research; or both. The monthly bulletins of the D.S.I.R. provide such measurements on a comparative basis for most significant areas of the country.

2. Pollution of the Land

In the broadest sense it can be said that the quality of the soil and/or surface of land (certainly in our insular climate) is principally affected in the following ways:

(1) by bad or ill-considered methods of agriculture, so as to cause a gradual deterioration in the structure and chemical content of the soil itself;

(2) by deliberate deposit of solid or liquid waste materials upon the land;

(3)   by the deposit of harmful substances carried either (i) in the air; or (ii) in water passing over, or percolating through, the soil.

A great deal of technical comment could be made about these three causes and the practicable methods of prevention, but the following semi-scientific discussion is included here merely for the purpose of illustrating the legal and administrative methods of control which exist, or which could be introduced. The three types of land pollution will now be separately discussed.

(1) *Pollution of land by bad or ill-considered methods of agriculture*

All types of husbandry which actively use the soil (that is, do not simply use an area of land merely as a concrete-surfaced or other barren area, as in, say, broiler chicken housing) rely upon the ability of soil to grow vegetation, whether this vegetation be grass, corn or root crops such as potatoes. Thus, the output even of a purely stock, or dairy, farm[8] is related to the soil structure and chemical content quite as much as an arable farm—save that, in

[8] The majority of stock and dairy farms tend to break the cycle of grass leys by growing barley, etc., in suitable fields.

modern stock-rearing and dairying, large quantities of food concentrates[9] are imported onto the farm.   Even in this case, however,
the total cost of imported concentrates is directly linked to the
volume and quality of grass, hay, silage and silo-fed grass produced;
and of barley and oats grown and milled on the farm for use themselves as concentrates.

Since the last war, and initially inspired by war-time needs for
intensive production, farmers (and other agriculturalists, including
horticulturalists) have tended increasingly to use the soil basically
as an inert growing medium in which crops are produced by the
addition of artificial fertilisers[9] containing all or any of the three
basic chemical requirements for plant growth, nitrates, phosphates
and potash, with essential " trace elements " often added.   The
tendency has been to avoid the application of old-fashioned farmyard manure or slurry for three principal reasons: (i) the cost of
labour involved; (ii) the tendency for manure to carry weed seeds
back onto the land; and (iii), in certain areas, the total absence of
stock from " corn farms."   In addition it has been fashionable in
many areas to burn stubble, rather than to plough it in.[10]

Whilst such methods, when combined with the continuing research and improvement of strains of grass, corn and rootcrops,[11]
have often produced vastly greater yields per acre, it is now clear
that, in many parts of the country, the soil structure is becoming
broken down, so that even increased applications of artificial
fertilisers do not maintain the yield, notably of wheat and barley.

This is, in the simplest terms, due to the need for humus, which
was once invariably supplied by the addition of farmyard manure
and/or by the ploughing-in of green crops.   Humus is required for
effective plant growth for two essential reasons: (1) it adds " body "
to the soil, so as to prevent the soil particles from becoming either
mere dust[12] or so compacted that water, oxygen and food chemicals
cannot enter; and (ii), equally important, it supplies one of the
essential needs in the physical process of plant growth in that it
supports the nitrogenous bacteria which live in the region of the
plant roots and convert the natural nitrogen in the soil to a soluble

[9] Many of which come from overseas.
[10] The ploughing-in of stubble does not, however, serve quite the same purpose
as the ploughing-in of green crops.
[11] Similarly, the hereditary factor is known to be of immense importance in stock
and milk production.
[12] And also thus subject to wind erosion: see p. 171.

form in which it can, by osmosis, be absorbed into those roots.[13]   In contrast, much land on which artificial fertiliser has been exclusively used for many years is becoming incapable of holding nitrates for sufficiently long in the region of the roots of a crop for it to be absorbed; in fact the nitrates in solution " leach "; that is, pass through the top soil and become lost in the sub-soil into which the roots never penetrate.

In short, it is possible to damage agricultural soil (i) by altering the chemical content, and (ii) by altering the physical structure.   In striking an economic and scientific balance between " traditional " agricultural methods and modern techniques it should not be forgotten that the British climate, whilst unreliable within limits, represents our greatest agricultural asset.[14]

The economic pressures which have influenced agriculturalists generally are, first, the ever-increasing cost of labour which causes a parallel tendency towards mechanisation; and, secondly, the policy of successive British governments since the 1939–45 war to provide " cheap food " by means of a system of grants and subsidies run in combination with the fixing of prices for home-grown agricultural produce.   This financial system has persuaded agriculturalists to increase their output per acre by the use of artificial fertilisers (as already discussed); by the use of maximum mechanisation which may, when heavy machines are used on soil during unsuitable weather conditions, cause a physical deterioration in soil structure; and also by the use, in order to prevent possible losses in the crop, of chemical insecticides and weedkillers.   The control of those insecticides and weedkillers which are potentially harmful to the ecology of a given area will be discussed later (at p. 172).   In any event, the change of policy away from subsidies as a result of entry into the European Economic Community will tend to alter the techniques employed in production.

It is hoped that this expedition into the science (or art) of agriculture will be forgiven by the reader, since its purpose is to illuminate the following series of comments.

At present, control of the agricultural techniques to be applied

---

[13] It should be noted that some grassland is " permanent pasture," never disturbed by the plough, which, due to nitrogenous bacteria, has its own perpetual, and often heavy, crops of grass.

[14] Particularly in terms of ability to grow grass, and more generally in the development and rehabilitation of fertile soils.

on any given farm or other agricultural holding is extremely limited. Indeed, the independence of character of most agriculturalists would cause them to be strongly opposed to a greater degree of governmental or local planning authority direction. The present elements of control are partly a matter of legal sanction and partly by means of financial inducement or coercion. They are principally as follows:

(i) *Control by the local planning and the local highways authorities* [15] is limited in the former case to exercise of aesthetic discretion in relation to buildings and trees; and in the latter to the generation, and movement and safety, of road traffic, as to which see Chapters 1 and 5.

(ii) *Control by the courts in respect of common-law and statutory nuisances*, as to which see Chapter 6 at p. 123 *et seq.*

(iii) *Control by the local authority under Public Health legislation* where the system, or lack of system, applied results in danger to human health, either from proximity of dwellings to unhygienic stock housing; or as a result of the contamination of milk, meat, vegetables or other produce. As to this see Chapters 1 and 6 (p. 131 *et seq.*).

(iv) *Control of an agricultural tenant by his landlord under the Agricultural Holdings Act*, 1948. This control is extremely limited.[16] A tenant of an agricultural holding, as defined by s. 1 of the 1948 Act,[17] has considerable—one might say immense—security of tenure. In the simplest (and therefore not entirely accurate) terms, whenever agricultural land is let for the purpose of agriculture, it will probably be construed, under the 1948 Act, as a type of tenancy from year to year which is automatically renewed without any initiative from the tenant, and can only be discontinued (*a*) with the approval of the Agricultural Land Tribunal [18]; or (*b*) for one

---

[15] Both these elements of local government are now co-ordinated at ministerial level in the Department of the Environment.

[16] Naturally, the war-time powers exercised between 1939 and 1945, whereby both owners of agricultural freeholds and tenants could be dispossessed for inefficient farming, no longer apply.

[17] This definition is linked to the definition of " agriculture " given in s. 94 (1) of the 1948 Act, which includes, in addition to the more common farming uses, horticulture, market and nursery gardening, fruit growing, seed growing and the cultivation of osier beds, hop gardens, etc.

[18] The machinery under the 1948 Act provides that, upon receiving a notice to quit, the tenant may within twenty-eight days issue a counter-notice under s. 24, requiring that the case be heard by the Tribunal. In any event, the notice to quit must be given prior to the appropriate anniversary date and then allow

of the seven statutorily defined reasons discussed below. The extent of this security of tenure becomes evident on considering s. 2 of the Act, which provides that even where the letting of agricultural land is for a period of less than one year it will be enlarged into a tenancy from year to year (as described above) except (*a*) where prior consent to a shorter, fixed period is obtained from the Minister of Agriculture, or (*b*) where the letting or licence is in contemplation of a use specified as one of the following: " for grazing or mowing during some specified period of the year " (s. 2 (1)), and even then, the agreement must not extend for longer than two seasons.

The seven situations which enable the landlord to give an effective notice to quit without prior reference to the Agricultural Land Tribunal are: where the tribunal have already, but for some other reason, given consent to a notice to quit; where planning permission for a non-agricultural use of the land has been obtained; where the tenant is not farming in accordance with the " rules of good husbandry " [19]; where the tenant is two months in arrear with rent after a demand has been made in writing [20]; where the tenant has committed any other serious breach of covenant; where the tenant becomes bankrupt; or where the tenant dies within three months preceding the giving of a notice to quit.[21]

(v) *Control by the Ministry of Agriculture, Fisheries and Food* by means of combined financial and administrative restrictions in making

twelve months before the holding be vacated.   Thus, if notice to quit is given one day after the anniversary date, possession will not be obtained for one year and 364 days.   The Agricultural Land Tribunals are drawn from local panels and consist of a legally-qualified chairman and one representative each of farm tenants and agricultural landowners, none having an " interest " in the case.

[19] The " rules of good husbandry " as set out in s. 11, and applied by the Agricultural Land Tribunal (under s. 27) allow the tenant considerable latitude: he is not necessarily required to be totally efficient, merely to avoid gross inefficiency. Where a Certificate of Bad Husbandry is relied upon, the Certificate must be actually issued before a notice to quit can be validly given.

[20] Farm rents are usually paid upon an annual figure but in half-yearly instalments, as for example, at Lady Day (25th March) and Michaelmas (29th September).   In such cases the rent normally becomes overdue to the extent required under the 1948 Act when the half-yearly instalment is two months overdue.

[21] Thus, providing the landlord hears of the death of his tenant and gives valid notice within the three months following, he can obtain possession without recourse to the tribunal.   If he fails to do so in time he may find that the tribunal will support an assignment or bequest to a third party made by the tenant in the event of his death.

improvement grants.[22] This aspect of the legal or quasi-legal control of farming techniques is, in a sense, more appropriate for discussion under Chapter 12 (The Needs of Landscaping and the Design of Buildings) or under Chapter 3 (The Countryside— Agriculture), to which reference should be made. However, for the sake of completeness here, the following short comments may be made.

Buildings, yards and fixed equipment.[23]—The use of these permanent or semi-permanent structures will clearly influence the method of use of the actual soil on the holding. Thus, the construction of, for example, a tower silo for chopped grass will tend (within the limited life of that structure) to cause the farmer to grow probably more grass and less corn. Conversely, the construction of either a tower silo for damp grain storage (for subsequent cattle fodder), or of a grain drier will commit the farmer to production of a certain acreage of corn. In this respect, therefore, the approval of a type of installation or building by the Ministry for purposes of a Farm Improvement Grant will influence the local use of the soil.

Natural features and ancient man-made features.—The presence of natural features, such as natural woodland and natural forms of land drainage, and equally the presence of ancient man-made features, such as Saxon hedgerows, medieval dykes, and planted or tended forestry, has a definite influence upon the soil conditions and micro-climate on any agricultural holding. The alteration of drainage (or the alteration of rainfall by the felling or planting of large areas of trees) through the increase or decrease of moisture in the soil will eventually affect the structure and chemical content of that soil. Such alterations tend, if carried out with forethought, to be advantageous, but it is, for example, possible to alter the balance of production on a holding. Thus, an ancient water meadow, which has long produced heavy crops of grass from a permanent pasture, may be altered by excessive drainage to a field suitable only for the production of corn requiring the use of artificial fertilisers, planting of seed and the use of heavy machines.

---

[22] The powers of the Ministry of Agriculture, Fisheries and Food are in very few cases mandatory and, by contrast, tend to be persuasive. In the United States of America, however, there is considerable power of positive control of farming methods in each State, under the combined influence of the State Boards of Agriculture, of Natural Resources, and of Health, and the Federal Department of Agriculture.

[23] This subsection, and also subsection (2) below, should be read in conjunction with Chapter 3.

Again, the grubbing-out of hedgerows (disregarding here the simultaneous infilling of ditches) can, where the fields thus created are extremely large, make the farmer absolutely reliant upon the regular and perpetual use of insecticides for the simple reason that those birds which act as natural predators upon insects do not, and physically cannot, include the field centre within their feeding range.

In terms of protection of the environment, there are effective means of protection of both individual trees, small groups of trees and of areas of woodland (see Chapter 15). There is also control of abstraction of water and, in practice to a more limited extent, control of land drainage (see Chapter 8). But there is, at present, no environmental control over the removal of hedgerows, no matter whether identifiable in Domesday Book or no, and it would be of advantage in some cases if, even though curious in description, a hedge were capable of registration as an ancient monument, as are tumuli and ancient stones. In recent years about 5,000 miles of hedgerow have been removed annually, either for the ever-increasing enlargement of fields, or as a means of reducing labour demand in hedge laying and trimming by replacement with barbed wire. Farm improvement grants can be given for this purpose, and the only form of sanction against hedgerow removal is by the refusal of such payment.

The use of chemical fertilisers, weedkillers, fungicides, and other chemicals. —It is increasingly clear even to the least informed layman that a proportion of chemical products used for these purposes are toxic not only to local flora and fauna but also to man. Insecticides of certain types can eventually build up within the bodies of insectivorous birds and thereby also poison hawks and other useful predators. Weedkillers used upon crops can, unless strictly controlled, drift onto adjoining land and there kill some or all of the natural flora. Such initial effects as these have a chain reaction. The absence of insects in an area will result in the absence of all insectivorous birds and of the birds and animals which prey upon them. The absence of weeds may remove both food and protective cover for further chains of bird—and animal—life. Thus the balance of nature is destroyed, and any later failure by man may permit, for example, an epidemic of insect pests uncontrolled by any natural predators.

At present there is no legal control of the manufacture or use of agricultural chemicals, although statutory means are under consideration. There exists the Advisory Committee on Pesticides and Other Toxic Chemicals, which has a continuous duty to keep informed and to advise the Minister of Agriculture, but restriction of use by the farmer is almost solely by restriction on availability of the chemical substance through manufacturers and merchants. In recent years the manufacturers have voluntarily withdrawn supplies and ceased generally to manufacture such products as Aldrin, Dieldrin and Heptachlor; and they have restricted the supply of DDT. The Farm and Garden Chemicals Act, 1967, does, however, provide for regulations to be made as to the clear labelling of such chemical products as to hazards in their use and application.

(2) *Pollution of land by the deliberate deposit of solid or liquid waste upon the land*

(*Note*: As to deposit of agricultural chemicals as part of the farming system, see the immediately preceding paragraphs.) Where the dumping can be clearly proved to be a trespass, or a public or private nuisance, or to result from an '' escape from land '' under the rule in *Rylands* v. *Fletcher*, and if the identity of the perpetrator can be established, an action will lie at common law. As to this see Chapter 6.

However, one by-product of the '' affluent society '' is the increasing tendency for persons unknown to dump waste, notably in the form of old cars, rubber tyres, and bedsteads either upon public land (roadside verges), or upon the private land of another. This tendency has been increased by the scarcity of large scale scrap dealers, particularly in rural areas.[24] In addition, the burning of rubber tyres is now strictly controlled [25] and cannot normally be carried out even in a scrap yard.

To meet the problem, the Civic Amenities Act, 1967, by s. 23, now requires the local authority (at urban or rural district level) to collect and dispose of such '' abandoned matter '' at the expense of the local ratepayer. Such a requirement will be of greatest importance, although of increasing expense, in the disposal of plastic food and drink containers, which are increasingly littering

---

[24] Thus, it may in fact be impossible even to give away a damaged or very old car. Further, for a scrap dealer to operate in a rural area upon an economic basis it must be possible to attract a sufficiently large volume of trade to justify the cost of car breaking and consolidation of waste materials for transport to industrial centres.

[25] See p. 160, *ante*.

the countryside.[26]   However, the Litter Act, 1958, and the Dangerous Litter Act, 1971, impose penalties of up to £100.   Further, by the Deposit of Poisonous Waste Act, 1972, and orders made thereunder, types of poisonous waste are listed—the Deposit of Poisonous Waste (Notification of Removal or Deposit) Regulations, 1972 (S.I. 1972 No. 1017)—and a general prohibition is imposed upon any deposit " liable to give rise to an environmental hazard " (s. 1).   The extent of civil liability is increased (s. 2) ; and a duty to keep records, and to notify the local authority of any such removal or deposit is imposed (s. 3).   Failure so to do is an offence subject to a fine of not exceeding £400.   As to the duty of disposal (but not collection) of all waste after the re-organisation of local government in 1974, the Local Government Act, 1972, provides that this shall become the duty of each county authority; the duty of collection remaining with the new districts.

Difficulties also arise where solid waste is deposited upon the private land of the possessor of the waste matter.   This situation has existed since early in the last century in relation to slag and other spoil heaps, but can be better discussed in the context of extractive industries; see Chapter 4.

In the case of liquid waste being spread upon land,[27] however, the problem should be considered here.   An aspect of increasing importance is the construction and use by agriculturalists of intensive stock housing.   The slurry or more solid waste produced in or adjoining buildings must annually be removed and disposed of. This can be either by the creation of a slurry or dung pit (the old " midden "), where the waste liquid tends to drain off into the adjoining soil; or by the construction of a slurry lagoon which is lined with polythene and has a large liquid surface area, whereby the contents is reduced in volume due to surface evaporation; or by the use of slurry pits and tanks which can be pumped out either into tankers or into a piped irrigation system.

It will be seen that the disposal problem arises either in the immediate vicinity of the slurry pit, or in terms of spreading the liquid or solid matter as manure, and there is therefore a tendency, in some cases, to poison soil by continuous and concentrated application of these substances.   However, the effect of a technique upon

---

[26] Certain types of plastic container are said to disintegrate in sunlight, but it is probable that they then produce toxic substances.

[27] As distinct from discharged into water, as to which see Chapter 7.

the user's own land is not subject to control except (i) where the waste liquid passes into underground water or any watercourse, as to which see Chapter 7; or (ii) where there is an offence under Public Health legislation, as to which see also Chapter 7. In regard to the spreading of dung or liquid manure upon land, it is also worthy of note that a mere temporary, although regularly repeated, nuisance by smell or the presence of flies is unlikely to provide a successful cause of action at common law.

(3) *Pollution of land by the deposit of harmful substances carried either (i) in the air; or (ii) in water passing over or percolating through the soil*

It will be evident that substances carried in the air will arise from those sources already discussed under " Pollution of the Air " (this chapter, section 1), but certain further aspects will be considered below. Again, the pollution of soil resulting from the presence, or passage, of polluted water must be directly related to the general subject of water pollution already discussed in Chapter 7, to which reference should be made. Further consideration is not required here.

The aspect of airborne pollution which may appropriately be considered at this point is the creation of quarry and industrial dust.[28] The creation of dust by quarrying or other similar activities is a statutory nuisance by virtue of s. 100 of the Public Health Act, 1936, under which the local authority must serve an abatement order on the person by whose act, default or sufferance the nuisance arises or continues; or, if that person cannot be found, on the owner or occupier of the quarry or similar premises (ss. 283–285). If that person is subsequently in default, or if the local authority reasonably believes the nuisance is likely to recur, the matter may either be brought before a magistrates' court, or legal proceedings for a mandatory order may be brought in the High Court. The Act provides that the former method is to be preferred where possible. The magistrates' court will then make a nuisance order and may also impose a fine not exceeding £20. If there is any subsequent failure to comply with the nuisance order a further fine will be imposed not exceeding £50 and £5 for each day on which the offence continues after conviction therefor. Lastly under the 1936 Act, the local authority is empowered, once a nuisance order has been made, to enter and abate the nuisance and subsequently to recover the cost

[28] See also Chapter 4, extractive industries; and Chapter 8 (1), air pollution.

from the person named in the order (s. 96). In the case of mines and quarries, however, it is specifically provided under the Act that where the " person named " in the abatement order is not the owner, then the person named may later recover the cost from the owner under s. 151 (3) of the Mines and Quarries Act, 1954.[28]

A rather similar type of land pollution occurs where there is an airborne deposit of dust, ashes or clinker from industrial or other sources, and provision is made for remedy under the Clean Air (Measurement of Dust and Grit from Furnaces) Regulations, 1971 (S.I. 1971 No. 161) and the Clean Air (Emission of Dust and Grit from Furnaces) Regulations, 1971 (S.I. 1971 No. 162). By these two sets of regulations it is an offence to emit more than a specified weight of solid matter resulting from combustion. The maximum amount permitted is related to the size of the furnace measured either in " Maximum Continuous Rating in pounds of steam per hour (from and at 100 deg. C or 212 deg. F)," or in thousands of British Thermal Units per hour. For example, a rating of 825 permits a deposit of 1.10 lb per hour if solid fuel is being burnt (only 0.25 lb. per hour if liquid fuel), whereas the maximum rating catered for by the Regulations of 475,000 (a large power station) may lawfully emit up to 250 lb. of solid matter per hour where solid fuel is burnt (or 57 lb. per hour if liquid fuel). The Regulations also restrict the maximum size of the particles of solid emitted.

Difficulties arise, however, where the source of pollution cannot easily be traced. Chemical liquids may be sprayed, particularly from aircraft, and carried by unexpected winds on air currents onto adjoining or other land and, in such cases, it may be impossible to prove adequately in a court of law that the defendant was responsible rather than some other party who was also using the same chemical spray. To remedy cases of this type, therefore, there might well be a valid argument for the setting-up of a suitable tribunal for the purpose of advising the appropriate Minister as to the need for restricting, or prohibiting, the use of the given chemical in a certain locality. In other words, the aggrieved party, upon proof of persistent pollution of his crops or land, could thereby obtain protection against the future activities of his several neighbours.

CHAPTER 9

POLLUTION BY NOISE;
NUCLEAR POLLUTION

1. Pollution by Noise[1] (and by Vibration)

Noise has been defined in the final report of the Committee on the Problem of Noise [2] as " sound which is undesired by the recipient." It may therefore arise from an immense variety of sources, but those of the greatest and most frequent significance to the ordinary member of the public are: (1) industrial processes; (2) road traffic; and (3) air traffic. These three will be discussed in some detail below.

The other, lesser, sources of noise range in the legal sense from, for example, explosive bird scarers designed to protect crops, through mobile sources, such as loudspeakers mounted on vehicles, to relatively common and permanent sources, such as church bells and railway shunting yards. At common law any noise may generally be actionable in nuisance (as to which see Chapter 6) provided it is sufficient to cause " substantial interference with health, comfort or convenience." [3] It is not necessary to prove a positive effect upon the physical well-being of the plaintiff.

A common-law action would nowadays tend to be brought in the Queen's Bench Division. In practical terms a nuisance by noise will be best remedied usually in that Division, although not by damages, but by an injunction to restrain the defendant. However the cost, and particularly the delay, involved in a civil action has prompted the passing of the Noise Abatement Act, 1960, which, by s. 1, declares noise or vibration [4] to be a statutory nuisance [5] under the

---

[1] The rather curious title of this section, which is presumably a shortened form of " pollution of silence by noise " (!), is taken from the classification of forms of pollution adopted by the Department of the Environment.

[2] Cmnd. 2056.

[3] *Vanderpant* v. *Mayfair Hotel Co., Ltd.* [1930] 1 Ch. 138. But see also *Christie* v. *Davy* [1893] 1 Ch. 316—the existence of " malice " may be taken into account.

[4] Since noise is merely a form of vibration, the dividing line in practice (and in physical effect) may on occasion be very narrow. See also the extension to the rule in *Rylands* v. *Fletcher* by the decision in *Hoard* v. *McAlpine, Ltd.* [1923] 1 Ch. 167—vibrations from pile-driving to be within that rule.

[5] With the specific exception, by s. 1 (7) of the 1960 Act, of noise from aircraft, this being covered specifically by the Civil Aviation Act, 1949, ss. 40 and 41, etc. (see (3) Air Traffic, *post*).

Public Health Act, 1936, Pt. III, as to which see Chapter 6 at p. 133. A statutory nuisance under the Public Health Act does, however, require to be proved upon the same basis as at common law; but the Act offers the advantages, first that the initiative can be taken (and is intended to be taken) by the local authority even without a prior complaint being lodged with them; and secondly that the offender may be suitably persuaded by means of successive fines.[6]

When remedial steps taken by the person responsible for causing a noise nuisance are deemed by the local authority to be ineffective, it will be a valid defence to subsequent proceedings under the 1936 Act to plead that reliance had been placed upon the advice of technical experts.[7]   Thus, this defence will apply to actions following the issue of an abatement notice[8] under s. 93 of the Act, and to those following the making of a subsequent nuisance order[8] by the local magistrates' court under s. 94 of the Act.   (But note that such a defence will not lie in a civil action for nuisance at common law.) So far as statutory nuisance only is concerned, where the " best practicable means " have been employed to abate it, the court may take into account, in deciding the issue, the cost of any further means of remedy relative to local conditions.[9]

In accordance with general principle, statutory undertakers are in no special position with regard to responsibility for noise: they have a duty to avoid creating it except where they are authorised to do so by Parliament; and, further, the " best practicable means " plea does not apply to them.

However, an extremely important change in the position of the liability to pay compensation which will be incurred in future by public works authorities—and notably in respect of new highways and of airports, as well as other types of works—is introduced by the Land Compensation Bill, at present before Parliament (December, 1972).   The Bill was inspired by an unfortunate history of adverse physical planning situations, such as those arising out of the construction of the Hammersmith flyover in London, in which the owners and occupiers of dwellings situated within only a few yards of the

---

6 Although these are, in some circumstances, not adequate where very prompt remedial action is to be encouraged.

7 *Saddleworth U.D.C.* v. *Aggregate Sand, Ltd.* (1970), 114 S.J. 931.

8 Abatement notices are issued by the local authority and, if not acted upon, application is made to the magistrates for a nuisance order.

9 *Walter* v. *Selfe* (1851), 4 De G. & Sm. 315.

new, elevated traffic route could obtain no compensation (other than *ex gratia*), unless some part of their property had, in fact, been acquired in connection with the highway construction. The provisions of the Bill are set out at p. 117, *ante*.

It is, perhaps, appropriate to mention here the provisions of s. 2 of the Noise Abatement Act, 1960, which seek to control a number of fairly common sources of noise. Thus, it becomes a statutory nuisance to operate a loudspeaker in the street between the hours of 9 p.m. and 8 a.m. or to operate one at any time for certain specified purposes, such as for advertising entertainment, trade or business. However, the same section provides that it shall be permissible to do so for police, fire, or other emergency reasons (s. 2 (2)); and it is also lawful for a travelling showman to operate loudspeakers on any land which is used for a pleasure fair.

The three specific sources mentioned at the outset of this Chapter will now be considered:

(1) *Noise from industrial processes*

In the case of noise produced by existing industrial plant, control is principally exercised through the Factory Inspectorate which is a body responsible to the Secretary of State for Employment (previously the Minister of Labour) under the Factories Act, 1961 (consolidating earlier Acts). Industrial noise is now " rated " by means of a British Standard method wherever a problem affects a mixed industrial and residential area; and this will be applied by the Inspectorate. However, it must also be noted that the " factory " must be as defined in s. 175 of the 1961 Act, namely premises in which people are employed in manual labour in the course of " trade or business " (i.e., there must be a profit motive, whether for personal gain or for charitable reasons) and the process must consist of either the making of any article,[10] or part of an article; or the alteration or repair, ornamenting, finishing, cleaning, washing, freezing, packing or canning, or adapting for sale, or breaking up or demolition of any article; or (without prejudice to the foregoing) the getting, dressing or preparation for sale of minerals or the extraction or preparation for sale of oil or brine. (The above is, in fact, a far less specific paraphrase of s. 175 of the Factories Act, 1961, but it is put in this form to show that it coincides, in effect, with the definition given by s. 66 of the Town and Country Planning Act,

[10] Of any description, e.g., includes a ship.

1971, and related Acts with regard to Industrial Development Control discussed below.)

Under the 1961 Act, inspectors have a right of access to factory premises and may even require a police officer to accompany them if necessary. They also have power to bring prosecutions under the Act in magistrates' courts (s. 164) and any fines imposed are to be deemed to be Exchequer moneys.

Planning Control.—Of greater significance, however, in the prevention of industrial noise, are the provisions for planning control, which may where appropriate prevent the construction or extension of an industrial building on any given site. These special means of control were introduced by the Town and Country Planning Act, 1962, in relation to the erection of both factories and offices. Subsequent provisions are now, however, " scattered about the Statute Book." [11]   They are to be found in ss. 66 to 72 of the Town and Country Planning Act, 1971, and ss. 19 to 22 of the Control of Office and Industrial Development Act, 1965; together with the Town and Country Planning (Use Classes) Order, 1972 (S.I. 1972 No. 1385), notably Class III and Class IV; and the Town and Country Planning General Development Order, 1973 (S.I. 1973 No. 31),[11a] notably Class VIII. In addition, s. 21 of the Local Employment Act, 1960, and the Public Health (Recurring Nuisances) Act, 1969, are relevant.

Where the proposed industrial development consists either of the erection of a building (other than mere replacement); or the change of use of a building so that, in both cases, the building together with any " related development " will comprise an " industrial " floor space [12] in excess of 15,000 square feet (in certain areas 10,000 square feet)[13] and is of a class indicated from time to time in regulations made by the Department of Trade and Industry, a certificate must be first obtained from the Department of Trade and Industry to the effect that the development will be consistent with the proper distribution of industry.[14] Such a document is known as an *Industrial Development Certificate* (or " I.D.C.").

[11] Sir Desmond Heap, *An Outline of Planning Law*, 1969, at p. 171.
[11a] Replacing the Town and Country Planning General Development Order, 1963, as amended.
[12] Town and Country Planning Act, 1971, ss. 68 (1), (2) and (3); S.I. 1972 No. 996.   See p. 47.
[13] See p. 45.
[14] Town and Country Planning Act, 1971, ss. 66 to 72.

The regulations governing the issue of I.D.C.s by the Department of Trade and Industry are the Town and Country Planning (Erection of Industrial Buildings) Regulations, 1966,[15] and it is at present prescribed that they shall apply to all types of "industrial building" as defined by s. 66 of the Town and Country Planning Act, 1971 (see p. 46).   But the term "industrial building" also means [16] any building used or designed for use for the carrying on of scientific research in the course of a trade or business.

Once an I.D.C. is obtained, it is then necessary to make a planning application in the normal way but also to furnish the local planning authority with a copy of the certificate; unless such copy is furnished, the application is to be of no effect (s. 67 (1) of the 1971 Act).

No appeal will lie from a decision by the Department of Trade and Industry against the issue of an I.D.C. (s. 67 of the 1971 Act). Further, the Department is empowered to attach conditions to the certificate (ss. 70 and 71 of the 1971 Act) and, in such cases, the conditions will be binding not only on the developer, but also on the local planning authority if that authority grants planning approval.

However, there is no onus upon the local planning authority to approve the development in the planning sense merely because an I.D.C. has been issued.   The principle is that the Department of Trade and Industry is concerned only with the overall national balance of industry and is not expected to consider more localised problems which, in many cases, must inevitably arise in the town and country planning sense.

Thus, a local planning authority to whom application for permission to develop is made, whilst required by statute to receive an I.D.C. in such cases, will otherwise ignore the existence of the certificate in arriving at a planning decision, unless that certificate contains conditions imposed by the Department of Trade and Industry.

(It may be appropriate to interpolate here the comment that a residential neighbour who creates noise as a result solely of a non-profitmaking mechanical pastime cannot be restrained by any provisions in planning legislation.   But action can, in most cases, be taken under the Public Health (Recurring Nuisances) Act, 1969, and at common law.)

[15] S.I. 1966 No. 1034.
[16] Town and Country Planning Act, 1971, s. 66.

It is, however, important to note that a loophole exists in the present planning controls which does, on some occasions, have most unfortunate consequences, especially in either Green Belt or predominantly residential areas. Under the General Development Order, Class VIII, it is permissible for an industrial building to be extended by up to one-tenth of its original capacity without seeking planning approval, provided that (i) the external appearance of the building is not " materially affected "; and (ii) an I.D.C. is not required (i.e., the total area of industrial floor space inclusive of the extension will not exceed 15,000 square feet).[17] The significance of the latitude permitted by the Order is most hardly felt either where the extension brings disturbing noise nearer to a dwelling, or where the extension becomes greater by means of reduction in the original industrial floor area in order to avoid the need to apply for an I.D.C. Further (with certain exceptions),[17a] where the right to extend by one-tenth is exercised, there is no provision whereby the local planning authority can require tree screening of the extension unless it first adjudges that the external appearance of the industrial building is " materially affected " by the extension.

(2) *Noise and vibration from road traffic*

The question of control of the flow and volume of road traffic is discussed in Chapter 5 on transport, but it is appropriate to comment here that there is still a need for greater thought and control in relation to the routeing of heavy vehicles, particularly so as to avoid certain types of urban or village streets, where the vibration and noise echo may be extreme, and may well not be adequately measured by the present system of measurement taken at ground level. However, the recent creation of the Department of the Environment will (by co-ordinating the functions of the previous Ministry of Transport and the Ministry of Housing and Local Government) make it possible to increase supervision of the use of highways in relation to the amenity effect upon adjoining land and structures.

Control of noise generated by road vehicles is exercised under the Motor Vehicles (Construction and Use) Regulations, 1973 (S.I. 1973 No. 24),[18] made by virtue of s. 40 of the Road Traffic Act,

[17] Or 10,000 square feet in London and other specified areas (*ante*).
[17a] Three National Parks (p. 294, *post*) and some Areas of Outstanding Natural Beauty (p. 308, *post*).
[18] See p. 165.

1972, which section is concerned with the regulation of weight, equipment and use of road vehicles.

By regs. 29, 106 and 107, it is an offence for any vehicle to generate when travelling upon the open road a noise in excess of 89 decibels (dBA)[19] at a horizontal distance of 25 feet[20] except (i) either where prior arrangement has been made with the Secretary of State [21]; or where the vehicle is a road roller (reg. 29 (2)).   However, further restriction is applied in the case of motor cars, which must not exceed 84 dBA; and motorcycles, where the permitted maximum is 86 dBA.

It is also the policy of the Department of the Environment to reduce these maxima to 80 dBA for lorries, and 75 dBA for motor-cars and motor-cycles, thereby approximately halving the noise apparent to the human ear.

Clearly, however, the ever-increasing number of vehicles using the roads in this country creates a mounting problem in relation to enforcement of the Regulations, especially since the police forces are considerably undermanned.   Once an offence can be established (which necessitates the use of the required apparatus) the maximum penalty is £50 upon summary conviction (s. 40 of Road Traffic Act, 1972).   But the most practicable means of control by the Department must lie at the stage of original construction of vehicles, both as to their design and as to their maximum size, and it is said that manufacturers have been persuaded to aim, in due course, for the noise criteria given above.   At the same time, however, heavy lorry manufacturers are seeking to increase the size of the largest lorries, upon the basis that these are necessary as part of the modern pattern of containerised cargo carried in ships, whereby cargo is packed in large containers at point of manufacture and is intended to remain so packed for subsequent handling and transport.

Under s. 40, the Secretary of State has power to regulate the

[19] The standard unit of measurement of sound is in decibels (dB), but for road traffic an " A " weighting scale is added, i.e., a factor to allow for the sensitivity of the human ear to a given band of frequencies: thus the unit of measurement to be employed for this purpose is signified as dBA.   Decibels work on a logarithmic scale; thus, e.g.: 80 dBA is creating ten times as much noise as 70 dBA; or an increase of 3 dBA roughly doubles the noise energy.   But the human ear judges an increase of 9 dBA to be about twice as loud.

[20] The method of measurement to be employed in relation to road vehicles is given in reg. 29 and Sched. 9.   This specifies the type, size and positioning of the noise-measuring apparatus.   Maxima for various types of vehicles are also now given.

[21] For example, for the movement of heavy bridge sections only transportable by special vehicle and by road.

maximum size of lorries permitted to use the roads, and he may thus prevent vehicles from overseas from operating in this country if of excessive size.   At present the maximum load licensed is 32 tons, but 44-ton vehicles have recently been in process of manufacture, and certain elements have been urging upon the Minister the commercial need for lorries of even larger size and pulling 12-ton trailers.   This is not to say that such vehicles could not be effectively silenced, but clearly other problems of traffic-flow require discussion in Chapter 5.

Future annual tests of roadworthiness (" MoT Tests ") are to include a check as to noise.

(3) *Noise from aircraft*

The Civil Aviation Act, 1949, in ss. 40 and 41 provides that civil aircraft shall be liable, in certain limited circumstances, for trespass, nuisance and surface damage, but there is an obvious, and often insoluble, problem in areas surrounding modern airports that the identity of an aircraft flying too low on take-off or descent cannot be readily established by those individuals who would wish to take action, either under the 1949 Act or at common law.

As already mentioned, provision is now to be made by new legislation in the Land Compensation Bill, both for compensation following upon adverse " physical factors " caused by public works, and specifically including amongst others airports and highways. In addition, the Bill provides for the making of grants to cover the cost of sound-proofing and other remedies, which have hitherto only been available at the discretion of the Secretary of State for the Environment.   For further details see pp. 117, 178, *ante*.

It has also been provided under the Airports Authority Act, 1965, that the Department of Trade and Industry may give instructions to the British Airports Authority as to noise abatement and sound-proofing schemes.[22]   The Act also provides for restrictions on the height of aircraft on approaching an airport, and for the compulsory use of minimum noise routes after take-off.[22a]   Further, the prior approval of the said Department must be obtained for the operation of any new type of aircraft from any given airport; and noise-limits are imposed upon aircraft after take-off, which are

[22] In 1966 grants were made for the sound-proofing of all dwellings in the near vicinity of London Airport (Heathrow).

[22a] Air Navigation (Restriction of Flying) Regulations, 1972 (S.I. 1972 No. 320).

lower limits by night than by day. It is also important to note that, under the 1965 Act, aircraft are required to reach a minimum height of 1,000 feet before passing over built-up areas, and, having reached that height, to throttle back.

Again, however, the letter of the law has been difficult to apply (even over Windsor Castle with the Sovereign in residence) and further steps were provided, still ineffectively, by the Civil Aviation Act, 1968, under which the then President of the Board of Trade required thirty-three airport authorities to provide " facilities for consultation with representatives of the local community on all matters concerning the management of the airport, including noise, which may affect them." (Yet it is significant that the existence of such a provision does not appear to be known even to reasonably well-informed persons in the vicinity of Heathrow.)

A further attempt to improve the quality of civilisation was made in the Air Navigation (Noise Certification) Order, 1970 (S.I. 1970 No. 823),[22b] which requires all aircraft landing in the United Kingdom to hold a certificate, from their country of registration, that they comply with certain specified noise maxima requirements related to their weight and size. Fines of up to £400 may be imposed.

A Parliamentary Committee set up in 1963 under the chairmanship of Sir Alan Wilson, with terms of reference to report on the problem of noise generally, found it necessary in the case of aircraft noise to develop and introduce a new scale of noise measurement, which is designed to gauge the distress caused to the population living near airports, and this is described as the Noise and Number Index (NNI). By this scale, the " maximum acceptable level " was deemed to be 50 to 60 NNI overhead during the day, and involved a mean noise level of 110 decibels of Perceived Noise (PNdB). In comparison the degree of noise required to produce only " moderate annoyance " at night was set at 45 NNI. If Heathrow airport is taken as a current example, the sector lying from Windsor in the west to Isleworth in the east, suffered in 1970 noise at night of 55 NNI, and there is prospect (unless affected by eventual construction of the third London airport at Foulness) of a progressive increase in night jet flights.[23]

[22b] As amended by the Air Navigation (Noise Certification) (Amendment) Order, 1972 (S.I. 1972 No. 455).
[23] There are 3,500 extra tourist flights from Heathrow in the period April to October in any year.

The most effective means of control of aircraft noise must lie in an international code designed to specify requirements in the construction of new aircraft and, possibly, in a right of individual countries to ground offending machines where a positive breach of noise regulations can be effectively proved.

It should be appreciated that no aircraft can be certain of being physically able to take a precise pre-arranged course on take-off, or for that matter at any other time, since it will always be at the mercy of cross-winds, head- and tail-winds, thermal currents and other factors. Thus, flight paths must, of necessity, be relatively broad.

2. Nuclear Pollution

The author takes the view that this specialised, but vitally important, aspect of control of pollution is unlikely to become the frequent concern of any non-scientific person—or protectionist body —since detection of this type of pollution requires the use of special instruments.   However, the effect of such pollution may, in a given case, eventually become evident through symptoms exhibited by vegetation and animal life.   The means of statutory control may be outlined very briefly as follows.

By the Radiological Protection Act, 1970, a National Radiological Protection Board was set up.   This Board took over (*a*) the functions of the previous Radiological Protection Service (which had been administered by the Medical Research Council); (*b*) those of the Radiological Protection Division of the United Kingdom Atomic Energy Authority's Health and Safety Branch; and (*c*) various other functions previously carried out under the Radioactive Substances Act, 1948.   The Board is subject to the directions of the Health Ministers (i.e., including the Secretary of State for Social Services, the Secretaries of State for Scotland and Wales, and the Minister of Health and Social Services in Northern Ireland).

The importation or production of most radioactive substances requires to be licensed.   Thus, by s. 1 (1) of the Nuclear Installations Act, 1965, as amended by the Nuclear Installations Act, 1969, no person may use any site for the installation or operation of a nuclear reactor (except where comprised in a vehicle as motive power!), or for the production or use of atomic energy, unless a " nuclear site licence " is obtained from the Minister.   Contravention of s. 1 (1) of the 1965 Act is punishable upon summary conviction by a fine of not exceeding £100, or imprisonment for not exceeding three months, or both; and, upon indictment, by a fine of not exceeding £500, or imprisonment for not exceeding five years, or both.

Nuclear site licences may be granted only to a body corporate (e.g., to a company; but never to an individual person), and the Minister may require notice of the licence to be served upon any local authority, any river authority, fisheries committee and any statutory water undertakers, or any other public or local authority. These recipients may make representations to the Minister within a period of three months from the date of service of the last-served notice (s. 3).   It should be noted that the Atomic Energy Authority Act, 1971, provides for the transfer of substantial undertakings from the Atomic Energy Authority to two private companies, British Nuclear Fuels, Ltd., and the Radiochemical Centre, Ltd., but does not transfer any patent rights.

Conditions may be attached to the licence (s. 4), and licences may be revoked at any time (s. 5).   A list of licensed sites is to be kept by the Minister (s. 6) and this list will also show sites previously used but now discontinued over the preceding thirty years.

Strict conditions as to operation of licensed sites are laid down (s. 7); and also, any " responsible party " has a duty to avoid being a carrier of " nuclear matter " (s. 11) (e.g., contamination on clothing, etc.).

Extremely wide provisions are made to ensure that any person who suffers damage from nuclear pollution can obtain compensation (s. 12), and—as distinct from other forms of civil liability—an action may be brought at any time up to and not exceeding thirty years from the date of the occurrence which gave rise to the action, or from the latest date in a series of such occurrences (s. 15).   In addition, special provision is made to establish liability on the part of " foreign operators," to obtain foreign judgments, and to share liability under foreign jurisdictions.

Licensed sites may be inspected at all reasonable times, and the Minister appoints inspectors under s. 24 of the Act.   Further, by s. 22 (5) and the Schedule to the Act, an inquiry (described as " the court " in para. 3 of the Schedule) may be held by a competent person appointed by the Minister.

Special arrangements are made in ss. 18 to 21 of the Act to ensure that financial cover is provided to the extent of potential liability at any given time but subject to certain specified maximum limits, including an aggregate maximum of £50 million in certain cases. This figure envisages, of course, international liability in the event of a catastrophe, and it suffices to say that any nuclear pollution which causes damage to persons or property will be adequately underwritten by the Government, subject, of course, to initial proof of liability on the part of a licensee.

Certain powers to operate nuclear reactors at electricity generating stations are provided under the Electricity (Amendment) Act, 1961, but this Act does not vary any of the statutory requirements already discussed.

CHAPTER 10

RESIDENTIAL AND SHOPPING AREAS

1. General

At first sight it may seem rather curious that dwelling-houses and retail outlets should be considered together, but the author's view is that, so far as influences upon the environment are concerned, the two general subjects are closely inter-related. Both housing and the provision of shops are influenced by broadly the same types of demand as to use, development and redevelopment. Thus, it may be said that, in the case of a run-down urban area, both houses and shops will be detrimentally affected by local economic decline; and, equally, in the case of entirely new development—that is, in general, of non-urban, agricultural (or other) sites—such new residential areas will require the services offered by new, or expanded, retail shops. The nationally known shopping centres, such as Oxford Street and Regent Street, or Knightsbridge and Kensington in London, and certain other large national and regional shopping centres elsewhere in Britain do, of course, present special cases and special problems.

Specific questions relating to the control of the design of new buildings, and of their setting in the landscape (whether a rural or an urban landscape), are discussed in Chapter 13; and other related questions, including the protection of buildings of architectural and historic interest, and the creation of conservation areas, are also considered in Chapter 13. The matter of the siting of new housing developments within the Metropolitan and other Green Belt areas is considered in Chapter 14. The present chapter, therefore, is designed to deal with the more general problem, or setting, within which these other special considerations may also arise.

Basically it may be said that, so far as protection of the environment is concerned, the objections to a given scheme for development, or for redevelopment of an area (urban or rural) may be that it will:

(a) cause the spoliation of open country or the demolition of, or obscuring from normal view of, structures or features of architectural, historic or aesthetic value; and/or (*b*) destroy a sense of local community (which may exist even in an impoverished area, such as the London dockland); and/or

(*c*) be proven to be unjustified in terms of economic, or alternatively social, value to the particular area.

Conversely, the basic factors which may be argued in support of a scheme for development or redevelopment of residential or shopping areas are:

(i) that it will improve the domestic conditions under which people live, or under which they shop; or alternatively in the case of a Green Belt area, that the character of the locality must be sacrificed to the national need in terms of shortage of housing; and/or

(ii) that a town, or an urban area within a large town or city, is declining, and will continue to decline, in terms of prosperity—and thus amenity—due to the fact that it is progressively less effective as a commercial magnet to attract trade from a surrounding area; and/or

(iii) that (as mentioned in Chapter 5, Transport) the prevention of eventual strangulation of a town or city by road traffic requires a division of the total urban area into cells, around each of which, traffic (other than delivery traffic or private cars reaching their home destination) will circulate unimpeded, in a one-way circulation system. Such a requirement suggests the separation of pedestrians from vehicular traffic and this, in turn, necessitates a radical redesigning of local communities—which consist of dwellings, shops, offices and other places of work.

So far as the redevelopment of urban areas is concerned, it must also be remarked that there should, in general, be a tendency towards various forms of higher-density housing (although not necessarily in high blocks of flats),[1] principally in order to decrease the pressure put upon development of open land outside towns—most of which is at present used for food

---

[1] But see p. 323, Recommendation 7, Appendix B. Also note Dartmouth Report, Section 3, paragraph 3.49: " The necessity for high densities in cities has so often been given as an excuse for building ever more high-rise flats. The open space released around them usually turned out to be useless, since mothers were understandably afraid to let small children play unattended fifteen floors below them, and miserable windswept concrete areas could hardly be described as adventure playgrounds for older boys and girls. Low densities (?) of 50 or 75 persons to the acre undoubtedly result in very attractive layouts with low-built houses or flats and a lot of greenery, which is difficult to achieve in crowded city centres."

production [2]—but also in order to provide more freedom of man-oeuvre within the constricted spaces available in existing urban areas.

It will therefore be evident that, when considering the environment in which we live, two questions arise. First, is there a predominant need to improve local living and working conditions, such as to warrant a radical and comprehensive scheme for redevelopment? And, secondly, and in contrast, is the predominant need to protect the existing physical features in the locality which, once lost, can never be regained? In deciding which of these two basic needs is likely to be afforded preference, it is necessary to have an understanding on the one hand of the basic concepts behind satisfactory town (or country) planning for housing and related, i.e., shopping, purposes; and on the other hand, to assess those factors which relate to the aesthetic value and/or the historical links of the area. It is not the function of this book to attempt to advise the reader as to matters of aesthetic judgment. Suffice it to say that in certain parts of the country (such as historic towns, some university towns, or centres of the arts) a far higher proportion of the population would grieve for the loss of a particular vista, façade, monument or tree than would even notice the change in less cultivated communities.[3]

It remains, therefore, to suggest simply those other factors which require to be taken into account by Ministers, local planning authorities, other local authorities, and private developers when assessing the financial and social viability of a scheme for development or redevelopment of a given area.

The majority of these factors relate also to specific proposals for schemes for comprehensive redevelopment of town centres. As such they are discussed in " Town Centres: Cost and Control of Redevelopment," Planning Bulletin No. 3, Ministry of Housing and Local Government, 1963, reprinted 1964.

In considering either an entire town, or an urban area within a town, it is necessary to assess the most suitable scale and type of future redevelopment and to base this upon evidence of:

the population of the town (or area), population growth, and immigration or emigration trends;

[2] At present almost fifty per cent. of the national food requirement is met from within Great Britain, and the balance imported accounts for a very significant proportion of national outgoings.

[3] *Strength* of local opinion is, however, a relevant planning consideration.

the nature and place of work of the majority of the residents, nature of local employment, average earnings and spending power, and general level of prosperity;

the communications, public transport, bus stations, road access, by-pass and car parking facilities—both existing and proposed.[4]

Within this framework, it is then necessary to assess the various standards of living accommodation available, and the standards both to be desired and reasonably supportable (including aid from the Exchequer) in the area. As to this, Recommendations 7 to 13 in Appendix B are particularly relevant.

The best relationship between residential requirements and the shopping characteristics suited to these requirements must then be deduced. In assessing these factors the status of the existing shopping centre (or area), if any, within the general catchment region must be gauged, and the existence of other competing regional centres taken into account, together with the comparative existing drawing power of each, and the likely effects of any future competitive development or redevelopment. This assessment is significantly applicable to, for example, a number of market towns where the market has ceased and shoppers from the surrounding villages and countryside may tend to go elsewhere. In such cases it is essential to arrive at a scale and type of commercial redevelopment which will attract increasing trade—if, indeed, this can be accomplished.

Shopping facilities can be divided into two categories, namely: (*a*) *main shopping centres*, i.e., a large number of shops and/or multiple stores grouped together and provided with public car parking facilities and pedestrian precincts; and (*b*) *neighbourhood shopping centres*, which may consist of a parade of shops, or even of one or two small general food stores strategically sited in relation to individual housing estates.

In deciding upon the practicability of a main shopping centre development, the question of existing and potential " drawing power " in competition with other regional shopping centres is, of course, of vital importance. But it is also necessary to relate this to any innate local advantages and disadvantages in terms of amenity, convenience (e.g., public transport and car parking),

[4] See Chapter 5; also Appendix B, Recommendations 22 to 29.

character, tradition (that is to say, habit—although this may be lost if the physical process of development causes stoppage of some, or all, of the existing trading), together with any other special local factors. The precise distribution and size of any established neighbourhood shopping centres within the catchment area of the major shopping centre development may also be of great significance.

The above characteristics must then be related to the physical attributes of the shopping area which it is proposed to renew. Thus, the structural condition and age of the property, any difficulties as to individual sites (e.g., shop-fronts for display purposes, access for customers and for delivery vans), and also the presence of any buildings of architectural or historic value, must all be taken into account.

The extent of existing shopping demand may be measured in relation to the number and approximate floor space of the existing town centre shops, the nature and proprietorship of those shops, the absence of any particular types of shops, and the possibility of any increase or decrease in proportion of these specific types following a comprehensive development scheme. It should also be noted that specialised or luxury shops are more likely to be opened in a shopping centre possessed of a large customer catchment area.

The analysis, as outlined, of the state of the existing shopping facilities will also include a careful and comparative note of trading values in relation to each other of premises in good, average and poor positions, in turn relative to, say, good positions but poor premises, and poor positions but good premises, etc. These assessments will be of importance in allocating to proprietors relatively equivalent sites in the new shopping centre. In addition, it may be assumed that the modern form and layout of shops will increase potential turnover to such an extent that the total number of new shops required to meet the estimated shopping demand will be less than the existing number of shops, so that some retailers—probably those in the poorest existing sites—should be encouraged (perhaps by financial inducement) to discontinue trading, and thus not to seek accommodation in the new development. In any event, the all-round increase in shop rents which almost invariably follows upon redevelopment will probably be sufficient to exclude traders having the smallest turnover.

Although the primary purpose of a shopping centre development is to improve the shopping facilities of the town, or urban area within a city, it must also be related to other commercial and professional interests in the area and to provision of substituted and additional office accommodation (including, for example, branches of the joint stock banks, Post Office, estate agents, etc.), which will probably affect the user of upper storeys, where these exist.   These commercial and professional interests, which are not retail outlets, in themselves act as specialised magnets for pedestrians and traffic of certain types.   Within this group of specialist activities, the siting of various key points is of great importance.   These include nationally-known chain stores, Post Offices, hotels, places of entertainment, and service trades, such as petrol filling stations and dry cleaners.

Lastly, in relation to the development or redevelopment of shops, brief mention should be made of the principal characteristics which affect the economics of an individual shop.   This is of particular significance in considering " neighbourhood shops."

The trading capacity of a retail outlet depends first upon having a site to which the customer can be attracted.   That is, either by being positioned in a street along which a large number of pedestrians pass, or being in a position adjacent to a car park.   (This latter example can, equally, relate to " out-of-town shopping centres," *post.*)   Secondly, the shape of the frontage and of the interior of the shop must be such as to encourage customers to enter, and not positively to discourage customers.   In this respect the modern concept of a " through " shop, having fronts onto, say, two streets, or onto one street and a public car park at rear, has obvious advantages.

Although there is, in the abstract, no ideal size or shape for a shop, certain criteria have been found to be commercially advantageous in various given conditions.   These criteria are of some interest in terms of protection of the environment, since they will motivate the proprietors of shops, or their landlords, in designing or extending a shop site in any given setting.   Thus, the desire to destroy an historic façade, or to demolish an adjoining building, will stem from a commercial assessment of the potential value of site based upon fairly accurate estimates of income from future retail sales.

In general, the value of a shop is directly related to the length of its frontage, so that a reduction, or expansion, in size of even a few feet may be of great significance.   For example, it has been found that, in the case of shops with, say, two storeys of office accommodation above, the loss of frontage resulting from providing a separate front entrance and stairs to the floor above will not normally be justified in terms of the rents receivable from those upper floors. It therefore follows that, with buildings of two or three storeys only (except in specialised positions), it will be preferable to have residential accommodation above shops in order to avoid the need for access from the street frontage.

The value of the frontage of a shop in turn tends to influence the desirable depth, since the value of the frontage increases with the volume of trade actually done, and this volume of trade is itself linked with the area of floor space available to customers. It is also a recognised principle in valuation of shops that the sales area is divided into zones, decreasing in value the further they are from the entrance—although this is largely negated in the case of " through " shops.

As to the pattern of existing shop sizes in Great Britain which has developed over the past 150 years, it has been found that certain dimensions tend to be preferred, as justified by trading records. It may thus be argued that development proposals which depart greatly from the norm will probably fail to be fully effective in trading terms. In the event of a planning appeal, the local planning authority and local objectors will therefore find that a balanced assessment will have to be made by the Inspector and the Secretary of State, wherein the effects upon the amenities of the surrounding area will be balanced against the commercial, and thus social, effectiveness of the proposed shop. The following dimensions are generally accepted as best suited to the various types of retail outlet:

Shops in villages, which have been purpose-built as opposed to the very large number created in the past from converted cottages, tend to have a relatively generous frontage, as a result of space being more readily available, of 18 to 20 feet. They tend to be roughly square in plan, and may often have rather too high a façade in relation to other elevations in the village scene. Suburban shops, other than those owned by the large, nationally-known chain store companies, tend to have an average frontage of about 18 feet, and frontages of less than 16 feet or over 23 feet have been shown to attract a markedly smaller proportion of traders. The appropriate depth for a frontage of 18 feet is about 50 feet, although on particularly valuable trading sites this may be greater.

In market towns (i.e., which attract custom from a large area of surrounding countryside) a greater range of frontage length is acceptable, since the variety of trades represented tends to be very considerably more than in suburban areas, the latter to a greater extent supplying foodstuffs and a smaller range of domestic equipment, fuel, etc.   However, the depth of shop sites in market towns averages about 60 feet, although this depth may be extremely variable from shop to shop.   In the case of well-known urban shopping centres, which draw custom from a fairly wide urban, or " commuter " area, but which are not specially-designed (i.e., modern) " shopping centres " competition has produced a variety of frontages, and a tendency for traders to increase these frontages whenever occasion arises to 25 to 30 feet or more, and to acquire depths of shop floor of frequently as much as 100 feet.   However, the very fact that the locality attracts a wide variety of customers, who may well visit it with a set purpose and a varied list of purchases and who may also be open to chance buying, also allows commercial viability for a very wide range of shop frontage and overall area.   (Compare the size of, say, a well-known chain store, next to which may exist a very small boutique.)

So far as the creation, or viability, of " neighbourhood groups " of shops is concerned, this will depend greatly upon local physical conditions—such as the form of the local road networks, ease of traffic-flow, the presence of steep hills, division by roads and railways, etc.   In the case of New Towns [5] of, say, 70,000 population, the plan for the town may include, for example, a central " shopping centre " (with a large pedestrian precinct, multi-storey car park, etc.), and five or six " neighbourhood centres," each catering for 10,000 to 12,000 people.   In the older towns, however, a total town population of 40,000 upwards would appear to begin to justify (in terms of trading returns) the creation of neighbourhood groups rather than to rely solely upon one principal town shopping centre, supplemented only by scattered local shops each tending to be similar in the nature of their stock to a village store.

It must also be remarked that the planned efficiency of a shop has a very dramatic effect upon profitability, and that a small shop tends to be much less efficient than one of larger size.   Further, the value of selling space per unit of area in a main centre may be as

[5] Created under the New Towns Act, 1946, as government strategy for the dispersal of over-populated cities.   The New Towns Acts, 1946 and 1953, are now repealed and replaced by the New Towns Act, 1965, as amended by New Towns Act, 1971.

much as four times greater than that in a subsidiary shopping centre. As one result of this it is found that in main shopping centres extremely large shop premises are at a premium, and that their letting (and also rateable) value is many times greater than their relative size.   It follows that there is an additional incentive for developers to attempt to create a main shopping centre as distinct from one of lesser magnitude.

Finally as to urban shop sites, but most important, it is nowadays essential that wherever possible rear access be provided both for new and for existing shops.   The value of this provision is reflected not only in terms of enhancement of trading capacity of the shop itself, but, even more significantly, in terms of traffic flow and town and country planning.   The removal of parked delivery lorries and vans from vehicular shopping streets will, clearly, make an immense difference to unimpeded traffic circulation.[6]

A concluding, but most significant, topic in this general discussion of shopping areas must now be considered.   During the past decade the American concept of the " *out-of-town shopping centre* " has been increasingly employed in Britain.   In a few cases this idea has been adopted as of value by local planning authorities, but the vast majority of proposals have come from speculative commercial companies—who have, on not infrequent occasions, resorted to utterly unscrupulous and sometimes illegal means of attaining their goal. This statement requires explanation.

The " out-of-town shopping centre," as developed in the United States and Canada, consists of a very large retail—or retail/wholesale —complex with abutting car parks, and often with mechanical moving belt delivery of goods from sales floor direct to the parking lot.   The original centres were developed by the largest agricultural combines[7] and are, by British standards, of immense size. They offer for sale foodstuffs and goods of every conceivable type, ranging from the smallest domestic expendable products to clothes and semi-durables, such as television sets, washing machines, etc.

The theory—which is, in fact, most effective in practice—is that

---

[6] See Chapter 5; also Appendix B, Recommendations 22 to 29.

[7] Agricultural combines in North America have arisen from the ability of the one-time " middle man " to buy extremely cheap grain in time of glut, and to convert it into profitable breakfast cereals, etc.   These middle men were then able to acquire the agricultural land—the farmers becoming their tenants—and to develop vast food empires owning both the sources of supply and the eventual retail outlets.

the customer can drive out of the town in which he lives to a rural, or quasi-rural, site and there easily purchase almost all his needs.   The customer therefore has the advantage that he can shop much more quickly by not having to move and park his car several times, and with expenditure of less personal energy.   The retailer has the advantage that the cost of the large site is immeasurably less than an equivalent urban site—which, in any event, would probably be un-obtainable on account of the large area required: to this advantage can be added the lower capital cost of construction, and probably of overheads.   However, the principal and exceedingly dangerous corollary is that, certainly in Britain, where an out-of-town shopping centre is developed it can readily undercut local shop prices, and can successfully draw off such a high proportion of resident custom from nearby towns and villages that many of their conventional shops are put out of business.[8]   In a country which is increasingly conscious of the rising cost of living, a superficial reaction may be to commend any cause of price suppression, but the author cannot emphasise too strongly that this is a false premise.   It must be borne in mind first that about 60 per cent. of households even in rural areas do not yet possess cars; and secondly that the inevitable cost to the local authority (i.e., ratepayers) and to the Exchequer of attempting to prevent the complete decay of a series of small towns of which the mainspring had been a market and shopping centre can be immeasurably greater than a marginal saving on retail prices.   Nevertheless, the incentive to make a relatively quick profit not infrequently causes mercantile adventurers to open out-of-town centres without seeking planning permission, with the object (*a*) of a high volume of sales before enforcement action by the local planning authority can force them to close; and (*b*) of attempting to persuade car-owning members of the local public to urge that planning permission be granted.

Housing.—A great deal of both sound and unsound theory has been propounded in recent years about the most suitable—or best compromise—conditions for housing families, individuals, old people and others.   In fact, the professional approach amongst modern architects now tends to take, as a starting point, the physical, psychological and social needs of the individual, rather than to stem from the older more artistic base of providing aesthetic satisfaction

[8] See Appendix B, Recommendation 33.

through the eye of the beholder. It would be inappropriate for a lawyer to discuss such matters at any length, and only a few remarks will be put forward.

The forms of human dwellings under modern living conditions range from the make-shift adaptation of basically unsuitable structures (such as most basement flats); through the traditional terrace or semi-detached or detached row of houses lining conventional (and now often outdated) traffic thoroughfares; to the recent concepts of blocks of high flats, or to special areas of low housing arranged round pedestrian precincts, courts or gardens, having vehicular access only on the periphery.

In short-term economics, it may often be illogical to retain, for example, monumental terraces of high-ceilinged Georgian housing; yet in terms of aesthetic and tourist trade value, and of a sense of history and social stability, such retention is usually fully justified—even at the cost of internal alteration and radical repair. In these cases, the weight of local or national public opinion can often be the deciding factor at a planning appeal.

The retention of traditional but uninspired and non-historic housing depends, in contrast, basically upon the existence of a nationally acute (although not always local) housing shortage. Each local authority, as housing authority, is required to keep a waiting list of persons resident and qualified who are in need of re-housing; and, in theory at least, the aim of each authority is to provide a sufficient number of housing units to clear their list. The expression " in theory at least " is not intended to imply that local authorities are failing to make a genuine effort to achieve this; it is rather that, in many areas, the grant of planning permission for housing development (whether given by the local planning authority, or refused but subsequently given by the Secretary of State) simply does not mean an easing of the housing list burden, since the developer seeks the best sale price for each dwelling, and such prices are, more often than not, paid by purchasers who were not living within, or even near, the housing authority area.

The policy of construction of extremely high tower blocks of flats has, until fairly recently, been pursued principally on the false assumption that the cost of each unit thereby provided would be less. It is, however, now generally accepted that on most sites the cost of each flat is considerably higher than would be the cost of equivalent accommodation in a " low-rise " block. Further, it is now amply appreciated (even by means of social records, such as those of the magistrates' courts) that the residents of high blocks often feel a sense of isolation and depression. A tower block does not form a community such as normally exists in a conventional and non-prosperous street.[9]

It has therefore more recently been considered that housing areas containing small " cells "—consisting of terraced houses, or low rise flats, grouped round a precinct or community garden—cater far more effectively in terms of social and amenity needs. However, in such cases " scale " is of great importance, as may be evidenced in a few of those of the New Towns in which this principle has been attempted. If the open spaces are too large, the sense of community is lost and is, indeed, replaced by a positive sense of insecurity. This psychological effect applies both to housing and to shopping areas.

Hotels.—Finally, it may be of value to mention a problem which relates largely to London, but which may well increase in significance in other parts of the country where there are strong tourist attractions, or where greater numbers of business visitors from abroad are anticipated.

In London, for the past decade or more, there has been an acute shortage of hotel accommodation. It is not proposed to discuss, within the already wide compass of this book, the provision of facilities for tourists and other travellers, but two environmental factors are of importance. First, the demand for hotel rooms (particularly for hotel rooms of the standard of air-conditioning and mechanical services to which citizens of the United States of America may be accustomed) has made the development of sites as multi-storey hotels one of the most profitable business propositions. These economic pressures have already been amply demonstrated by the erection of large numbers of " landscape " type windows sited so as to provide a fine view of the private grounds of Buckingham Palace! Secondly, several blocks of flats, or flatlets, in or near the West End of central London have, by a variety of means, been converted into hotels. This process has, of course, involved the migration of the previous tenants, and has therefore added to the housing shortage.

The pressures involved should not be underestimated. In 1970,

[9] See p. 190, footnote 1.

it was calculated that the then annual total of tourist visitors to London amounted to five million, and that this figure would double by 1975. In the final quarter of 1970, there existed about 73,000 " bed spaces " (to use the expression commonly employed), with a further 12,500 bed spaces for which planning permission had been given; yet it was anticipated that an additional 30,000 bed spaces would be needed by 1975—a total being required by that year of about 115,000.

The cost of providing such bed spaces can be estimated at approaching £15,000 per room, the majority of which would contain two beds, the cost stated including supporting restaurant and other services. In arriving at the appropriate daily charge for a room it is common practice to divide the capital cost by 1,000; thus, on the assumption that the room is let for every night of the year, the annual gross return on capital will be 36·5 per cent. The net profit will, of course, depend upon the cost of services offered and supplied.

At the end of 1970, about 100 hotels were either in process of construction or awaiting planning permission.

In so far as the provision of hotel accommodation in appropriate places serves to increase the national income from international tourism, it is a significant and important factor in the national economy. However, it must be stressed that indiscriminate and excessive development can permanently destroy many of the original tourist attractions, in terms principally of general atmosphere. For example, those Americans who have visited London over a period of years are already beginning to make comment that much of the atmosphere of history and classical architecture is being destroyed, or rendered nugatory, by unsympathetic development. Hyde Park Corner may be the next case in point.

2. Legal Aspects

Since both houses and shops are structures, many related legal aspects (such as the protection of Scheduled Buildings) will be found elsewhere in this book. It is proposed to consider here merely two principal topics: (i) the general powers exercisable by a housing authority to clear and improve sub-standard housing areas; and (ii) the statutory controls which govern the change of use from one type of shop to another, and the control of design of shop fronts and of shop signs.

(i) *Sub-standard housing areas.*—Statutory control of housing conditions and public health has existed since the early nineteenth century, and it was, in fact, from these sources that the more modern approach to human living conditions now represented by town and country planning stemmed. However, the original legislative approach has survived (now in parallel with planning statutes) in the form of the Housing Acts; notably the Housing Act, 1957 (the Principal Act), as amended by the Housing Acts of 1961 to 1971, the Housing Subsidies Act, 1967, and the Public Health Acts, 1936 and 1961.

So far as the repair of insanitary houses is concerned, s. 4 of the Housing Act, 1957, lays down an eight-point standard concerning structural repair, stability, freedom from damp, ventilation, natural lighting, water supply, drainage (and water closets) and facilities for the storage and preparation and cooking of food. The house is to be " deemed unfit for human habitation if and only if it is so far defective in one or more of the said matters that it is not reasonably suitable for occupation in that condition " (s. 4 (2)). In such cases the housing authority (normally the district or borough council) is empowered to enforce, or itself to take, certain specified action.

In the case of houses which are generally both " unfit for human habitation " (i.e., which do not comply with all the eight points referred to above), and are incapable of being rendered " fit " at reasonable cost, the housing authority has certain powers relating to demolition and reconstruction. It is felt that, since these powers inevitably have an effect upon a wider environment than that of the individual occupier, the matter should now be discussed, but it may also be of advantage briefly to consider the preliminary situations, which will relate to lack of repair and means of coercion to obtain the reasonable co-operation of owners in carrying out such repairs.

In the case of urban housing areas which require urgent improvement, it is first necessary to consider whether the defects can be rectified at a reasonable cost for each dwelling. But, even if repairs and improvements would not be justified upon purely economic grounds, it will still be broadly true to say that an acute local shortage of housing will validate expenditure in order to improve conditions, and to provide a further life of such dwellings generally of fifteen years or more; in exceptional areas, a lesser length of life can apply. Therefore, except in the case of the most patent slum areas, local housing authorities will tend to start by giving notice to repair to " persons having control " of such houses (i.e., owners, or lessees, or agents) where it is believed that this can be done at reasonable cost (ss. 9 to 15 of Part II of the Housing Act, 1957, as amended). Rights of appeal against such notices lie to the county court (s. 11), but if the court finds that repairs cannot be completed at reasonable cost, then the housing authority will automatically have power to acquire the dwelling-house either by agreement or by compulsory purchase (s. 12). If no appeal is made and the repairs are not carried out, the housing authority may themselves carry out the necessary work and recover the cost from the owner of the property as a civil debt (s. 10). Certain provisions are also made for contribution by a lessor of a house where the tenant incurs expense following a notice to repair (s. 13).

Where the property is in an extremely dilapidated condition, however, certain other provisions apply under the Public Health Acts, 1936 and 1961, and these measures disregard the question of whether or not it may be capable of repair at reasonable cost. If the house is in such a state as to constitute a " statutory nuisance," [10] then the local magistrates' court may make an order prohibiting use of the premises until they are rendered fit, and the local public health inspector may take action under s. 92 of the 1936 Act in order to abate the nuisance. The 1961 Act, however, introduced a form of expedited procedure applicable to cases where the premises constitute a danger to health or a nuisance but where the normal procedure would cause " unreasonable delay." In this more rapid process, the local authority must serve a notice under s. 26 of the 1961 Act specifying the defects which they intend to rectify. The person in control of the property must then, within seven days, serve a counter-notice to the effect that he intends to carry out the work; and if he fails to serve such counter-notice the local authority may then act and charge the costs to the person responsible. Provisions are also made in ss. 25 and 27 of the 1961 Act for local authorities to take emergency steps in the case of dangerous, or ruinous and dilapidated structures and sites.

The purpose of the preceding paragraphs has been to indicate, very briefly, the steps which may be expected in dealing with substandard or slum housing areas before a (partially) planning decision is put into effect by clearing and redeveloping either individual

[10] As defined by the Public Health Acts: see p. 133.

housing sites, or an entire area of obsolete dwellings. The question of such demolition now remains to be considered.

In cases of individual houses which are " unfit " for human habitation (i.e., they fall short of the eight-point standard, *ante*), and which cannot be rendered fit at reasonable cost, the local authority are empowered under s. 17 of the Housing Act, 1957, to make a *demolition order*, although they are also permitted, as an alternative, to refrain from so doing and to make a *closing order* instead. So far as *Scheduled Buildings* are concerned a considerable measure of protection and control by the Department of the Environment is afforded, but as to this see Chapter 13.

Before making a demolition order, the local authority must first serve a notice on the person having control of the dwelling-house (in the case of tenement blocks there may be several such persons), and also upon anyone who has lent money upon mortgage of the property. This procedure is governed by s. 16 (1) of the 1957 Act, and the section also provides for the local authority to accept undertakings as to the repair and future use of the premises in lieu of demolition (s. 16 (4) to (6)). These undertakings are to be given at a hearing called by means of a " Notice of Time and Place " originating from the local authority, and such notices are usually given before the final decision as to a demolition order is made. If, however, the required undertakings are not then given, the local authority must, as specified by the Act, forthwith make a demolition order.

Following the making of a demolition order, the premises must be vacated not later than a date specified in the order, which must be not earlier than twenty-eight days from the date of service of the order. The demolition must be carried out within six weeks of the demolition order becoming operative, or alternatively within six weeks of vacation of the premises: this also must be stated in the order.

It should be noted that the occupier, if he is not the owner, must also be separately notified by the local authority, who will normally offer alternative housing accommodation. In addition, it is normal practice for the same authority to explain to the owner or tenant of the house what improvement grants can be made available, since these may assist that person in deciding whether to undertake to repair. In the case of a change of mind on the part of the owner, the local authority is permitted (s. 24) to postpone or revoke the order where an undertaking to reconstruct is given.

This discretion may also be applied in relation to " any other person who in the opinion of the local authority is or will be in a position to put his proposals (for reconstruction) into effect "—s. 25 of the Housing Act, 1961.

When demolition takes place, the local authority may sell the materials remaining, and set the value of these off against the costs to be recovered from the " owner " (s. 23 of the 1957 Act).

Rights of appeal to the county court exist in the case of both closing and demolition orders, but where the occupier is merely a tenant with less than three years of his lease to run, or a tenant from year to year or lesser periodic tenancy, no appeal is permitted.[11] In any event any appeal must be made within twenty-one days of the order (s. 20 of the 1957 Act).

It may also be of significance in matters affecting the environment that s. 72 of the Housing Act, 1957, empowers a local authority to demolish any " obstructive building " (i.e., which, due to its contact with, or proximity to, other buildings, is dangerous to health). Again there is a right of appeal to the county court.

In the instances referred to so far, the owner of such sub-standard housing will be left with ownership either of a site following demolition, or (temporarily) with a structure upon which a closing order has been made and which is therefore not to be used until defects are corrected. It is evident that a proportion of owners will be unable to finance the necessary works and that others may simply refuse to incur expenditure. In such cases it is provided, by s. 17 of the 1957 Act, as amended by the (now) Town and Country Planning Act, 1971, that the local authority must then acquire the house and/or site either by agreement or by compulsory purchase. It is not possible, however, within the limited field of this book, to discuss matters of compulsory purchase and compensation.[12]

Where whole areas of unfit housing are concerned, the powers of local authorities are rather different from those so far described. As has been mentioned in Chapter 1, in discussing the broad principles of town and country planning, a development plan may, clearly, provide for renewal of a housing area—or for removal of the

---

[11] In regard to the terms of leases with over three years yet to run, the county court has power to vary or determine, upon an application being made by a landlord or tenant affected.

[12] As to this the reader is referred to *The Encyclopedia of Compulsory Purchase and Compensation* (Sweet & Maxwell); and to *Compulsory Purchase and Compensation* by Lawrance (Estates Gazette).

housing accommodation to some other part of the development plan area and replacement by commercial or industrial developments. However, this process may not be best suited to a more urgent situation, and reliance will then be placed upon provisions for slum clearance under the Housing Acts, 1957 to 1969, and the Housing (Slum Clearance Compensation) Act, 1965. These provisions are primarily concerned with the financing of slum clearance through Exchequer and local authority funds, together with the payment, where applicable, of compensation to persons displaced from their homes, but this aspect of compensation will not be discussed in this work.

Part III of the Housing Act, 1957, provides for the clearance and redevelopment of areas of unfit housing. The local authority may either *declare a clearance area under s.* 42, or *compulsorily purchase the area.*

The effect of declaration of a *clearance area* is that the owners of any property in the area are required to demolish it. If they fail so to do, the local authority may enter, demolish, and sell the materials, then charging the balance of the cost *pro rata* to each owner. To achieve this purpose a " clearance order " must be made; but before making such an order the local authority is required to ensure that suitable alternative accommodation exists. Further, a copy of the council's resolution making the order must be sent to the Secretary of State for the Environment before any further action is taken; and this copy must include details of the number of occupiers affected.

In practice, an area may be cleared piecemeal, that is, by means of a planned series of clearance orders; but, since the area remains the property of the original owners, such a scheme must be designed to assist those owners in arranging for suitable redevelopment through private sources. It may well be that owners of poor quality housing will be unable to finance such a project, and that they will require to approach investment companies or development companies.

The procedure for creation of a clearance area is set out in s. 44 of and Sched. 5 to the 1957 Act, as amended by the Housing Act, 1961, and the Public Health Act, 1961. The order must be in prescribed form and must be related to a map of the area to which it applies. Before submitting the order to the Secretary of State, the local authority must publish, in one or more local newspapers circulating in the area, a notice in prescribed form, which will include a description of the area affected and will say where the order and supporting map may be inspected.   In addition, the local authority must serve on every owner, lessee or occupier (except tenants for a month or less period than a month) and on every mortgagee a notice stating the effect of the order and indicating the time within which and manner in which objections may be made.   The Secretary of State must, if objections are made and not withdrawn, hold a public inquiry, and upon consideration of his Inspector's report, " shall make such order in the matter as he thinks fit."   Notice of this decision must be served on the persons previously served and any others who appeared at the inquiry, and must also be published in the local newspapers.   The order will, in fact, come into effect six weeks after the date of such publication.

Lastly, the method of dealing with areas which are predominantly residential and in which the living conditions " ought to be improved by improvement of the amenities of the area or of dwellings therein " is provided in s. 28 in Pt. II of the Housing Act, 1969, and the Housing Act, 1971, whereby general improvement areas may be declared. These areas and clearance areas are mutually exclusive (1969 Act, s. 29).   The process of creating such general improvement areas is similar to that required for a clearance area, and is set out in s. 28 (2) of the 1969 Act.   Once the area is formally in existence the local authority becomes empowered (s. 32) to carry out works on land owned by them, and to " assist (whether by grants or loans or otherwise) in the carrying out of any works on land not owned by them."   They may also acquire land by agreement and may let or otherwise dispose of land for the time being owned by them. Special provisions are made for the Secretary of State to approve contribution to expenditure by a local authority upon such general improvement areas, if he deems this desirable (s. 37 and the 1971 Act).   Aid may also be applied in " intermediate areas " and in " areas of derelict land," by virtue of the Housing Act, 1972.

(ii) *Control of the use and design of shops.*—Planning controls relate, as already discussed in Chapter 1, to " development "; and development, as defined in s. 22 of the Town and Country Planning Act, 1971, may consist of—

(*a*) the carrying out of building, engineering or mining operations, or other operations in, on, over or under land (subject to certain exceptions, as specified in s. 22 (2), such as works of maintenance to buildings and to highways, etc.); or (*b*) the making of any material change of use of any buildings or other land.

It is evident that the construction of, or adaptation to, a shop will constitute a building operation, and nothing further will therefore be said here as to (*a*) above, save that the matter of the display of advertisements will be considered later in this chapter.

However, the major problems in interpreting the law in relation to shops arise out of sub-paragraph (*b*), that is, questions of " material change of use." To what extent is the existing or proposed use of a shop for a specific type of trade controlled?

It must first be stressed that a change of use, in relation to any building or land, will only be subject to control if it is deemed to be a " *material* change of use." In general, minor changes, such as (to take dwelling-houses as an example) a small increase in the number of occupiers of a single dwelling,[13] will not require planning permission save for such changes as are specified in the Act. A material change of use must be " substantially " different from the previous use; and " substantial " has been defined, in the case of *Palser* v. *Grinling* [1948] A.C. 291 (H.L.) as " considerable or big."

However, the Town and Country Planning (Use Classes) Order, 1972 (S.I. 1972 No. 1385), by art. 3 and the Schedule to the Order, together with the Town and Country Planning General Development Order, 1973 (S.I. 1973 No. 31), by art. 3 and Sched. 1, Class III, to that Order, provides that within certain groups of user listed in each of nineteen " use classes," a change of use shall not require express planning permission. Class I of the Schedule to the Use Classes Order provides that the interchange of use for all types of shop shall not be deemed to involve " development " except where the change is to any of the following types of shop:

  a shop for the sale of hot food
  a tripe shop
  a shop for the sale of pet animals or birds
  a cats' meat shop or
  a shop for the sale of motor vehicles.

It is evident that the first four types are likely to cause objection

---

[13] This should not be confused with the occupation of a dwelling-house (which includes a flat, etc.) by a single family becoming occupation in a number of separate units by several families, even though remaining entirely residential in nature. By s. 22 (3) (*a*) of the 1971 Act, the use of a single dwelling-house for the purposes of two or more dwellings is declared to constitute development.

upon grounds of smell; that the third may also be related to noise; and that the primary possible objection to the selling of motor vehicles would be upon grounds of traffic (in the form of congestion either caused by customers or by delivery and movement of vehicles for sale) and of noise.

Although Class I is concerned with " shops " as defined in the Act—namely, " a building used for the carrying on of any retail trade or retail business wherein the primary purpose is the selling of goods by retail "—the public conception of shop premises is rather wider, and extends, for example, to estate agents' offices, banks, and betting offices. The Town and Country Planning Acts and various Orders and circulars have given fairly clear indications of the limitations of Class I. Thus, hairdressers, undertakers, ticket agencies, and premises used for receiving dry cleaning, washing or repairing, are declared to be " shops "; whereas petrol-filling stations, offices, betting offices, fun fairs (arcades, etc.), garages, hotels or " any other premises (other than a restaurant) licensed for the sale of intoxicating liquors for consumption on the premises " are not " shops."

If the primary use of premises (even if of shop design and layout) has been for office purposes, then it is made clear in Class II of the Order that it may be changed to another form of office without application for planning permission. It may not, however, change to any form of shop without such permission. Thus, an estate agent's office may become a bank, or a solicitor's office. However, neither a retail shop, nor an office, nor any other premises for that matter, may be converted to a betting " office " without obtaining both a licence from the local magistrates and also planning permission. This latter limitation is clearly concerned with the effect upon a neighbourhood of the type of client who may frequent the betting office.

So far as changes to office use (other than betting offices) from any other type of use is concerned, the reader is referred to Chapter 11, Offices.

*　*　*　*

There remains to be considered one important influence which a shop may exert upon its immediate environment; that is, the question of the *display of shop signs and related advertisements*. Advertisements, including shop signs, are by virtue of ss. 34, 35 and 63 of the Town and Country Planning Act, 1962—now consolidated in ss. 63

and 109 of the Town and Country Planning Act, 1971—subject to the Town and Country Planning (Control of Advertisements) Regulations, 1969 (S.I. 1969 No. 1532).[14]   An " advertisement " is

> " any word, letter, model, sign, placard, board, notice, device or representation, whether illuminated or not, in the nature of, and employed wholly or partly for the purposes of, advertisement, announcement or direction (excluding any such thing employed wholly as a memorial or as a railway signal), and . . . includes any hoarding or similar structure used, or adapted for use, for the display of advertisements."

References to the display of advertisements are to be construed accordingly (reg. 2 (1)).

The basic approach of the Town and Country Planning Acts, 1962 and 1968, which are now consolidated in the 1971 Act, is that express permission is required for all advertisements, subject to a large number of defined exceptions as set out in the Advertisements Regulations.   There is also a proviso that the exceptions shall be upon different bases according to whether or not the advertisement is to be situated (a) within an " area of special control," or (b) in any other area.

By s. 63 of the 1971 Act and Part VII of the Advertisements Regulations (regs. 26 and 27) and Sched. 2, local planning authorities are required to consider which parts of their total planning area ought to be defined as areas of special control, and are empowered to define such areas (reg. 26), subject to consultation with other local authorities which may be affected, together with any " associations " if so directed by the Secretary of State (reg. 26 (3)). The Secretary of State may himself define an area of special control if he deems this necessary (reg. 26 (2)).   It is also directed that, where possible, local planning authorities should give consideration to redefinition of these areas at about five-yearly intervals.

The process of creating an area of special control is set out in Sched. 2 to the Regulations.   The local planning authority must first consult with other local authorities affected, and then commence the procedure by making an order, defining an area by reference to a map annexed thereto, and submitting such order to the Secretary of State for approval, together with a statement of their reasons for proposing that the area be an area of special control.   The local

---

[14] As slightly amended by S.I. 1972 No. 489.

planning authority must then, forthwith, publish in the *London Gazette* and in each of two successive weeks in one or more local newspapers, a notice (in a form prescribed in Sched. 3, or substantially to like effect) describing the area, stating that the order has been submitted to the Secretary of State, and naming a place or places where a copy of the order and annexed map may be inspected, during a period of at least twenty-eight days from the date of the first advertisement. During this time, objections or representations may be sent in writing to the Secretary of State.

If objections are not withdrawn, the Secretary of State must, before approving the order, either cause a public local inquiry to be held, or provide some other opportunity for objectors to appear before a person appointed by him; and similar rights of hearing will apply to the local planning authority. The Secretary of State may then approve the order, with or without modification; but if modifications are contemplated, similar provisions must be made for publication of notices and for hearing further objections and representations. Once the order is approved, the local planning authority must publish a notice to this effect, again in the *London Gazette* and for two successive weeks in one or more local newspapers, this notice stating also where the order and annexed map may be inspected. The order will come into force on the date of publication in the *London Gazette*.

An area of special control having been created, it follows that within that area no advertisements shall be displayed unless specially excepted (reg. 27). The special exceptions are laid down in regs. 9, 12, 14 and 23; and in reg. 27 (2). In the case of those under reg. 27 (2) express consent must be obtained. The types of advertisements thus permissible in an area of special control are as follows:

Regulation 9 refers to advertisements relating to Parliamentary and local government elections, to other advertisements specifically ordered by Parliament, and to authorised traffic signs. These advertisements are to be of defined sizes, and those relating to elections shall be removed within fourteen days.

Regulation 12 refers to the control of advertisements within buildings (*post*). Those which are within buildings and are also within the requirements of this regulation may be displayed in an area of special control.

Regulation 14 refers to advertisements of " specified classes," and these will be discussed more fully later. They include, for example, boards showing the name of a shop, and plates indicating the presence of a professional office.

Regulation 23 refers to a special case, that is, travelling circuses and fairs, and these are thereby permitted to display advertisements of limited size, subject to removal within seven days.

Regulation 27 (2) (i.e., permissible in an area of special control only with express consent) refers to hoardings or similar structures for display of notices relating to local events; to advertisements giving directions to, for example, public libraries and museums; and to those in the interests of public safety. Provisions are also made in this regulation for limitations as to time, and for directions as to removal, even of expressly approved advertisements.

There now remains to be considered the situation affecting advertisements in areas other than areas of special control. As already stated, the general rule is that display of all advertisements requires consent (reg. 6) but that this may be either (*a*) express or (*b*) deemed consent. The advertisements which may be displayed by deemed consent are defined in Part II of the Regulations, which includes regs. 9, 12 and 14 (as mentioned earlier in relation to areas of special control) and regs. 10, 11, 15 and 16. Of these, further reference must now be made to regs. 12 and 14. Regulation 12 relates to display of advertisements within a building, and requires that express consent will be required in certain cases where the advertisement is visible from outside the building, namely: where it is illuminated; or where the building is used " principally for the display of advertisements "; or where the advertisement is within one metre of any external door, window or other opening through which it is visible from the exterior. In the latter case, therefore, consent may be required for the fairly common practice employed by " cut price " stores of affixing numerous price reduction signs to the glass of their windows.

Regulation 14 relates to advertisements of specified classes as follows:

Class I—Functional advertisements of local authorities, statutory undertakers and public transport undertakers. These include, for example, bus stop signs and signposts indicating the whereabouts of museums, libraries, railway stations, etc.

Class II—Miscellaneous advertisements relating to the premises on which they are displayed and (*a*) for the purposes of identification, direction or warning with respect thereto, being not exceeding 0·2 square metre in area; or (*b*) relating to any person, partnership or company separately carrying on a profession, business or trade at the premises, and not exceeding 0·3 square metre in area (limited to one advertisement on a maximum of two frontages if both have entrances); or (*c*) relating to any institution of a religious, educational, cultural, recreational or medical or similar character, or to any hotel, inn or public-house, block of flats, club, boarding house or hostel situate on the land on which any such advertisement is displayed, and limited to one advertisement of not exceeding 1·2 square metres in area (on a maximum of two frontages if these have entrances).

Class III—Certain advertisements of a temporary nature including " for sale " and " to let " signs; auction and other notices; advertisements as to those engaged in building or construction projects, etc.; advertisements of local events and agricultural demonstrations.

Class IV—Advertisements on business premises which relate wholly to the business carried on, or the goods sold, or the services provided on those premises, together with the name and qualifications of the proprietor, i.e., this includes notably shop signs.   However, it is provided that no such advertisement may be displayed on the exterior wall of a shop, unless the wall contains a shop window; and that it shall not be displayed " so that the highest part of the advertisement is above the level of the bottom of any first-floor window in the wall on which it is displayed"; and that if the advertisement is in an area of special control only, it shall not exceed 0·1 of the overall area of the face of the wall upon which it is displayed up to a height of 3·6 metres from ground level, and the area shall be computed in the case of a projecting advertisement as if it were placed flat against the building.

Class V—Advertisements displayed in the forecourts of buildings are limited as to the aggregate of their area to 4·5 square metres.

Class VI—Advertisements in the form of flags attached to a single flagstaff in an upright position on the roof of a building, and which bear no inscription or emblem other than the name or device of a person or persons occupying the building.   (One assumes that the Union Jack is not yet proscribed!)

However, these classes having been specified by reg. 14, provision is made by reg. 15 for the Secretary of State to exclude the application of reg. 14 where he deems this desirable: in other words, the degree of exemption may be reduced. Further, by reg. 16, advertisements which are displayed by deemed consent generally (i.e., under regs. 9, 12 and 14) may be required to be discontinued by means of the local planning authority serving a " discontinuation notice," following which the usual rights of appeal to the Secretary of State will apply. Rather similar provisions are made in respect of revocation or modification of express consent (regs. 24 and 25).

Applications for express consent are made under Part IV of the Regulations (regs. 17 to 22) and the procedure is broadly similar to that for planning applications.

In terms of control of existing advertisements, two factors apply. First, the display of advertisements may be limited as to time or by means of conditions; and both express and deemed consent may be withdrawn and a " discontinuance notice " served. Secondly, penalties for unlawful display of any advertisement are laid down in s. 109 of the 1971 Act, being a fine of not exceeding £100 upon summary conviction and, in the case of a continuing offence, £5 for each day during which the offence continues after initial conviction.

CHAPTER 11

OFFICES

1. General

The siting and use of office premises is not of such great importance in the context of protection of the environment as the siting and control of industry, yet it frequently has a significant effect upon the planning or " improvement " of an area. The existence of a large number of office jobs in any locality will influence the demand for transport and other services, for shopping facilities and, at least within a catchment radius, for housing of office workers.[1] In Inner London, for example, the incorrect siting of a sky-scraper office block would cause acute pressure to be exerted upon public transport serving that area, and would greatly increase the load upon postal services and upon restaurant facilities (if no effective canteen or restaurant were provided within the building). In so far as private cars and vehicles delivering to an urban office block are concerned, it should be noted that most urban (including country town) authorities have, for a considerable number of years past, laid down as a permanent condition of planning permission that for a given area of new office floor space a specified proportion of vehicle parking space be provided.

At the present time, the demand for planning permission for office development in prospering city centres is considerable,[2] due, it is submitted, principally to the immense profits to be made in terms of speculative investment. (The author here ventures to suggest that the grossly inflated rents paid by office tenants seeking " prestige " accommodation are very largely the product of the present system of taxation, wherein rent, no matter how exorbitant, is deductible for tax purposes.)

It is therefore of particular importance that the development of new urban centres, and equally the comprehensive redevelopment of outdated town centres, are, in fact, normally the subject of development plans. These development plans are drawn up in the usual

---

[1] See Appendix B, Recommendations 32 and 38.
[2] Even justifying the expense of jacking up and moving 14th-century buildings to new sites!

way by the local planning authority (in consultation with any lesser authorities affected), are then submitted to the Secretary of State for approval, and are subject to a local public inquiry.[3]   So far as office development is concerned it is significant that the finally approved plan for any given area will specify the precise total area of office floor space to be constructed.   An additional control—in this case directly by central government—has been imposed by the Control of Office and Industrial Development Act, 1965, now replaced by ss. 73 to 86 of the Town and Country Planning Act, 1971.   This provision requires that whenever development is proposed which includes office premises[4] exceeding a total of office floor space (measured externally) of 10,000 square feet or more in those areas designated from time to time by the Secretary of State for the Environment,[5] it is necessary that an Office Development Permit be obtained from the Secretary of State for the Environment as an essential condition precedent to an application for planning permission.   Under the 1965 Act this requirement was due to lapse during 1972, but it has now been extended (unless otherwise varied by Parliament in the interim) until 5th August, 1977.   For a more detailed discussion of this statutory control, see p. 221, *post*.

Whereas it is within the statutory powers of a local planning authority to undertake the development, or redevelopment, of a town centre at its own expense (reserving all profits which may arise to the benefit of the local ratepayers), it is an almost invariable practice for the local authority to operate through commercial development companies.   The principal reasons for this method of

[3] For a short general discussion of development plans see Chapter 1.

[4] " Office premises " is defined in s. 73 (1) as either (*a*) premises whose sole or principal use is to be use as an office or for office purposes; or (*b*) premises to be occupied together with those as in (*a*), wholly or mainly for purposes of the activities of the premises as in (*a*).   The definition is thus related to the meaning of " office purposes," which is interpreted in s. 73 (5) as including the "purposes of administration, clerical work, handling money, telephone and telegraph operating and the operation of computers, and ' clerical work ' includes writing, book-keeping, sorting papers, filing, typing, duplicating, punching cards or tapes, machine calculating, drawing and the editorial preparation of matter for publication."   Thus, for example, a bank or a duplicating agency will constitute an " office " and may require an O.D.P.

[5] The areas designated at present (1973) include the whole of the South East Economic Planning Region, but no longer include other parts of England, which had been designated between 1965 and 1969.   (The South East Economic Planning Region does, of course, also include Greater London and the remainder of the " Metropolitan Region," the exemption limit for the former being increased from 3,000 square feet by S.I. 1970 No. 1824.)

operation are discussed elsewhere [6] but, in brief, the prime advantage lies in the fact that the independent developer will form a means of protection against any possible loss which may occur either in terms of unexpected construction costs or in terms of a lower total rental being obtained than had been anticipated. Thus, the contractual terms must be drawn up with the greatest care in order to guard the rate fund. For this reason, it is equally essential that conditions be imposed as to the quality of design and construction, and as to dates for completion of the various stages in the development, together with the terms and periods of lettings which will result. Again, the contract will generally include a form of long lease to the developers which will secure reversion of all property rights (i.e., legal, although not *de facto*, possession) to the local authority at the end of a specified period (or periods as to parts of the site).

A further considerable advantage in arranging comprehensive development through specialist development companies is that the initial stages involve a specified competition between those accepting an invitation to enter, wherein those developers having sufficient resources at the given time submit proposed schemes to the local authority in whose district, borough or county borough the development area lies [6a]: in the former two cases, that is, county districts and boroughs, the submission is also thus indirectly made to the local planning authority. The schemes submitted are then judged in terms of both amenity (including practical use) and cost (including quality and value for money); and the selected proposals are then submitted, *via* the local planning authority, to the Secretary of State for approval. Before approving any such scheme the Secretary of State must first afford an opportunity to objectors—who may be existent property owners affected by the scheme, amenity or other societies, etc., and the general public—to be heard, invariably at a local public inquiry of some magnitude.

It will be observed that this method offers the advantages that a wide variety of sources of architectural and planning ideas may be tapped without undue expense to the local authority, and that sources of finance may also be more widely available.

There is, nevertheless, an important problem which tends to be

[6] Chapter 10.
[6a] Until 1st April, 1974: see Chapter 1.

aggravated by the employment of private developers in comprehensive redevelopment areas. As has recently been recognised by the Secretary of State in regard to London,[7] new office buildings tend to be let, so far as possible, in large units; that is, generally to larger firms or the branches of large companies. There is, accordingly, a shortage of small and reasonably inexpensive office accommodation, which is frequently necessary to meet the needs of the local public in terms of accessibility to professional services[8] and to some branches of the service industries.[9] This difficulty may be, in part, catered for in a central area redevelopment plan by specifying that a defined number of small-sized office units be designed and provided, so as at least to accommodate those firms already existing in the pre-development area. But, even here, the considerable increase in rents frequently charged may be well beyond the capacity of a small professional partnership or service company. In some types of area, therefore, the use of independent developers may tend to act to the detriment of the local community in terms both of office occupiers and of the local inhabitants served by them.

It must also be remarked that, as in the case of certain well-known sites in London, private developers have constructed multi-storey office blocks and have then, quite deliberately, refrained from letting the whole, or part, because it is now (regrettably) a financial fact of life that the value of money is falling so rapidly that the book value of property tends to soar. Thus, an empty office block may double its book value (upon security of which further capital may be borrowed and re-invested) within, say, four years. Certain steps may be taken by the relevant local authority, including the decision that the " void " building be rated as if occupied, but a discussion of these is beyond the scope of this book.

It should also be noted that a distinction should be drawn between the general methods of planning discussed above and the requirements in relation to New Towns, which are referred to elsewhere.[10]

The amenity of an existing area, whether in town, village, or open country, may, of course, be affected by the introduction of an

---

[7] See Chapter 1.
[8] Say, solicitors' offices.
[9] Say, duplicating services or typing agencies.
[10] See Chapters 1 and 10.

office use. Yet, in many instances, this may be the only economic means of financing the cost of maintenance of a large mansion (or even a town house). In the case of a country house it is evident that, short of continuation in use as a dwelling, the important amenity factors to be considered are: first, that at least the exterior, together with the setting of the building, be well maintained; and, secondly, that the presence of an office establishment should not generate excessive road traffic. Adequate statutory provisions exist for the listing of buildings of sufficient architectural or historic importance,[11] but difficulties may occasionally arise as to enforcing adequate maintenance and suitable external decoration. The building, whilst being the principal feature in a village or stretch of open country, may not be deemed by the government experts to merit listing.[12] Nevertheless, it is possible for a rather gaunt and not over-attractive building to be of some value in an otherwise featureless landscape; and certainly it is possible for the same building to be rendered an eyesore by inappropriate treatment, which may be intended merely to catch the eye for commercial purposes. If the area is, in general, not attractive, the possible alternative means of control by declaration of a conservation area [13] will not be available to the local planning authority. However, the second problem, that of road traffic, can, to an extent, be met by the imposition of limits on the size (i.e., preferably by width, since this is more readily checked than weight) of vans and lorries using minor roads in the immediate area, by means of an order made by the Secretary of State (or other " appropriate minister ") by virtue of s. 16 of the Road Traffic Regulation Act, 1967. A person who drives a vehicle, or causes or permits a vehicle to be driven, in contravention of such an order is liable on summary conviction to a fine not exceeding £20 (s. 16 (5)).

In the cases of both town houses and country houses of particular architectural merit there is, inevitably, a loss to interior design and decorative qualities in many cases of office use. The principal problems arise in connection with the alteration of size of rooms. In many instances the original height of ceilings is far greater than is desired for office use, and this is further emphasised where larger rooms are divided by partitions. Thus, it is possible that the interior

[11] Chapter 13, at p. 239.
[12] Chapter 13.
[13] Chapter 13, at p. 270.

plaster mouldings in a Grade I or Grade II* building are protected, but that the architectural effect is rendered ridiculous by partitioning, or by the erection of false, suspended ceilings.

In relation to the conversion, or extension, of existing buildings in order that they may be used as offices, it has become evident in many significant areas that local planning authorities (in particular certain London Boroughs) have experienced great difficulty in persuading, or attempting to persuade, property owners to retain major internal features, such as entrance halls and staircases, in high-quality listed buildings.[14]   As will be explained,[15] statutory protection may be imposed upon the interiors of certain Grade I and Grade II* buildings, but, in practice, it is often necessary for a local planning authority to arrive at an effective working arrangement with the owner (or potential purchaser) of such a building. For example, the only real financial hope for preservation of a building may sometimes lie in the prospect of purchase by a large concern who will only acquire it if they are assured that permission for certain alterations will be, or has been, given.   Again, the conversion of a terrace, or terraced side to a town square, for office use will provide the owner with a larger floor area for letting, and thus a higher return on capital, if he can succeed in dismantling the majority of entrance halls and staircases.   Clearly the loss of such major features may, in a few decades' time, be taken as a point in argument to obtain permission for demolition of the entire building, as being no longer of top quality as a specimen of its particular architectural period.

In this respect, a further hazard exists in the strict requirements of modern Building and Fire Regulations.   The office layout will be influenced by the need for a ready means of escape, and also by the construction of fire-resistant partitions and self-closing doors, which may entirely destroy any merit in preserving many architectural features.

The above-mentioned difficulties would be reduced by an increase in the availability of Exchequer grants, and it might often be of assistance to a local authority to be able to apply for additional financial aid purely upon the basis that a building served a special amenity need in the locality, even though it be of fair but not outstanding quality.

National allocation of office premises.—It will be seen from subsequent

14 Notable in certain well-known London squares.
15 Chapter 13.

discussion of the purpose and use of the system of Office Development Permits that there is a means of central governmental control over the national allocation of office premises. In effect, this additional control has tended to be exercised rather more in order to limit excessive speculative office building, in for example London, rather than positively to encourage new office users in provincial areas in fact deficient in such accommodation.

Offices can, for this purpose, be divided into two categories: those directly concerned with industrial manufacture or export and requiring to be sited accordingly; and those not so connected, which are almost invariably related to the service industries. Offices dealing with manufacture will generally seek to be sited either in the locality of the factory, or at a port of export or some alternative major centre of commerce, such as the City of London, Liverpool or Southampton; whereas professional or service industry offices (such as estate agents or travel agents) will wish to be situated at a central point of a catchment area from which they draw their clients or customers. So far as applications for the granting of office development permits for the latter use are concerned, the tendency will have been discouraged in recent years (rightly or wrongly) by the imposition of Selective Employment Tax,[16] now due to be abolished in April, 1973. At the same time, however, the Government has actively engaged, through the Location of Offices Bureau, by direct advertising and other means, in encouraging the relocation of London-based offices in rural, or semi-rural, areas. As a result of many techniques developed by the electronics industry (including the use of tape recordings, microfilm recording of documents, the use of computers for rapid calculation, and private telephone lines) many city-based companies handling a considerable volume of information and documents now tend to set up very large clerical and records departments in the provinces, thereby saving both in terms of building and accommodation costs, and in rates of pay.

2. Legal Controls

It had become evident by the mid-1960s that some form of central government control of office development was increasingly necessary for two inter-related reasons. First, speculative developers were tending to concentrate upon office construction in certain most profitable areas (notably in central London), to the detriment

[16] No rebate being available to service industries, including professional firms.

of progress in development or redevelopment in other parts of the country.   And, secondly, that, as a result of such an influence, the absence of office accommodation in various provincial areas was resulting in a local shortage of jobs for office workers.

Parliament therefore passed, in August, 1965, the Control of Office and Industrial Development Act, of which Part I relates to office development and Part II to industrial development (as to which see Chapter 2).   This Act was repealed, but re-enacted without material alteration, by Part IV of the Town and Country Planning Act, 1971, of which ss. 73 to 86 and Scheds. 12 and 13 relate specifically to the provisions of the 1965 Act.   This legislation introduces an additional control over office development, which is, in fact, to be exercised not through the medium of local planning authority decisions (although these do still separately apply to applications for office development) but directly by central government by means of permits to be obtained from the Secretary of State for the Environment (although originally the Chairman of the Board of Trade under the 1965 Act).   These permits are to be described as *Office Development Permits*, frequently referred to as "O.D.P.s."

Whenever it is proposed to develop " office premises " (as defined in s. 73 (1) of the 1971 Act)[17] which exceed a " prescribed exemption limit " (s. 75 (7), *infra*), in terms of "office floor space" (as defined in s. 85 (3)),[18] an O.D.P. must first be obtained from the Secretary of State.[18a]   In deciding upon whether or not to grant or withhold such a permit, the Secretary of State " shall have particular regard to the need for promoting the better distribution of employment in Great Britain " (s. 74 (3)).   However, as already mentioned, office developments which are sufficiently small to be below the " prescribed exemption limit " (s. 75 (7)) will not require an O.D.P.   The exemption limits may be varied from time to time in accordance with national and regional needs by order of the Secretary of State.[18a]   There is, however, a requirement in the Act (s. 75 (8)) that the Secretary of State shall not reduce the prescribed exemption limit to less than 1,000 square feet.   He may vary the

---

[17] See p. 216, footnote 4 for definition, which is related also to use for " office purposes."

[18] " Office floor space " is defined, by s. 85 (3), as the gross floor space comprised in office premises, ascertained by external measurement, whether that space is to be bounded by the external walls of a building or not; party walls are to be included up to their vertical centre line.

[18a] Secretary of State for the Environment.

exemption limit in any selected part of the country for purposes of control particularly in relation to employment.

It must, however, be emphasised that although it is a requirement of the Act that an O.D.P. be obtained as an absolute condition precedent to making a planning application involving office development (i.e., office development exceeding the prescribed exemption limit), it is still completely at the discretion of the local planning authority nevertheless to refuse planning permission.

Since this work is primarily concerned with the control of the environment and does not purport to consider the regulation of employment or the law of town and country planning in general, it is not proposed to discuss the statutory provisions which are now contained in ss. 73 to 86 (Pt. IV) and Scheds. 12 and 13 to the Town and Country Planning Act, 1971, in exhaustive detail. However, two essential matters must be mentioned. First, the areas of control (Metropolitan and otherwise) may be varied by order of the Secretary of State for the Environment according to national needs from time to time. And, secondly, careful provision is made in the Act so as to prevent developers from creating additional office space by piecemeal development. An attempt to develop a site in separate parcels of under 10,000 square feet will not avoid the need to obtain an O.D.P., because the Act stipulates that any " related development " must be added for the purposes of this calculation: furthermore, the conversion of an existing building, or any parts of an existing building, into office premises will equally require an O.D.P.

In cases where the proposed development includes office and industrial premises, both an O.D.P. and an Industrial Development Certificate (" I.D.C.") may be required, even though only a single planning permission may be all that is subsequently necessary for the site. However, provision of office space can be a *condition* in an I.D.C., in which event a separate O.D.P. will not be necessary.

The definition of " office premises " is essentially related to premises intended to be used for " office purposes." [17] There is no appeal from a decision by the Secretary of State for the Environment to refuse an O.D.P. save on a point of law to the High Court.[19]

[19] As to the matter of claims for compensation for refusal of planning permission (which is a subject beyond the scope of this book) it should be noted that no provision is made for such claims following refusal of an O.D.P.; claims will, however, arise in relation to I.D.C. refusal.

The general policy as to the control of office development has been clearly stated in Circular No. 64/65 (issued by the Minister of Housing and Local Government on 25th August, 1965). In this circular it is emphasised that O.D.P.s will equally be required in relation to areas of comprehensive development (or redevelopment); and, further, that any development proposed to be carried out by a local authority will require such a permit, which must be obtained from the Department of the Environment in the usual way.

The office development to which the Act applies is development of any kind; that is, it may include the rebuilding of an office, provided such rebuilding is of such a type that, under general town and country planning legislation, planning permission is required. Further, a permit will be required even for premises which are not to be used directly for office purposes but which are ancillary to an office, as for example an office canteen, or a garage for office employees or clients: but such ancillary uses must be (as assessed by the local planning authority) occupied and used " wholly or mainly " in conjunction with the actual offices (ss. 73, 74).

Restrictions and conditions upon permission for office development may be imposed by two separate and parallel means; that is, both in connection with the granting of an O.D.P., and also as part of the related planning permission. Thus two separate sets of qualifying provisions may apply to the same site, but it is provided (s. 77) that any restriction or condition imposed by the Department of the Environment must be accepted and implemented by the local planning authority. The Department is empowered to impose restrictions upon the qualification of the applicant for subsequent planning permission. Thus the O.D.P. may, for example, restrict the persons by whom it may be used; or it may limit the period of its own validity. Equally, the Department of the Environment may also impose conditions upon the office development. Such conditions must be listed in the second schedule to the Permit itself, but it will be open to the local planning authority to impose more (but not less) severe conditions in relation to subsequent planning permission if they so desire. In the case of a planning application in a designated area for a building for mixed use in which the office user is stated to be intended as under 10,000 square feet (the exemption limit, so that an O.D.P. is not required) it is nevertheless open to the Department of the Environment to impose a condition (by s. 79) that at no time shall other parts of the building be brought into office use so as to exceed the exemption limit, unless an O.D.P. is first obtained.

In the case of contravention of O.D.P. conditions the usual means of enforcement action (under general town and country planning legislation) will apply.[20]

It should also be noted, in so far as the Metropolitan Region[21] only is concerned, that developers may have certain latent rights, in relation to the construction of offices on particular sites, of which the general public in the area affected may not be conscious. These may exist for the following reasons. The 1965 Act (s. 3), being concerned with the extreme pressures at that time exerted upon the Metropolitan Region, provided for certain retrospective restrictions. The Act laid down (as now by the 1971 Act) that, in this Region, even where planning permission had been granted prior to the Royal Assent, an O.D.P. need not be issued. In these cases, the planning permission still exists, and may be acted upon at any time in the future as soon as an O.D.P. is, in fact, granted: an earlier refusal to grant an O.D.P. need not influence future decisions as to O.D.P.s on the same site. This is now provided for by s. 83 of and Sched. 12, paras. 1 and 2, to the Town and Country Planning Act, 1971. Equally, an earlier planning permission may become effective when the necessity to obtain an O.D.P. upon any given site ceases to exist: that is, either at such time as ss. 73 to 87 of the 1971 Act are repealed (or lapse); or (and significantly) if the Secretary of State decides that the area in which the site in question lies shall no longer be subject to the requirement that an O.D.P. be obtained (i.e., by removal of the named borough or district from Sched. 13 to the 1971 Act). This latter situation will also arise where the Secretary of State by order raises the exemption limit to an area greater than that affecting the relevant site, as has already occurred by the increase of exemption limit in the Metropolitan Region from the original 3,000 square feet to 10,000 square feet.

Finally, reference should be made to the means of enforcement of restrictions upon office development. This is laid down, in common

---

[20] But with the stipulation (s. 82 (2)) that it shall not be open to the person concerned to appeal upon the grounds that planning permission " ought to be granted."

[21] The Metropolitan Region, for the purposes of this Act, comprises all the area of Greater London together with such areas as are set out in Sched. 13 to the 1971 Act (s. 85 (6)), and these range from Aldershot in the West to Southend-on-Sea in the East, and from Luton in the North to Horsham in the South.

with all other means of general planning control (Pt. III of the 1971 Act) and additional control in special cases (Pt. IV of the 1971 Act), in Pt. V of the 1971 Act, whereby an enforcement notice must first be served (s. 87), with a right of appeal to the Secretary of State (s. 88). The penalties for failure to comply with such an enforcement notice are a fine not exceeding £400 upon summary conviction, or an unlimited fine upon conviction on indictment. If the enforcement notice relates to discontinuation of the *use* of office (or any other) premises, failure to comply may result in the imposition of the penalties as already stated and if the offence continues a fine not exceeding £50 per day of continuation upon summary conviction, or an unlimited fine upon conviction on indictment.

CHAPTER 12

VISUAL AMENITY:
THE CONTROL OF ARCHITECTURAL
DESIGN AND OF LANDSCAPING

THE purpose of this chapter is to consider the basic question of the protection of visual amenity in a locality.

In general, local and national economic requirements are the concern of commercial interests, and are therefore thoroughly analysed from the standpoint of profitability. Further, the siting of manufacturing or other commercial enterprises—certainly upon a national or regional basis,[1] and frequently within more localised urban or rural environments—tends to receive the active attention of planning authorities. In contrast, however, matters of aesthetic judgment, or of other solely amenity factors (such as additional, but not measurably excessive, noise; or of minor additional pollution of air or water), may tend to be insufficiently stressed both at elected planning committee level [2] and at subsequent planning appeals.

The word " amenity " is frequently in the minds both of the public and of local planning authorities, yet the legal significance of the term is uncertain. The word is used in s. 51 (1) of the Town and Country Planning Act, 1971, yet the Act gives no formal definition of it. One meaning was, in fact, discussed in the specific context of the phrase " with a view to securing the amenity of the area . . ." (as used in s. 59 (1) of the Housing, Town Planning, etc. Act, 1909) in the judgment of Scrutton, L.J., in *Re Ellis and Ruislip-Northwood U.D.C.* [1920] 1 K.B., at p. 370 (C.A.), in which he said: " The word ' amenity ' is obviously used very loosely; it is, I think, used in an Act of Parliament, and appears to mean ' pleasant circumstances or features, advantages.' Wide streets and plenty of air and room between houses seem clearly to be amenities, and a provision securing them by setting back houses to a given line seems to me to be a provision with a view to *securing* amenity." In the same case,

---

[1] As to the bodies concerned with the national and regional siting of industry, and the significance of Development Areas, see Chapter 2.
[2] More particularly at delegated planning authority level, e.g., boroughs, U.D.C.s and R.D.C.s.

Bankes, L.J., in a dissenting judgment, said, "... 'amenity' is a term of such very wide significance. ..."

It could be maintained that it would be both difficult and, in practice, unsatisfactory to attempt a precise (and thus restrictive) interpretation of the word "amenity." The above judicial descriptions, for they can be said to be nothing more, turn upon the meaning of the word "pleasant"; and what (apparently) pleases some may well be repellent to others.

It is submitted, however, that the "provision" of amenity may, as generally understood, be taken to have two meanings. Thus, it may consist either (*a*) of rendering a locality (or individual physical environment) pleasant, or more pleasant; or (*b*) of reducing, disguising or totally concealing aspects of a locality which would otherwise be unpleasant. Thus, the planting of tree screens is an "amenity factor."

Whether or not, therefore, the meaning of "amenity" is to be equated to the new but perhaps wider expression "physical environment" which was introduced in s. 2 (3) (*a*) of the Town and Country Planning Act, 1968,[3] is an open question. However, if "amenity" may be accepted as a broadly descriptive term for the purposes of this chapter, it may then be said that the prime weaknesses in the present arrangements for the protection of such amenity arise from the following factors:

(i) The cost of land scheduled, or likely to be scheduled, for development is now so high that financial pressure causes developers to attempt to obtain planning permission for a considerably greater density than that known to be preferred, as a matter of policy, by the local planning authority. Many members of planning committees (which are, of course, purely voluntary and unpaid) have suffered the experience of monthly applications by the same developer for the same site continuing, at slowly decreasing density, for as long as eighteen months. However, this situation only arises, in general, where the developer is of sufficient size to afford surplus drawing office capacity.

(ii) The existence of outline planning permission on any site (which is granted under the 1971 Act, s. 42 and art. 5 (2) of the Town and Country Planning General Development Order, 1973 (S.I. 1973 No. 31)) is the principal cause not only of the situation stated in

---

[3] Now s. 7 (3) (*a*) of the Town and Country Planning Act, 1971.

(i) above, but also of many other attempts to obtain detailed planning permission of a type which would not have been envisaged at the time of the granting of outline permission.[4] The continuous escalation of land prices causes frequent changes in ownership of such undeveloped sites, and is a constant inducement to subsequent purchasers to seek what would initially have been considered over-development. Thus, frequent attempts are made to convert what should be small and visually insignificant sites into higher density and/or unusual, and thus more expensive, developments. The conclusion to be drawn from this is that outline planning permissions should not only be given as sparingly as possible, but also that there should be some clear directive that, where necessary, the provision in the second paragraph of art. 5 (2), requiring the submission of " further details " as to various " particular matters," be applied before outline applications are considered for approval. More particularly, this requirement should relate to the total floor area and total height proposed for any building.

An obvious example of the problems currently arising can be given. An outline permission for a " block of flats " should, in almost every case, specify a maximum number of dwellings, so as to leave the applicant in no doubt as to the speculative land value of the site. If this were mandatory in every outline permission a great deal of delay in development, and of cost incurred in local planning authority work, would also be saved by avoidance of a subsequent succession of detailed applications. Bearing in mind the very acute shortage in local authorities of trained planning staff, this measure would be of benefit to all members of the public. Doubtless s. 42 of the 1971 Act, in limiting the time for which outline permission will be valid, will assist in this respect. By this section, an outline permission for building or other operations granted before 1st April, 1969, for which the development to which it refers has not been begun before 1st January, 1968, is limited as follows: (a) any matter specifically reserved by the permission for later approval must be applied for and dealt with within three years of 1st April, 1969; and (b) the actual development must be begun within five years of 1st April, 1969, or within two years of " the final approval " of

---

[4] The giving of outline planning permission commits the local planning authority to allowing some form of the proposed development on the site. For general guidance to developers and local planning authorities see Circular 48/59, paras. 42–51 and p. 14 thereof.

any reserved matter, whichever period be the longer. As to the exact date of the "final approval," this is to be taken as the official date of granting by the local planning authority, that is, not the date of a planning committee resolution, but the date upon which formal notification *in writing* of the approval is given to the applicant. In the case of a successful appeal, the relevant date becomes the date upon which approval is granted by the Secretary of State in accordance with s. 43 (5) of the 1971 Act. However, the above time-limits will be overridden by any express condition in an outline permission granted before 1st April, 1969, where this has specified that commencement or completion of the development, or alternatively approval of detailed plans, shall be before a given date (s. 66 (3) of the 1968 Act).

In the case of outline permission granted after the coming into force of s. 42 (previously s. 66 of the 1968 Act) on 1st April, 1969, the same general principles apply: namely, that a requirement shall be made (or will be deemed to have been made, if omitted) that detailed approval will be obtained within three years[5] of the date of the outline permission; and that development will be commenced within five years of the date of outline permission or within two years of the date of detailed permission, whichever be the longer period.

It will be seen that the time factors of three years and five years are more readily related to the general needs of the new style Structure Plans and Action Areas (introduced by the 1968 Act)[6] than to the question of site value-density-amenity, as specifically discussed in this chapter. In fact, the very mention of a five-year limit may have the effect of encouraging prolonged negotiation over density in relation to the detailed plans. However, shorter or longer periods may be specified by the local planning authority if they so desire.

(iii) Matters of design and of scale of development on any given site are, obviously, influenced by the needs and intentions of the architects. Those laymen who particularly appreciate the importance of an aesthetic judgment in the design of any structures[7] which are likely to impinge upon the day-to-day life of local inhabitants for decades or centuries to come, no doubt also sympathise with the professional (and principally financial) problems

[5] Section 42 (2) (*a*).
[6] Now in Part II of the 1971 Act.
[7] See Appendix B, Recommendations 10 to 13.

which face the architect under modern conditions. The designers of buildings may be constantly tempted to create structures which are principally intended as emphatic forms of self-advertisement. Thus there is pressure to design in such a way that a development will stand out from surrounding structures or natural features, by means either of marked contrast in scale, or of balance, or of texture or colour of materials. The standard form of argument put forward at planning inquiries in favour of such treatment of a site is that the designer's intention is to record for posterity the manners and social values of the present day and age. It should, however, be borne in mind by those concerned with the granting of planning permission that the technical advances, both in the methods of construction and in the variety of building materials available, now enable an architect to create a structure which is in no way related to its natural environment. By contrast, for example, the great houses built in past centuries can be seen, in virtually every case, to be suited to their setting, not only because their designers generally so intended, but also because of the then technical limitations upon structure and materials. Imbalance was thus more difficult to achieve; and materials of stone, brick, tile and slate tended to be appropriate to the locality in which they were both obtained and used.

Under modern conditions, the final selection of facing and cladding materials for walls and roofs is not infrequently left by the planning committee to the discretion of a local planning officer. This can, clearly, be of embarrassment to that official, and examples can be quoted in which the sample material submitted as matching the existing neighbouring structures either has not, in fact, done so, or has not matched the eventual bulk delivery to the site. The effect of a design, as shown on the elevational drawings seen by the planning committee, can be radically altered by changes in colours or textures of materials. The answer to this problem might be that a colour range (or ranges according to the physical and natural characteristics of the planning authority area) be approved and published by the Department of the Environment, so that it would then be open to a planning authority to indicate that, in their view, facing or cladding should be within certain, numbered, ranges of colours or tones. Such ranges would, by definition, not attempt to be precise to the extent of British Standard colours, but would be shaded so as to indicate limits of brilliance and contrast.

It may be said that a Ministerial directive of this nature would be too restrictive upon the designer, but the very existence of such colour charts would, in fact, render it possible for a developer to appeal more readily to the Minister upon a specific question of colour, and to do so simply by means of written representation.[8]

The (then) Minister of Housing and Local Government has, of course, correctly published a statement of broad advice to those concerned with the aesthetics of the design of buildings and other structures in *Selected Planning Appeals*, Second Series, Vol. V (1963), in the Preface to Section 1, " Design." In this advice, it is remarked that: ". . . it is not possible to lay down rules defining what is good and what is bad; and much may in any event turn on the site. Moreover, opinions, even expert opinions, can often differ." Further reference to the matter of expert opinion is made in paragraph (iv) below, but here it is necessary to stress the importance of such guidance, particularly in view of the Minister's further comment in the same advice: " Planning control should not be used to stifle initiative and experience in design; a design is not bad because it is new and different—it may be very good. Designs should be rejected only if the objection is clear and definite and can be explained. It is not enough to say that a design will ' injure the amenities ' or ' conflict with adjoining development '; it must be explained why it will do so." To this comment one would in no way take exception, save that, where it so happens that a committee consists principally of persons whose education has not included the opportunity to acquire a sufficient degree of artistic experience or judgment, then such concepts as whether or not a building is " fussy, or ill-proportioned " may be inexplicable to the voting members, no matter how efficient and skilled may be the advising local government officer present at the meeting.

There are also many examples of buildings of excellent modern design which have been approved in isolation and have thus been sited unsuitably in areas in which the predominant characteristic was originally one of historical charm or interest, and which should have been retained without disruption. In some cases the existence of mature tree screens has been taken into account, disregarding the

---

[8] The appellant from a refusal of planning permission generally has the option of continuing to a local public inquiry or, alternatively, of putting his case in writing for decision by the Minister without subsequent oral argument.

fact that the particular trees may have a far more limited life than the existing or proposed buildings which it is intended shall be protected by means of the screen.

(iv) At this point it is relevant to consider the effects of the existence of honorary panels of architects. Some local planning authorities have set up permanent panels of local architects in private practice to advise upon the architectural merits, or demerits, of designs if and when such designs are submitted to them by the planning committee (or, in some cases, an area sub-committee). They deserve the gratitude of the general public since their function is essentially honorary. The general method of operation is that an individual architect will not attend a panel meeting either where his own design is to be considered, or where the site in question is close to the base of his practice. In addition, the planning application drawings are so presented to the panel by the planning officer as to preserve the anonymity of the designer. However, it must be remarked that the weakness in this otherwise most helpful system often lies in the totally inadequate reimbursement of panel members. Whilst travelling expenses are provided, no allowance is made for loss of professional time. Since the practice of architecture has on average in recent years become (as shown by statistics) relatively poorly rewarded in comparison to other professions, such a loss of working hours can be significant. This may influence the time devoted to deliberation; and also, perhaps, the standard of ability of those local architects both willing and able to serve. Under the present national economic conditions, local planning authorities are hard-pressed to find money to finance the repair of historic buildings, let alone for reimbursement of architects' panels to any worthwhile extent.

Pressure upon the financial resources of local authorities in the general planning sphere is also now increased under the Civic Amenities Act, 1967, by the introduction of Conservation Areas, although the protective effect of such designations is greatly to be welcomed. In the long-term, the ability of planning authorities to cast a protective aegis over such areas will result in a reduction of unsuitable planning applications and will also encourage the continuation of certain skills in design and craftsmanship. But, at the present moment, planning authorities are incurring very considerable expense, both in completing surveys of such areas prior to consideration for designation, and in financing improvements to those structures owned by the local authority which are not, at present, suited to the new Conservation Areas in which they stand.

Conservation Areas, whilst appropriate to the subject of this chapter, are separately discussed in Chapter 13 (2), Conservation Areas and Buildings of Architectural and Historic Interest.

(v) Whereas the design and construction of a single building of a scale common to a surrounding urban area may not greatly alter the character of a town, the question of infilling in many villages is of critical significance. The whole nature of a village centre can be radically altered by the erection of, for example, a single bungalow in inappropriate materials. This factor is of particular importance in the light of the Minister's Development Control Policy Note, No. 4, " Development in Rural Areas " (1969), in which para. 6 states, ". . . Some villages are suitable for considerable expansion; others have special qualities which are worth preserving and this may restrict new building to minor ' infilling ' and replacements." No advice is given, however, as to the qualities desirable in these new structures in relation to the village entity; although it is stated, in para. 7 of the same Note, that " reference should be made in each case to the local planning authority's stated policy for the area and to any detailed plans they have prepared to guide development in particular villages. Planning Bulletin No. 8 ' Settlement in the Countryside ' explains the purposes of such plans and how they are drawn up." [9]

However, it should also be noted that, even in rural areas, the decline in the required size of the agricultural labour force has resulted in a shortage of employment in the immediate vicinity of many villages. As the old local families leave to find work elsewhere, the village tends to become a dormitory or retirement area, and to be increasingly inhabited by people who are often unaware of local character and atmosphere and to whom the existence of relatively large gardens or allotment areas is of little interest. Problems therefore arise, for example, in connection with " back land " development and unsympathetic infilling.

(vi) It is, perhaps, also relevant to mention the recently published

---

[9] The Council for the Protection of Rural England publication *The Future of the Village* (1970) emphasises the need to preserve villages, and that many of special merit are already being lost, due to their streets becoming parts of major traffic routes. The publication proposes various practical means of protection.

comment by the Buchanan Standing Joint Committee [10] to the effect that the level of town and country planning research (as at 1970) carried out by the then Ministry of Housing and Local Government " is far too small in relation to present needs, and that the gathering and storage of information is fragmented and lacking in co-ordination." It was therefore recommended by the Committee that a research organisation for planning and environment generally be set up upon similar lines to the Road Research Laboratory and the Building Research Station: and, further, that a central national pool of statistical information be made available to local government planning departments.

(vii) The importance of a careful consideration of the matters of amenity discussed here will be progressively increased as a result of the Report of the Committee on Public Participation in Planning (the Skeffington Committee), published by the then Ministry of Housing and Local Government under the title " People and Planning," 1969. The view expressed in the report is that members of the public in general, and of voluntary organisations concerned with special interests (ranging through a gamut including such varied interests as nature conservation, noise abatement, architectural and archaeological conservation, recreational sports, etc.) shall be encouraged actively to discuss each significant local planning problem during the time of its active consideration by the local planning authority. But it should be borne in mind that local societies formed to encourage, protect and enjoy specialised interests tend to become extremely zealous in the furtherance of their particular concern, sometimes regardless of wider town and country planning considerations. In the end it is the local planning authority which has to form a fully balanced view; and, frequently, a firm and early decision may be necessary, not least by reason of financial factors affecting the project itself. The existence of a local exhibition relating to a particular development (say, a school) will, no doubt, stimulate constructive and useful comment; but it will also stimulate criticism in the minds of those members of the local population who have had no real experience of the problems involved, and who may be stimulated to comment and sometimes to obstruct, to some extent as a mere pastime. It is all the more

[10] Consisting of five professional bodies representing architects, surveyors, town planners and engineers, and set up following Professor Colin Buchanan's report " Traffic in Towns " (1963).

important, therefore, that local planning authorities should be aware of the need to make their decisions only after having evaluated (*a*) the need for progress (commercial and scientific); (*b*) the natural desire of the average man to retain a sense of personal security which relies upon a locality with which he is familiar; and (*c*) the need to aim, so far as possible, for perfection in the " amenities " offered by any local environment.

CHAPTER 13

BUILDINGS, STRUCTURES AND LAND OF ARCHITECTURAL OR HISTORIC INTEREST; CONSERVATION AREAS

THE destruction or other despoliation of buildings or monuments of architectural or historic interest has, of course, occurred throughout history and has included such varied activities as the reduction of so-called strong-points by Parliamentary troops in the seventeenth century, and the deliberate breaking-up (by means of enormous bonfires) of monoliths at Avebury and elsewhere whenever stone for a local building was required. Steps were taken to protect ancient monuments towards the end of the last century[1]; and the National Trust for England and Wales and Northern Ireland was created by statute in 1907[2] in order to provide for the acquisition and management of buildings, structures and land for the benefit of the nation. The value of this function has progressively increased in parallel with the eroding effects of estate duty upon the traditional ownership of landed estates.

Despite this it became increasingly evident, and more particularly since the rapid increase in size and capacity of development companies, that other means of protection were also required. The Town and Country Planning Act, 1947, therefore introduced Building Preservation Orders, to be made by local planning authorities or by the then Minister of Housing and Local Government when a building of architectural or historic interest was seen to be in danger. However, many unfortunate demolitions succeeded in avoiding discovery until too late, and the Town and Country Planning Act, 1962 (s. 32, now consolidated in s. 54 of the Town and Country Planning Act, 1971), therefore introduced a requirement that the Minister (now the Secretary of State for the Environment) draw up lists of buildings to be afforded protection against demolition, damage or alteration. Further provisions to

---

[1] Ancient Monuments Protection Act, 1882, followed by subsequent legislation now extant in the Ancient Monuments Acts, 1913 to 1972 (*post*).

[2] The National Trust for Scotland, 1931.

assist and extend these powers were made in the Civic Amenities Act, 1967, which created Conservation Areas; together with certain other statutes, now largely consolidated in the Town and Country Planning Act, 1971.[3]   Thus, the protection afforded to buildings and their settings can be divided into:

1. Buildings, structures and land of architectural or historic interest; and
2. Conservation areas.

1. Buildings, Structures and Land of Architectural or Historic Interest

(*Note.*—Reference is made in this section to the distinct and separate powers and duties of (*a*) county planning authorities, (*b*) county authorities generally, (*c*) district (delegated) planning authorities, and (*d*) district authorities generally.   However, as from April, 1974, with the reorganisation of local government under the Local Government Act, 1972, *all* these powers and duties will be with the New Districts—unless specially reserved in individual cases either to the county or to the Secretary of State for the Environment in any given case.)

The range of protection under this general heading can be further divided under the following headings:

(*a*)   Listed buildings[4] (miscalled " scheduled buildings ");
(*b*)   Building Preservation Notices[5];
(*c*)   Buildings subject to grants and loans for repairs or maintenance;
(*d*)   National Trust property;
(*e*)   Ancient Monuments;
(*f*)   Churches and other ecclesiastical buildings;
(*g*)   Public Health legislation; Rates Relief;
(*h*)   Historic Buildings Bureau.

In considering these headings, however, the reader should also refer to the Recommendations (numbers 14 to 21) put forward by the Dartmouth Committee, for the text of which see Appendix B hereto; but in so doing, it may be found preferable to read initially the remainder of this chapter.

---

[3] Conservation areas are now dealt with in s. 277 of the 1971 Act.
[4] Listed buildings are those placed upon special statutory lists for purposes of protection and record.
[5] Building Preservation Notices may be issued to provide temporary protection pending " listing " of a building.

(1) *Listed buildings* ("*scheduled buildings*")

To take first the enactment having the principal effect in terms of the protection of buildings of special merit, the Town and Country Planning Act, 1971 (consolidating earlier Acts), requires buildings of architectural or historic interest to be "listed" (s. 54). The original lists created under this and preceding statutes were divided into Grade I, Grade II* and Grade II lists, which were afforded varying degrees of protection (*post*); but provision was also made for a "supplementary list," described as Grade III,[6] which contains buildings of architectural or historic interest which were, at the time of original listing, thought not to be of sufficient value to warrant protection if it were also borne in mind that there exists an emergency method open to the local planning authority in the form of the Building Preservation Notice (*post*). However, the original form of listing has been found to be inadequate in two principal respects. First, it has become evident that the lists require to be extended in order to include late Victorian, Edwardian and even quite recent buildings, where these are of special value in terms of architectural merit or historical connection. This process of chronological extension was commenced in 1969. Secondly, and even more importantly, it has become evident that the inclusion of a building in the Grade III list (i.e., unprotected), or within the confines of a Conservation Area (*post*) without being statutorily listed, has frequently induced early demolition by unscrupulous developers who wish to avoid any danger of subsequent statutory protection. This became evident to many local authorities, and is commented upon in the Dartmouth Committee Report.[7] Steps have accordingly been taken not only to afford greater protection within conservation areas—by means of provisions in ss. 7 to 9 of the Town and Country Planning (Amendment) Act, 1972 [8]—but also by revision of the present lists in order gradually to abolish the present Grade III category. Thus, many of the present Grade III structures will become Grade II and protected; but a few may cease to be listed. However, the process of revision involves careful inspection by expert assessors employed by the Department of the Environment, together with, in many cases, painstaking historical research, and it

---

[6] Grade III buildings may, however, form a "Grade II Group," yet this will not afford statutory protection (s. 54 (9), (10) of 1971 Act).

[7] Appendix B, p. 324, *post*.

[8] See p. 272, *post*.

is unlikely to be completed in less than fifteen years. The revision is, however, being carried out area by area and thus buildings in certain parts of the country have already been re-graded (i.e., as Grade I, Grade II* and Grade II only), whereas other areas will continue to contain Grade III buildings for many years to come.

The purpose of listing is to preserve buildings or structures which offer good, or special, examples of periods of architecture or of the work of particular architects; or which demonstrate the development of engineering or building techniques; or which are in themselves of outstanding artistic merit; or which illustrate special types of user or occupation related to industry (including agriculture); or which may illustrate a local or specialised dwelling.[9] It is also possible to list small separate features, such as a market cross; or to include any features lying within the curtilage of a larger, listed building.[10] It is also important to note that special provisions apply in cases where the listed building forms part of a conservation area. Such instances are now treated, broadly speaking, as if the proposed development were contrary to the local development plan.[10a]

As already stated, Grade I, Grade II* and Grade II lists are described as statutory lists, and owners of any buildings included in these lists are required to be notified of the fact of listing by the Secretary of State (s. 54 (4) of the 1971 Act). Owners of Grade III buildings may, however, be unaware of the listing. It is also important to note that churches, scheduled ancient monuments[11] and Crown property (the latter unless leased[12]) may be listed, *but are not* thereby protected. However, with the exception of these last three categories, buildings already listed " non-statutorily " as Grade III can be protected by the local planning authority by the issue of a building preservation notice (s. 54 of the 1971 Act). This can be removed by the Secretary of State after consultation with the local planning authority, which authority is bound then to inform the owner of the property of the removal of protection.[13]

[9] Such as weavers' cottages, fishing villages, etc.
[10] If within the curtilage, structures will be automatically included in the listing (s. 54 (9) of 1971 Act).
[10a] By the Town and Country Planning (Listed Buildings and Buildings in Conservation Areas) Regulations, 1972 (S.I. 1972 No. 1362).
[11] Excluded by s. 56 (1) of 1971 Act; but see p. 262.
[12] But tenants of Crown property must apply for Listed Building Consent (s. 266 (4) of 1971 Act) if they wish to demolish, alter or extend.
[13] Schedule 11, para. 10, to the 1971 Act, and Circular 61/68 of Department of the Environment, Appendix 54; also see *post*, pp. 249–250.

The effect of " listing " (i.e., other than if Grade III) is that no demolition, alteration or extension of the listed building may be carried out, if this is to be " in any manner which would affect its character," without obtaining listed building consent (s. 55 of the 1971 Act). Thus, the General Development Order, 1973, will not be applicable[14] to listed buildings and, further, the latitude permitted in all other cases in relation to " material development "[15] cannot be used; for example, unusual exterior painting, or the removal of glazing bars from sash windows is not permissible in the case of listed buildings. In addition to making an application for a listed building consent, it is necessary (through the local planning authority)[16] to notify the Royal Commission on Historical Monuments (England) or where applicable, the Royal Commission on Ancient and Historical Monuments (Wales and Monmouthshire) or such other body as the Secretary of State may direct (s. 55 (2), (3) of the 1971 Act). Two further provisions may also apply. Where the listed building is owned by a local planning authority, the application for listed building consent must be made to the Secretary of State for decision. In such cases it is also reserved to the Secretary of State (ss. 270 and 271 of the 1971 Act) that at any time he may, by regulations, lay down further requirements as to any listed property, in terms of consultation with other bodies, or in terms of the need to obtain his consent. In any event, where applicable, the estate owner of the fee simple of the property, and any tenant of it, must also be informed and a " Section 27 certificate,"[16a] given by the applicant[17] to the effect that this has been done, must be lodged

[14] The General Development Order, 1973, describes 23 classes of " permitted development," for which planning permission will not normally be required; these include notably permitted extensions within the curtilage of a dwelling-house (Class I), and development of agricultural buildings within certain limits as to size, etc. (Class VI).

[15] For a definition and further explanation see Heap, *An Outline of Planning Law*, 5th ed., Chaps. 7 and 8. The Town and Country Planning General Development Order, 1973 (S.I. 1973 No. 31), gives automatic planning permission for certain types of development.

[16] But it is now proposed in the reorganisation of local government to place Listed Building Consent entirely in the hands of the new District Councils (subject to approval by the Department of the Environment). This is opposed in the Dartmouth Committee Report; see Appendix B, Recommendation 19.

[16a] Under s. 27 of the Town and Country Planning Act, 1971, which repealed and re-enacted s. 16 of the 1968 Act, under which reference used to be made to a " section 16 certificate."

[17] Who, of course, need not be the owner or tenant.

with the local planning authority simultaneously with the application.

It must, however, be emphasised that there is a very significant exception to the arrangements described above, namely, *where planning permission is granted which includes, and expressly authorises, alteration or extension (but not demolition) of a listed building, this will operate, without more, as a listed building consent* (s. 56 (2) of the 1971 Act).   (See, however, footnote 16, p. 241.)

In any event, in the case of a planning permission related specifically to a listed building, or in the case of a simple listed building consent, conditions may be imposed so as to limit the benefit of that consent to specified persons (Sched. 11, para. 1 (2), to the 1971 Act); to preserve specified features either *in situ*, or elsewhere; or secure that any reconstruction or repairs be carried out in the original, or similar, materials (s. 56 (4) and (5) of the 1971 Act).

Further safeguards are afforded by reg. 4 and Circular 61/68, paras. 8, 9 and 10, whereby, in the case of proposals relating to Grade I, Grade II* and Grade II buildings, any intention to demolish, to alter or to extend must be advertised in the local press, and site notices must be displayed for at least seven days.   In both forms of publicity at least twenty-one days must be allowed for the making of representations or objections.   In addition, where the proposals relate to these three grades (other than to interior alterations to Grade II buildings unless the building has benefited from an historic buildings grant),[18] the Secretary of State must be informed.   And, further, where demolition of the whole or part of a Grade I, Grade II* or Grade II building is proposed, it is required (by para. 8 of Ministry of Housing and Local Government Circular No. 61/68—" Historic Buildings and Conservation ") that no less than six national bodies be notified, namely:

    The Ancient Monuments Society

    The Council of British Archaeology

    The Georgian Group

    The Society for the Protection of Ancient Buildings

    The Victorian Society

and either

    The Royal Commission on Historical Monuments (England) if in England, *or* The Royal Commission on Ancient and Historical Monuments (Wales) if in Wales or Monmouthshire.

[18] Historic Building Grants and Loans, see *post*, p. 250 *et seq.*

In the case of the two Royal Commissions, the notification must be accompanied by the relevant extract from the statutory list so as to describe the building.

(As to advertising and site notices only, a rather similar requirement applies to Conservation Areas: see *post*, p. 270.)

The local planning authority are urged (and presumably the expense is thereby justified) to obtain and to follow expert professional advice, and either to employ expert consultants, or to set up an Historic Buildings Department (Ministry Circular No. 61/68).

If the local planning authority intend to grant listed building consent, such intention must be notified to the Secretary of State, together with the criteria influencing their decision.[18a] These criteria must include reference to: (*a*) the relative importance or (local or national) rarity of the building; (*b*) its value when seen as part of a group of buildings or townscape; (*c*) the architectural merit of the design and historical associations (including any illustration of social history in relation to a pattern of living or of a past technology); (*d*) the condition of repair, cost of repair, and availability of grants and the economic value, or potential use, if put into repair; (*e*) any alternative uses in contemplation for the site, including the desirability of redevelopment in rundown localities; (*f*) the probable effect of such redevelopment upon any other listed buildings in the vicinity (Sched. 11, para. 3, and s. 31 (2), (3) of the 1971 Act, with Circular 61/68, paras. 9 and 10).

After consideration of this information, the Secretary of State is empowered, if he so desires, to call in the application and decide the matter himself. The decision to call in the application will be influenced by the existence, or not, of representations from the six national bodies already referred to. In arriving at a decision, the Secretary of State is to " have regard to " any professional advice made available to the local planning authority, and there is an assumption that he " will not be disposed to approve " a listed building consent, in relation particularly to demolition, where this is contrary to the views of the local planning authority. Nevertheless, once a decision to call in is made, both the local planning authority and/or the applicant is then entitled to request a local public inquiry to be conducted by a Department of Environment Inspector,

---

[18a] But see S.I. 1973 No. 273, exempting the Greater London Council, the Court of Common Council and councils of London Boroughs.

and at which any local civic or preservation society should also be heard (Sched. 11, para. 4 (4) to the 1971 Act).   Where the local planning authority delay, a similar provision is made to that for normal planning applications, namely, the application to be dealt with within two months of being made or, failing this, that there shall be a " deemed refusal " upon which the applicant can appeal to the Secretary of State (Sched. 11, para. 9).

Where the application for listed building consent is refused by the local planning authority, there is a right of appeal upon the basis of argument that the particular building is not, in fact, of (sufficient) architectural or historic interest.   In the case of protection not by listing but by mere building preservation notice,[19] the same argument and system of appeal will apply (Sched. 11, para. 8 (2), and s. 54 (1) of the 1971 Act).

In terms of the degree of strictness of control, it should be noted, first, that where the application relates only to such alterations, etc., as would be covered by the provisions of the General Development Order, 1973,[20] and the said " permitted development " is refused either by the local planning authority or by the Secretary of State, then compensation will be payable by the *local authority* [20a] as to any potential loss of value which results directly from the decision (s. 263 of the 1971 Act); secondly, the powers of delegation by local planning authorities to district authorities [20b] are considerably restricted in relation to listed buildings, and any proposal to delegate such a power must first be submitted to the Secretary of State for approval (s. 3 (1) of, and Sched. 11 to, the 1971 Act).

Demolition, alteration or extension of a " listed building " (" Statutory " grades, i.e., I, II* and II, but not Grade III) is an offence under s. 55 (1) and (4) of the 1971 Act, and is punishable upon summary conviction by a fine of up to £250 or up to three months' imprisonment, or both; or, upon indictment, by up to twelve months' imprisonment and/or an unlimited fine.   Further, the fine imposed is to be related to the financial gain obtained by the

[19] *Post*, p. 249.
[20] Such as, e.g., development within the curtilage of a dwelling house of not exceeding 50 cubic metres (1,750 cu. ft.) or one-tenth, whichever is the greater, subject to a maximum of 115 cubic metres (4,000 cu. ft.) (Class I); or development in relation to agricultural buildings, etc. (Class VI).
[20a] Not necessarily the *planning* authority.
[20b] Until reorganisation of local government in April, 1974, by virtue of the Local Government Act, 1972.

offender. The section does, however, provide that it shall be a defence to prove that the works carried out were urgently necessary for safety (or health), and that the local planning authority had been notified as rapidly as possible of the state of affairs.

Repairs Notices.—Where the owner or occupier of the listed premises fails to repair or maintain the structure to an extent reasonably necessary for preservation, the local planning authority or local authority (i.e., district council) or the Secretary of State may issue a repairs notice (s. 115 of the 1971 Act), which may specify the precise work to be carried out. If such repairs are not commenced, the local planning authority or local authority may, after two months, compulsorily purchase the property, paying only " minimum compensation " (*post*). Within this two-month period it is, of course, open to the owner to apply to the local authority for a grant or loan, in the ordinary way; and, if the facts of the situation warrant such a grant, the local authority will be expected to consider the matter favourably. However, even if the property is so neglected that it has to be demolished, the power of the local authority to acquire at minimum compensation value will remain. The onus of proof of the progressive neglect lies on the local planning authority (s. 117 of the 1971 Act) and it may be necessary to produce dated and attested photographs to illustrate this. Further, the precise effect of a compulsory purchase order at such minimum compensation must be clearly explained to the owner at the time of the issue of the repairs notice (s. 117). The effect would, in fact, be that only the value for the unrepaired listed building would fall to be paid in compensation, and that any higher value for potential redevelopment would certainly not be obtainable.

There is a ground of appeal against a minimum compensation notice on the basis that any neglect to repair had not been deliberate (i.e., that it was either unintentional or unavoidable), and this appeal will be heard initially in the local magistrates' court, with further appeal to the Crown Court (s. 117 (6) of the 1971 Act).

Enforcement Notices.—Where the listed building has not been demolished, but other unauthorised works materially affecting the character of the structure have been carried out, the local planning authority,[21] or the Secretary of State after reference to the local planning authority, can serve an enforcement notice on the owner

[21] Unless this power has been specifically delegated to a district authority.

or occupier to take effect within twenty-eight days (or specified longer period: ss. 96 and 100 of the 1971 Act and Sched. 5 to the 1968 Act) requiring them to reinstate the structure as it was before alteration.

Upon receipt of the enforcement notice, the owner or occupier of the listed building may appeal to the Secretary of State, stating the facts upon which he bases his appeal. Both the appellant and the local planning authority are, in these circumstances, entitled to ask for a formal hearing if they wish, and the notice will be of no effect pending decision of the appeal. There are eight grounds of appeal only, and these are now specified in s. 97 (1) (*a*) to (*h*) of the 1971 Act, namely: (*a*) that the building is not, in fact, of special architectural or historic interest (i.e., it ought never to have been listed); (*b*) that the matters alleged do not, in fact, contravene s. 55 of the 1971 Act, i.e, the work carried out will not materially affect the architectural or historic character of the building; (*c*) that the works were urgently needed in the interests of safety or health, or for the preservation of the building; (*d*) that listed building consent ought to be granted for the particular works done,[22] or that any relevant (specified) condition of a listed building consent ought to be " discharged " (i.e., removed) or other conditions substituted; (*e*) that the notice was not correctly served; (*f*) that the requirements of the enforcement notice are excessive in terms of rectifying the effect of the unauthorised works; (*g*) that the period specified in the notice for such corrective work is unreasonably short; and (*h*) that the steps specified to be taken would not, in fact, restore the building to its former state.

If the Secretary of State so decides he may either " de-list " the building (thereby removing all other than normal planning restrictions and provisions applicable to a non-listed site); or he may grant consent for the appellant's works; or he may discharge (remove) or change any condition made in the enforcement notice (s. 97 of the 1971 Act). Where, however, such an appeal is not successful, or where the enforcement notice is not complied with (including at the expiry of the permitted time after an appeal) the offender may be tried summarily and a fine of up to £400 imposed: if tried on indictment the fine is unlimited. Where the corrective work is still not done after conviction, a further offence is thereby committed and a

[22] This criterion permits the introduction of a general discussion of the relative merits of the building in terms of justification of its listing.

penalty of £50 per day from the date of the subsequent conviction may be imposed, to continue until completion of the remedial work. Alternatively, a conviction on indictment following an earlier conviction (summary or on indictment) may result in a fine to which there is no limit (s. 98 (1) of the 1971 Act). In all the above instances, where the person named in the enforcement notice has transferred ownership of the listed property to another, who was made fully aware, by the vendor, of that notice and its effects, the original owner may plead this as a defence, and the subsequent owner may become liable to conviction in his stead.

Additionally or alternatively, the local planning authority, or the Secretary of State, is empowered (s. 99 of the 1971 Act) to enter and carry out the work specified in the enforcement notice and may subsequently recover the cost from the owner, together with expenses incidental to the process.

Listed Building Purchase Notice.—In cases where listed building consent is refused, revoked, or later modified, or is given conditionally, and the owner claims that the building has become incapable of "reasonably beneficial" use in its existing state, and also that it cannot be so rendered by such future works (if any) as have been approved, the owner may serve on the "local council" a listed building purchase notice (s. 190 of and Sched. 19 to the 1971 Act) to include not only the listed structure but also any contiguous or adjacent structure which is substantially inseparable from it. The council must then (Sched. 19, para. 1 (1)), within three months from date of service, reply by service upon the owner of their own notice to the effect either: (*a*) that the council are willing to purchase; or (*b*) that another local authority or statutory undertaker has agreed with the council to purchase in their stead; or (*c*) that the council are not willing to purchase and have not found any other body to act as in (*b*), and further that they have transmitted a copy of the purchase notice to the Secretary of State. This latter notice must include the reasons for the decision, and also the date of transmission to the Secretary of State.

It should be noted that in arriving at a decision the council are to take no account of any prospective changes of use or development of the listed property, unless the local planning authority (or delegated planning authority) or the Secretary of State have already undertaken to permit them, and the owner has been so informed (s. 192 (2) of the 1971 Act). The fact that the property is let will militate against the approval of a purchase notice.   Also, the service of a repairs notice (*ante*) has the effect (s. 115 (1) of the 1971 Act) of preventing, for three months, effective service of a purchase notice.   If, within that period, the Secretary of State approves compulsory acquisition of the property, a purchase notice will then be of no avail.   Further, the question to be resolved by the council is simply whether the land in the existing state is capable of *reasonably beneficial use*, not whether it is of less use (or value) to the owner than it would be if developed by alteration, or demolition and reconstruction.

Upon receipt of the copy of the purchase notice, the Secretary of State has very considerable freedom of action.   He may (Sched. 19 to the 1971 Act) either confirm or not confirm (i.e., refuse) the purchase notice; or he may amend any conditions applicable to the purchase; or he may grant listed building consent (i.e., to demolish or alter) in lieu of purchase; or he may direct that planning permission be granted in respect of work on the said land or on adjacent land; or he may otherwise modify the terms of confirmation in the light of the probable ultimate use of the building or cleared site.

The Secretary of State is, however, required to deal with any purchase notice within a maximum of nine months of the service of the purchase notice on the " local council," or within six months of receipt of the application from the said council by the Department of the Environment, whichever be the shorter period.

Where the Secretary of State arrives at a decision to confirm a purchase notice, but legal proceedings are then taken in the High Court, under Part XII of the 1971 Act,[23] the owner is prevented from serving any further purchase notice.

Modification or Revocation of Listed Building Consent.—Existing listed building consent may be modified or revoked where the development plan and any other " material considerations " make this expedient, but the Secretary of State must be consulted and his confirmation, or variation, obtained (Sched. 11, Pt. II, paras. 10 to 12).   Where the consent is revoked or modified and the person interested in the building has either incurred expenditure in preparing plans or carrying out works rendered abortive, or has

---

[23] Presumably an application to the High Court by local or other objectors for an injunction to restrain demolition; and, rarely, by the local planning authority, or other local authority.

otherwise sustained loss or damage thereby, the local planning authority shall pay compensation (s. 171 of the 1971 Act).

The process of modification or revocation of a listed building consent is as follows (Sched. 11, Pt. II). The local planning authority make an order, but this is to be of no effect until confirmed by the Secretary of State. When the order is submitted to the Secretary of State for consideration, the local planning authority must serve a notice on the owner and on the occupier of the listed building and " on any other person who in their opinion will be affected by the order," the recipients being allowed at least twenty-eight days to make representations by appearing before " a person appointed by the Secretary of State for the purpose." The power to revoke or modify a listed building consent may be exercised at any time before the relevant works have been completed, but cannot be retroactive so far as works already carried out are concerned (Sched. 11, para. 10 (4)).

Alternatively, where matters have not proceeded as far as confirmation by the Secretary of State (i.e., the order has been made, the persons affected notified, and consultation only with the Secretary of State has taken place) *and the owner, occupier and other persons apparently affected have agreed in writing that they have no objection*, and also it " appears to " the local planning authority that no claim for compensation is likely to arise, then the order must be advertised in the local press, specifying that any other persons affected by the revocation or modification may give notice that they wish to appear before a person appointed by the Secretary of State. The period for such notification of objection must be at least twenty-eight days (Sched. 11, para. 12 (*e*)), but the order may also specify that it is to come into effect (pending an inquiry) within a shorter period (if deemed advisable) providing this be not less than fourteen days from the date of the advertisement. A copy of this advertisement is to be sent to the Secretary of State (Sched. 11, para. 12 (4)) within three days of publication; and if, within the first-stated period (minimum twenty-eight days, as above), no objections are received and the matter is not called in by the Secretary of State, the order will come into effect.

(2) *Building preservation notices*

A building preservation notice may be given by a local planning authority in order to afford protection to an *unlisted* building, if they deem it to be of special interest and in danger of demolition or alteration (s. 58 of the 1971 Act).   The notice is served on the owner and the occupier of the building and must include an explanation of its effect, namely, that there shall be deferment of demolition or alteration, etc., for six months, to enable the Secretary of State to consider whether or not the building should be listed (*ibid.*). Before serving such a notice, the local planning authority must establish (and resolve as to) whether or not the structure appears to be of architectural or historic interest and whether or not it is in apparent danger, such as being subject to a planning application involving demolition or alteration.[23a]

If the Secretary of State refuses to list the particular building, the local planning authority are required to inform the owner and occupier of this decision; and a subsequent building preservation notice cannot be validly served within a further twelve months.

The six months' protective period which automatically follows issue of a building preservation notice is, however, applicable whether or not the building is eventually listed, and it is an offence (under ss. 55 and 98 of the 1971 Act, and punishable as at p. 244, *ante*) for the owner or occupier to carry out any unauthorised (i.e., damaging) work.   Equally, any enforcement notices served during the six-month period remain valid until the period expires, even where the decision of the Secretary of State not to list the building is made and notified in a shorter time.   At the end of the period, however, all enforcement notices related to building preservation notices will cease; although the local planning authority, or the Secretary of State, remain empowered to enter and carry out the prescribed repairs and to recover the cost thereof.

It should, however, be emphasised that although the serving of a building preservation notice does not give rise to a claim for compensation, liability to compensate may arise if the building fails to be listed, providing the owner or occupier has had to cancel a contract for building works, and has thereby incurred expense.

(3) *Grants and loans for repairs and maintenance*

These fall into three main categories:

(i) *Historic Buildings Grants and Loans* may be made available by local planning authorities, or by county district authorities, by

---

[23a] Although, if a building is, in fact, already listed, the granting of planning permission will override that protection!

virtue of the Local Authorities (Historic Buildings) Act, 1962, and earlier related statutes.[24]   (In the case of " buildings of *outstanding interest* " or " ancient monuments," other grants and loans are available direct from the Secretary of State for the Environment: *post*, p. 252.) [25]

The Local Authorities (Historic Buildings) Act, 1962, enables local planning and district authorities:

(a) as they think fit, to contribute to the expenses of repair or maintenance of a listed building (s. 1 (1) (*a*));

or

(b) with the consent of the Secretary of State, to make a similar contribution in regard to other buildings which appear to be of architectural or historic interest (s. 1 (1) (*b*)).

This contribution may either be an outright grant (s. 1 (1)); or it may be by way of loan " upon such terms and conditions as the local authority may determine " (s. 1 (2)), and in this case it will be within the power of the local authority to dispense with payment of interest or, at any time, to renounce their right to repayment of any balance of the debt still due.   The local authority may, if they deem fit at the outset, impose conditions as to creation of a public right of access, although this access will generally be limited in terms of the part or parts of the premises concerned, and as to hours of the day and days of the week.   If, within three years of the date upon which the grant is made, the grantee disposes of his interest in the property (e.g., by sale of the freehold, or of his entire lesser share in the property), or if he lets the property for a term of not less than twenty-one years, the local authority are empowered to recover the amount of the grant, or such proportion of it as they think fit. But, where the grantee disposes of his interest by gift, the recipient of the gift is to be deemed to step into the shoes of the grantor (s. 2) and thus to be liable in regard to any repayment in the case of a loan, or as to sale of the property within any balance of the three-year period then still to run.   As to this, it should be noted that Circular

[24] Which supplements the power of a local authority under s. 11 of the Ancient Monuments Consolidation and Amendment Act, 1913, as to ancient monuments, and of the Minister of Works (now Secretary of State for the Environment) under s. 4 of the Historic Buildings and Ancient Monuments Act, 1953, as to buildings of outstanding historic or architectural interest, to make grants for the preservation of " buildings " (structures), their contents, and also adjoining land.

[25] Loans by the Department of the Environment were authorised by the Civic Amenities Act, 1967.

68/62 does indicate that it would be permissible for a local authority to make a loan where a preservation society intends to purchase a building with the declared intention of carrying out repairs and then re-selling.   In such cases the local authority would expect to recover their loan less any of the society's costs not recouped out of the sale price.

The local authority are not required to notify the Secretary of State at the time of their approval of each grant, but are to inform him of all grants and loans made within every twelve months, such information to be in the hands of the Secretary of State not later than the 30th June in every year (Ministry Circular No. 61/68, para. 14).

It should also be observed at this stage that, in the case of groups of buildings, the local authority may prefer to avail themselves of the opportunity to invite the Secretary of State to make a grant under the Historic Buildings and Ancient Monuments Act, 1953, since, although individual buildings within the group may not be categorised as of " outstanding historic or architectural interest," it is provided (by para. 15 of the Ministry Circular No. 61/68) that a group within a " town scheme " may possibly merit the description of being thus " outstanding."   For such purposes annual agreed sums are paid (in arrear) by the Secretary of State but to a limit of 25 per cent. in value of the grants made, the balance being payable as to 25 per cent. by the local authority, and 50 per cent. by the owner of the property.   It is also open to the local planning authority (county council) and the district authority to bear the contribution as to 25 per cent. jointly between them (Local Authorities (Historic Buildings) Act, 1962).

The local authority are also instructed, by para. 25 of Ministry Circular No. 61/68, to give informal advice to owners about repairs or alterations to listed buildings, and to suggest other sources of guidance, such as the Society for the Protection of Ancient Buildings.

(ii) *Grants and loans made solely by the Secretary of State* under the Historic Buildings and Ancient Monuments Act, 1953, may, at discretion, be available for the repair or maintenance of buildings and their contents which are adjudged to be " of outstanding historic or architectural interest," and they may extend to the up-keep of surrounding land.   It should be noted, however, that the mere fact of listing (i.e., under the provisions of s. 54 of the 1971

Act) does not establish that the building is of "outstanding interest" under the 1953 Act. By s. 4 (1) and (4) of the 1953 Act, the Historic Buildings Council is to be consulted, and any repairs carried out under a grant must be to the satisfaction of architects on the staff of the Department of the Environment. It is usual to require proof that the applicant is incapable of meeting the full cost out of his own resources, and such loans generally relate to work to be carried out on an entire building rather than upon a part only. They are not available for works of modernisation. Further, they will, almost without exception, be dependent upon an agreement providing for access by the public (s. 1 (3) of the 1953 Act).

As an alternative to the making of a grant or loan, the Department of the Environment may, by agreement, acquire the building, contents and land (s. 5 (1) of the 1953 Act); or may, after consulting the Historic Buildings Council, make grants to local authorities to enable them to acquire properties (s. 6 (1) of the 1953 Act, and s. 114 of the Town and Country Planning Act, 1971). Such authorisation by the Department of the Environment does, however, depend not only upon the building being of sufficient merit to justify classification as of outstanding architectural or historic interest but also upon (*a*) the existence of listing; or (*b*) the existence of a building preservation notice [26]; or (*c*) the fact that it is a structure capable of being protected by a building preservation notice: that is, *it cannot apply to ecclesiastical buildings* (other than parsonages) *which are in use*, or structures already covered by the Ancient Monuments Acts (*post*, p. 261), or buildings on Crown land (unless otherwise agreed by the " appropriate authority " which will be, dependent upon the land, either the Crown Estate Commissioners, or the Chancellor of the Duchy of Lancaster, or the Duke of Cornwall, or a specific government department—s. 266 of the Town and Country Planning Act, 1971, and especially s. 266 (4)). In addition, special Parliamentary procedure is required in the case of National Trust property (see pp. 258 *et seq.*, 309). Provision is, however, made to ensure that building preservation notices can be made upon land and buildings included in a settled estate under the Settled Land Act, 1925 (s. 275 of the Town and Country Planning Act, 1971).

(iii) *Grants for the improvement, or creation (by conversion) of dwellings.* A third type of grant may be made available in cases where the

26 Made under s. 58 of the 1971 Act.

building which it is intended to preserve is, or is intended to become, a dwelling.[27]   The Housing Act, 1969, provides for grants of this type, but these provisions have been varied, by the Housing Act, 1971, in the case of such property which is either in Development Areas (*post*) or in Intermediate Areas (*post*), as will be explained later.   The 1971 Housing Act is to be effective only until 23rd June, 1973, after which date (in the absence of any intervening legislation) the rates of grant in those areas will revert to those empowered by the 1969 Act, which is continuing for the remainder of the country.

Under both the 1969 and 1971 Acts, provision is made for three types of grant, namely: (*a*) discretionary " improvement grants " (which are made available at the discretion of the local housing authority); (*b*) " standard grants " (which can be claimed as of right where the property meets certain requirements as to structural soundness); and (*c*) " special grants " (which are, again, discretionary, but are given in addition to (*a*) or (*b*)).

The distinction between dwellings qualifying under the 1969 Act and those under the Housing Act, 1971, is, thus, geographical only.   *Development Areas* are those areas of the country specified by the Secretary of State for Trade and Industry (as successor to the former Chairman of the Board of Trade), by orders made under the Local Employment Act, 1960, s. 1, and the Industrial Development Act, 1966, s. 15, as requiring special measures to encourage " the growth and proper distribution of industry."   *Intermediate Areas* are those areas specified similarly by order by the Secretary of State for Trade and Industry under the Local Employment Act, 1970, s. 1, as having less acute problems than those in development areas but nevertheless requiring encouragement of the proper distribution of industry.

In the case of *improvement grants* and *special grants* the local authority may make a grant towards the cost of works of improvement or repair where these are such as to produce a high general standard of improvement and also generally provide a dwelling with an expectation of a thirty-year life (although there is discretion to reduce this period in cases of housing shortage).   In both cases the works must not be commenced until the grant has been formally approved.

(*a*) *Improvement grants.*   If the local authority are acting under the

---

[27] As to increases in rates chargeable following improvements, see Appendix B, Recommendation 8.

1969 Act, the recipient of the grant is to contribute an equivalent sum towards the total cost of those parts of the works which qualify for the grant (i.e., a 50 per cent. grant); but, if the local authority are in an area where the Housing Act, 1971, applies, a contribution of only 25 per cent. is required from the property owner (i.e., a 75 per cent. grant). There are, however, ceiling figures as to grant. Thus, under the 1969 Act (i.e., the greater part of the country) the maximum grant in the case of single houses is £1,000; or, in the case of conversion to form additional dwellings (e.g., division of a single house into several flats, or of some other non-domestic type of building into flats) the maximum will be £1,200 for each separate dwelling provided. Under the 1971 Act [27a] (i.e., in Development and Intermediate Areas) the limits are raised to £1,500 and £1,800 respectively, providing that the local authority are satisfied that the total grant is justified in any given case. Further, by Circular 63/71, para. 11, the Secretary of State has indicated that he is prepared to consider a possible increase in these latter two limits in any exceptional case, where supported by the local authority. Provisions have also been made (by way of amendment to the Housing Act, 1959) for various increases in Exchequer contributions to local authority expenditure in relation to grants and loans (s. 37 of the Housing Act, 1971).

It should be noted that provisions are made in the Housing Act, 1971, for all increases in grants and loans to apply not only to England and Wales, but also to Scotland. Since all areas in Scotland now have either development area or intermediate area status, the Act applies throughout Scotland, although it is (as in England and Wales) only effective until 23rd June, 1973. There is no provision, however, for automatic extension of the Act to any parts of England and Wales declared to be development or intermediate areas after the inception of the Act, unless the Order creating these areas so directs. In relation to the general town and country planning approach, it should be observed that the delimitation of development areas and intermediate areas is upon a basis of employment exchange areas, and is not directly related to local planning authority or other local authority areas. Thus it is possible for the benefit of the Housing Act, 1971, to extend to only

---

[27a] See also the Housing (Intermediate Areas) Order, 1972 (S.I. 1972 No. 422); and, as to Scotland, the Housing (Improvement of Amenities of Residential Areas) (Scotland) Order, 1972 (S.I. 1972 No. 457).

part of a local government area or district, the remainder continuing under the 1969 Act.

(*b*) *Standard grants* are the second type available through the local authority, as authorised by ss. 7 to 12 of the Housing Act, 1969. These grants may be claimed as of right by the owner of a dwelling where the estimated future life of that dwelling will normally exceed fifteen years after repair and improvement. Such standard grants are unlikely to be of particular significance in terms of the preservation of buildings of special merit, although it is possible that they may very occasionally be of incidental assistance, more particularly in relation to the preservation of areas of cottage dwellings (e.g., as in fishing villages). In any event, they are not payable additionally to improvement grants (*ante*); that is, if a standard grant happens to be paid before an improvement grant is approved, the total of standard grant so paid will be deducted from the improvement grant.

Standard grants relate only to provision of "standard amenities," and are available only when any such amenity does not exist in the dwelling house. Thus, strictly speaking, the presence of a Victorian bath having no piped water and with a waste pipe merely to a soakaway, would exclude a standard grant for a bath, although not for piped hot and cold water or suitable drainage. The 1969 Act allocates (Sched. 1, Pt. I) specific sums of money to be granted for each missing standard amenity, and these are set out in Appendix C of this book (p. 328).

(*c*) *Special grants* are provided for by ss. 13 to 15 of the 1969 Act. A local authority may approve an application for a special grant " in such circumstances as they think fit " (s. 14 (1)), provided that the applicant has either a fee simple absolute, or a term of years absolute of which not less than five years remain unexpired. The grant may not exceed one-half of the total cost of the proposed works, but, if any of the works consist of standard amenities (application not having been made separately for a standard grant (*ante*)), then each standard grant will be paid at full rate (as set out in Appendix C hereto), the balance only being subject to (maximum) grant of 50 per cent.

It is, perhaps, appropriate to comment finally as to grants, that whereas the clear purpose of all three types of grant is to increase the total housing stock available in the United Kingdom, it is also necessary for local authorities to exercise certain discretion. For example, the over-free availability of improvement grants or special grants for roof repairs may tend to encourage landlords to be less prompt in carrying out small repairs at their own expense, in the hope of qualifying for a grant at a later stage.

General Improvement Areas may be created by local authorities, by virtue of s. 28 (1) of the Housing Act, 1969. They must be predominantly residential in character, and the purpose of the declaration of such an area is to enable the local authority to assist in the improvement of land in private ownership.[28] The principle to be applied is that of a general raising of the living standard of the area, and this the local authority may do by means of loans and grants and also by traffic regulation, road closures, provision of car parking and of open spaces, planting of trees and the acquisition of property: they may also assist private property owners by organising composite building contracts for their benefit. Although it is not necessary for the local authority to obtain the approval of the Secretary of State for the Environment, they are required to send to him a copy of their resolution together with a copy of the report which is required to be made to the local authority prior to their resolution, and a map, together with a statement of the precise number of dwellings in the area. In addition, a notice of the resolution must be published in two or more local newspapers, and this notice must also indicate where, at all reasonable times, a copy of the resolution, report and supporting map may be inspected. It is provided, by s. 29 of the 1969 Act, that general improvement areas and clearance areas[29] shall be mutually exclusive.

Reference having been made to clearance areas, it may be advisable also to refer, in passing, to compulsory purchase of the area, which may be imposed as an alternative by order of the local authority under Pt. III of the Housing Act, 1957. In this case the local authority will acquire the entire area under the Compulsory Purchase Act, 1965, and will demolish and subsequently redevelop

---

[28] As to increases in rates chargeable following improvements, see Appendix B, Recommendation 8.

[29] i.e., broadly, areas declared by the local authority to be clearance areas as a result of the dwellings therein being technically " unfit " for human habitation (see p. 206). Upon such a declaration the owners of property are required to demolish and clear the area. Subsequently such owners obtain the benefit (which may or may not be adequate) of re-development, generally by combining in a scheme. For these purposes " unfit " is a technical term and is defined by s. 4 of the Housing Act, 1957.

the area.   Such redevelopment is more commonly by the introduction of independent developers, rather than by direct labour.

In the case of individual property which has become '' unfit '' [30] for human habitation, where the house is capable of repair at reasonable cost, a notice to repair may be served under ss. 9 to 15 of Pt. II of the Housing Act, 1957, or summary action may be taken in certain circumstances under the Public Health Acts, 1936 and 1961, whereby the local authority will carry out necessary works and charge the cost to the owner.   Where the house is incapable of repair at reasonable expense the local authority may make either a closing order or a demolition order under the 1957 Act.   As to these it must be noted that where the house is listed, or where the Secretary of State has given notice to the local authority that it is of sufficient [31] architectural or historic interest, then a closing order must be made in lieu of (or in substitution for) a demolition order (Housing Act, 1957, ss. 17 and 26).

(4) *The National Trust for England and Wales, The National Trust for Scotland, and The National Trust for Northern Ireland*

The National Trust for Places of Historic Interest or Natural Beauty was incorporated as an Association [32] in 1894 in order to promote the permanent preservation for the benefit of the nation of lands and buildings of beauty or historic interest, including the natural features, and animal and plant life upon such lands.   In order to extend the powers of the Trust, the Association was converted to a body corporate (with perpetual succession and having a common seal) by the National Trust Act, 1907.   By this Act the Trust was empowered to purchase, take (i.e., by gift, etc.), hold, deal with and dispose of property; and provision was made for four classes of membership (ordinary, life, honorary and local corresponding members), and for power to fix rates of subscription and generally to carry out the business functions necessary in running such a body.   It was also provided, however, that the affairs of the Trust be administered by a council consisting of a president and fifty members, of whom twenty-five are elected annually from among the members.   The balance of twenty-five members of the

[30] See p. 202.

[31] i.e., to render it '' inexpedient that the building be demolished pending any decision as to listing.''

[32] i.e., an '' Association not for profit '' under the Companies Acts, 1862 to 1890, liability of members being, at that stage, limited by guarantee.

council are appointed by (variously) the president, trustees or vice-chancellor, of twenty-two major national institutions or universities.[33] The council's powers of management of the Trust's property are extremely widely drawn, and include " all such proceedings as they may deem desirable in the furtherance of the objects of the National Trust " and " all such provisions as may be beneficial for the property or desirable for the comfort or convenience of persons resorting to or using such property. . . ." However, the 1907 Act also provides (s. 21 and Sched. 1) that certain properties listed in the Schedule shall be inalienable, and further that once the council of the Trust has specified (from time to time) any further property as " to be held for the benefit of the nation," this also shall become inalienable.

However, the powers of the Trust have been further extended in a number of directions, although not in regard to inalienability, by subsequent legislation, namely, the National Trust Charity Scheme Act, 1937, the National Trust Act, 1939, and the National Trust Act, 1953, as amended and supplemented by the National Trust Act, 1971.

Thus, although property may be rendered inalienable, it remains within the power of the Trust to grant leases or to grant easements or other rights over it (ss. 8 and 12 of the 1939 Act). The Trust may enter into restrictive covenants in order to prevent the alteration or demolition of property (s. 8 of the 1937 Act). Money may be raised by way of mortgage of Trust property (ss. 22 to 24 of the 1907 Act), and power is also given to charge for admission to Trust property (s. 30 of the 1907 Act), provided that such charges are " reasonable " and, further, that no charge is made for admission to common land held by the Trust as special trustees. As would be anticipated, the Trust is empowered to make byelaws both as to lands and buildings (s. 33 of the 1907 Act and s. 24 of the 1971 Act).

The National Trust Charity Scheme Confirmation Act, 1919,

---

[33] Two members by each of: the National Gallery, the Royal Academy of Arts and the British Museum; one member by each of: the Universities of Oxford, Cambridge, London, Edinburgh, Glasgow, St. Andrew's and Dublin; the County Councils Association, the Commons Preservation Society, the Society for the Protection of Ancient Buildings, the Royal Institute of British Architects, the Royal Society of Painters in Watercolours, the Society of Antiquaries of London, the Linnean Society, the Entomological Society, the Royal Botanic Society, the Kyrle Society, the Selborne Society, and the Trustees of Public Reservations, Massachusetts, U.S.A.

confirmed a scheme whereby the Trust is enabled to operate as, and to receive the benefits of status as, a charity, thereby having advantages in terms of taxation and in relation to saving in estate duty which would otherwise be payable by any donors of property.

The powers of the Trust were extended in other respects by the 1937 and 1939 Acts, as follows. By virtue of s. 4 (*a*) of the 1937 Act it became possible to acquire additional land which was, of itself, not of special beauty or historic interest, but which would assist in the maintenance or preservation of any other part of the Trust property. Further, s. 4 (*b*) provides for acquisition in any manner, and retention of any investments (if " trustee investments ") intended for the provision of income or appreciated capital for the preservation or maintenance of Trust property. Assistance from local authorities, including county or county borough or urban or rural district councils, is provided, by s. 7 (1) as to the donation of land, and by s. 7 (2) as to financial contributions; but in both cases the consent of the Secretary of State for the Environment (in 1937 the Minister of Health in relation to Town and Country Planning) is required.

The 1939 Act was designed to enable the tenant for life under a settlement (who would otherwise be subject to the requirements of the Settled Land Act, 1925) to grant, by virtue of s. 3, gratuitously or otherwise, to the National Trust in fee simple absolutely, or for the whole of any lesser estate other than a leasehold (i.e., mainly the usual interests of a life tenant), the following:

(*a*) the principal mansion house and pleasure grounds and the park and lands (if any) usually occupied therewith;

(*b*) any lands occupied or enjoyed for the purposes of agriculture, sport or afforestation, where this is deemed desirable by the council of the National Trust, for preserving the amenities of the principal mansion house; and

(*c*) either an annual sum charged upon any other lands or buildings comprised in the settlement (i.e., the settlement under which the tenant for life benefits) or any settled (money) interest on such property, or any capital moneys which are subject to the same settlement.

Such an arrangement must, however, be subject to a certificate, given by the (now) Secretary of State for the Environment that the said mansion house is " a building of national interest or architectural, historic or artistic interest " (s. 4 (*b*)); and also that the written permission of the trustees of the settlement is obtained (s. 4 (*a*)). But the National Trust is required (s. 4 (*d*)) to maintain the property only " so far as there shall be funds available . . . from the endowment but no further."

Having acquired property, the National Trust may (s. 5 (1)) lease it for such term and at such nominal or other yearly rent as the trustees of the settlement may approve (or the court may approve), providing that (s. 5 (2)) there shall be contained in the lease a covenant to admit the public to a specified part or parts of the demised premises.

Finally, the National Trust Act, 1953, amended the powers of the council of the National Trust so as to enable the variation from time to time of the subscription of " ordinary subscribing members " of the Trust; and also extended the powers of the council in relation to the investment of Trust funds beyond the restricted field of trustee investments previously permitted by s. 1 of the Trustee Act, 1925.

See also Chapter 15, The Countryside—II.

(5) *Ancient monuments*

Ancient monuments, for the purposes of the relevant legislation, consist of ancient buildings, structures or earthworks, but exclude those ecclesiastical buildings which are in use,[34] and also houses unless occupied solely by a caretaker.[35] In terms of age, an " ancient monument " generally pre-dates 1714, although no precise year is laid down by statute and a high proportion date from prehistory. The Ancient Monuments Act, 1931, by s. 15, defines " ancient monument " and thereby extends the application of protection beyond the original list given in the Act of 1882. Thus, an " ancient monument " is to consist of any monument listed in the 1882 Act, and also any monument for the time being specified in a (subsequent) list published under s. 12 of the 1882 Act, and also any other monument or group of monuments which in the opinion of the (now) Secretary of State for the Environment is of " like character," or of which the preservation is " in the opinion of the [Secretary of State], a matter of public interest by reason of the

---

[34] Other than " parsonage houses," which are specifically made eligible for inclusion as ancient monuments. But see next note.

[35] Thus, it appears that " parsonage houses " which are " in use " (i.e., occupied by more than a caretaker) are in a special category as " houses."

historic, architectural, artistic or archaeological interest attached thereto."

The means of protection, whether by "guardianship," or by purchase, or by grants for repair, are provided now by the Ancient Monuments (Consolidation and Amendment) Act, 1913, the Ancient Monuments Act, 1931, and the Historic Buildings and Ancient Monuments Act, 1953, together with the power of compulsory purchase under s. 59 of the Town and Country Planning Act, 1968 (which relates also to the Acquisition of Land (Authorisation Procedure) Act, 1946, and the Ancient Monument Protection Act, 1882), and is not repealed by the Town and Country Planning Act, 1971. In addition, special legislation was passed in 1972, in the form of the Field Monuments Act, which is designed to safeguard such ancient earthworks as are listed from time to time under s. 12 of the 1913 Act, in order to protect them from damage due to agricultural or forestry operations.

As to ancient monuments of all types, the Act of 1913 provides that the Secretary of State for the Environment (previously the Minister of Public Building and Works) or the local authority may *purchase* ancient monuments *by agreement*, or may accept them as a gift or bequest (ss. 1 and 2). Alternatively the owner of a monument may, by agreement, constitute the Secretary of State or the local authority as "*guardian*" of the monument[36] and thus responsible for repair (ss. 3 and 4).

Where a monument is in danger of damage by neglect, or of removal, the Secretary of State has a number of alternative courses of action. He may make a preservation order; and/or he may offer grants for repairs and maintenance; or he may negotiate and purchase the monument (but not compulsorily). A *preservation order* is made by virtue of ss. 6 and 7 of the 1913 Act and s. 11 of the 1953 Act. Under such an order no demolition, alteration or addition to the structure may be carried out without the specific consent of the Secretary of State (*ibid.*); and if neglect continues the Secretary of State may compulsorily become "guardian" of the monument (s. 7 of the 1913 Act and s. 12 (5) of the 1953 Act) for so long as the preservation order remains in force.[37]

As to the cost of repairs in cases where a preservation order applies, the Secretary of State may accept voluntary contributions (s. 9 of

[36] About 200 such cases of guardianship existed in 1971.
[37] Only four such orders appear to have been in force in 1971.

the 1913 Act) and the Department or the local authority may themselves undertake repairs, or may contribute to the cost when these
are carried out by the owner, provided that plans and specifications
have previously been submitted, with a request for a contribution,
to one of the Ancient Monuments Boards (s. 11).

The three Ancient Monuments Boards, constituted separately
for England, Wales and Scotland, were set up by virtue of s. 15
of the 1913 Act, and are essential to the administration of the provisions of that Act, and of the subsequent Acts of 1931 and 1953.
Although the ownership, or guardianship, of ancient monuments (if
either of these applies) is vested in the Secretary of State for the
Environment, it is the prime duty of the Ancient Monuments
Board to record, supervise, and arrange for repair of such monuments. In this the Board is assisted by the Inspectors of Ancient
Monuments, appointed by virtue of s. 16 of the 1913 Act. The
Secretary of State can, if he thinks fit, give advice as to the treatment
of any monument, and may superintend any repairs, these functions
being free of charge, save for out-of-pocket expenses.

The powers of protection and supervision exercised by the
Department of the Environment were increased by the Ancient
Monuments Act, 1931. Section 1 of that Act enables the Department to prepare " preservation schemes " which relate not only to
the monument itself, but also to the area adjacent to the site, in
order to restrict building thereon, and to control the height, design,
materials and colour of such structures if, in the view of the Secretary
of State,[37a] these would detract from or otherwise affect the monument. However, such preservation schemes cannot be retroactive, in
that they may not (s. 1 (4)) affect any structures erected before the
date of publication in the *London Gazette* of a formal notice of intention
of the Secretary of State to confirm the scheme. Any building contracts made, but not completed, by such date are also not subject to
restriction by the scheme. It is also provided (by s. 18 of the 1913
Act) that the Secretary of State may give consent to the relaxation,
by the relevant local authority in any specific instance, of the
National Building Regulations if these would otherwise impede
" the erection of new buildings in a style of architecture in harmony
with other buildings of artistic merit existing in the locality."

To assist in the application of these measures it is made an

[37a] Originally the Commissioners of Works, the duties of whom are now vested in
the Secretary of State for the Environment.

offence (by s. 6 (2) of the 1931 Act) to demolish, alter or add to any monument listed under the Ancient Monuments Acts[38] without a notice of intention having been given to the Secretary of State, and a further three months allowed after such notice before commencement of any operations, unless urgent necessity is established.

A further degree of control is added by the Historic Buildings and Ancient Monuments Act, 1953, ss. 10, 11 and 12, whereby an *interim preservation notice* may be served by the Secretary of State for the Environment upon the owner and occupier where there is immediate danger of destruction of an ancient monument (s. 10 (1), (2)). The notice puts the monument under temporary protection immediately upon service; but seven days' notice is required before inspection is carried out. Compensation, resulting from delay caused by the notice, may become payable.

The interim notice will lapse after twenty-one months (unless earlier revoked, or upon the making of a preservation order) (s. 10 (3) (*c*)). A preservation order may be made (s. 11) either in lieu of, or subsequent to, an interim preservation notice, but is subject to " special parliamentary procedure "[39]; it may, however, be revoked at any time by further order published in the *London Gazette* (or *Edinburgh Gazette* if the monument is in Scotland).

In the case of both interim preservation notices and preservation orders, a person who has " an interest in the whole or a part of a monument " which is injuriously affected by service of the notice or the making of an order, or who suffers damage or undue expenditure as a result, may claim compensation " as may be appropriate in the circumstances " (s. 12 (2)). The compensation is payable by the Exchequer and is assessed by the Lands Tribunal.

The combined effect of the 1931 Act and the 1953 Act is that a penalty can be imposed, upon summary conviction, of £20 per day during which contravention of either Act occurs or continues (s. 1 (6) of the 1953 Act); and, if contravention continues after such period as the court shall determine, the Secretary of State may take any remedial action necessary and recover the cost thereof from the offender, including the owner of a monument (s. 1 (7)).

In practical terms two further points should be particularly

[38] Not merely under the Town and Country Planning Acts, 1968 and 1971.
[39] See the Statutory Orders (Special Procedure) Act, 1945; and as outlined in *Local Government and Administration* by Sir William Hart, 8th ed., at p. 334 *et seq.* The procedure is extremely lengthy and, dependent upon pressure of Parliamentary business, may take between one month and three months.

noted. The definition of " ancient monuments " was re-stated in s. 15 of the 1953 Act and was then extended so as to include structures relating to the Industrial Revolution.[40]   Secondly, it is provided by s. 13 of the 1913 Act that all monuments either owned by, or under the guardianship of, the Secretary of State for the Environment shall be open to public access, " except in cases where the owner's consent is required," or where the deeds relating to ownership by the Department, or guardianship, were executed before the coming into force of the 1913 Act.[41]

Lastly, in regard to the special provisions under the Field Monuments Act, 1972, for the protection of earthworks and other monuments from damage or destruction in the course of agricultural or forestry operations, " acknowledgement payments " may be made by the Secretary of State for the Environment to the *occupier* of such land, following upon an acknowledgement payment agreement.   In return for this payment in compensation for future loss in agricultural production, the Secretary of State may enforce the rights of protection of relevant field monuments as provided for in the agreement as if he were " the absolute owner in possession of the land." However, the 1972 Act relies upon the occupier (and owner) entering into such voluntary agreement, which in many cases may be refused by the occupier, and further legislation is to be introduced in order to afford powers of compulsion.

(6) *Churches and other ecclesiastical buildings*

These (with the exception of parsonages) have, apparently, been excluded from control and grant aid on the principle that the members of the body of the Church should subscribe to support of the buildings appertaining to their faith; and that the Established and other Churches within Great Britain should not receive support from the Exchequer which would not be available to other sects and religions.   Whatever may be the logical justification of this policy, the result under modern circumstances is that many churches, chapels and other meeting houses, having small congregations, cannot meet the current high costs of maintenance and repair.   The National Assembly of the Church of England accordingly passed the Pastoral Measure of 1968, which

---

[40] The study of " industrial archaeology " has received increased attention in recent years.

[41] 15th August, 1913.

was approved by Parliament, setting out the procedure to be adopted for dealing with those churches of the Church of England declared from time to time to be redundant.   The process is divided into three stages.

The First Stage consists in a " declaration of redundancy," made in a " pastoral scheme " originating from the Pastoral Committee of the diocese concerned, and making recommendations to the bishop (s. 3 (2) of the Pastoral Measure, 1968), but subject to the statutory requirement that all " interested parties," including the local planning authority, be consulted.   These recommendations will include the possibility of an alternative use for a suitable purpose, such as a museum, upon the basis that, after completion of the redundancy process, the structure may become the subject of a grant either as a listed building or as an ancient monument.   Such consultations must also include reference to the Council for the Care of Churches, and the obtaining from that council of full information about the historical and architectural factors relating both to the church in question and to other churches in the area (s. 3 (4)).

Within the first stage and following the above process of consultation, the Pastoral Committee may make recommendations as " draft proposals " for submission to the bishop (s. 3 (5)) and, if the bishop approves them, these are then to be submitted as a " draft scheme " to the Church Commissioners (s. 3 (6)).   The Commissioners are required to send a draft of the redundancy scheme to relevant local planning authorities, supported by the views of the Advisory Board for Redundant Churches.   If the views of the Commissioners and of the Board are in conflict, reasons for the difference in opinion are to be stated.   Following receipt of the draft scheme, the local planning authority may, within twenty-eight days, request an oral hearing by the Church Commissioners.   Any amendments to a draft scheme are to be subject to the same process as set out above.   To ensure reasonable public participation in this rather negative form of planning, s. 5 of the Pastoral Measure requires publication in one or more local newspapers circulating in the locality of a notice stating the objects of the draft scheme, naming a place or places at which it may be inspected, and inviting written representations.

A draft scheme can be made, therefore, merely with the consent of the bishop of the diocese concerned, and under his seal; but a scheme (proper) will only come into effect after submission for confirmation by Her Majesty in Council (s. 8 (1)). Appeals against such schemes may be made by those who have earlier made written representations by lodging notice of appeal with the Clerk of the Privy Council within twenty-eight days, beginning with the day after the date of the first publication of the notice that the scheme is to be submitted to the Privy Council (s. 8 (2)). Such appeals are heard by the Judicial Committee of the Privy Council, who subsequently report by way of a proposal to Her Majesty in Council that the appeal be allowed or dismissed, or that the scheme be returned to the Church Commissioners for further consideration (s. 8 (4) and (5)). The latter may then amend the scheme and re-submit it (s. 8 (6) and (7)).

If the Order in Council is made, it is then sent to the relevant local planning authority (provided that the planning authority have, in fact, made earlier representations), and the scheme will come into effect upon the date of a notice of confirmation being published in the *London Gazette*. However, this does not complete the process, since a Second and a Third Stage is required.

The Second Stage consists initially of a waiting period (s. 49 (1)), during which time the church building passes into the care of the Diocesan Board of Finance for a minimum of one year. In this period the Diocesan Redundant Churches Use Committee, or the Church Commissioners, are to endeavour to find (s. 42 (2)) a suitable alternative ecclesiastical use for the building. If no suitable ecclesiastical use can be found the actual redundancy scheme is then prepared (s. 50 (1)) and copies of this are to be sent to the Diocesan Board of Finance, the local planning authority, and the Advisory Board for Redundant Churches. In cases where the proposal is that the building be cared for and maintained the Redundant Churches Fund is also to be supplied with a copy.

The Third and Final Stage requires that, between one and three years following the declaration of redundancy, the Church Commissioners may still decide that, even where no suitable use can be found for the structure, it may yet be placed in the care of the Redundant Churches Fund (s. 51 (1) (*b*)). If no other alternative can be found, the redundancy scheme may provide for the demolition of the church, and disposal of materials and of the site. In such cases further and final consultation is required with the bishop, the Diocesan Board of Finance, the Advisory Board of Finance, the

Advisory Board of the Redundant Churches Fund (if care or maintenance of any part not to be demolished is involved), and the local
planning authority, again with the right of making representations
within twenty-eight days (s. 51 (1) (*c*) and (2) and (3)).

It may appear as an anti-climax, that, in cases where the Advisory
Board for Redundant Churches certifies that the building is of such
small historic or architectural interest that there should be no
objection to demolition, a *shortened procedure* is permitted (s. 49
(1) (i)).   In such cases the one-year waiting period may be
dispensed with by the Church Commissioners, and further latitude
is allowed in that particular features of architectural or historic
value may be incorporated in another, or new, church.   However,
similar safeguards as to consultation with local planning authorities
(as already cited) are to apply, even in the use of the shortened
procedure.

Finally, it must be emphasised that although churches which are
in use do not qualify for the various grants available for other special
buildings (*ibid.*), they are, nevertheless, protected by listing under
the Town and Country Planning Act, 1971, read together with the
Redundant Churches and other Religious Buildings Act, 1969,
from demolition, alteration or extension, so that *listed building consent
is still required even after the building ceases to be in " ecclesiastical use "*
(s. 249 of the 1971 Act) *until the redundancy scheme procedure is completed
following consultation with the local planning authority.*   (As to the
parallel requirements as to listed buildings consent and de-listing,
see pp. 241–242, and 244, *ante.*)

(7) *Public Health legislation; rates relief*

Returning to buildings in general, there is *public health legislation*
(notably the Public Health Act, 1961) which may override the
various provisions for protection already discussed.   Where a
building is dangerous and immediate action is necessary, the local
authority may take such steps as they deem advisable (s. 25), but
they must, if reasonably practicable, notify the owner and occupier
before taking action: it is specifically provided that the surveyor of
the local authority may personally exercise these powers (s. 25 (1)).
In cases where the building is not positively dangerous, but is so
ruinous or dilapidated as to be seriously detrimental to the amenities
of the locality, the local authority are empowered to serve notice
on the owner to repair or restore the premises or, if the owner so

wishes, to demolish them. But, where the owner chooses to demolish rather than to repair, and the building is either on the statutory lists,[42] or is an ancient monument, the consent of the local authority, and in some cases the Secretary of State for the Environment, must first be obtained (*ante*, pp. 241 and 262).

Financial assistance, over and above the making available of grants for repair and improvement, is afforded to occupiers and/or owners in the form of *relief from liability to pay rates*. The General Rate Act, 1967, with Sched. 9, para. 68, to the Town and Country Planning Act, 1968 (which latter paragraph is not repealed by the Town and Country Planning Act, 1971) enabled rating authorities to exercise the option of rating unoccupied premises after they have been vacant for three months: however, by s. 17 of and Sched. 1 (2) to the said Act, this option may not be exercised in respect either of buildings on the statutory lists[42]; or of those notified to the rating authority by the Ministry as being " a building of outstanding architectural or historic interest "[43]; or any other buildings which are subject to building preservation orders or to notices or lists under the Ancient Monuments Acts, 1913 and 1953. However, buildings on a " provisional list " only (i.e., including both Town and Country Planning Act, 1971, listing, and also as to ancient monuments) may be rendered liable to rates, at the rating authority's discretion.

(8) *Historic Buildings Bureau*

To assist in finding uses for statutory listed buildings generally,[44] the Department of the Environment has set up an Historic Buildings Bureau [45] which is to accept particulars from those owners who wish to sell, or let on lease, listed buildings. But this may be done only after the building has been in the hands of ordinary estate agents for at least two months and these estate agents have been informed by the owner of his intention to approach the Bureau. In order to avoid commercial competition with agents, the Bureau will never be concerned with matters of price or rent; and, having made the

---

[42] i.e., listed as Grade I, Grade II * or Grade II (but not Grade III) under ss. 54 and 55 of the Town and Country Planning Act, 1971 (previously s. 32 of the 1962 Act and s. 40 (1) and (10) of the 1968 Act).

[43] i.e., under the Historic Buildings and Ancient Monuments Act, 1953 (*ante*, p. 262).

[44] i.e., Grade I, Grade II* and Grade II only.

[45] Address: Caxton House (West), Tothill Street, London, S.W.1.

necessary introduction between the owner and purchaser or tenant, will leave negotiations to the parties or their agents. Further, the Bureau is to make no charge for its services.

The Bureau normally circulates information to a wide variety of bodies, including the professional institutions of estate agents, local authorities, the National Trust, amenity societies, universities and industrial or commercial concerns.

2. Conservation Areas

The Civic Amenities Act of 1967 was designed (*inter alia*) as " an Act to make further provision for the protection and improvement of buildings of architectural or historic interest and of the character of areas of such interest . . . ," etc. Therefore Part I of the Act provides for the designation by local planning authorities of " Conservation Areas "; and also for further protection of listed buildings (as already discussed). The only section relating to conservation areas (namely, s. 1 of the 1967 Act) is now replaced by s. 277 of the Town and Country Planning Act, 1971, although merely by way of consolidation.

The practical purpose in empowering local planning authorities to create conservation areas is to render it possible to go beyond the preservation of individual buildings, and to afford " blanket " protection over a defined (designated) urban or village area. There is, in fact, a positive direction to the local planning authority that they shall " from time to time determine which parts of their area are areas of special architectural or historic interest the character or appearance of which it is desirable to preserve or enhance, and shall designate such areas as conservation areas " (s. 277 (1)). It is further provided that the Secretary of State may " after consultation " give directions to a local planning authority so to act (s. 277 (2)). Thus, reluctant authorities may be required to take action; yet it should be noted that although there are now about 1,600 conservation areas in Britain, there is at present considerable variation between the number of conservation areas which it has been seen fit to designate in adjoining counties or boroughs. However, it should be appreciated that two inter-related problems arise in the designation process; the first is the matter of cost, and the second the consequent need to choose between areas which may well be extremely similar in their merits at the time of selection.

In the preliminary stages it is necessary for the local planning authority to carry out pilot surveys as to suitability for conservation throughout their entire county or county borough. Only by this means is it possible to ensure that a fair selection is made (and thus to avoid unnecessary discontent on the part of ratepayers, including those living in areas not eventually designated); and equally to ensure that the ultimate total cost will be not unreasonable. The cost of such surveys is, in itself, relatively high, but, once conservation areas are created, it becomes essential that they be seen to be actively and effectively conserved. Thus, the local planning authority should particularly apply enforcement action (or compulsory purchase where necessary) to buildings within conservation areas; and should, in addition, seek to set an example by the replacement, where necessary, of unsuitable (or ill-sited) public equipment and fixtures, etc., such as signs, litter containers, bus shelters, trees, etc. Section 277 (5) states: " Where any area is for the time being designated as a conservation area, special attention shall be paid to the desirability of preserving or enhancing its character or appearance in the exercise, with respect to any buildings or other land in that area, of any powers under this Act, Part I of the Historic Buildings and Ancient Monuments Act, 1953, or the Local Authorities (Historic Buildings) Act, 1962."

It should also be borne in mind that the designation of a conservation area may affect adjoining areas. Thus, a public park not within but adjacent to a conservation area may require to be improved in standard and in management. Further, and of greater significance, there may be an increase in applications for permission to develop or redevelop adjacent sites, the property value of which (in urban areas) will have been increased as a result of their proximity to a conservation area. Thus (as in the city of Bath) considerable pressure from developers may arise, with the object of constructing multi-storey blocks of flats or offices in which " landscape " windows will offer magnificent views of the conserved areas, but will in themselves seriously detract from the visual appearance from other viewpoints. Again, the designation of a number of (urban) conservation areas within a county borough will allow the introduction of a point of argument upon application for planning permission in relation to other sites; that is, that the site in question is *not* within a conservation area and must therefore, by inference, be of lesser quality: this will in fact be by no means always a valid assertion, since the limitation in size and number of designated areas is enforced by cost.   Therefore, it is submitted that in the case of several cities in Britain which can be seen, even in monetary terms, to represent an asset by the attraction of foreign exchange obtained from overseas visitors, there should be special provision made for very large block grants from the Exchequer. Whereas a mediaeval street may be appreciated in proximity to a Victorian shopping parade, it will become pathetically incongruous if overshadowed by a multi-storey steel and concrete block—as indeed may the modestly monumental eighteenth- and nineteenth-century buildings at Hyde Park Corner in London, when certain proposed developments take place.

Provision has now been made, by s. 9 of the Town and Country Planning (Amendment) Act, 1972, to enable the Secretary of State to make direct grants or loans in order to benefit any specific areas of " outstanding architectural or historic interest " (s. 9 (1)), and these may cover either the whole or part of the expenditure by the relevant local authority.

Turning to positive means of protection, it has been the experience of local planning authorities that the effect of the original system of listing of buildings has, as already mentioned,[46] been unsatisfactory in terms of prevention of demolition where Grade III structures have been concerned.   Buildings of this grade frequently form part, if not the whole, of conservation areas, and such areas can be grossly devalued, in a matter of hours, by the removal of such old or merely unusual structures.   Similarly, much of the value of a single statutorily listed building could be lost by the demolition of an adjoining, or adjacent, structure.   This comment was also made in the Dartmouth Committee Report,[47] and legislative action has now been taken in the Town and Country Planning (Amendment) Act, 1972, ss. 7 to 9.   By s. 7, all buildings within a conservation area other than listed buildings or " excepted buildings," [48] may be protected by the local planning authority giving a direction that a specified building be subject to control under this section so as to prevent demolition.   The direction is validly made only where it is " in the interests of preserving the character or appearance of any

---

[46] See p. 239.

[47] See Appendix B, Recommendations 14 and 19.

[48] " Excepted buildings " are those which are excepted from local planning authorities' powers to serve building preservation notices otherwise available under s. 58 (2) of the Town and Country Planning Act, 1971, such as Crown property.

part of their area which is for the time being a conservation area."
Such a direction requires to be confirmed by the Secretary of State
for the Environment (s. 7 (3)), and will normally take effect only
on the day on which it is so confirmed by him. However, special
provision is made for cases of extreme urgency, in which the local
planning authority may specify in the direction and notice that it
shall have immediate effect (s. 7 (4)). Provision does not appear
to have been specially made for the payment of compensation in the
event of a decision on the part of the Secretary of State to refuse to
confirm such an immediate designation.

CHAPTER 14

GREEN BELT AREAS

REFERENCE has already been made[1] to the fact that the greater part of the practical application of statutory law relating to our environment (and also to other functions of local and national government) is now heavily overlaid by ministerial directives in the form of Circulars and other papers. These documents, which are sent to local authorities and to departments of central government, generally purport to be advisory in nature and to set out the town and country planning and other policies which the relevant Minister would " wish " to see applied. They thus tend to be almost binding upon the local authority (certainly in so far as local government officers are concerned), yet to have no force in law in committing the Minister as to any future decisions he may make.

The significance of this quasi-administrative law is perhaps most marked in relation to protection of the Green Belts, which now surround (totally or partially) a large number of our towns and cities. For example, in arguing any given case against development of a site within a Green Belt, it is almost essential to quote from a number of ministerial circulars which have been issued during the past twenty years—even though they be merely persuasive in effect in so far as the Secretary of State for the Environment is concerned.

It is therefore thought advisable to divide this chapter into three sections:

1. The factual situation and policy considerations in relation to Green Belts;

2. Statutory provisions controlling Green Belt land; and

3. Persuasive statements of ministerial policy, in the form of (i) circulars and similar publications; and (ii) administrative tribunal (i.e., planning inquiry) case law (including also published Appendices).

Thus, section 1 is designed to offer a general picture of the current trends in protection of the Green Belt, and sections 2 and 3 are

[1] Chapter 1, at pp. 4 and 5.

intended to offer respectively a statement of the law and sources of persuasive argument.

1. The Factual Situation and Policy Considerations in Relation to Green Belts

The principle of the Green Belt is now generally accepted as an important element in the planning of both large urban areas and also of the rural, or semi-rural, parts of the country surrounding conurbations.

The idea was introduced into town and country planning by the Green Belt (London and Home Counties) Act, 1938, which purported to be " an Act to make provision for the preservation from industrial or building development of areas of land in and around the administrative county of London, to confer powers for that purpose upon the [then] London County Council and certain other authorities and persons, and for other purposes."

In the post-1939–45 war period it became evident that a greater degree of positive town and country planning was necessary in order to secure tolerable living conditions and essential services in these small and highly-populated islands. Thus, development plans for every area throughout Britain have become of increasing importance, and many of these have included provision for Green Belts round the major cities and sometimes other towns of lesser size. At the same time, however, the demand for (and value of) housing land has risen very rapidly, and most Green Belt areas, more particularly in the Metropolitan Green Belt, have been increasingly threatened and despoiled by developers. There is, clearly, a greater incentive to apply for planning permission to build houses or flats in a Green Belt, where the very name may add substantially to the potential selling price, than to seek to develop urban waste land, such as redundant railway siding sites.

The nominal Metropolitan Green Belt,[2] which encircles London, covers a considerable area, varying from six to ten miles in width and amounting to about 850 square miles. This nominal Green Belt had been so agreed by the then Ministers as parts of a series of county development plans principally during

---

[2] The greater part of the area of proposed Green Belt still awaits formal approval by the Secretary of State, and no clear Parliamentary statement as to policy has yet been made. A total of 1,200 additional square miles has been requested by adjoining county authorities. See, however, p. 280, *post*.

the period 1950 to 1959; but additional areas have since been allocated (subject to ministerial confirmation) by the individual local planning authorities, and have awaited formal approval for many years. As to this, further reference is made at pp. 279–280 *post*.

The principal purposes of Green Belts throughout the country were defined in 1955 by the (then) Ministry of Housing and Local Government Circular No. 42/55 (see *post*, p. 287; and Appendix D). The three basic aims given in the circular have been recently reiterated by the Under-Secretary of State for the Environment in answer to a Parliamentary Question,[3] as follows: " *First to contain the growth of larger built-up areas; secondly, to prevent the coalescence of towns; thirdly to preserve the special character of particular towns.*" He further added: " Of these three objectives, the first two apply to the London Green Belt. There is no doubt that Green Belts have always been understood to have the aim of preserving the countryside so that it is within reach of the townsmen." That is, in the case of very large conurbations, the function of a surrounding Green Belt is not only to prevent (at least temporarily) the tendency to produce an unplanned sprawl of development from spreading either into the countryside or along the lines of transport routes, but it is also intended to provide an area of open country within a reasonable distance from the city centre which may be enjoyed (at least visually) by urban dwellers. In this latter respect, the recreational value of any Green Belt has been further increased by the various provisions now made for access to open country, and for establishing and increasing the rights of the general public to use footpaths, bridleways, etc. This question of public access to the countryside is discussed in detail in Chapter 15, The Countryside—II: Conservation and Recreation.

It must also be remarked that so far as Green Belts designed primarily to prevent coalescence of urban areas are concerned (as, say, between the cities of Bristol and Bath), the relatively firm maintenance of the principle up to the present time may be the result of the relevant local planning authority having been, in most cases, a rural-minded county. Since reforms of local government involve the formation of large mixed urban and rural planning authorities [3a] there will be greater need of vigilance in the protection

[3] *Hansard*, 11th June, 1971, col. 1471: " London Green Belt."
[3a] Local Government Act, 1972.

of Green Belts on the part of the Secretary of State. This increased vigilance may also require to take the form of directives so as to avoid the granting of planning permissions by local planning authorities—against which latter action there cannot, of course, be any appeal by local objectors.

However, it is within Green Belts that the most hotly-contested plans for development tend to arise, notably in connection with the use of virgin land for housing.[4] Thus, as already stated, in the Metropolitan area, developers, both small and large, tend, in so far as housing construction is concerned, to concentrate upon finding sites in the Green Belt rather than within the Greater London urban area. This position is further aggravated by the fact that the older houses lying within the Green Belt and which existed before creation of the statutory Green Belt area (1938), tend to have been built in the approximate period 1880 to 1930. They frequently have extensive grounds of, say, one to four or more acres. Unless such grounds have been deliberately designated as Green Belt by the local planning authority (and subsequently confirmed as such by the Secretary of State) they will be automatically zoned as " residential " land. Thus, for example, even a domestic orchard of, say, one acre, lying at a distance of many hundreds of yards from the original dwelling-house, may be developed as a housing estate without real impediment, since the orchard may be designated as " residential." (Also, where land is zoned as " white land," that is as land which it is expected will continue in its present use, say for agriculture, and abutting on to the Green Belt, it will receive no special protection.)

In the situations discussed above, the normal statutory requirements as to application for planning permission do, of course, apply, but the tendency is for developers to go to appeal even where the chances of success may be slight. This inclination is encouraged by our system of taxation, whereby the cost of representation and of divers professional witnesses can be legitimately set against tax as business expenses. It must further be remarked that a large development company will tend to follow a policy of employing the best possible counsel and firms of expert witnesses, whereas in contrast local planning authorities tend, on occasion, to be represented

[4] The Dartmouth Committee Report, in Recommendation 9 (see Appendix B hereto) states, " The development of virgin land should be more strictly controlled, especially where there is derelict or under-utilised land in urban areas."

by solicitor-members of their staff whose experience of advocacy may, in many cases, tend to be limited by comparison.[5] The planning authority may also tend to be, to an extent, handicapped in that the usual practice is to use their own specialist officers as professional witnesses who are, of necessity, vulnerable in two respects: first, their evidence is generally drawn from comparisons within their own authority area—whereas the appellants' witnesses will often draw from a wider field of recently obtained information; and secondly, cross-examination may tend to infer (generally without justification!) that they are partial witnesses due to their original involvement in initial advice given to the planning committee in relation to the appeal case.

Thus, it is submitted that, whatever may be the stated purpose of the Green Belt, the line is not at present being effectively held; and more particularly in cases where there is any remotely conceivable possibility that an appeal site could be described as " in-filling," whether this be in-filling in the heart of a village, or in-filling of an enclave of open land on the perimeter of a village.

At the present time (1973) the Government is striving to achieve two contrasting aims; that is, to increase the stock of building land, whilst at the same time asserting in regard to the Green Belt generally as follows [6]: " The general position is that all development control policies applying within the Green Belt entail a very strong presumption against buildings, except particular buildings that have a direct relevance—for example, farm buildings in rural areas and special developments for sport.   The presumption always is that there should be a very strong argument against the Green Belt being infringed."   To this may be added the statement given in Circular 10/70, Land Availability for Housing,[7] in para. 6: " One of the most important aspects of the duty of local planning authorities is the release of adequate land for house-building.   In many cases they have made appropriate proposals in their development plans.   But in some areas there remains a need for urgent action to release land *now*.   In order to have a significant effect on the problem, the Secretary of State considers that releases of land should be sufficient to meet housing needs already existing and

---

[5] It is also not uncommon for local planning authorities to omit one or more legitimate grounds from their case.

[6] *Hansard*, 11th June, 1971, col. 1474: " The London Green Belt."

[7] 14th December, 1970.

foreseeable for at least the next five years; and that the land required to meet these needs should be released at once so as to keep the supply of land well ahead of demand. The Secretary of State accordingly looks to local planning authorities to make generous additional releases *wherever this can be done without detriment to other important planning objectives, e.g., the safeguarding of Green Belts.*" [8]

However, a significant number of recent decisions by the Secretary of State following planning appeals, and often contrary to the recommendations of the Inspectors concerned, would seem to indicate that the Metropolitan Green Belt at least is not to be so well guarded. A clear statement of the balance to be struck between the opposing needs for housing land and Green Belt amenity should be the subject of urgent Parliamentary consideration.

It must also be emphasised that any Green Belt can only continue to exist in practice where there is a willing body of farmers and other agriculturalists, including forestry owners, to continue to cultivate the land. This section of the community is continually discouraged by the incursions and depredations of the large urban communities in their localities, and they suffer harm not only from deliberate damage and carelessness, but also from the possibility that a flow of members of the public may well carry disease onto their land. It is hardly surprising, therefore, that many farmers may be greatly attracted by offers of " building land value " for their fields in cases where planning permission is at all likely to be obtained. At the present time building land value in the Metropolitan Green Belt may be up to £60,000 per acre, by comparison with a relatively high agricultural value of up to £1,000 per acre. There will also, clearly, be a ready market in the sale and purchase of options[9] for substantial sums as a deliberate gamble in the hope that permission to develop within the Green Belt may, by some means or other, be eventually obtained. In addition, an agriculturalist who lives in hope of the taking-up of an agreed option is far less likely to spend money on large-scale improvements to buildings and fixed equipment which would be necessary for modern economic production on the holding.

The future of the Metropolitan Green Belt is in process of clarification, and a clearer statement of policy by the Secretary of State

[8] The latter phrase is italicised by the author.

[9] i.e., a contract whereby one party is to have the first option to purchase land at some future date.

may be anticipated in the near future. To date an increase in area of about 50 per cent. (472 square miles) upon the previous total of 850 square miles has been agreed, to give a total of 1,322 square miles; but further additions may be expected in the counties of Berkshire and Essex. It appears that the total figure will be less than the combined total requested by the several development plans, etc., of the adjoining county authorities [10] for an increase of about 147 per cent., or to about 2,050 square miles. Many areas of the existing Metropolitan Green Belt have already changed radically in character as a result of housing developments, and it is to be hoped, in view of the relatively small expansion in area now permitted by the Government, that greater restraint of building ventures can now be anticipated. Certainly, at the present time, there is a general feeling of unease in the minds of many people fortunate enough to live in the Green Belt itself as they see both amenity and some of the more expensive property values declining, where this relies upon a rural setting. However, the decline in the value of property is not, of itself, a " planning consideration " in terms of application by the Secretary of State or his Inspectors, save in so far as it influences the strength of local " public opinion," which latter factor is a relevant planning consideration.

2. Statutory Provisions Controlling Green Belt Land

(a) *Statutory creation of the Metropolitan Green Belt and special controls relating thereto*.—In 1938, the year in which the Green Belt (London and Home Counties) Act was passed, general town and country planning legislation had developed to the stage that, by virtue of the Town and Country Planning Act, 1932, " town planning schemes " of a rather rigid nature could be made by local authorities, subject to confirmation by the (then) Minister. The 1932 Act introduced, for the first time, the principle that planning could be applied to areas of land which were unlikely, in the foreseeable future, to be developed; whereas, under earlier legislation, provision had been made only for the planning of areas either already in course of being developed, or which were expected shortly to be built over. But no provision was made for interim development control [11] under the 1932 or earlier Acts except where the area was

---

[10] Essex, Kent, Surrey, Berkshire, Buckinghamshire and Hertfordshire.
[11] Introduced by the Town and Country Planning (Interim Development) Act, 1943.

subject to a town planning scheme. Further, local authorities exhibited very considerable reluctance to prepare these schemes, since they would result (as the law then stood) in liability to pay compensation to owners of land whose interests therein had been injuriously affected by the scheme. (In this instance the term " injuriously affected " relates to the effect of any town planning provisions in the scheme, or the doing of any work under it—subject to various specific exclusions of the right to compensation. It did not relate solely to the modern meaning of " injurious affection," which now applies either (*a*) to the indirect effects of compulsory acquisition (e.g., severance by a road), or (*b*) to injuries or detriment caused by works carried out upon land adjacent to the claimant's land, but where the claimant's land has not, in fact, been acquired.)

As a result of the deficiencies in town and country planning powers existent at that time, the method adopted to secure and promote the Green Belt in the Green Belt (London and Home Counties) Act, 1938, is as follows. (And it should be noted that all material powers provided under the Act are still valid.)

By s. 3 of the Act of 1938 together with s. 120 in Pt. VI of the Town and Country Planning Act, 1971, local authorities [12] may enter into agreements with persons interested in land in their area for the purpose of regulating the development or use of the land either permanently or for limited periods. Specific power to enforce such restrictive covenants is provided for by s. 22 (1) of the 1938 Act, which section also excludes the power of the Lands Tribunal to discharge or modify them, which would otherwise exist upon the mutually agreed application of interested parties under s. 84 of the Law of Property Act, 1925.

In addition, a local authority may, by s. 3 (*c*), acquire land " for the purpose of establishing a Green Belt round London," either by purchase, gift, lease, exchange or otherwise. In the case both of agreements for regulating development or user, and of agreements to acquire, the section specifically requires that no lessee may validly bind the land unless he first obtains the written consent of " the person entitled for the time being to the reversion immediately expectant upon that lease." In other words, there must first be a complete chain of written consents leading back to the freeholder.

---

[12] For this purpose, by s. 3 (*a*), (*b*), including a parish council; but in most cases, subject to subsequent approval by resolution of the relevant county council (i.e., local planning authority): s. 32.

Equally, any restrictions imposed by an agreement made under s. 3 cannot derogate from the rights of any lessee, tenant, or even licensee of the person entering into the covenant (s. 29). It is, however, provided by s. 18 that a private owner of an estate in the Green Belt may enter into an agreement with the local authority to the effect that in the event of himself or any of his successors in title wishing, at a later date, to sell his estate or interest in the land (or any part of it), it will first be offered to the local authority at a price to be determined by whatever means are provided for in the agreement. Such agreements must be registered as land charges. It is also made clear, by s. 19, that the right under s. 18 may be exercised by a tenant for life[13] or a trustee for sale,[14] but may not be exercised without an order of the High Court, or (in the case of a tenant for life) the consent of the trustees of the settlement, or (in the case of a trustee for sale) the consent of all the beneficiaries under the trust who are of full age and are not under disability.

In the case of land held on charitable trusts, however, no power under the 1938 Act may be exercised if at variance with the purposes of the trust without an order of either the High Court or the Charity Commissioners.

On completion of an agreement or an acquisition the local authority must deposit plans of the relevant land with the Department of the Environment.

Once land has been protected by agreement, or acquired under the 1938 Act, it may not subsequently be alienated in any way from Green Belt purposes without the consent of the Secretary of State (s. 5). In obtaining this consent the local planning authority must publish a notice of their intention in one or more local newspapers, serve a copy of such notice on every contributing[15] local authority and on the county council (where relevant), and also " seek " the consent of such local authority and/or county council. The Secretary of State will then consider any objections and " may (s. 33) hold or cause to be held such (public or private) inquiries as he may consider necessary." The decision of the Secretary of State is to be made by means of an order (s. 5). This order may contain such conditions " as shall appear to him to be just "; and

---

[13] i.e., a tenant for life under the Settled Land Act, 1925.

[14] i.e., a trustee for sale within the meaning of the Law of Property Act, 1925.

[15] i.e., district or parish councils which have contributed to the cost of the agreement or purchase of land.

it may, equally, cause the land to be freed, from a specified date, from any restrictions imposed upon it, including any covenant entered into providing this were for the purposes of the Act.[16] Specific provision is made for the appropriation of any land which is subject to a 1938 Act covenant—where this is for purposes of development under a development plan—by s. 112 of the Town and Country Planning Act, 1971. In addition, s. 6 of the 1938 Act provides a saving in relation to certain powers of acquisition of Green Belt land subject to the Act where the local authority seeks to acquire land for use under various statutory powers other than for highway purposes. Provision for such acquisition or use for highway purposes is made under s. 8 of the Act, and this includes acquisition for purposes of construction (including ancillary works) or improvement of a road. However, in all cases of acquisition by local authorities it is provided (s. 9) that any restrictions imposed upon the land for the purposes of the 1938 Act shall not be taken into account when arriving at the compensation payable by either local authorities or statutory undertakers.[17] Statutory undertakers are permitted to acquire Green Belt land, but their use of that land may be restricted and, further, they may be required to provide other land, in substitution, for Green Belt use (s. 7 (1)). In order to provide this substitute land they may acquire it by agreement under powers originally provided by earlier Town and Country Planning Acts, but now by virtue of s. 120 of the 1971 Act.

Where land " becomes " (i.e., is approved subsequently from time to time as) Green Belt land after such land is already subject to various orders for intended improvement in connection with a highway, then such road improvements shall lawfully continue (s. 8). Similar savings are provided in the 1938 Act in relation to main sewers; piped watercourses; electric cables (including overhead cables), substations and transformers (s. 11); and also for the protection of the Post Office in relation to telephones and telegraph wires, etc. (s. 30). Latitude is also provided in relation to use for educational purposes (s. 20).

---

[16] i.e., the Secretary of State can only deal with covenants entered into specifically by virtue of the 1938 Act. Any other restrictive covenants can only be altered by voluntary reference to the Lands Tribunal made under s. 84 of the Law of Property Act, 1925.

[17] " Statutory undertakers," for the purposes of the 1938 Act means any persons authorised by an enactment or order to construct, work or carry on any railway, canal, inland navigation, dock, harbour, tramway, gas, or electricity undertaking.

The two provisions in the Act which are of prime importance relate, first, to user of Green Belt land (s. 27), and secondly to restrictions imposed upon erection of buildings (s. 10). By s. 27, nothing in the Act shall prevent the use of Green Belt land for purposes of recreation or for purposes of agriculture (here defined as a use as arable, meadow or pasture land, or for the growth or sale of underwood) (s. 27 (*a*)); nor for " camping by means of tents " (but subject to this being in accordance with any byelaws or later enactments regulating camping generally, such as the Physical Training and Recreation Act, 1937 and 1958) [17a] (s. 27 (*b*)); nor in relation to the letting for any of the above purposes by a local authority or parish council (but not private owners) of land vested in them (s. 27 (*c*)).

Finally, as to restrictions to be imposed upon the erection of buildings within a Green Belt, special problems arise and must be considered here in some detail. In the case of land previously acquired by local authorities or subject to a negotiated restrictive covenant, by s. 10, no building may be erected on the said Green Belt land (other than ancillary to a previously approved use of that land) without the consent of the Secretary of State and of *every* " contributing local authority." [18] Thus, in the case of sites acquired by, for example, a county authority with the aid of contributions from a district or districts, the county must not then erect a building upon it unless permission is first obtained from the said other local authorities and from the Secretary of State for the Environment. It should, therefore, be noted that, in the case for example of a recreation ground, or camping site, purchased jointly by local authorities and lying within the Green Belt, it will be necessary to obtain the agreement of all local authority contributors to any proposal to construct buildings upon it. Further, no building may be erected in contravention of any local byelaw (s. 10 (2)).

(*b*) *Application of general Planning Controls under the Town and Country Planning Acts where Green Belt Land is involved.*—The question of obtaining the approval of contributing authorities and the Secretary

---

[17a] Or Class V of the General Development Order, 1973 (S.I. 1973 No. 31).

[18] " Contributing local authority " here means any local authority which has either before or after commencement of the 1938 Act, contributed, or agreed t contribute, towards the cost incurred in the acquisition of that land or c negotiated restrictive covenants upon that land.

of State must, however, be clearly distinguished from the normal requirement, applicable to all areas of land whether Green Belt or no, that planning permission under the Town and Country Planning Acts must also be obtained.

The normal considerations to be taken into account in relation to the granting of planning permission (as already considered in Chapter 1) will of course be equally applicable to a site consisting of Green Belt land, but in addition, the local planning authority will be expected to bear in mind the stated government policy in relation to protection of Green Belt areas, and they will therefore lean towards refusal of permission, and will only grant it " in very special circumstances " (*post*, p. 330). Application of this criterion has, however, led to curiously contrasting situations. In many rural areas local planning authorities have felt obliged to refuse applications by farmers about to retire to construct bungalows upon their own land, even upon secluded sites and solely for the purpose of ensuring that they may continue to live in the same community after retirement.[19] Yet, in other parts of the country, and notably near centres of large populations, permission is much more freely given for purely speculative development, generally upon the grounds that the particular piece of Green Belt land is not fully effective in that it has become partly surrounded by other development. Thus, the frontiers of urban areas advance by means of a form of what may be described as " serrated leapfrog."

However, in cases where permission is sought for development for a special purpose which is not incompatible with the principle of the Green Belt, local planning authorities are able, in certain given legal circumstances, to grant permission subject to specified conditions (these conditions being, however, only valid if they are included as conditions in the written notice of planning approval). A brief reference to the present case law governing planning conditions has been made in Chapter 1, but there is one leading case of special importance in relation to Green Belt sites. In *Fawcett Properties, Ltd.* v. *Buckingham County Council* [1960] 3 All E.R. 503 (H.L.) planning permission was given for the erection of two cottages in the Green Belt, but subject to a particular condition, namely, that " the occupation of the houses shall be limited to

---

[19] It should, however, be noted that planning permission has on occasions been obtained upon this basis of argument when the real intention (subsequently proved by action) was to obtain profit by re-sale.

persons whose employment or latest employment [20] is or was employment in agriculture as defined by s. 119 (1) of the Town and Country Planning Act, 1947 [now replaced by s. 290 of the 1971 Act], or in forestry, or in an industry mainly dependent upon agriculture and including also the dependants of such persons aforesaid." Fawcett Properties subsequently wished to avoid this condition and contended that it was, in fact, invalid upon a number of grounds but principally that the effect of the terms of the condition was too wide in that it did not " fairly and reasonably " relate to the type of permission granted. The learned judge in the court of first instance accepted this contention, but was overruled in the Court of Appeal. Upon further appeal to the House of Lords, the validity of the planning condition was again upheld,[21] and the appeal accordingly dismissed. The validity of the particular condition was held to be based upon the fact that it was germane to the grant of planning permission. Four principles emerge from the speeches (judgments), as follows:

(i) A condition must fairly and reasonably relate to the permitted development [22] (and, in this instance the purpose of the condition was, validly, to protect the Green Belt). As to this, the author wishes to add, with respect, the comment that, in other physical circumstances, e.g., where a pocket of Green Belt land has become isolated by recent surrounding development, it may be argued that protection of the Green Belt will no longer provide a valid ground for such a condition, and the condition may therefore be rendered invalid.

(ii) A condition must not be " wholly unreasonable "; that is, in the light of the principles of town and country planning, which are not concerned with, for example, maintenance of property values. The term " wholly unreasonable " means (*Kruse* v. *Johnson* [1898] 2 Q.B. 91, at p. 92) such as could find no justification in the minds of reasonable men.[23]

---

[20] i.e., to allow for retiring agricultural workers.

[21] Lord Reid and Lord Upjohn dissenting.

[22] *Pyx Granite Co., Ltd.* v. *Minister of Housing and Local Government* [1958] 1 All E.R. 625; reversed in part only [1959] 3 All E.R. 1.

[23] See also *Associated Provincial Picture Houses, Ltd.* v. *Wednesbury Corporation* [1947] 2 All E.R. 680; *Hall & Co., Ltd.* v. *Shoreham-on-Sea U.D.C.* [1964] 1 All E.R. 1; *Alnatt London Properties, Ltd.* v. *Middlesex County Council* (1964), 15 P. & C.R. 288; *Minister of Housing and Local Government* v. *Hartnell* [1965] 1 All E.R. 490; *Kingsway Investments, Ltd.* v. *Kent County Council* [1969] 1 All E.R. 601.

(iii) But a restriction may validly be imposed which restricts the use of premises to certain types of occupier, or even personally by name to one occupier or group of occupiers. Thus, it is possible to grant permission limited to an individual occupier which will cease upon his death or vacating the premises: this being particularly relevant where there may be a reasonable need for a particular specialised trade to continue in the area, but where also the site is unsuitable for indefinite user for that purpose having regard to the surrounding area.

(iv) That, as stated by Lord Morton of Henryton in his dissenting speech, a condition may be void for uncertainty.[24]

3. Persuasive Statements of Ministerial Policy

(i) *Circulars and other publications.*—In addition to the recent re-iteration of policy by Ministers in Parliament and elsewhere, as referred to in Section 1 of this chapter, it is necessary to refer to the original statements of intent in regard to the creation and preservation of Green Belts which have been made from time to time by successive governments. These publications show a remarkable consistency for the entire period from at least 1952. Consistency has not, however, applied in terms of planning consents (whether on appeal or otherwise) upon Green Belt sites during this period.

The sources referred to in Appendix D range from 1955 to 1963 but are constantly relied upon, where deemed expedient, when arriving at planning decisions. The sources are:

Circular No. 42/55—Green Belts (Issued by Ministry of Housing and Local Government, 3rd August, 1955).

Circular No. 50/57—Green Belts (Issued by Ministry of Housing and Local Government, 19th September, 1957).

Circular No. 37/60—The Review of Development Plans (Issued by Ministry of Housing and Local Government, 25th August, 1960).

Command Paper, Cmnd. 1952—London—Employment: Housing: Land. (Presented to Parliament by the then Minister of Housing and Local Government and the Minister of Welsh Affairs by command of Her Majesty, February 1963.)

---

[24] " As my noble and learned friend, Lord Simonds, said in *London and North Eastern Rly. Co.* v. *Berriman* [1946] 1 All E.R., at p. 270, ' A man is not to be put in peril upon an ambiguity.' . . ."

Circular No. 10/70—Land Availability for Housing (Issued by the Department of the Environment, 14th December, 1970).

Such sources are appended hereto (p. 329 *et seq.*) in case they may be desired when presenting a case in relation to development of a Green Belt site.

(ii) *Administrative Tribunal (i.e., Planning Inquiry) Case Law.*—It must be emphasised that the body of precedents, in the form of earlier planning appeal decisions, which has been built up over the past three decades differs radically in its application from case law as it is applied in the courts operating under the English legal system (whether at home or abroad). Planning appeal inquiries are administrative tribunals: therefore their preceding decisions can never be more than persuasive, in that policy considerations may be introduced by the Secretary of State in arriving at an (administrative) decision which is based upon national economic, sociological and political factors which lie beyond the argument presented at the inquiry.

Therefore, in the same way that Ministry circulars may be quoted merely as a persuasive point in argument, reported decisions following planning inquiries are in themselves merely persuasive.

The communication of the Secretary of State's decision (or of the Inspector's decision where such power is delegated to him by the Secretary of State by means of s. 36 of and Sched. 9 to the Town and Country Planning Act, 1971) is in writing to the appellant and to other interested parties. This normally takes letter form, and first sets out the Inspector's summary of the facts of the case and his recommendation, which are followed by further comments by the Secretary of State (save in the case of decision by the Inspector, as above), and the final decision to allow or to dismiss the appeal, or to allow the appeal subject to the imposition of certain planning conditions (say, as to re-siting, design, user, etc.). A summary of such decisions, in cases selected by the Ministry only, is published in a series of bulletins and issued from time to time. These consist (as at February, 1973) of: a First Series of thirteen bulletins (English and Welsh cases) issued between September 1947 and April 1958; a series of Scottish selected appeal decisions issued between October 1952 and October 1959; and a Second Series of five bulletins (English and Welsh cases) issued between June 1959 and June 1963. The total of cases covered in these bulletins includes twenty-nine decisions on Green Belt sites, of which twenty relate to houses, two relate to factory extensions, and one each to broiler houses, dog breeding establishments, limestone working, offices and training school, sand working, limestone working and workshops.

The decision in each case is related not merely to the fact that the site lies within a Green Belt but also to a variety of other factors relating to the individual planning application, including obscurity of the site, demand for housing, etc. It is therefore of limited value to discuss the principles applied from time to time, but the reader is referred to the *Encyclopedia of the Law of Town and Country Planning*[25] for ready access to these bulletins (see vol. 3, Part V—A thereof) and also for an excellent Digest of Planning Decisions (see vol. 3, Part V—B thereof), in which Green Belt decisions are discussed under the heading: " V. Development Related to Dwelling-houses and Residential Areas . . . (E) In a Rural Area, Green Belt and agricultural use " (Encyclopedia index reference 5-2156 to 5-2159).

Further and most important, it will be observed that many of the cases referred to in the Digest are reported in the *Journal of Planning and Environment Law*[26] and are therefore drawn from a less restrictive range of cases than are the selected decisions published by the Ministry.

The principal conclusions to be drawn from an analysis of planning appeal decisions over the past twenty years are as follows. The existence of a Green Belt is generally essential to the protection and improvement of amenity both of towns and of rural areas. Agricultural land is, in any event, scarce in Britain, and planning decisions must be based upon considerations which include the quality of such land and the efficiency of the holding (farms, market gardens, orchards, etc.). The nature of the development proposed is, however, also relevant in terms of its effect upon local amenity, and further in relation to any strong local need for the specific type of development. The local need may be represented either by a general requirement on the part of the community (such as for a hospital), or by the need relative to ownership of other land (say, for a gardener's cottage on a small estate). It should also be noted that, where there is a housing need (and this need exists in most,

---

[25] Published by Sweet & Maxwell, Ltd.
[26] Published by Sweet & Maxwell, Ltd. Cases reported in the *Journal of Planning and Environment Law* are often submitted by solicitors and others concerned therein. They are referred to, by way of example, thus: " [1953] J.P.L. 252 ": the names of the appellant and local planning authority are *not* used.

although not all, parts of the country), the Secretary of State may be disposed to allow a small, single dwelling on the grounds that it represents no " significant incursion into open space land."

Greater latitude may also be allowed on Green Belt land where the proposed development represents " in-filling " within the natural confines of an existing village—although this is less likely to meet with favour in the case of a small and scattered hamlet.

In so far as the erection of a dwelling-house is concerned, the form of employment of the proposed occupier is significant: the need for a cottage for an agricultural worker on (or near) a particular farm, market garden or even horse breeding stud, may be recognised, although the tendency is to favour agricultural workers rather than others engaged in a local trade not directly related to continuation of the Green Belt.   Further, it is often necessary for an appellant to produce sound economic evidence to the effect that a farm, or other agricultural unit, really requires the presence of an additional worker—say as a result of the setting-up of a new farming enterprise within the general conduct of the farm.[27]   In the case of market gardens or smallholdings it may well be possible to succeed upon the basis that the present owner/manager needs to live on the holding and not at a distance.   This will now particularly apply with the increased use of greenhouses and cloches, which require supervision and protection from weather conditions.

It should also be remarked that, although the presence of industry is generally deemed to be incompatible with the Green Belt, this has not precluded the Minister from granting planning permission where other factors have, in his view, rendered it desirable.   Such considerations may particularly apply in cases of applications to extend existing factories, and notably where these factories have an origin in some special local craft or skill, or are sited in order to make best use of natural resources, such as a water supply of a particular quality.[28]

---

[27] As to this, the Ministry of Agriculture, Fisheries and Food is normally invited to comment through the Ministry's local officials.   Since 1969, however, this comment takes the form purely of a statement of assessment of fact from an agricultural standpoint and does not include a recommendation.

[28] See Chapter 2, Industry.

CHAPTER 15

THE COUNTRYSIDE — II:
CONSERVATION AND RECREATION

THE purpose of this chapter is to consider the balance at present struck between the need for conservation (whether in terms of flora and fauna, or of matters of historical, architectural or sociological importance), and the national need to allow access to the country-side for recreational purposes. In contemplating these problems, it is now necessary to bear in mind the recommendations of the Dartmouth Committee, in regard to recreation and the reader should therefore refer to Appendix B, Recommendations 39 to 46. It will also be clear that the content of this chapter cannot be considered purely in isolation and that reference should be made to other chapters, and notably to those dealing with: the general needs of British agriculture (Chapter 3); the Green Belt principle (Chapter 14); and conservation areas (Chapter 13 (2)). However, it is also appropriate to consider here the effects of recreational activities in the countryside upon the practical needs of farming and forestry.

In 1949 the National Parks and Access to the Countryside Act was passed, having the primary objective of enabling those people not fortunate enough to live in rural surroundings to have access to open country for the purpose of physical and mental recreation. The Act seeks to secure maximum reasonable access for urban dwellers and also makes provision for the definition (and, if necessary, compulsory acquisition) of certain sites offering facilities for outdoor sports (such as sailing, water-skiing or rock climbing) whilst at the same time preserving, so far as possible, the " rural atmosphere " desired by both countrymen and others seeking relaxation. In this respect, the existence of Green Belts round large urban areas—whilst still of great value in limiting the growth and the merging-together of towns, and in offering rural or semi-rural scenery—do not *specifically* provide for increased freedom of access. Thus, the benefit of their scenic attraction must largely be appreciated from public highways. (For a detailed consideration of the Green Belt principle, see Chapter 14).

The statement " trespassers will be prosecuted " is now generally realised by the layman to be a legal impossibility.[1]   Yet the occupier's right to request a trespasser to leave by a reasonable route and, upon refusal, to use reasonable force to eject him, and further to bring a civil action for damages, has greatly limited the extent of public access to the countryside.   The 1949 Act therefore made provision for the securing of public rights of access, as set out below, but subject to the continuing right of the occupier of land to bring a civil action for damages against an individual, or group of individuals, for physical damage to his property or for deliberate and continuous annoyance by identifiable defendants.

First, by Part I of the 1949 Act, a National Parks Commission—now called the Countryside Commission [2]—was set up, and provided with certain powers in relation to: National Parks; the creation or definition of public rights of way; and the creation of Nature Reserves and Areas of Outstanding Natural Beauty.

1. National Parks

By Part II of the 1949 Act, ten National Parks were brought into being.   These constitute a total area of about 5,250 square miles, or one-tenth of the area of England and Wales.   The Parks were named as follows:

Brecon Beacons	Northumberland (Roman
Dartmoor	Wall)
Exmoor	Peak District
Lake District	Pembrokeshire Coast
North Yorkshire Moors	Snowdonia
	Yorkshire Dales

However, the mere designation of a tract of land as a National Park does not, of itself, confer upon the public any general rights of access: such rights, save in the case of " open country " (*infra*), can only be created by the making of Access Orders by the local planning authority (*infra*).   Neither is there any change in ownership (or occupation) of the land, except in " special circumstances " when the Countryside Commission may acquire land by compulsory purchase, necessitating a public inquiry, etc.   Such compulsory acquisition is by virtue of s. 14 of the 1949 Act.

[1] i.e., with the exception of Ministry of Defence land, etc., trespass to land is not a crime.

[2] Countryside Act, 1968, s. 1.

In short, it is the intention of the Act that, so far as possible, the normal life of the area within any National Park should continue without hindrance, but that special steps are also to be taken by individual National Parks Committees (which are statutory bodies controlling each separate Park), and by the local planning authority, to conserve the natural beauty and amenity of the countryside within the boundary of the Park. The working relationship between a National Park Committee and their local planning authority or authorities is laid down by s. 8 (2) of the 1949 Act, as amended by the Countryside Act, 1968, Sched. 4. Where the National Park is situated in more than one local planning authority area, the Act requires that a joint planning board be set up except where the Secretary of State decides that such a joint board is unnecessary in the particular case. The setting-up of a board requires to be authorised by order made by the Secretary of State.

In the absence of a joint planning board the relevant local planning authorities are themselves required to consult with the Secretary of State and, upon the basis of this, to arrange either (*a*) to set up their own National Park Planning Committee (which will be concerned only with such parts of the Park as lie within the local planning authority's area) reporting direct to the council of the county, or county borough; or (*b*) more usually, to set up a National Park Sub-Committee, reporting to the planning committee of the local planning authority, which will in turn make recommendations to the county, or county borough, council.

In addition to the alternatives (*a*) or (*b*) above, Sched. 4, para. 2, to the Countryside Act, 1968, enables two or more local planning authorities, upon their own initiative, to form joint advisory committees for such purposes as are provided by Pt. II of Sched. 2 to the Town and Country Planning Act, 1971, in relation to joint consultation (but not administration) as to matters affecting the National Park.[2a]

It should also be noted that (by s. 8 (1) of the Countryside Act, 1968) the arrangements as to planning administration or consultation as mentioned above are subject also to prior consultation with the Countryside Commission. In addition (s. 8 (6)), the composition of a joint planning board, a joint advisory committee, or an individual National Park planning committee (or sub-committee)

[2a] See also Chapter 1 as to Joint Advisory Committees for collaboration as between adjoining local planning authorities.

shall be, as to one-third at least,[3] made up of persons nominated by the Secretary of State after consultation with the Countryside Commission. This one-third is in fact appointed, following such nomination, by the joint action of the local planning authorities (or authority) concerned. Such persons are to be appointed for not less than one year nor more than three years, although re-appointment is not excluded and is a normal occurrence.

Where the National Park contains more than one county district, it is possible (s. 8 (7)), if desired, to create a " united district."

Subject to any effect of the above arrangements, a local planning authority in preparing or proposing to alter or add to a development plan affecting any part of a National Park must consult the Countryside Commission (s. 9).

The extent of " reasonable public access " to land within a National Park is to be defined in the context of a National Park; that is, a greater degree of access to private land is to be required. Nevertheless, it is clearly laid down in the 1949 Act that due regard must be had specifically to the needs of agriculture and forestry, and the economic and social needs of rural areas; the need to protect water against pollution; and the need to conserve the natural beauty and amenity of the countryside. As a safeguard, the Countryside Commission receives general directions from the Secretary of State, and is also required to submit to him, and to publish, an annual report.

Whatever the type of body acting under the above arrangements as the local planning authority for a National Park, no additional planning powers are provided (except in the three National Parks referred to in the next paragraph). The local planning authority are, however, required to be more stringent in the exercise of planning control, and only very moderate growth of villages within a Park is to be permitted. Where development does take place, traditional designs and materials are to be used, except where the cost would be unduly high. It is, however, significant that (s. 14) " where, as respects any land in a National Park, the Minister is satisfied that it is expedient so to do, he may with the consent of the Treasury acquire the land by agreement, whether by way of purchase, lease or exchange."

In three out of the ten National Parks, namely, the Peak District,

[3] But, by the same subsection, the Secretary of State may reduce this to one-quarter.

the Lake District, and Snowdonia, however, additional powers are conferred upon the local planning authorities in relation to " permitted development." In all normal parts of England and Wales certain defined types of " development " are permitted by virtue of the General Development Order, 1973 (S.I. 1973 No. 31), the purpose being to reduce the volume of applications for planning permission required to be considered by planning authorities. Thus, under this Order, and by way of example, it is permitted to carry out a limited extension within the curtilage of a dwelling house (i.e., not exceeding 50 cubic metres (1,750 cu. ft.) or one-tenth, whichever is the greater, subject to a maximum of 115 cubic metres (4,000 cu. ft.) and to certain other limitations: Class I of the Order of 1973). Again, under Class II, gates, fences, and walls may be erected up to a height not exceeding 2 metres, or 1 metre where they abut onto a road used by vehicles. Also, under Class VI and Class VII special provisions are made to allow for the carrying out of building and other operations relating respectively to agricultural units or to forestry. It will be seen, therefore, that the special scenic requirements in certain National Parks could be imperilled by the actions of a developer carrying out building or engineering operations under the Order, which he would be perfectly entitled to do without informing the local planning authority of his intention.

In the Peak District, the Lake District and Snowdonia, therefore, the Landscape Areas Special Development Order, 1950 (S.I. 1950 No. 729), has been made applicable. This Order requires that, whenever a " permitted development " is contemplated, the developer must give fourteen days' notice of his intention to the local planning authority, and the authority may then require (if they deem it necessary) that a formal planning application be made.[4]

A further provision is made to assist in the good management of National Parks by the National Parks and Access to the Countryside (Grants) Regulations, 1954 (S.I. 1954 No. 415), which provide that the cost of the provision of positive works, such as car parks, caravan sites, picnic sites and living (including camping) or other accommodation (including meals and refreshments), together with the planting

---

[4] Since the committee's decision as to whether or not development may proceed as " permitted development " must be made within fourteen days, delegated powers as to this will often be exercised by the committee chairman or by a small, standing sub-committee.

of trees and the treatment of derelict land, the acquisition of land or of access to land, and also payment of compensation to secure the discontinuance or modification of uses of land or the alteration or removal of buildings, shall be supported to the extent of 75 per cent. by Exchequer grant, the remainder being provided by the local (planning) authority. The initiative, however, lies largely with the said local authority, who may be subsequently asked to justify such expenditure to their ratepayers.

Lastly, in relation to National Parks *per se*, it is possible to restrict the use of signs and advertisements by creation of " areas of special control " by virtue of reg. 26 of the Town and Country Planning (Control of Advertisements) Regulations, 1969 (S.I. 1969 No. 1532), as to which see pp. 209–214.

2. Nature Reserves

Part III of the National Parks and Access to the Countryside Act, 1949, created Nature Reserves, of which 106 now exist, amounting in total to 271,404 acres. A further 11,896 acres of Naturalists' Trusts nature reserves also exist. In relation to the operation of these Reserves, certain powers were given to the then Nature Conservancy, now the Natural Environmental Research Council.[5] Such areas are not strictly wildlife sanctuaries (although the public may be excluded if it is deemed necessary), but they are individually concerned with the support of certain species, and may therefore require the scientific control or destruction of other competitive fauna or flora.

Although the Natural Environmental Research Council is required to take the initiative as and where necessary in the creation of Reserves, it is also provided, by s. 21 (4) of the 1949 Act, that local planning authorities may take such action themselves (either separately or jointly with other local planning authorities) in consultation with the Research Council.

The Natural Environmental Research Council may enter into agreements with landowners as to the management of land as Reserves (s. 16 of the 1949 Act); or the Council may compulsorily acquire land for the same purpose (s. 18 of the 1949 Act), whether or not an agreement (under s. 16) has previously been made. If such an agreement exists at the time of compulsory purchase, provision

[5] By s. 3 (3) of the Science and Technology Act, 1965.

is made for arbitration in accordance with the provisions of the Arbitration Act, 1950 (s. 18 (4)). In addition, the Council is empowered (s. 20) to make byelaws for the protection of each Nature Reserve, subject to the requirement (s. 23) that they keep the local planning authority informed of any such measures.

It may be appropriate to comment here that the natural condition of a Nature Reserve may be severely altered as an indirect result of planning decisions in relation not to the Reserve itself, but to other land in the vicinity. The development of an industrial or residential area, even at a considerable distance, may have a direct effect upon the wildlife in the Reserve. For example, the case of the male glow-worm beetle, which is attracted by street lamps and other illuminations! A further interesting example of considerable economic importance is that of the Glastonbury Levels in Somerset, where drainage and peat-cutting are expected radically to alter the local flora over a period of years.

3. Public Rights of Way

Part IV of the 1949 Act makes provision for research into the existence of, and future continuation of, any alleged public rights of way. By s. 27, county councils (i.e., " rural " counties) were required to carry out a survey of all land alleged to be subject to *then existent* public rights of way, and to draw up (s. 29) *draft maps and written statements* defining and commenting upon such rights of way for the Secretary of State's consideration and approval.

The permanent imposition of such rights of way clearly affects the concomitant rights of ownership or occupation of land, and extensive provision is made for representations and objections prior to approval by the Secretary of State. On completing preparation of the draft map and statement, the " surveying authority " (county) must notify the Secretary of State and cause a notice to be published in one or more local newspapers and in the *London Gazette* indicating that copies may be inspected by the public, and also that representations and objections may be made within a specified period, this to be not less than four months (s. 29 (1)). During this period the owner or other person " interested in " such land, and any other objector, may require information as to all documents (if any) creating or modifying such rights of way, and this must be provided within fourteen days of such requirement (s. 29 (2)).

Any objection or representation made during the stated period is to be heard by a " person appointed " by the surveying authority, who must then serve notice of his decision on behalf of the authority upon the objector (s. 29 (3)) (referred to as the " original objector " in the following paragraph).

In cases where the surveying authority then decide to modify the particulars already given in the draft map and statement by deletion of a way shown as a public path or road used as a public path, or to modify it by the addition of a way, they must give notice of this, again in one or more local newspapers and in the *London Gazette*, specifying a further period, in this case a minimum of twenty-eight days, within which objections must be made to the authority.   If then any objection is made, the authority must inform the " original objector " (see preceding paragraph) of the effect, and must also provide similar facilities for a hearing both of the original and subsequent objections by a person again nominated by the authority, who may either maintain or revoke the modification (s. 29 (4)).

In addition, any person who is aggrieved by the determination of the surveying authority on completion of the above process may, at any time within twenty-eight days after the service of the notice of the determination upon him, himself serve a notice of appeal on the Secretary of State and on the surveying authority.   In such cases the Secretary of State will appoint an inspector to hear both appellant and the surveying authority, and will subsequently arrive at a decision (s. 29 (5), (6)).

On completion of such of the foregoing measures as apply, the surveying authority are to prepare *provisional maps and statements* (s. 30) and shall again give notice in the local press and *London Gazette* as to the availability for inspection.

At this juncture a further element of appeal process is introduced (s. 31).   At any time within twenty-eight days of publication of the above notice the owner, lessee, or occupier of any land shown on the map as being subject to a right of way may apply to the Crown Court[5a] for a declaration that the existence or extent of such rights as are shown on the provisional map in a given case are incorrect in

[5a] Previously quarter sessions, but, by s. 8 of and Sched. 1 to the Courts Act, 1971, such appellate jurisdiction was transferred to the Crown Court; also see Public Rights of Way (Applications to the Crown Court) Regulations, 1972 (S.I. 1972 No. 93).

relation to earlier statements of the legal position and decisions. Such applications do not, of course, relate to any administrative policy decision, since this cannot be arrived at by a court of law (which is not an organ of administration in such cases). A right of further appeal to the High Court under s. 20 of the Criminal Justice Act, 1925, is provided by s. 31 (7) of the 1949 Act, such appeal being only by way of case stated on a point of law.

The final stage in the process is for the surveying authority to prepare definitive maps and statements (s. 32) containing all the particulars already given in the provisional maps and statements, and to furnish a copy to the Secretary of State. Once this stage is reached the definitive map shall constitute conclusive evidence of the existence of any footpath and of any bridleway or road used as a public path.

Provision is made for periodical revision of maps and statements (s. 33), including a power of the surveying authority to revise the definitive map on receipt of fresh evidence (s. 33 (2) (3)), with similar rights of objection to the authority and thence, on appeal, to the Secretary of State and on a point of law to the High Court.

The foregoing considerations relate to public rights of way which have had a legal basis for existence prior to (and, thus, independently of) *the* 1949 *Act*. In addition, powers are given to the councils of both county districts and county boroughs to create *new public rights of way* either on foot or on horseback, where they consider there is a need for it (s. 39 (1)). This may be done either by agreement or by compulsory creation. In the first case (s. 39 (2)) a " public footpath agreement " may be made with the owner of land, etc., provided that the approval of the local planning authority is first obtained, and it may be arrived at upon payment or otherwise. Compulsory creation of a public right of way (s. 40) is possible after due consideration of both the extent of value to the public, and of the precise effect which such creation may have upon the rights of persons interested in the land (s. 40 (1) (*a*), (*b*)). These factors must also be taken into account in arriving at the compensation to be paid. The approval of the local planning authority must also be obtained.

The 1949 Act provides for the *diversion* (s. 42) and *closure* (s. 43) of existing public paths being now the concern of county borough and county district councils, subject to confirmation by the Secretary of State, and thus the previous methods requiring the posting of notices on church doors and application to the local magistrates' court, etc., become unnecessary.

In regard to all aspects of creation, alteration, diversion or closure of public rights of way, the 1949 Act provides, by s. 84, that it is the duty of all local authorities to have due regard to the needs of agriculture and forestry. However, the extent of the burden, if any, to be borne by the landowner, or other persons interested in the land, has been increased (or clarified) by further legislation in the Countryside Act, 1968, which both supplements and amends the 1949 Act. Section 28 (1) of the 1968 Act imposes a statutory duty upon the owner (not occupier) of land to maintain any stile, gate or similar structure across a footpath or bridleway " in a safe condition and to the standard of repair required to prevent unreasonable interference with the rights of the persons using " the way. If such duty is not complied with, the highway authority may give fourteen days' notice of their intention and then take all necessary steps for repairing and making good the stile or other works, and may then recover all reasonable expenses from the owner. However, if the owner duly complies with s. 28 (1), the highway authority must contribute " not less than a quarter of any expenses . . . reasonably incurred " (s. 28 (3)). Also (s. 28 (4)) the highway authority may enter into a written agreement to maintain any such structure without charge to the landowner. In addition, the local planning authority are required to pay *compensation* based upon the amount of depreciation in value of the land affected by an access order [6] (s. 70). However, such compensation must be assessed upon the evidence of the effect of the first five years of access; that is, a period of five years must, in practice, elapse before a claim can be assessed (s. 71), but nevertheless, the intention to claim must be notified not later than six months from the date of the authority's order (National Parks and Access to the Countryside Regulations, 1950 (S.I. 1950 No. 1066)). There is also, however, provision (under s. 73) for payments on account, in cases of special hardship.

A further duty is imposed upon the landowner by s. 29 (1) of the 1968 Act which requires that, whenever a footpath or bridleway is ploughed up, the surface must be reinstated (as required by s. 119 (3) of the Highways Act, 1959) within a period of six weeks from the date of a notice of intention to plough being given; or, if no such

[6] Or land held together with such land. As to access orders, see *post*, p. 304.

notice is given, within a period of three weeks from the time of commencement of such ploughing up. Nevertheless, by s. 29 (2), where a notice of intention has been given, the said period of six weeks may be extended, if in the interests of good agriculture, by means of an order for temporary diversion of the path until a specified date. If the owner subsequently defaults, or if the owner has no legal right to plough (presumably in the case of a prior agreement not to plough), then the highway authority may, again with fourteen days' notice of their intention, carry out the reinstatement and recover the reasonable cost (s. 29 (7)).

By s. 30 of the 1968 Act a further public right (and private imposition) is provided, whereby " any member of the public shall have, as a right of way, the right to ride a bicycle, not being a motor vehicle, on any bridleway, but in exercising that right cyclists shall give way to pedestrians and persons on horseback." This, however, does not permit of cycle racing (s. 30 (6)), neither does it increase the highway authority's liability as to maintenance (s. 30 (3)).[6a]

The public use of footpaths and bridleways is to be facilitated by a duty imposed upon the highway authority by s. 27 of the 1968 Act, which requires the authority to erect signposts along the route and at every point where it leaves a metalled road, such signpost merely indicating the existence of a footpath or, as appropriate, a bridleway. It is also made an offence subject to a fine on summary conviction not exceeding £5, and £2 per day of continuation after conviction, for any person to place or maintain near such ways a notice which may deter the public from using the way.

Finally it should be noted that, in order to establish that a public right of way has come into existence at law (other than by statute) it is necessary to prove that the right has been exercised as of right [7] and for so long a time that it must have come to the notice of the landowner that the public were using the way as of right, thus justifying the inference that the landowner was consenting (i.e., not objecting).[8]

Long-distance routes.—In addition to the provision of ordinary footpaths and bridleways, the 1949 Act makes provision for the

---

[6a] A potentially onerous burden upon the landowner if the path is very frequently used by cyclists.

[7] *Nec vi, nec clam, nec precario* (without force, without secrecy, without permission): and *Hue* v. *Whiteley* [1929] 1 Ch. 440, at p. 445.

[8] *Greenwich District Board of Works* v. *Maudslay* (1870), L.R. 5 Q.B. 397, at p. 404.

setting-up of " long-distance routes " (ss. 51 and 52) where it appears to the Countryside Commission that the public " should be enabled to make extensive journeys on foot or on horseback along a particular route . . . which for the whole or the greater part of its length does not pass along roads mainly used by vehicles. . . ."   In the course of preparation of a report showing such routes, the Commission was required to consult every joint planning board, county council, county borough council and county district council affected. The report was then submitted to the Secretary of State (s. 51 (5) and s. 52) for his approval, modification or rejection.   No provision was made under these two sections for the lodging of objections or for representations.

To assist the function of long-distance routes, ss. 53 and 54 of the 1949 Act also respectively empower the highway authority to provide and operate ferries; and the local planning authority to provide accommodation, meals and refreshments along the route, provided that these are, in fact, found to be facilities otherwise lacking (s. 54 (2)).[9]

4. Access to Open Country

By Part V of the 1949 Act, provision is made for public access to " open country " by means either of *access agreements* or *access orders*. Open country is defined as (s. 59 (2)):

> " any area appearing to the authority with whom an access agreement is made or to the authority by whom an access order is made or by whom the area is acquired, . . . to consist wholly or predominantly of mountain, moor, heath, down, cliff or fore-shore (including any bank, barrier, dune, beach, flat or other land adjacent to the foreshore)."

To these categories have now been added, by the 1968 Act, wood-lands (s. 16 (1)), and rivers and canals and their banks (s. 16 (2) to (10), but with certain important exceptions).[10]   At the same time, however, s. 16 (7) of the same Act requires that, where the land is within a National Park, the local planning authority must first

[9] The Forestry Commissioners are also endowed with considerable and extended powers to trade in this manner by s. 23 of the Countryside Act, 1968: see p. 308, *post*.

[10] i.e., save for the property of the Inland Waterways, who have separate statutory powers and may open their waters and/or banks if they wish.   Reservoirs and their banks belonging to statutory undertakers are also excluded, but may, again, be opened at the latter's discretion.

obtain the consent of the Countryside Commission and of the Natural Environmental Research Council. Thus, " open country," as defined for the purposes of the 1949 and 1968 Acts, is limited to those areas of the above-mentioned types of land which have been made subject to access agreements, access orders, or compulsory acquisition for the purpose. It must further be noted that land used for certain specified purposes is classed as " *excepted land*," and even an access order (i.e., in the absence of the agreement of the owner) will not give the public a legal right of access to it. " Excepted land " is defined by s. 60 of the 1949 Act, and may be described briefly (and approximately) thus: agricultural land other than rough grazing land; land declared to be a Nature Reserve; land covered by buildings or within the curtilage thereof; land used as a park, garden or pleasure ground; land used for the surface working of minerals; a golf course, racecourse, aerodrome; land covered by works of statutory undertakers; land in course of being developed; and (broadly) land registered as common land under the Commons Registration Act, 1965, but of the type over which the public do not have a right of access. (The existence or not of a public right of access stems largely from s. 193 of the Law of Property Act, 1925, and it should be realised that the term " common " relates to agricultural rights held in common, and that it does not mean " common to all members of the public.")

Access agreements are made between the local planning authority and " any person having an interest in land, being open country, in the area of the authority " (s. 64 (1) of the 1949 Act), but are subject to the approval of the Secretary of State. The agreement may include an undertaking by the authority to make payments in consideration of the agreement itself and/or in respect of contribution to expenditure incurred by the landowner, tenant or occupier (s. 64 (2)). The agreement may also be made irrevocably or be subject to revocation or variation, if so specified in the document (s. 64 (3)). In addition, special provision is made to enable tenants for life who have entered into forestry dedication covenants under the Forestry Act, 1947, nevertheless to make access agreements (s. 64 (4)). Where woodlands are already subject to an access agreement, the Secretary of State may, by s. 79 of the 1949 Act, either revoke the agreement or vary it so as to exclude any part of the land; and, even if the person interested in the land does not wish the agreement to be revoked or amended, the Secretary of

State may require the local planning authority nevertheless to make a revocation or suitable order to this effect. Where, however, the land (of any type) is in a National Park, the Countryside Commission must be consulted.

Access Orders can be made (by virtue of s. 65 (1)) in the event of access agreements not being reached, and they cannot be made where such an agreement exists (s. 65 (2) (*a*)), nor without a prior approach to secure an agreement (s. 65 (2) (*b*)). As in the case of access agreements, the confirmation of the Secretary of State must be obtained. The access order must contain a scale map and also any such descriptive matter as the local authority shall deem to be necessary. The procedure for the making of such an order is set out in Pt. I of Sched. 1 to the 1949 Act, this being common not only to access orders, but also to orders designating National Parks, public path orders, diversion orders, and extinguishment orders, and the method to be adopted is set out below at p. 305. Access orders may only be made upon land in National Parks after prior consultation with the Countryside Commission: and in instances where the Commission, rather than the local planning authority, wish to take the initiative, they may request the local planning authority to make such an order on National Park land. But, in both these instances, the Secretary of State for the Environment is to be consulted and may either himself make an order, or direct the local planning authority so to do.

There is also a special provision (s. 69) for the temporary suspension of public access where application is made to the Minister of Agriculture, Fisheries and Food requesting this on the grounds of exceptional risk of fire. This is clearly of particular value in relation to woodlands (in dry, windy seasons), and also to standing corn.

To allow for flexibility, s. 110 (2) of the 1949 Act provides that access orders may be varied or revoked, although the total area of land affected may not be increased without an entirely fresh order. Further, the Secretary of State (by s. 79 (1)) may refuse to confirm an order where either it will prejudice the growing of timber for commercial purposes, or it may reduce the amenity value of woodlands in a given neighbourhood.

The position of the landowner where either access agreements or access orders apply is as follows. He may not carry out any work on the area if this substantially reduces public access, *except where this work will convert the land into "excepted land" (ante)* (s. 66 (1)). But in other respects his liability at law for acts or omissions affecting the state of land or of adjoining land is to be in no way increased by the Act; thus, for example, the extent of the liability of the occupier towards persons coming upon his land who may be injured by accident is no greater as a result of the existence of an access agreement or access order.

Procedure for the making of orders designating National Parks; public path orders; diversion and extinguishment orders and access orders is laid down in Pt. I of Sched. 1 to the 1949 Act. The authority making the relevant order must first give notice in the prescribed form stating the effect of the order and naming the places in the locality to which it relates and including the places at which the order and supporting map and descriptive documents may be inspected. In the case of public path orders and access orders this notice must be published in at least one local newspaper and in the *London Gazette,* and must be served on every owner,[11] lessee and occupier (except tenants for a month or any period less than a month),[12] with certain special exceptions. In the case of orders designating National Parks (or varying such orders), it is not required that the notice be served on owners, lessees or occupiers, but it is laid down that publication is necessary in two national newspapers, and at least one local newspaper in the area of every local planning authority to which the order relates. In the case of diversion or extinguishment orders, notification must be as in the case of public path orders and additionally, a copy of the order must be served upon every county, county borough, county district or parish council (including parish meetings if no parish council) thereby affected, and a copy of the notice must also be displayed prominently at the ends of the section of path to be diverted or extinguished.

In all these cases, if no objections or representations are then made (or are made and withdrawn), the Secretary of State may, if he thinks fit, confirm the order, with or without modifications. If they are made and not withdrawn, the Secretary of State shall hold an inquiry where a local authority is the objector; if any other objector, he may hold such an inquiry or, alternatively, he is to afford some

---

[11] In the case of land belonging to an ecclesiastical benefice notice is also to be served on the Church Commissioners.

[12] Thus excluding tenants of " holiday lettings."

other opportunity of being heard (para. 2 (2) of the Schedule), and may then confirm or modify the order. Special provisions are, however, made in the case of the land of statutory undertakers, whereby the order is subject to special parliamentary procedure. In addition (by para. 2 (3)) the Secretary of State must not confirm or make an order which is such as to affect land not subject to the original form of order as submitted to him without notification to the public, followed by a local inquiry if there are then objections or representations.

As soon as may be after the order is confirmed or made by the Secretary of State, he shall publish a notice (on similar lines as described above for the earlier stages), stating that this has been done, and that copies of the order may be inspected; and, further, copies of the notice must be served on the owners, lessees or occupiers concerned, and upon other persons who have made a request in writing to receive copies. Finally, copies of the notice must be posted upon the land or public path, as indicated for the earlier stages of the process.

Provision for public access to, and enjoyment of, the countryside, was further extended by the Countryside Act, 1968 (reference to which, in specific instances, has already been made). In addition to the alteration of title of the National Parks Commission to that of the *Countryside Commission*, s. 1 of this Act enlarged the functions of this body, and gave power to make charges for their services, to accept gifts or contributions and " to do all such things as are incidental to, or conducive to the attainment of the purposes of, any of their functions." These functions are set out in s. 2, and include the improvement of facilities for enjoyment of the countryside, conservation and enhancement of natural beauty,[13] and the securing of public access (*ante*). The Commission are also to advise any Minister having functions under the Act, and shall make recommendations to local planning authorities.

The Commission now have a degree of overall national authority (subject to the overriding powers of the Secretary of State) for conserving and enhancing the countryside and for securing facilities for the public. The freedom of action is considerable, in that they may also make grants and loans to persons other than public bodies

[13] In some National Parks regular bus services have been provided to carry visitors from strategically sited car parks to places of special attraction, thereby avoiding a sprawl of parked cars marring the scenery.

(s. 5), and further may undertake experimental projects which may require and include the compulsory acquisition of land, construction of buildings, and the ownership and management of works, equipment and services (s. 4).

The 1968 Act also empowers local planning authorities to set up Country Parks (ss. 6–8),[14] to provide facilities therein, including parking places, shelters, lavatories, refreshments, and arrangements for open air recreation generally. Such Country Parks may be either on land owned by the authority; or by agreement on other land; or on land acquired by compulsory purchase. It may be worthy of note that such areas may be of indirect value in agricultural areas in helping to contain those members of the public who might otherwise tend to cause harm to the normal processes of farming—as by the wanton disposal of bottles and polythene bags which tend to injure or kill livestock. They may also be of value in enabling the local planning authority to exercise a greater degree of control and provision of amenity services at well-known beauty spots or rural points of tourist attraction.

As a further measure, ss. 6 and 9 together with Sched. 2 to the 1968 Act empower the local planning authority to exercise similar controls over public commons, and to make byelaws for the purpose.

Lastly in relation to special places of public visitation (" beauty spots," etc.), special provision can be made for parking and for picnic sites for the accommodation of motorists and other road users, by virtue of s. 10 (2); and byelaws may also be provided to control them (s. 41). This has the advantage that motorists can be encouraged to park in such a way as to see the view, rather than to become part of it and thus detract from the enjoyment of their fellows. In this respect, a further measure of vehicle control is provided by s. 32 of the 1968 Act, which enables the local planning authority, in consultation with the highway authority, to make traffic regulation orders (under the Road Traffic Regulation Act, 1967) upon roads " contiguous to " National Parks, Areas of Outstanding Natural Beauty, Country Parks, Nature Reserves, Areas of Experimental Interest to the Countryside Commission, and National Trust land.

Areas of Outstanding Natural Beauty may also be designated at the initiative of the local planning authority or of the Countryside

[14] See Appendix B, Recommendation 43.

Commission by virtue of ss. 87 and 88 of the 1949 Act.   The purpose of this provision is to protect those areas of outstanding natural beauty which cannot, or cannot immediately, be contained in a National Park.   Thus, small areas of outstanding merit which would not, by their size, warrant the creation of a Park, or to which public access would not be justified, can be controlled by the Countryside Commission which may do " all such things as appear to be expedient for preserving and enhancing the natural beauty of the area." Grants may be made for this purpose.   However, the powers to provide facilities for public enjoyment (as in National Parks) do not apply to Areas of Outstanding Natural Beauty.

In addition, certain Areas of Outstanding Natural Beauty are protected against " permitted development " of agricultural buildings (which otherwise applies under Class VI of the General Development Order, 1973).[15]   Thus, in the areas of natural beauty specified by the Town and Country Planning (Landscape Areas Special Development) Order, 1950 (S.I. 1950 No. 729), fourteen days' notice of intention to carry out such " permitted development " must be given to the local planning authority, who may at any time during that fourteen-day period intervene and require an application for planning approval to be made.   The areas so far specified are, for convenience, scheduled as entire county districts (rural or urban), and lie in the counties of: Caernarvon (three districts), Chester (one district), Cumberland (five districts), Derby (three districts), Lancaster (one district), Merioneth (four districts), Westmorland (four districts).

Forestry Commission woodland is discussed in more detail in Chapter 3 (Forestry) but, by virtue of s. 23 of the Countryside Act, 1968, the Commissioners now have powers to provide a very significant contribution to public use of their woodland areas.   They may " provide or arrange for, or assist in the provision of, facilities and any equipment, facilities or works ancillary thereto," including living accommodation, camping and caravan sites, provision of meals and refreshments, picnic places, viewpoints, car parks, nature study and other walks, information and display centres, shops (!) in connection with the aforesaid facilities, and public conveniences.   The Commissioners may make such charges for each of these facilities as they think reasonable.

---

[15] As to this type of " permitted development," see p. 63.

Further, to enable any of the above, the Minister of Agriculture, Fisheries and Food may acquire land " in proximity to land placed by him at the disposal of the Commissioners." Such acquisition is (apparently) to be upon the basis as set out in s. 24 (2) of the Act (which amends the Forestry Act, 1967), whereby there is provision for purchase, feu,[16] lease, or exchange, but not by compulsory purchase.

5. National Trust Land

The final category of land having a special relationship to the general public is land and buildings owned by the National Trust for England and Wales (or the separate National Trusts for Scotland and Ireland). The former originated as an Association in 1894 and, by the National Trust Act, 1907, obtained powers to acquire " by purchase, gift or otherwise," and subsequently to manage, either land previously private land, or open spaces and places of public resort. Thus, the powers of acquisition by the Trust are extremely wide, and have assisted in preserving, to the benefit of the general public, many houses or estates which have fallen prey to the ravages of estate duty, and would otherwise have been destroyed by fractional sales, demolition or simple inability to finance essential repairs.

The National Trust is not a Government body and is not subsidised by the Exchequer, save through the usual systems of grants and loans which are available to private owners. The Trust is an association incorporated by Act of Parliament, and is registered as a charity so that advantages as to income tax and estate duty are obtained. The powers and duties of the National Trust are discussed in some detail in Chapter 13, Buildings and Land of Architectural and Historic Interest, etc., at p. 258 *et seq.*

The National Trust for England and Wales now owns the freehold of about 365,500 acres, and leasehold of about 21,750 acres. The Trusts for Scotland and Northern Ireland hold 4,067 acres and over 82,000 acres respectively.[16a] In recent years a most significant contribution to the protection of the environment in England and Wales has been the Enterprise Neptune scheme organised by the Trust, under which coastal areas have been purchased under the general powers of the Trust. This acquisition of a

[16] In Scotland.
[16a] In both latter countries, principally owned, not leased.

total, so far, of 32,000 acres of coastline, headland and coastal farms, etc., has extended protection against development and provided a number of public facilities. The scheme is still open.

In terms of public access to open " land " it should, finally, be noted that the foreshore round the British coastlines (i.e., the land between high and low water marks, being limited landwards to the medium line of high tide between spring and neap tides)[17] is vested in the Crown. There is a public right of navigation and of fishing (and rights ancillary thereto) but no common-law right to bathe from the foreshore [18] or to shoot from it.[19] Further, permitting the public to wander on the sand of the foreshore does not imply dedication to the public.[18]

It is now necessary to turn from the various rights of access which have been bestowed upon the general public, and to consider a number of special means whereby the owner, or local inhabitant, of an area may be protected against undue incursions by the public.

6. Caravans and Caravan Sites

In 1970 about three million people took camping or caravan holidays, and there are now over 200,000 static holiday caravans in Britain. Many caravan sites were developed shortly after the 1939–45 war, often by tenant farmers who had discovered that the terms of their tenancy failed to exclude such a use of their land. Until the passing of the Caravan Sites and Control of Development Act, 1960, there were few effective powers to enable local authorities to influence the siting and management of caravans.

The control of caravan sites is now governed by the Act of 1960 just mentioned and (principally in relation to gypsy encampments) the Caravan Sites Act, 1968; and the law on this subject can be surprisingly complicated in certain circumstances. For this reason the reader who may be faced with a specific problem arising from a local site should take legal advice. However, the means of control can be said to be broadly as follows.

Caravan sites are subject to a dual system of controls; namely the normal requirements relating to planning permission, and also a requirement to obtain from the local authority, at district level, a site licence. It will be appreciated that, so far as planning permission

---

[17] *Philpot* v. *Bath* (1905), 21 T.L.R. 634, at p. 636 (C.A.).
[18] *Brinckman* v. *Matby* [1904] 2 Ch. 313 (C.A.).
[19] *Lord Fitzhardinge* v. *Purcell* [1908] 2 Ch. 139, at pp. 166, 167.

for development of any type (i.e., not only caravan sites) is concerned, the applicant for planning approval need be neither the occupier nor the owner of the land—he may be a person with no direct interest in the site: in the case of caravan sites, therefore, for this or other reasons, once planning permission is given there may be lack of sufficient planning control of the management or use of the site.   Permission can, of course, be given subject to conditions, and in terms of the person to whom it is granted; but, nevertheless, even a person so specified may in practice delegate responsibility.   In addition, many other problems can arise in relation to mere temporary (say over-night) use by individual mobile caravans, and also in relation to whether or not a particular structure or vehicle is, or is not, a caravan.   For these reasons it was found necessary to introduce the parallel system of site licensing, and to define both "caravans" and "caravan sites."   A *caravan* is any structure (not being a tent or a railway carriage standing on a railway) designed or adapted for human habitation which is capable of being moved from one place to another (by being towed or transported) including a motor-vehicle so designed or adapted (s. 29 (1) of the Caravan Sites and Control of Development Act, 1960).   However, the Act excludes from the above definition a "twin-unit" caravan if the dimensions thereof exceed 60 feet in length, or 20 feet in width, or (as to the living accommodation) 10 feet in height.   A *caravan site* is defined as any land on which a caravan is placed for purposes of human habitation, and extends to include any land used in conjunction therewith (s. 1 (4) of the Caravan Sites and Control of Development Act, 1960).

Since the purpose of a site licence is to control the manner of use of the site in terms of good management, it issues to the *occupier* of the land, and not to an owner not in occupation except where the total site consists of not more than 400 square yards and is let under a tenancy granted with a view to its use as a caravan site, in which latter case the "occupier" is deemed to be the immediate landlord. The licence sets out certain conditions with which the occupier must comply.   Failure to do so renders him liable to a fine of £100; or, for a second or subsequent offence, to a fine of £250.   On a third or subsequent conviction the local magistrates' court may make an order revoking the licence and, in this event, the local authority will have no power to issue a fresh licence within a subsequent period of three years.   Thus, if the use of a caravan site is found to be on three occasions in breach of a condition stated in the site licence, the site will cease to be usable for caravans for at least three years and, at the end of that period, a new licence may, or may not, be granted.

The application for a site licence must be made in writing by the occupier to the district (or borough) authority, and must include certain particulars as required by the Caravan Sites (Licence Applications) Order, 1960 (S.I. 1960 No. 1474). Planning permission must be obtained before this licence application is made, but the licence must be issued within two months of the granting of planning permission (unless the applicant has had a site licence—on any site—revoked within the preceding three years). In considering the granting of planning permission, the local planning authority must consult with the licensing authority (which may, of course, be the same local authority),[19a] in order to ensure that there are no objections in terms of probable future management. For this purpose, and others, the licensing authority are required to keep a register of site licences.

It will thus be evident that it will, in many respects, be more appropriate for conditions as to user to be imposed by means of the licence rather than as terms in planning permission—which latter may, in any event, be subject to a planning appeal. The conditions to be attached to the site licence are related to the interests not only of the general public living in, or visiting, the locality of the site, but also of the caravan dwellers themselves, and these are indicated in the Model Standards for Caravan Sites (Circular No. 42/60) published by the Department of the Environment. They particularly relate to: the total number of caravans to be permitted on the site at any time (or at specific periods); the size, type, state of repair, etc. of the caravans; positioning within the site itself, amenity features (including tree screens or bushes); sanitary facilities, land drainage, etc.; and fire regulations. At present there is generally no legal provision for the control of the colour of caravans, although the possibility of so doing was referred to as long ago as 1960 in Circular 42/60. The Dartmouth Committee believes this would be advantageous, but recognises that road-safety factors may apply. It may be of particular value to note that it is a compulsory condition in every site licence that a copy of the licence must be displayed on the

[19a] And will be the same authority in any event after 1st April, 1974.

site itself, except where the site is restricted to not more than three caravans.

If the occupier is dissatisfied with the site licence conditions he may appeal, within twenty-eight days of the granting of the licence, to the local magistrates' court; as, equally, may any other " person aggrieved." The court may vary, or cancel, the conditions if they are deemed to be " unduly burdensome," but, in so doing, the court must relate their decision to the Model Standards for Caravan Sites. Subsequently, site licence conditions may be altered on the initiative of the licensing authority, subject again to a similar right of appeal to the magistrates. The licence itself is an important document, in that any transfer to a subsequent occupier—which can only be obtained with the permission of the licensing authority—must be indorsed upon it. If, on any occasion, there is an alteration in conditions these must also be so indorsed on the licence.

In order to ensure compliance with the conditions in any site licence, the authorised officer of the local authority has a right of entry, upon giving twenty-four hours' notice to the " occupier " of the site; and obstruction of such an officer is an offence. So far as sites of area 400 square yards or less are concerned, where the " occupier " in terms of the site licence is not, in fact, in direct occupation of the site (*ante*), the " occupier " has an immediate right of re-entry (i.e., to dispossess his site tenant) in the case of a breach of a condition of the site licence: this provision is necessary, since it will be the licensed " occupier " who will be liable to a fine, or to forfeiture of the licence.

There are a number of exceptions to the requirement of a caravan site licence, as set out in Sched. 1 to the Caravan Sites and Control of Development Act, 1960. Broadly speaking these are related either to very small numbers of caravans on a small site and/or a use of limited duration. Thus, for example, a single caravan may be used without a licence within the curtilage of a house for the benefit of that house; or caravans may be used for seasonal occupation by agricultural workers; or they may be used temporarily in relation to building or engineering operations.

It is lastly necessary to note that special provisions govern caravans used by migrants—that is, gypsies and other travellers. By the Caravan Sites Act, 1968, s. 10, in areas designated under the Act, it is an offence for " any person being a gypsy " to station a caravan for the purpose of residing for any period on land within the boundaries of a highway (e.g., including verges); on any other un-occupied land; or on any occupied land without the consent of the owner. However, it shall be a defence (s. 10 (2)) to prove that the caravan was so stationed in consequence of illness, mechanical breakdown, or other immediate emergency and that it was removed (or is intended to be removed) as soon as reasonably possible. The penalty upon summary conviction is not exceeding £20, and £5 per day in respect of a continuation after conviction. By s. 11, a magistrates' court may, on the complaint of a local authority, by order authorise that authority to take such steps as may be specified in the order to remove the caravan or caravans from the area. In such cases, notice of the summons must be given by the local authority to the owner and occupier, if any, of the land (unless not reasonably ascertainable). Obstruction of local authority officers in carrying out the order is an offence subject to a fine not exceeding £20 upon summary conviction, or £50 on a second or subsequent conviction. It must, however, be re-emphasised that the provision of this Act will apply only to *areas designated* by the Secretary of State for the Environment, following an application by a council of a county, county borough, or a London borough (s. 12). The making of such an order will be related to the availability of suitable alternative sites officially provided by the local authority for the accommodation of gypsies. Finally, the term " gypsy " extends well beyond the true Romanies (s. 16) and includes other " persons of nomadic habit of life."

7. Miscellaneous Protective Measures

The *preservation of buildings* of architectural or historic interest (which may, of course, be of a simple, even rudimentary type but indicative of a specialised or ancient occupation) can be of value in open country as much as in urban or village areas. The statutory protection afforded under the Civic Amenities Act, 1967, is con-sidered, together with other provisions of that Act and other legisla-tion, in Chapter 13, Conservation Areas and Buildings of Architec-tural and Historic Interest.

The *preservation of trees* and areas of woodland is discussed in Chapter 3, 3. Forestry, but it should be noted here that the effect of the imposition of a tree preservation order has been extended by s. 13 of the Civic Amenities Act, 1967, whereby the owner of land on which a tree subject to such an order dies, is removed, or is destroyed, will be required to replace that tree with another of a type to be approved by the local planning authority. The planning authority may, however, absolve the owner from this responsibility or, if they intend to enforce these provisions, an appeal lies to the Secretary of State[19b] and subsequently, on a point of law only, to the High Court (s. 14 of the 1967 Act).

Protection of flora and fauna.—It should also be emphasised that the activities of the public, as also of the rural community, in relation to (*a*) certain special localities to which attention has been paid by local authorities and Parliament, and (*b*) certain of the rarer or imperilled species of flora and fauna, are governed by a number of specific Acts of Parliament. Thus, there is, as one example of many, the Lindsey County Council (Sandhills) Act, 1939, which was passed in order to protect a specific local area. Such Acts are distinct from orders made by the Home Secretary under the National Parks and Access to the Countryside Act, 1949, or (as to bird sanctuaries) under the Protection of Birds Acts, 1954 to 1967, such as the Humber Wildfowl Refuge Sanctuary Order, 1955 (S.I. 1955 No. 1532), the Southport Sanctuary Order, 1956 (S.I. 1956 No. 692), etc. Again, control may be by local byelaws made by the local planning authority, also under the 1949 Act, ranging from the Aberlady Bay Nature Reserve Byelaws made in 1952, to the Tentsmuir Point Nature Reserve Byelaws made in 1962. It therefore follows that it may be advisable, in any specific case, to inquire of the local authority as to the existence of a special Act, order or byelaws.

As to the protection of species of flora and fauna, there exists a long chain of current legislation, but the following statutes may be of particular interest. The Local Government Act, 1933, empowers county and borough councils to make byelaws for the protection of wild plants. In all except nine of the counties in England and Wales, such byelaws have been made.

The protection of animals (birds and mammals) is divided according to whether they be game or other. The Game Acts, 1772 to 1960, afford to the police, gamekeepers and owners or occupiers rearing game, certain powers to prevent poaching, including the right to confiscate guns, and to arrest persons found in actual pursuit of game. However the fact of " actual pursuit " may, on occasions, be difficult to prove.

[19b] The weakness here is that an unscrupulous owner could obtain the opportunity of a second appeal to the Secretary of State by surreptitiously poisoning the tree!

For the purposes of these Acts, " game " includes hares, pheasants, partridges, grouse, heath or moor game, black game, bustards, woodcock and snipe: it does not include wildfowl (i.e., duck and geese). A similar type of protection is applied to game fish, i.e., salmon, trout and migratory trout, by means of a series of Acts, the Salmon and Freshwater Fisheries Act, 1923, Tweed Fisheries Acts, 1857 and 1859, Salmon Fisheries (Scotland) Act, 1933, the Salmon and Freshwater Fisheries (Protection) (Scotland) Act, 1951, and the Salmon and Freshwater Fisheries Act, 1972.

The combined effect of this legislation is to regulate the method of taking both game and other freshwater fish (including eels) by prohibiting " destructive methods " of fishing (such as stunning of fish in a stretch of water by explosives); and by providing for closed seasons which, so far as game fish are concerned, vary from river to river.   There is also provision for prevention of water pollution such as to harm the fish therein, but this is now, in practice at least, largely superseded by the overall application and effect of the Rivers (Prevention of Pollution) Acts, 1951 and 1961 (see Chapter 7, Pollution of Fresh Water).   The administration of the provisions of these Acts is largely local and is in the hands of the River Authorities [20] who are enabled to make byelaws relating to any special circumstances.   They may also maintain, improve and develop fisheries; and may purchase or lease land for the purpose, including the development of establishments for the artificial propagation or rearing of salmon, trout or other freshwater fish. In order to carry out their protective function, the River Authorities and District Boards may appoint water bailiffs, and may petition the Secretary of State for the alteration of dates in any annual close season, whether relating to rod fishing or to the estuary and river mouth netting of (migratory) fish.

Special provision is also made for the protection and regulation of native wild species of deer.   The Deer Act, 1963 (which applies to England and Wales only), declares close seasons for deer and prohibits the taking or killing by certain devices.   It also restricts the use of vehicles for that purpose.   In Scotland, the Secretary of State for Scotland may make regulations under the Deer (Scotland) Act, 1959, to prevent the illegal taking and killing of all species of

---

[20] In Scotland this function is carried out by District Boards, although such Boards so far exist in under half of the 108 Salmon Fishery Districts into which Scotland is divided.

deer, but provision is made for the protection of agricultural and forestry interests. There are separate statutory close seasons for each species of deer, and for the hinds and stags of each species.

Turning to other birds and mammals which are not traditionally classified as game, a number of separate statutes apply. The Protection of Birds Acts, 1954 to 1967, make it an offence to kill or injure, or to attempt to kill or injure, any wild bird or to take their eggs; but subject to a large number of clearly defined exceptions. These excepted species may (by s. 9 of the Act) be varied by order of the Secretary of State, and are at present governed by the Wild Birds (Various Species) Order, 1970 (S.I. 1970 No. 678). The method of application of the order is by amendment of the first four Schedules to the Act. The First Schedule is divided into (Part I) species which are protected at all times (at present reduced to approximately sixty, including, e.g., avocet, all eagles, most hawks, hoopoe, etc.); and (Part II) species protected only during the close season (six of the rarer species of duck, and the whimbrel). The Second Schedule lists species which may be killed or taken at any time but by authorised persons only,[21] consisting principally of the "vermin" type (e.g., rooks, crows, jays, magpies), some types of gull, some types of pigeon, house sparrows, starlings, etc. In certain areas the bullfinch and oyster-catcher are included. The Third Schedule lists those species which are permitted to be killed or taken only outside the close season, namely, snipe, plover, woodcock, capercaillie, eight species of duck and five species of geese. In addition there are restrictions upon the sale of live or dead birds and their eggs, unless bred in captivity.

At present there appears to be little general statutory protection for wild animals other than deer; although by the Conservation of Seals Act, 1970 (replacing the Grey Seals Protection Act, 1932), this species is now protected along the coasts of both England and Wales, and Scotland, by means of a close season, which extends from the 1st September until the 31st December. A person who wilfully kills, injures or takes a seal during the close season or attempts to do so, is guilty of an offence punishable upon summary conviction by a fine not exceeding £50, or in the case of a second or subsequent

---

[21] " Authorised persons " include owners and occupiers of land on which the action is taken; or a person authorised in writing either by the local authority or by River Boards, the Nature Conservancy, and some similar public authorities.

offence, by a fine not exceeding £100 (ss. 2, 5 and 6 of the Act). Further, by s. 3, the Secretary of State may by order prohibit the killing, injuring or taking of seals in any given area, where he considers this to be necessary for the " proper conservation of seals." The Act also provides for the apprehension by a constable of offenders and powers to search and to seize firearms, poisons, etc.; and for the entry upon land for up to eight weeks by a person authorised in writing by the Secretary of State to investigate possible offences, or possible damage by seals to fisheries, etc.

In addition, two Bills have recently been placed before Parliament, namely the Protection of Otters Bill and a Bill for the Protection of Badgers.

Pest Control.—The reverse side of the coin, that is, the protection of the countryside against the ravages of pests, should also be briefly considered. The Pests Act, 1954, enables Rabbit Clearance Orders to be made, which designate areas to be cleared so far as may be practicable. (However, the Nature Conservancy is permitted to re-introduce rabbits onto special reserves for purposes of research.) Considerable damage has been caused in a variety of ways by various species of animal imported into Britain largely during the past century or half-century. These are now controlled, and importation or keeping prohibited, by the Destructive Imported Animals Act, 1932, together with a series of orders made thereunder, relating to: muskrats (1933), grey squirrels (1937), non-indigenous rabbits (1954), mink (1971), coypus (1971). (The latter species are harmful in that they burrow extensively in, and therefore weaken, river embankments and dykes.) In addition to these measures, blanket coverage is offered by the Animals (Restriction of Importation) Act, 1964, which is principally designed to protect the world's rarer species.

The protection of insect life in terms of the use of insecticides is discussed under pollution (see p. 172), but protection *against* harmful insects is provided for by the Destructive Insects and Pests Acts, 1877–1927, under which two orders have been made. First, prohibiting the importation of forest trees without special permission, and, secondly, prohibiting the importing of all unbarked coniferous timber, since several species of pest beetles and several varieties of fungus infection would otherwise pass undetected.

Litter Control.—The Litter Act, 1958, and the Dangerous Litter Act, 1971, make it an offence punishable upon summary conviction by a fine not exceeding £100 for any person to throw down, drop or otherwise deposit in, into or from " any place in the open air to which the public are entitled or permitted to have access without payment, and leave " (i.e., not pick up again!) " any thing whatsoever " so as to deface that place by litter. Proceedings against an offender may be instituted by the local authority (e.g., district council, county council, etc.) or, in National Parks, by the joint board, or alternative relevant Park committee. National Parks Boards or committees are also empowered to appoint wardens to secure compliance with the Litter Act, although in practice they normally have additional functions in terms of public relations.

In the case of deposit of *poisonous* waste, heavier penalties have recently been imposed by the Deposit of Poisonous Waste Act, 1972, and regulations made thereunder, as to which see p. 174, *ante*.

APPENDIX A

Meaning of " development " and " new development " under the Town and Country Planning Act, 1971

PART III

GENERAL PLANNING CONTROL

Meaning of " development " and " new development "

22.—(1) In this Act, except where the context otherwise requires, " development," subject to the following provisions of this section, means the carrying out of building, engineering, mining or other operations in, on, over or under land, or the making of any material change in the use of any buildings or other land.

(2) The following operations or uses of land shall not be taken for the purposes of this Act to involve development of the land, that is to say—

(a) the carrying out of works for the maintenance, improvement or other alteration of any building, being works which affect only the interior of the building or which do not materially affect the external appearance of the building and (in either case) are not works for making good war damage or works begun after 5th December 1968 for the alteration of a building by providing additional space therein below ground;

(b) the carrying out by a local highway authority of any works required for the maintenance or improvement of a road, being works carried out on land within the boundaries of the road;

(c) the carrying out by a local authority or statutory undertakers of any works for the purpose of inspecting, repairing or renewing any sewers, mains, pipes, cables or other apparatus, including the breaking open of any street or other land for that purpose;

(d) the use of any buildings or other land within the curtilage of a dwellinghouse for any purpose incidental to the enjoyment of the dwellinghouse as such;

(e) the use of any land for the purposes of agriculture or forestry (including afforestation) and the use for any of those purposes of any building occupied together with land so used;

(f) in the case of buildings or other land which are used for a purpose of any class specified in an order made by the Secretary of State under this section, the use thereof for any other purpose of the same class.

(3) For the avoidance of doubt it is hereby declared that for the purposes of this section—

(a) the use as two or more separate dwellinghouses of any building previously used as a single dwellinghouse involves a material change in the use of the building and of each part thereof which is so used;

(*b*) the deposit of refuse or waste materials on land involves a material change in the use thereof, notwithstanding that the land is comprised in a site already used for that purpose, if either the superficial area of the deposit is thereby extended, or the height of the deposit is thereby extended and exceeds the level of the land adjoining the site.

(4) Without prejudice to any regulations made under the provisions of this Act relating to the control of advertisements, the use for the display of advertisements of any external part of a building which is not normally used for that purpose shall be treated for the purposes of this section as involving a material change in the use of that part of the building.

(5) In this Act " new development " means any development other than development of a class specified in Part I or Part II of Schedule 8 to this Act; and the provisions of Part III of that Schedule shall have effect for the purposes of Parts I and II thereof.

Development requiring planning permission

23.—(1) Subject to the provisions of this section, planning permission is required for the carrying out of any development of land.

(2) Where on 1st July 1948 (in this Act referred to as " the appointed day ") land was being temporarily used for a purpose other than the purpose for which it was normally used, planning permission is not required for the resumption of the use of the land for the last-mentioned purpose before 6th December 1968.

(3) Where on the appointed day land was normally used for one purpose and was also used on occasions, whether at regular intervals or not, for another purpose, planning permission is not required—

(*a*) in respect of the use of the land for that other purpose on similar occasions before 6th December 1968; or

(*b*) in respect of the use of the land for that other purpose on similar occasions on or after that date if the land has been used for that other purpose on at least one similar occasion since the appointed day and before the beginning of 1968.

(4) Where land was unoccupied on the appointed day, but had before that day been occupied at some time on or after 7th January 1937, planning permission is not required in respect of any use of the land begun before 6th December 1968 for the purpose for which the land was last used before the appointed day.

(5) Where planning permission to develop land has been granted for a limited period, planning permission is not required for the resumption, at the end of that period, of the use of the land for the purpose for which it was normally used before the permission was granted.

(6) In determining, for the purposes of subsection (5) of this section, what were the purposes for which land was normally used before the grant of planning permission, no account shall be taken of any use of the land begun in contravention of the provisions of this Part of this Act or in contravention of previous planning control.

(7) Notwithstanding anything in subsections (2) to (4) of this section, the use of land as a caravan site shall not, by virtue of any of those subsections,

be treated as a use for which planning permission is not required, unless the land was so used on one occasion at least during the period of two years ending with 9th March 1960.

(8) Where by a development order planning permission to develop land has been granted subject to limitations, planning permission is not required for the use of that land which (apart from its use in accordance with that permission) is the normal use of that land, unless the last-mentioned use was begun in contravention of the provisions of this Part of this Act or in contravention of previous planning control.

(9) Where an enforcement notice has been served in respect of any development of land, planning permission is not required for the use of that land for the purpose for which (in accordance with the provisions of this Part of this Act) it could lawfully have been used if that development had not been carried out.

(10) For the purposes of this section a use of land shall be taken to have been begun in contravention of previous planning control if it was begun in contravention of the provisions of Part III of the Act of 1947 or of Part III of the Act of 1962.

Recommendations of the Working Party on the Human Habitat

Presented to the Secretary of State for the Environment in January, 1972. (Published as " How Do You Want to Live? A Report on the Human Habitat," H.M.S.O., 1972.)

(*Note.—A number of these recommendations are now comprised in recent legislation, to which reference is made in the text of this book.*)

People and Planning

1. When planning authorities consult interested parties on planning decisions, they should offer alternatives. The financial and environmental consequences must be made clear and the choice should be put before the public in simple language.

2. There should be a specific, universal, and named procedure to give local publicity to all planning proposals beyond the merely trivial.

3. It should be standard practice for outside representatives to be co-opted on to local planning committees.

4. The Press should also be admitted to planning committees; all non-elected persons could be asked to leave when delicate financial matters are being discussed.

5. The Department of the Environment, together with the Civic Trust, the Town and Country Planning Association, and other bodies, should make a series of films on different aspects of planning to be shown to local authorities throughout the country.

6. The Government should amend the laws relating to compensation:

   a. So that property just outside the line of a new road, but seriously affected by it, can be acquired.

   b. To enable grants to be made to owners for sound-proofing and similar work without acquisition.

   c. To allow more flexibility in assessing compensation payable to small traders who at present suffer hardship due to redevelopment of their area, or due to other planning decisions.

Housing and Architecture

7. The Government should offer additional financial incentives to encourage rehabilitation and environmental improvements in older housing areas; and to encourage the return of a resident population to the centres of our towns and cities.

8. The Government should give extra financial encouragement for the improvement of individual dwellings, and rate increases on improved houses should be delayed for five years.

9. The development of virgin land should be more strictly controlled, especially where there is derelict or under-utilised land in urban areas.

10. The Government should give new incentives to ensure that special

facilities and landscaping are provided to coincide with the completion of new housing projects.

11. The architectural profession should instigate further research into the design of homes which could be easily expanded or contracted according to the changing needs of the occupants.

12. Architectural competitions should be encouraged.

13. We suggest that the Secretary of State for the Environment sends a circular to all local planning authorities urging them to interpret the existing Planning Acts for the maximum protection and enhancement of the habitat.

Conservation Areas and Historic Buildings

14. We welcome the new proposals for legislation for the greater protection of unlisted buildings in conservation areas.

15. Local authorities should follow the example of the Government by establishing a cleaning fund for the regular cleaning of public buildings; they should give owners percentage grants from this fund towards the cost of cleaning privately-owned buildings.

16. Each local authority should set up a special sub-committee of their planning committee with its own budget, to be concerned with conservation, historic buildings, and town improvements.

17. Suitable measures should be taken to increase the supply of architects, builders and craftsmen with skills in the repair and adaptation of historic buildings. .

18. The new District Councils should take urgent steps to obtain skilled professional advice on the historic buildings which will become their responsibility. In some cases they could use County Council staff as their agents. Under the Act, the Secretary of State for the Environment should require District Councils to make arrangements which he considers to be satisfactory.

19. We also ask the Government to reconsider that part of the new legislation which removes all historic buildings powers from County Councils. There should, however, be opportunities for preservation at both levels of local government, provided that the arrangements of the authorities concerned satisfy the Secretary of State.

20. More Historic Building Trusts, and a National Buildings Conservation Fund, should be established without delay.

21. The Government should consider the whole question of tax rebates and estate duty in relation to historic buildings.

Traffic

22. Local authorities should not allow town centres to be used as through roads for traffic. " Loop " [1] and other systems should be examined for confining through traffic to circumferential roads.

---

[1] Section 5, para. 5.23 of the Report:

In Norwich . . . " the central area road pattern will eventually be based on a ring and loop system. The inner ring road . . . will provide for vehicle circulation around the city centre. Penetration into the central area by private cars

23. More ring roads should be developed, to allow as many streets as possible within the ring to be physically closed to through traffic.

24. Local authorities should examine schemes of neighbourhood environmental management for the exclusion of local through traffic from residential areas in towns and cities.

25. Local authorities should exercise powers to control or restrict town centre parking, since this is the most effective way of limiting car commuting.

26. The Government should accept the principle of public subsidy of public transport. Only if public transport undertakings receive suitable funds for development can they continue to play their part in holding down the social costs of urban congestion.

27. Private bus operators should be more freely licensed to provide services in deprived rural and suburban areas.

28. More local authorities should introduce reserved bus lanes to speed the flow of public transport.

29. Foot streets should be established without delay in all towns and cities.

Industry and Commerce

30. Because of the growing scale of industrial plant and the tendency to agglomerate, the cumulative effect should be anticipated by assessing the environmental capacity of an area to absorb them.

31. With so many major industrial installations gravitating to the coast and towards deep water facilities, a policy of development inland from these points should be adopted whenever possible, rather than to allow industrial growth to proliferate along the coastline.

32. In areas of commercial pressure the capacity of the area to contain massive increases in office floor space should be more strictly assessed, with a greater emphasis on the environmental consequences.

33. While recognising the need for changes in the structure of retailing, major out-of-town shopping centres or hyper-markets should only be allowed in exceptional cases and where no damage to existing nearby town centres would result.

34. There should be a faster rehabilitation of inherited areas of dereliction, more assistance to local authorities whose areas have suffered economic decline as a result, and grants for rehabilitation of derelict land in private or in industrial ownership.

35. The National Farmers Union and the Department of the Environment should co-operate to draw up a form of planning control for farm buildings.

36. We recommend greater research be undertaken into energy

is to be confined to loop roads, and only buses will be allowed to use cross-centre links. This system will enable the main shopping areas and the historic areas to be virtually traffic free during the major part of the day. Service vehicles will only be allowed access during limited periods. The main purpose of the loop roads is to provide access to car parks, whose size will be determined by the environmental capacity of the loop roads."

transmission methods and transportation of products, with particular reference to the transmission of electrical power and underground pipelines.

37. In economic policies towards depressed areas, greater efforts should be made to achieve positive environmental improvements.

38. There should be a general shift of emphasis from predominantly economic and technical, to social and human criteria, for new development of all kinds.

Recreation

39. Existing parks should have increased facilities for active recreation and be made generally more attractive. Landscaped areas, small gardens and walkways should be created in all our towns.

40. In built up areas, the Government should investigate the provision of Leisure and Sports Centres by a partnership of local authorities and private enterprise.

41. Museums should have flexible opening times, better lighting, more seats and general comforts. Treasures should be arranged in a more exciting and more artistic way so that visitors would be attracted by the atmosphere of beauty, relaxation and fun.

42. Local authorities should clear canals, put locks into working order, and make the best of them for sport and recreation. There should be public access to all river banks and canal towpaths.

43. Country parks of all types should be encouraged. Facilities should include landscaped car parks, nature trails and special areas for picnics and barbecues.

44. Derelict land unsuitable for building should be more quickly reclaimed for public enjoyment and recreation. Central and local government should combine to step up this work which could vastly improve the urban environment.

45. There should be new planning control to cover touring caravans and tents.

46. All caravan and camping sites should be more carefully located, have improved facilities, and better landscaping, in order to protect the interests of both caravanners and local residents.

Environmental Education

47. Environmental education and the exercise of citizenship go hand-in-hand: the opening-up of opportunities for public participation in decision-making is the most important of all means of environmental education, which should aim at developing a critical, moral and aesthetic awareness of our surroundings.

48. The professional organisations and the institutions of environmental education at the professional level should review their practices and encourage a more effective interdisciplinary, team-work approach. Their policies towards professional education should be in line with the inter-disciplinary requirements of environmental management. Opportunities should be extended for the mid-career education of professionals in environmental studies.

49. School children must be encouraged to learn about the environment

n practical ways. Project work, both in the rural and in the urban environment, should become more widespread at all levels of ability. Consideration hould be given to the establishment of urban centres for environmental tudy, along the lines already familiar in countryside studies.

50. There should be a wider application of team-teaching methods to study of the environment, bringing together the perspectives of different subjects and different teachers, in which the art department has a special ole to play.

51. Audiovisual methods should be more widely used. Perhaps the resources and expertise of the Department of the Environment and the Open University might be applied to the production of a much greater variety of high quality films, tapes and other materials for environmental education in further education and in the schools.

52. There should be more research into the means by which the general public forms its attitudes to environmental issues, and the lessons incorporated into teacher-training courses.

53. Television companies should think hard about the possibility of dramatising environmental issues in popular television fiction.

54. Decision-makers in both local and national government should be given more opportunity to learn about how their decisions can affect the environment, and a National Centre should be created to service this and all other aspects of environmental education.

Standard Grants (Sections 7 to 12 of the Housing Act, 1969)

Standard amenities and relevant amount of grant are one only of each of the following (col. (b) relates to Development Areas: p. 255, *ante*):

	(a) £	(b) £
A fixed bath or shower	30	45
A hot and cold water supply to a fixed bath or shower	45	67·50
A wash-hand basin	10	15
A hot and cold water supply to a wash-hand basin	20	30
A sink	15	22·50
A hot and cold water supply to a sink	30	75
A water closet	50	75
	£200	£330

The maximum total of standard grants shown above is thus £200 (£330). Of this, if all amenities are provided, the hot and cold water supplies will receive £95. But the total of £200 may be further increased to an upper limit of £450 (£675) by the addition of (i) half the cost of providing a piped water supply where none has existed before; and (ii) half the cost of construction or conversion to a new bathroom, provided this will be attached to the dwelling; and (iii) half the cost of installing a septic tank or cesspool[1] for a water closet, where main drainage is not available.

It is no longer necessary to provide facilities for storage of food as a condition of the grant[2]; but the bath or shower must, where possible, be in a separate bathroom; failing this it must never be in a bedroom. The water closet must, where reasonably practicable, be in the dwelling and accessible from inside.

It is further provided by the Act that a standard grant will only be available where:

(a) the dwelling was in existence prior to 3rd October, 1961; and

(b) the standard amenities will be for the exclusive use of the occupants of the relevant dwelling; and

(c) the local authority are satisfied that, on completion of the work, the dwelling will be in a satisfactory state of repair, having regard to its age, character and the locality in which it stands; and that it will be in all other respects fit for human habitation and likely to remain in that condition and available for use for at least fifteen years. Decorative repair is not, however, to be taken into account.

However, where the dwelling is situated in an improvement area (i.e., declared by the county, county borough or county district under Part II of the Act), a generally more extensive level of improvement will be required.

[1] Cesspools require to be emptied periodically; septic tanks do not.
[2] Refrigerators being now commonplace.

APPENDIX D

Green Belt Policy Statements

1. *Command Paper, Cmnd. 1952:*—" *London—Employment: Housing: Land* "
(Presented to Parliament by the Minister of Housing and Local
Government and Minister for Welsh Affairs by command of
Her Majesty, February, 1963.)

" *The Metropolitan Green Belt*

64. The Government believe that the green belt should remain a permanent feature of the planning policy for London. They will maintain the approved green belt without substantial change, and they will make extensive additions to it. They believe that, with the co-operation of the local planning authorities, enough housing land can be provided within range of London without damage to the structure of the green belt.

65. But the approved green belt covers 840 square miles, and the extensions proposed by the local planning authorities would increase it to nearly 2,000 square miles. Not all of this is essential to the purposes of the green belt nor has it all high amenity value. It cannot reasonably be maintained that none of this land should be considered for development, however serious the housing shortage may be and whatever this may mean in terms of hardship. The Government feel it inevitable, in the light of the land demands that have to be met, that some changes may have to be considered. Any modifications which may be necessary are likely to be small in relation to the whole area of the approved green belt; and should, in the main, be on land with little amenity value. There is no question of allowing development on the fine countryside which forms an important part of the green belt.

66. They do not propose to allow ' nibbling ' into the belt; a more selective approach is needed. The intention is that the planning authorities themselves should be asked initially to consider, in the light of the needs set out in this Paper, what additional areas would be suitable for housing. Any proposals put forward would be the subject of a public local inquiry.

67. The local planning authorities have proposed large additions to the approved green belt; the extent of these can be seen on the map attached to this Paper. The Government propose to strengthen the approved green belt by adding substantially [1] to it; but the size and boundaries of these additions cannot be settled at this stage.

Conclusions on Land

68. More land must be found for London housing over the next 10 years.

---

[1] As observed in Chapter 14, this " substantial " addition has now been fixed at fifteen per cent. (!) giving a final total of only 980 sq. miles (see p. 280, *ante*).

Dispersal of work and population will be an essential ingredient in this. But dispersal by itself cannot meet the need. Since the amount of land which London itself can provide is limited, a good deal of land has to be found for Londoners in the outer areas, over and above local needs. It should be possible to find most of this land outside the approved green belt, and such changes as may be necessary should not affect it substantially."

2. *Circular No. 42/55—Green Belts*
(Ministry of Housing and Local Government, 3rd August, 1955.)

" 1. Following upon his statement in the House of Commons on April 26th last (copy attached), I am directed by the Minister of Housing and Local Government to draw your attention to the importance of checking the unrestricted sprawl of the built-up areas, and of safeguarding the surrounding countryside against further encroachment.

2. He is satisfied that the only really effective way to achieve this object is by the formal designation of clearly defined Green Belts around the areas concerned.

3. The Minister accordingly recommends Planning Authorities to consider establishing a Green Belt wherever this is desirable in order:

(*a*) to check the further growth of a large built-up area;

(*b*) to prevent neighbouring towns from merging into one another; or

(*c*) to preserve the special character of a town.

4. Wherever practicable, a Green Belt should be several miles wide, so as to ensure an appreciable rural zone all round the built-up area concerned.

5. Inside a Green Belt, approval should not be given, *except in very special circumstances*,[2] for the construction of new buildings or for the change of use of existing buildings for purposes other than agriculture, sport, cemeteries, institutions standing in extensive grounds, or other uses appropriate to a rural area.

6. Apart from a strictly limited amount of ' infilling ' or ' rounding off ' (within boundaries to be defined in Town Maps) existing towns and villages inside a Green Belt should not be allowed to expand further. Even within the urban areas thus defined, every effort should be made to prevent any further building for industrial or commercial purposes; since this, if allowed, would lead to a demand for more labour, which in turn would create a need for the development of additional land for housing.

7. A Planning Authority which wishes to establish a Green Belt in its area should, after consulting any neighbouring Planning Authority affected, submit to the Minister, as soon as possible, a Sketch Plan, indicating the approximate boundaries of the proposed Belt. Before officially submitting their plans, authorities may find it helpful to discuss them informally with this Ministry either through its regional representative or in Whitehall.

8. In due course, a detailed survey will be needed to define precisely the inner and outer boundaries of the Green Belt, as well as the boundaries of

---

[2] The phrase is italicised by the author: it is a technical expression frequently used in this connection, but of which no clear definition appears to exist.

towns and villages within it.   Thereafter, these particulars will have to be incorporated as amendments in the Development Plan.

9. This procedure may take some time to complete.   Meanwhile, it is desirable to prevent any further deterioration in the position.   The Minister, therefore, asks that, where a Planning Authority has submitted a Sketch Plan for a Green Belt, it should forthwith apply provisionally, in the area proposed, the arrangements outlined in paragraphs 5 and 6 above."

Annex to Circular No. 42/55

Statement by the Rt. Hon. Duncan Sandys, M.P., Minister of Housing and Local Government, in the House of Commons on 26th April, 1955:

" I am convinced that, for the well-being of our people and for the preservation of the countryside, we have a clear duty to do all we can to prevent the further unrestricted sprawl of the great cities.

The Development Plans submitted by the local planning authorities for the Home Counties provide for a Green Belt, some 7 to 10 miles deep, all around the built-up area of Greater London.   Apart from some limited rounding-off of existing small towns and villages, no further urban expansion is to be allowed within this belt.

These proposals if strictly adhered to, should prove most effective.   For this the authorities in the Home Counties deserve much credit.

In other parts of the country, certain planning authorities are endeavouring, by administrative action, to restrict further building development around the large urban areas.   But I regret that nowhere has any formal Green Belt as yet been proposed.   I am accordingly asking all planning authorities concerned to give this matter further consideration, with a view to submitting to me proposals for the creation of clearly defined Green Belts wherever this is appropriate.

However, I do not intend on this account to hold up my approval of Development Plans already before me.   Additional provisions for Green Belts can be incorporated later."

---

3. *Circular No. 50/57—Green Belts*

(Ministry of Housing and Local Government, 19th September, 1957)

(*Author's Note*: This circular concerns the principles to be applied by local planning authorities when defining the Green Belt areas within their total development plan.)

" 1. I am directed by the Minister of Housing and Local Government to refer to Circular No. 42/55 about Green Belts.

2. A number of sketch plans have been received and considered, and the authorities can now proceed with formal proposals for the alteration of their Development Plans.   This circular gives advice on the form of the submission.

Boundaries of Green Belts

3. The one-inch County Map will show the whole area of Green Belt falling within the County, apart from any areas covered by Town Maps. On the outer edges of a Green Belt it should be possible to choose a suitable boundary along roads, streams, belts of trees, or other features which can be

readily recognised on the ground and which appear on the one-inch base map.

4. On an inner boundary, however, where the edge of the notation will mark a long-term boundary for development, treatment at a larger scale will be necessary. Where such boundaries fall in Town Map areas no difficulty of scale will arise; but where they do not, authorities are advised to adopt the 1 : 25000 (approximately $2\frac{1}{2}$ in.) scale, seeking the Minister's permission under Regulation 3 (2) of the Development Plan Regulations, 1948,[3] for the submission of a section of the County Map at the larger scale. This larger scale inset is still legally part of the one-inch County Map and should show no more detail than is normally shown on that map.

5. The definition of a long-term boundary for development may involve detailed adjustments (either inwards or outwards) in the boundary of the area already allocated on a Town Map. Where land allocations are to be deleted or additional land allocated for development within the Plan period, the adjustments can be included in the same submission as the Green Belt proposals.

6. There may be some pockets of land, between the town and the Green Belt, which are not to be developed within the present Plan period but which could be developed later without prejudice to the Green Belt. It would be misleading to allocate such areas now, but to include them in the Green Belt for the time being might give rise to difficulties and undermine public confidence in the Green Belt at a later date if it were then decided to allocate the land for development. Such areas may well be left as pockets of ' white ' land. They are then bound to be especially attractive to developers and it will be desirable to set out in the Written Statement the authority's policy for such areas in order to make it clear that they are not available for development at the present time.

Existing settlements

7. Where it is proposed to allow no new building at all, the Green Belt notation can be simply carried across the settlement. Where it is proposed to allow ' infilling ' but no extension of a settlement, and the form of the present settlement is such that it is clear what ' infilling ' would apply, the Green Belt notation can similarly be carried across the settlement. These settlements, however, will need to be listed in the Written Statement in order to distinguish them from the first category.

8. The need to map the limits for development of a settlement is likely to arise only where the authority propose to allow some limited measure of expansion, or where the existing development is scattered and the authority consider it necessary to show in the Plan their precise intentions, e.g., to permit the closing of some gaps by ' infilling ' but not others. In such cases a County Map inset on the 1 : 25000 (approximately $2\frac{1}{2}$ in.) scale will normally be needed.

---

[3] The current regulations are the Town and Country **Planning (Struc**ture and Local Plans) Regulations, 1972 (S.I. 1972 No. 1154).

Notation

9. The notation suggested for County Maps in revised (Circular No. 92) notation is an edging and open horizontal hatching with the initials GB where necessary. For County Maps in the full colour (Circular No. 59) notation, an edging and open horizontal hatching in Green (2) is suggested.

Written Statements

10. The Written Statement forming part of the proposals for the alteration of the Development Plan should state:

(*a*) the reason for defining the Green Belt.

(*b*) the kinds of development which the Council would be prepared to approve in the Green Belt. It will normally be appropriate for this statement to refer only to the categories of development listed in paragraph 5 of Circular No. 42/55, and to make no reference to the possibility of allowing other development in exceptional circumstances. These other exceptional cases would thus become proposals for development not in accord with the Development Plan and so be treated in accordance with the normal procedure in such cases.

(*c*) the Council's intentions for development control in any border areas of ' white ' land for the kind referred to in paragraph 6 above.

(*d*) the Council's intentions for development control in settlements where they are proposing to allow infilling or expansion.

Authorities may also care to include a reference to the special attention which will be paid to visual amenity when they consider proposals for development which will be in the Green Belt or conspicuous from it.

11. Most Green Belts will lie in the areas of more than one planning authority. It will clearly be desirable in such cases to secure a consistent development control policy over the whole Green Belt, and authorities will wish to consult with the other authorities concerned to secure such a policy. Specimen forms of words are set out in the Appendix to this Circular in order to provide a basis for co-operation in the drafting of Written Statements.

Rural Areas generally

12. It is important that the specially strict control in the Green Belts (and in the areas of landscape value) should not result in permission being given elsewhere for development which is inappropriate or detrimental to the countryside."

---

4. *Circular No. 37/60—The Review of Development Plans*
(Ministry of Housing and Local Government, 25th August, 1960)

" 8. Special considerations apply where a Green Belt has been established or proposed. A Green Belt is a long-term restriction of development in a defined area, and it must be matched by adequate provision for balanced and compact development elsewhere. This means the intensive use to its full capacity of land in the areas contained by the Green Belt, and the selection of adequate land for development beyond the Green Belt— avoiding wherever possible the use of good agricultural land."

5. *Circular No. 10/70—Land Availability for Housing*
(Department of the Environment, 14th December, 1970)

" *Release of Land*

6. One of the most important aspects of the duty of local planning authorities is the release of adequate land for house-building.   In many cases they have made appropriate proposals in their development plans.   But in some areas there remains a need for urgent action to release more land *now*.   In order to have a significant effect on the problem, the Secretary of State considers that releases of land should be sufficient to meet housing needs already existing and foreseeable for at least the next five years; and that the land required to meet these needs should be released at once so as to keep the supply of land *well ahead* of demand.   The Secretary of State accordingly looks to local planning authorities to make generous additional releases *wherever this can be done without detriment to other important planning objectives, e.g., the safeguarding of Green Belts.* [4]   Where the amount of land being released provides also for longer-term needs (more than, say, seven years ahead) the Secretary of State will be prepared to support measures by the local planning authority to achieve the phasing of development.   The Secretary of State will consider on their merits planning applications which come before him on appeal or on the exercise of his discretion and will be prepared to give weight to the need, where it exists, for the urgent release of more land for house-building."

----

6. *Circular No. 71/71—Development of Agricultural Land*
(Department of the Environment, 28th September, 1971)

The text of this Circular is not set out here in full, but it seeks principally to indicate to local planning authorities that the role of the Ministry of Agriculture in relation to planning deliberations is to be reduced, but that:

" 4. . . . it remains the Government's policy to ensure that as far as possible land of a higher agricultural quality is not taken for development where land of a lower quality is available and that the amount of land taken is no greater than is reasonably required for carrying out the development in accordance with proper standards.   The arrangements under which the professional services of the Ministry of Agriculture are available for consultation by local planning authorities in their development plan work will continue to be the principal means for giving effect to this policy."

" *Consideration of agricultural views*

8. Local planning authorities are requested to give full consideration to the views expressed by the Divisional Surveyor and to make every effort in cases falling within paragraph 7 (a) and (d) " (i.e., as to (a), an opinion given in writing as to why, in agricultural terms, a development would be undesirable; and as to (d) a " conditional acceptance," usually, for example, relevant to mineral workings which are to be reinstated on completion of extraction) " to effect reconciliation with him in cases of disagreement. Exceptionally when opposing views cannot be reconciled request may be made to the appropriate Secretary of State to call in the application for determination by himself after a local inquiry."

[4] The phrase is italicised by the author.

Provision is also made, in paragraphs 9 and 10, to enable the Ministry of Agriculture to enter either a *formal objection* or a " *conditional acceptance* " in the event of a planning application going to appeal at a planning inquiry. This is to be done by letter. If the substance of the agricultural objection is not set out in the local planning authority's Rule 6 Statement,[5] a copy of the Ministry of Agriculture's letter must be sent to the appellant.

[5] That is, the formal statement of the grounds for refusal relied upon by the local planning authority, as required by r. 6 of the Town and Country Planning (Inquiries Procedure) Rules, 1969 (S.I. 1969 No. 1092).

INDEX